SKETCHES OF CHRISTIANITY IN NORTH INDIA

SKETCHES OF CHRISTIANITY IN NORTH INDIA

REV. M. WILKINSON

GYAN

Published by

Gyan Publishing House
5, Ansari Road
Daryaganj, New Delhi-110002
Phone: 011-47034999, 9811692060
E-mail: books@gyanbooks.com

Distribution Network
gyanbooks.com
India, USA, Canada, UK, Australia

ISBN: 978-93-6780-306-6 (PB)

First Published, 1844

2nd Impression 2024

Printed at: Gyan Press, Delhi.

SKETCHES OF CHRISTIANITY IN NORTH INDIA
Author: REV. M. WILKINSON

SKETCHES OF CHRISTIANITY IN NORTH INDIA.

SKETCHES OF CHRISTIANITY IN NORTH INDIA.

BY THE REV. M. WILKINSON:
MISSIONARY.

"Her report hath travelled forth into all lands."
"The coming of the Lord draweth nigh."
"Even so come, Lord Jesus, come quickly."

SEELEY, BURNSIDE, AND SEELEY,
FLEET STREET, LONDON.
MDCCCXLIV.

PREFACE.

Over the continent of India, teeming with beings, whose destinies for eternity roll on with the stream of time, the Christian philanthropist has long cast his eye; and with an intensity of interest known to him who has felt the value of a Saviour, watched the united efforts of the Christian Church to arrest the abominations of idolatry, and witnessed with concern the zeal and life of missionaries, together with the funds of benevolence, poured out on the altar of faith, without producing those results which anticipation in the fulfilment of Prophecy delighted to recognize as near at hand.

That, however, which the mere politician and sceptic would denominate a failure, is nothing more than the barrenness of the ground between the period of sowing and that of germination, and cannot, by the servants of the blessed Jesus, be regarded as the sterility of the soil. Holy men of God, and full of faith, like Brown, Martyn, Corrie, and Thomason, &c., have cast in the seed, and entered into rest, in the sure and certain hope, that the period shall arrive, when sower and reaper shall rejoice together, bringing their sheaves with them.

Others are now humbly following in their track, and, though the season of sowing is not yet past, they are occasionally delighted to see, here and there, an *oasis* rising up in the moral desert (surely indicating the approach of Messiah's reign), and which shall encroach on the surrounding wastes, till the wilderness shall blossom as the rose, and the desert sing for joy. For Jehovah hath said it, that "As the rain cometh down, and the snow from heaven, and returneth not thither, but watereth the earth, and maketh it bring forth and bud, that it may give seed to the sower, and bread to the eater;—so shall my word be that goeth forth out of my mouth: it shall not return unto me void, but it shall accomplish that which I please, and it shall prosper in the thing whereto I sent it." (Isa. v. 10.) The Lord hasten it in its time!

CONTENTS.

A. D.		PAGE
1706.	Frederick, King of Denmark sends B. Ziegenbalg and H. Plutcho, Missionaries to Tranquebar	2
1716.	Society for Promoting Christian Knowledge sends them assistance	3
1728.	The Society sends J. F. Kiernander to Cudalore ...	3
1758.	Mr. Kiernander goes to Calcutta	4
	The first Church built in 1715	5
	The Mission School opened	7
1768.	P. F. Bento de Silvestre renounces Romish errors,	14
1769.	Rev. Mansol Joze da Costa arrives	14
	An account of his life	15
1771.	Mr. Da Costa dies	17
	Mr. Bento de Silvestre appointed catechist	17
	Captain John Griffin dies	18
	Famine in Bengal	19
	Mission Church completed	19
1772.	Francis Joseph Hanson renounces popery	21
1775.	Rev. John Christman Diemer arrives	24
	Ganeswan Dass baptized, ...	25
1783.	Mr. Diemer returns to Europe, ...	30
1787.	Mr. Kiernander goes to Chinsurah, ...	32
	Mr. Charles Grant, ...	38
	John Christian Obeck	39
1788.	Sir William Jones arrives and studies Sanscrit ...	41
	Moravians send Missionaries	44

A. D.		PAGE
1783.	Mr. John Thomas arrives in Calcutta, ...	44
	Military Orphan Asylum established	46
1786.	Rev. David Brown, ...	48
1787.	St. John's Church finished, ...	64
1792.	The Native Hospital founded, ...	75
1793.	The Mission Church enlarged, ...	79
1794.	Sir William Jones dies, ...	83
	Rev. Dr. Buchanan, ...	89
1796.	Appointed Chaplain by the East India Company, and arrives at Calcutta, ...	94
	Lord Mornington governor, ...	100
1800.	College of Fort William established, ...	106
	Mr. Obeck dies, ...	113
1803.	Dr. Buchanan proposes an ecclesiastical establishment for India, ...	117
1806.	Dr. Buchanan proposes to translate the Holy Scriptures into fifteen oriental languages, ...	125
	Rev. H. Martyn and Rev. D. Corrie arrive at Calcutta, ...	125
	Memoir of Bishop Corrie, ...	130
	Memoir of Mrs. Corrie, ...	133
1808.	Lord Minto governor, ...	143
	Letter and Diary of Mr. Brown, ...	162
	Rev. T. T. Thomason arrives, ...	174
	Mr. Martyn finishes the Hindostanee New Testament, ...	181
1810.	Bible Society established at Calcutta, ...	187
	Letters of Mr. Martyn, ...	193
	Conversion of Abdol Messeh, ...	202
1812.	An earthquake—The Printing Office at Serampore destroyed by fire, ...	203
	Rev. Mr. Brown dies, ... 81,	204
	Mr. Thomason revises the Arabic Bible with Sabat,	207
1813.	East India Company grant £1250. towards printing the Bible in Malay, ...	208
	Earl Moira governor, ...	209

A.D.		PAGE
	Dr. Middleton appointed first Bishop of Calcutta, ...	209
	Arrives in India, ...	215
	The Hindoo College, and the School Book Society, established, ...	218
	Church Missionary Society send Rev. W. Greenwood,	219
1816.	Native Schools established, ...	225
1819.	Rev. Messrs. Jetter and Deer arrive at Burdwan, ...	226
1821.	Rev. John Perowne arrives at Burdwan, ...	227
	Conversion of a Brahmin, ...	229
	History of James, a native catechist, ...	230
	The Calcutta mission, ...	233
	Krishnagur, ...	235
	Benares, ...	236
	Cawnpore—Christian Translation Society—Native Female Orphan Asylum, ...	242
1826.	Meerut—Rev. H. Fisher, ...	245
	Conversion of Matthew Prabu Din Naick, ...	248
	Letter from Bishop Middleton, ...	251
	Agra—Bishop Corrie, ...	265
	Rev. Dr. Parish—Agra Relief Society, ...	266
	Agra Orphan Institution, ...	268
	Christian Knowledge Society—Bishop Middleton, ...	275
	Society for Propagation of the Gospel in Foreign Parts,	278
	Bishop's College—Marquis of Hastings, ...	280
	Dr. Mills' History of Our Lord, in Sanscrit verse, ...	284
	Bishop of Calcutta visits Jangera and Barripore, ...	304
	Examination of Catechumens, ...	308
	Tallygange Mission, ...	314
	Cawnpoor and Futtehpoor, ...	321
	Account of Calcutta and its establishments, ...	325
	Definitions of Brahma, ...	337
	Description of a Sabbath at sea, ...	350
	Escape of Rev. H. Fisher, ...	353
	Memoir of Rev. Charles Knorpp, ...	364
	Loss of life at a Bathing Festival at Benares, ...	375
	Journal of a Missionary at Benares, ...	377

A D. PAGE

Obituary of Stephen Laprimaudaye, Esq. 399
Memorial of Captain W. 400
Death of Mrs. Schneider, ... 404
Memoir of Sir Henry Blosset, ... 407
A Visit to the Female Orphan Refuge, Agriparrah, 411
Conversion of a Native, ... 414
Notes of a journey to Bombay, ... 415

SKETCHES OF CHRISTIANITY IN NORTH INDIA.

A HISTORY

OF THE PROGRESS OF

CHRISTIANITY IN NORTH INDIA.

An invaluable History of the spread of Christianity in the South of India having been given to the world by the Rev. Mr. Hough, formerly chaplain to the Hon. East India Company, many have been led to inquire for a history of Christianity in North India. The following sketch is intended to supply this want.

The obscurity in which the early periods of history are involved is a subject of regret to every lover of useful knowledge, but is especially to be lamented when it affects the records of those events which concern the eternal interests of mankind. The period when Christianity was first introduced into India, and the circumstances attending its introduction, are involved in considerable obscurity; but there is good ground for believing that Christianity was introduced into India at a very early period of the Christian era, and that it prevailed to a considerable extent. The remarkable coincidence of some of the stories related in the Hindoo Purāns, with part of the Christian Scriptures, could scarcely have been accidental; and the proof which the late Colonel Wilford has adduced, of some at least of the Purāns being of a date posterior to the

Christian era, seems to sanction the opinion of the having been constructed according to notions then current, derived from the Christian scriptures. There are two sects now existing in North India, certainly of modern origin, which evidently shew in their writings a knowledge vastly superior to Hindooism, either ancient or modern, in things pertaining to God and salvation. The names of the leaders of these sects are Kawir and Nānik Shah.

But whatever of true Christian knowledge now prevails in India, may be traced to labours of a comparatively recent date. The Portuguese were first in the order of European nations who attempted to establish Christianity in India, but the corrupt form of it which that people had adopted from Rome, assimilated more to Hindooism than to the simple religion of Jesus Christ its founder. This sketch therefore will be confined to the labours of Protestant Christians.

Amongst these, the honour of being first to erect the standard of the cross in India, belongs to the Dutch. In the beginning of the seventeenth century, they obtained possession of the whole coast of Ceylon, and took immediate measures for the dissemination of primitive Christianity. They settled among the people faithful and pious missionaries, evangelists, 'messengers of the Churches,' by whom they were sent forth. Schools were quickly instituted in various parts of the island, &c. and by the end of the century, 300,000 of the natives were numbered among the members of their churches. Soon after the commencement of the eighteenth century, Frederic, the fourth king of Denmark, in consequence of the recommendation of one of his chaplains, resolved on establishing a mission for the conversion of the heathen on the coast of Coromandel. With a view to this, he engaged and sent out Bartholomew Ziegenbalg, and Henry Plutcho, two young men who were educated for the ministry at the university of Halle, in Saxony, and who arrived at the Danish settlement of Tranquebar, in July 1706.

Thesemissionaries corresponded with some of the first characters of that age, both in Denmark and in England, on the subject of their mission,* and in 1714, Ziegenbalg visited both these countries with a view to obtain help for the great work in which he was engaged. In England he was received with the greatest kindness by all ranks. He was honoured with an audience by George the First, the Archbishop of Canterbury, and the Bishop of London, who promised to afford the mission the utmost assistance in their power. In consequence, the Society for Promoting Christian Knowledge, which had been established only a few years before in London, was led to patronize the mission at Tranquebar, and has ever since that period been the principal instrument of supporting and extending the undertaking.

That Society, in 1716, published a collection of letters from the Protestant missionaries and other worthy persons in the East Indies, relating to the mission, and with a view to draw the attention of the English nation to the more extensive propagation of the gospel in India. At first, assistance was sent from the society to the Danish missionaries, but afterwards new missions were undertaken under the express sanction and immediate superintendance and at the sole expense of the Society for Promoting Christian Knowledge.

The first of these missions was established at Fort St. George in 1728, and was extended to Cudalore in 1737. Among the missionaries sent out by the society to Cudalore, was John Frederic Kiernander. He was a native of Sweden, and completed his education at the university of Upsal. In 1735, he became latin teacher in the university of Halle, in Saxony, under Dr. Franke, and after four years was recommended by him to the Society for Promoting Christian Knowledge, as a suitable person to be sent to India as a missionary. He accordingly set out for London, and from thence em-

* See Buchanan's Christian Researches, p. 154.

barking in the Colchester Indiaman, arrived at Cudalore on the 20th of April, 1740, where he continued to labour till May 1758, when that settlement was taken by the French under the command of Lieutenant-General Count Lally.

After the capitulation Mr. Kiernander was informed by that impetuous General, that the services of a Protestant missionary were no longer required at that settlement, and a passport being offered him, he accepted it, and retired to the Danish settlement of Tranquebar.

No immediate prospect appearing of the restoration of Cudalore to the English, Mr. Kiernander turned his attention to Bengal, where the English power had now obtained a considerable ascendancy, and on the 29th of September, 1758, he arrived in Calcutta.

On his arrival he was received by the then Governor Clive, and the other members of the government, with great kindness, and a house was appropriated on the part of government for his residence, rent free, which was continued to him for eight years. This may be justly considered a new era in the religious history of Calcutta. Up to that period it is probable that the ordinances of religion had been administered very irregularly.

In the early charters granted to the East India Company, a clause had been inserted requiring them to maintain a chaplain and a schoolmaster, wherever a European regiment was stationed. It was also enacted, that the chaplains of the company should qualify themselves to afford Christian instruction to the Hindu and Portuguese servants of the company in their native languages. But the continual struggle for existence which the local government had to maintain with the native powers, added to the spirit of amassing wealth which usually attends men in the situation of the first English settlers in Calcutta, would greatly obstruct the operation of such enactments; and, in fact, it does not appear that either then or for a long period afterwards, any steps were taken to carry the provision of the charter, as it respected the native servants of the company, into execution. The English, however, had not wholly neglected the necessary provision for public worship among themselves. A writer who signed himself '*Asiaticus*,' who had resided long in India, and who published a small volume a short time before his death (1802) has recorded a few particulars of the early state of European Calcutta, which he collected from eye-witnesses, as from authentic tradition.

From that author it appears, that a church was erected in Calcutta in or about the year 1715, at which time the English had been there about twenty-five years. In a note, Asiaticus gives an extract from the travels of Capt. Alexander Hamilton, published in 1727, who spent his time in trading in various parts of the East Indies from the year 1688 to 1723. 'About fifty yards from Fort William (now the New Custom House) stands the Church, built by the pious munificence of the merchants residing there, and the Christian benevolence of a few sea-faring men, whose affairs called them to trade there ; but ministers of the Gospel being subject to mortality, very often young merchants are obliged to officiate, and have a salary of £50 per annum, added to what the Company allows them for their pains in reading prayers, and a sermon on Sunday.'

Nor were the destitute offspring of Europeans wholly unheeded by the British inhabitants of Calcutta of that day. Before, or about 1732, a subscription was set on foot for the maintenance and education of twenty boys, to which subscriptions were added the sacramental collections, and a Mr. Bourchier, sometime master-attendant at Calcutta, afterwards Governor of Bombay, on the establishment by charter of a Mayor's Court in 1726, built a lower-roomed house on the site of the present Scotch Church, which house he conveyed to Government, on condition of paying 4000 arcat rupees per annum to support a charity-school, and for other benevolent purposes.

In consideration of the great additions afterwards made to the Court-house, chiefly by the liberality of the inhabitants of the town, government agreed to give 800 rupees per mensem to the school, and when the ruinous state of the building made it necessary to pull it down, Government generously agreed to pay that sum in perpetuity.

A furious hurricane, which occurred in 1737, attended by a violent earthquake, levelled the English Church with the ground, did immense damage to the shipping, and otherwise much injured the town of Calcutta. The church was rebuilt not long after, and information thereof was sent to the Society for Propagating the Gospel in Foreign Parts. To this communication an answer was sent expressive of their approbation of what had been done. A silver cup was also sent by the Society, with an appropriate inscription commemorative of the event.

No further record of the religious history of Calcutta from that period till 1756 remains, when, among the other devastations, committed by the army of the Nawab of Bengal, the church was demolished. It lay contiguous to the old fort at the west end, where the writers' buildings now stand.

The two chaplains to the Government then at Calcutta perished ;—one in the black hole, and the other during the mortality which broke out among the fugitives from Calcutta at Fulta ; and during the whole of 1757, there was no Protestant minister at Calcutta. In 1758, of the two chaplains stated to have arrived, one did not belong to this presidency, but had been detained on the emergency by the governor. These circumstances would render the prospect of a permanent ministry among them very acceptable to the reflecting part of the community, and accounts very naturally for the cordial reception Mr. Kiernander met with. From his first arrival he seems to have taken a share in the public offices of religion equally with the chaplains, and kept a register of all occasional duties, which is still referred to as an official document. After the demolition of the church in 1756 till 1787, a small Bungalow (single-floored residence) situated in the old fort, was the only place of worship for the Presidency, except a church, raised by the efforts of Mr. Keirnander. This is not the only instance in which new settlements have been indebted to missionary piety and zeal for the blessings of a regular Gospel ministry; and it is practically important that the present race of inhabitants of Calcutta, who are so highly favoured in respect of religious opportunities, should know how much they and their ancestors are indebted to the missionary zeal of the Church of England.

Mr. Keirnander, on his settlement in Calcutta, set himself diligently to fulfil the object of his mission. It does not appear that he consulted the Society, under whose directions he had proceeded to India, respecting his removal from the coast to Calcutta; but, on being informed of the circumstances, &c., that led to it, the Society for Promoting Christian Knowledge continued their support to him. Accordingly, in the Report of that Society, published in 1761, they express their obligations to Messrs. Butler and Cape, chaplains of that settlement, for their very friendly reception of Mr. Keirnander—for their procuring large subscriptions toward carrying on the good work he is engaged in; and for the Christian offer they make of assisting him in the peculiar offices of a minister of the gospel.

The Rev. Henry Butler, in a letter of the 12th of January 1761, bears testimony to the good behaviour of the Society's missionary, and recommends it to them to send a person of industry and unblemished morals to assist him in the school, not doubting, but that whatever stipend they shall allow him will be considerably augmented in Calcutta.

Aided by the large subscriptions here acknowledged, Asiaticus states, that Mr. Keirnander opened a school at Calcutta, called the Mission School, on Dec. 1, 1758, and by the end of the following year, 175 children had been received by him, thirty-seven of whom had been clothed and maintained, as well as educated. Among these, it is probable, were included twenty children, supported by the Town Charity, previously existing. In after years these were included in the account of the mission, under a distinct head; and it is known, that afterwards Mr. Keirnander, and his assistant, had the superintendence of the Town Charity until the time when the present free-school was established.

In the Report made to the Society for Promoting Christian Knowledge, of the mode of instruction used in the school, it is stated, that the scholars were all taught in the English language, in reading, writing and arithmetic, and were all, whether of heathen, Mohamedan, Roman, or Protestant parents, equally catechized and instructed in the Christian religion. One of the Bengalees (a Brahmin) had in the year read through the Bishop of Man's instructions for the Indians,* the English Bible, and the Whole Duty of Man. Hence, a hope is expressed, that when they grew up, they would embrace the truth of our holy religion. Some of the descendants of the Romanists already declared they would never be Papists. Many of them, from fifteen to twenty-five years of age, who had been before neglected by the Romish priests, who gave them no instruction, but rather chose to keep them in ignorance, had applied to this school, and were more disposed and apt to learn than those on the coast.

It is further stated that Mr. Kiernander had offered his services to the Portuguese, some of whom belonged to the old congregation at Cudalore; and at their request, with the consent of the governor and English chaplains, he had begun, June 3rd, at such hours as did not interfere with the English service, to preach in Portuguese. His congregation was yet but small, consisting of (beside the school-boys) five from Cudalore, and eleven of Calcutta, and his own family. The wife of a German

* Bishop Wilson.

soldier, with her two children, had been received into his congregation. He had also preached and administered the sacrament at Frederick-Nagore, or Serampore, when desired, as the Danes had there no chaplain; and, when requested, had read prayers and preached in the English church, besides which he occasionally visited the Swedes and Germans in the company's service.

The constant attendance on the school had prevented him from learning the Bengalee language so as to address himself to the natives in their own tongue, but he gave the preference to the education of children, having more hopes from their tender minds than from those who had grown old in ignorance and sin. And he expressed his desire that thus opening a door to young persons might, as hitherto, be attended with God's blessing; adding, that he would be heartily glad of a fellow labourer; that one of them might apply himself to the Bengalee language, and the other to the Hindostanee.

In August, 1759, a Dutch ship from Batavia arrived in the river Hoogly, filled with troops, and others followed, bringing in all 700 Europeans and 800 Malays. The arrival of such a body of men, without any visible occasion for their service, alarmed the local English government, who, in the precarious situation of their affairs with the native powers, could not but feel to what danger they should be exposed were so formidable a reinforcement to take part against them. Measures were accordingly taken, by which nearly the whole of the Europeans were taken prisoners. It appears that of these about 400 of the Dutch soldiers volunteered into the company's service, so that the greatest part of the garrison of Fort William were acquainted with the German tongue. At their desire, and with the consent of the colonel commanding, Mr. Kiernander, in the January following, reported that he had begun to give them a sermon on Sundays, and had a considerable congregation, both of soldiers and their officers, and likewise of other Germans of the place.

In another letter from Calcutta, the 29th Feb. 1760,

he informed the society that the number of his scholars increased monthly, of the Portuguese children of Roman Catholic parents.

The above statements give a favourable impression of the prudence and zeal with which Mr. Kiernander pursued the important objects of his mission: the due respect paid to those in authority not only procured him easy access to the European soldiers, who, but for his pious care must have remained destitute of Christian ordinances, but also gained their favourable support to the more immediate objects of his mission.

Some reference to an attempt on the part of the Roman Catholic Portuguese to dispossess him of the place in which his school was kept, the particulars of which are not recorded, indicate that his labours were not without a portion of that opposition which such attempts have ever experienced. "Whilst the strong man armed keeps his house his goods are in peace; but when a stronger than he comes" to reclaim the spoil, a contest begins, which the messengers of the Gospel must be content to maintain, using only those weapons with which their divine Master has supplied them. These are principally, patience in imparting instruction; humble faith, and persevering prayer.

In this spirit Mr. Kiernander seems to have commenced his work in Calcutta, nor were his labours confined to public preaching and teaching in the schools; books and tracts were also distributed by him, and copies of an address in manuscript, which he circulated among the Roman Catholics of Portuguese origin, are yet in existence, in which the erroneous tenets of the Church of Rome were plainly and affectionately set forth, and many were led to attend to the instruction thus given them. It may be here noticed, that Mr. Kiernander continued to the end of his life, to labour for the good of this class of the Calcutta population.

He for some years kept up a regular correspondence with the Society for Promoting Christian Knowledge, though but few particulars respecting the progress of his labours are published. From these however we learn the pleasing fact, that the conductors of that venerable institution, were much alive to the spiritual interests of India, and from what is still experienced of the expense and difficulty with which similar supplies are obtained, the school-books, tracts, and medicines, put by them at Mr. Kiernander's disposal, must have been of inestimable benefit to the poorer classes of Christians of that day in Calcutta.

At the end of 1760, being the second year of his abode in that city, Mr. Kiernander gave the following account of his school and ministry: 'that there remained 231 scholars, all of whom are taught reading, writing, cyphering, and the principles of Christianity;' and, he says, 'their inclination to learn, and the emulation that he perceives among them, make him go on with pleasure in his labour.' The number increasing obliged him to employ more assistants, and he was supplied with them from those brought up in the school. This is a pleasing fact in this early part of the history of the mission. It is further stated, that he had been enabled to supply 154 rupees monthly, for the salaries of those assistants, besides books, ink, and some small wages for servants, all which large expence had been defrayed, without putting the Society to any charge. He was at that time under some difficulty with regard to a house in which he might have his school.

He had baptized, beside children of Portuguese, German, and Dutch parents, one adult Tamul-can, seventeen years old, and was preparing three other adults for baptism. Of his Portuguese congregation, two adult persons and four children had died. He had that year sixty-one communicants; he continued preaching in the Portuguese language, had no time to apply himself fully to learn the language of the country, and was desirous of an associate to assist him in his growing labours.

At the end of the year 1761, there remained in the

school 242 scholars. Of these one hundred were maintained by the town charity, twenty paid for their learning, and 122 were instructed and furnished with books, &c. at the expence of the society, and thirteen of the poorest of them had an allowance monthly, towards their clothing and diet. Some of those who had left the school were serving their masters faithfully.

The church in the old fort being taken up in the morning by two services, English and German, and in the afternoon by English prayers, the Portuguese sermon was continued on Sundays in the afternoon in the school-room for want of a more convenient place.

There had been baptized this year, besides others, eleven adults from among the heathen. At this time the Portuguese language was taught to all the adults receiving instruction, that language having become almost general in its use, in transactions of business, and occupied the place of the languages of the country, as English now does.

Thus after three years' residence in Calcutta, besides many children and youth of both sexes, who were presented for baptism by persons personally interested in their welfare, Mr. Kiernander was able to report the baptism of twelve adult *natives*.

Visiting the sick and instructing the catechumens, occupied Mr. Keirnander's evenings after school-hours, in which he was assisted by one of his pupils, who understood both English and Portuguese. He had this year to lament the loss of two valuable friends to himself and the mission—the English chaplains, Butler and Cape; but he writes, 'God hath made up their loss in the Rev. Mr. Samuel Hanely, who is appointed chaplain in their stead, who with an equally good zeal, ardently endeavours to promote the cause of Christianity.'

To those who are familiar with the history of this presidency at that period, it will not be matter of surprise, that during the years 1763-4, there should be no account of any visible success attending Mr. Kiernander's labours, as in other years. A state of public agitation is necessarily unfavourable to the progress of that religion which is, first pure, then peaceable. The pious missionary no doubt expressed the feelings of many in Calcutta at that period of danger and disquietude, when in a letter addressed to the Society, dated October 8, 1763, he thanked God that the worst was past, and hoped that Providence would, out of these troubles, bring much good, by opening a door for the entrance of the gospel among the heathen. It was perfectly natural too, that Mr. Kiernander, in reporting the progress of his mission, should express his gratitude to God for making Lord Clive the happy instrument of restoring peace and tranquillity to the country.

The contentions which had agitated the minds of Europeans around him, he must have felt very unfavourable to the benevolent purposes for which he came among them; whilst the animosities excited in the natives against the British, must preclude the going amongst them for the purpose of imparting to them the blessings of Christianity. But now that peace was established, a door of hope presented itself to the mind of this good man, and devoted servant of his Master. At this time the German volunteers returning to the presidency, his ministration among them was again called for.

During the year, the Portuguese congregation had increased by the addition of twelve converts from Popery, and of eight adult heathen natives of Bengal.

This congregation is described as consisting of a variety of nations—Bengalees, Hindostanees, Peguans, Malayans, Wadugas, &c. These were severally instructed in the Portuguese language, as a general medium by which to convey to them a knowledge of Christian doctrine, &c., and a hope is expressed that some from among them would become ministers of the same blessed truths to their own nations respectively in their own language.

During the year, the Society for Promoting Christian Knowledge had supplied Mr. Kiernander with a considerable number of English, German, and Portuguese books and tracts, which were extensively distributed, and the result is stated to be an increased spirit of devotion in the congregation, and a growing practice of real godliness.

At the close of 1766, Mr. Kiernander reports an increase of twenty-seven persons to his congregation, who had renounced the errors of Popery.

Besides these successful efforts among the adult population, Mr. Kiernander expressed a hope at this time that his labours in the schools were not wholly in vain; but had been of great and real service in giving education to several who were then capable of taking useful and influential employments and situations under government, which circumstance he trusted, from the good conduct he might warrantably calculate upon, from the Christian principles in which they had been instructed, would recommend the school to the favour and fostering care of those in authority.

It may be proper to state in explanation, that Mr. Kiernander became possessed of considerable property on his second marriage. He was also greatly patronized in all his useful labours by the European residents.

Another letter dated Feb. 25, 1768, relates the deliberate conversion of a priest of the Church of Rome, forty years of age, of the order of St. Augustin. His name was P. F. Bento de Silvestre. He understood the French, Portuguese, Bengalee, and Hindostanee languages.

About this time Mr. Kiernander was applied to for copies of the Psalms and New Testament in Arabic, by some persons connected with the court of *Shah Allum*, and they were so well received by his Majesty's moollahs, that he transmitted to Allahabad, where the court was then held, all the Arabic Psalters and Testaments in his possession.

In the beginning of June 1769, there arrived in Calcutta another clergyman, formerly of the Romish persuasion,—the Rev. Mansol Joze Da Costa, who had been privately received into the Protestant Church at

Madras, on Nov. 21, 1768, and who read his public recantation in Mr. Kiernander's Portuguese congregation.

The following interesting account of him is given by the missionaries to whom he first addressed himself at Madras :

'He was a native of Coimbra in Portugal, aged forty-four years at the time he renounced Popery, of the order of the Dominicans, and had been admitted into that society, and ordained before he left Europe. After he came into Asia, he was near seven years at Goa, from whence he was sent to Dice, near Surat, invested with the power of an inquisitor, and afterwards to Siam. Hither he brought some doubts with regard to the Popish doctrines, and becoming acquainted with a Jesuit priest named Antonio Rodrigues, whom he observed to entertain the like scruples with himself, they opened their minds to each other. Here he got, for the first time in his life, a sight of the Bible in Latin. This he studied, together with some Protestant books which Providence threw in his way, and there gained so much insight into the errors of the Church of Rome, and was so far convinced that the Protestant doctrines were agreeable to the word of God, that during the six years he resided at Siam, he mentioned these things privately to many of the Portuguese that were there, and he gave in a list of forty-three persons, who accordingly came over from the Romish to the Protestant persuasion.

'Father Rodrigues, with whom, as long as he lived, D'Costa secretly kept up an intimacy, actually separated himself from the Church of Rome, and leaving the Jesuits, put himself under the protection of the Dutch, who had then a factory at Siam. Upon this his brethren excommunicated him, and Padre D'Costa received likewise an order from Goa to send Rodrigues from Siam to the inquisition ; but the execution of this order was very well dispensed with on account of the latter being protected by the Dutch. Sometime after, Rodrigues, being dangerously ill, the Jesuits went to him, and offered him a plenary absolution ; but he refused both that and the extreme unction. They were however very busy about him to his last moments, and when he was dead, gave out that he had returned to the communion of the Romish Church, and buried him with the usual ceremonies.

'Padre D'Costa's inclination to the Protestant religion could not long remain concealed from some suspicious persons at Siam. Happening therefore to be confined to his bed by sickness, he was visited by one of his own order, who seized upon his escritoir, and finding in it a paper, wherein he and Rodrigues had noted many errors of the Church of Rome, took it away, together with his Protestant books, and other effects, and got him on board a vessel bound for Goa, in order to be put into the Inquisition. A Moor of his acquaintance however set him on shore at Jausolen, from whence he came to Cobolam.

'Here he found that his being sent from Siam was providentially a benefit to him, as he thereby escaped the danger in which others were involved, when the King of Ava and Pegu invaded that country. Soon after this he went to Tranquebar, on purpose to discover himself to the Danish missionaries; here, though he lived with the Roman Padre, he found means to get several Portuguese books printed in the mission, and going frequently to Parreiana, where the missionaries have a church, he there met with the Rev. Mr. Weidebrock, but feared to disclose himself, lest it should come to the ears of the bishop of the French mission at Siam, who was then at Pondicherry, and who might hinder the design he had of introducing the Protestant religion among his old congregation. He therefore quitted his intention of embracing Protestantism at Tranquebar; determining to go to Madras, to find Mr. Fabricius; and came in disguise to Vepery, in the month of October, 1766; but as that missionary was not then at home, he did not think fit to discover himself to Mr. Breilhaupt.

The secession of these two missionaries from the

Romish church excited no little stir among the members of that communion in India; and in the month of July 1769, a priest arrived in Calcutta from Goa, authorized to excommunicate Mr. Bento de Silvestre unless he should recant. A letter was sent him demanding an answer in twenty-four hours, to the several charges laid against him. He returned an immediate answer, requesting that it might be read publicly in the Romanist church, but, aware that this request would not be complied with. he distributed several copies of it to the people in the town, and thus his reasons for leaving their communion being made public, much discussion was excited, and some good produced among those of better understanding.

It may be sufficient to add here that these two converts continued for many years to manifest the sincerity with which they had embraced the Protestant faith, by being content to live in great poverty, whilst they assisted considerably and cheerfully in the instruction of the congregation over which Mr. Kiernander presided.

Mr. D'Costa suffered much from ill health, and died in 1771, after a long illness. To the last he had a great desire of returning to Siam, in the hope of being successful in undoing part of what through ignorance he might have done amiss, and of turning many unto God. Mr. Bento de Silvestre was received as a catechist by the Society for Promoting Christian Knowledge, at a salary of £50 a year, and continued to labour faithfully in the service of the mission, till his death in 1786.

Several affecting accounts were rendered to the Society of the pious and exemplary lives and happy deaths of several of the mission congregation of both sexes during this year. Among the adult converts was one Thomas, a native of Bengal, aged twenty-four years, who had made such proficiency in the Portuguese language and in the knowledge of Christianity, that he had been employed as a catechist to instruct his countrymen, &c.

Another was a Chinese from Canton, a sea-faring man of the age of twenty-two years, and who desired to settle in Calcutta. The other two were women, also natives of Bengal, the one aged twenty, the other sixteen years.

Among the converts from popery was one Antonio Soaffery from Leghorn, who had resided at Calcutta twenty-nine years, and was then fifty-two years of age. He had for some time entertained doubts concerning popery, and expressed his thanks to God, that seeing his error, he had been led into the knowledge of "the truth as it is in Jesus."

The Rev. Mr. Bento de Silvestre had for some time been engaged in translating the catechism and some prayers into the Bengallee language, and was at this time upon the point of finishing what promised to be an important acquisition to the Bengalee converts, &c.

In 1770 a Captain John Griffen died, who by his will bequeathed the residue of his estate to the church then being erected, and directed that the yearly interest should be available for the repairs of the church, and to supplying the salaries of one or two missionaries and school-masters, appointing the Society for Promoting Christian Knowledge, jointly with the Rev. Dr. Knapp, director of the Orphan-house at Halle, Saxony, trustees for the right application of the bequest.

On communicating this circumstance, Mr. Kiernander renewed his request that two more missionaries might be provided and sent to Calcutta by the earliest opportunity. This application was favourably received, and communication entered into with Dr. Knapp of Halle, desiring him to look out for two suitable persons to be sent as soon as it should be deemed advisable. The affairs of Captain Griffen were found to be in some disorder, and though the legacy is spoken of in subsequent reports, it does not appear ever to have been realized to the mission.

The year 1771 was remarkable in Bengal for the excessive distress and calamity which the generality of the natives underwent. During the first part of the year, from January to June, were continual fires, to the ruin of thousands of families, and the entire consumption of many plentifully-stored granaries of rice and other provisions which had been collected together in the prospect of an approaching dearth. No rain had fallen in Bengal for a period of nine months, and in the upper provinces for a longer period. A famine succeeded, and thousands died. The number of those who perished is stated on good authority to have been at least 1,400,000; others state the mortality to have been much greater. The streets and roads in Calcutta were daily strewed with dead bodies, &c. At Mushadabad (Patna) and other places the mortality was even greater.

In such a scene of distress and suffering and death, the Christian missionary's heart and hands were open to sympathize and to relieve. Mr. Kiernander, in a letter to the Society, acknowledges with the warmest expressions of gratitude to God, the more than fatherly care and kindness experienced during this season of scarcity and contagion. Not only were his own wants supplied, but he was enabled to administer to the wants of many.

In this communication the completion of the church is noticed. It was consecrated and solemnly set apart to the service of God as a *Mission Church* on the fourth Sunday in advent of that year. Instead of 20,000 rupees, as at first calculated, the cost amounted, owing to an enlargement of the original plan, to 60,000 rupees and upwards, which sum was met by Mr. Kiernander out of his own private resources, excepting a few subscriptions amounting to not more than 1800 rupees.

Hitherto Mr. Kiernander had ministered in his own dwelling-house; from henceforth public service was uniformly conducted in the church; in the morning in English and Portuguese, and again in the afternoon in Portuguese, besides prayers on Wednesdays and Fridays with catechising. A pamphlet published in Calcutta by a person signing himself *Asiaticus*, and known to the writer of this sketch, says, in allusion to the church, 'The edifice was named *Beth-Tephillah*, a house of prayer. Thus after a lapse of fourteen years, Calcutta once more beheld an English church completed at the expense of a stranger.'

Without detracting from the praise due to Mr. Kiernander for his liberality, it is but justice to add, that that stranger was sent to India at the instance and expense of the Society for Promoting Christian Knowledge; that his connection with that society recommended him to persons of the greatest influence in the presidency, &c., and that much of his resources was derived from his official services among the friends of that society in Calcutta.

During the year Mr. Kiernander baptized, besides children, eleven adult heathens, seven of whom were natives of Siam, the other four were natives of Bengal. Three more heathens were preparing for baptism, one a native of *Bengal*, the other two from *Batavia*. In the course of the year, fourteen Papists also were received into the Protestant church. The communicants in the English congregation were eighty-five, in the Portuguese sixty-nine, and ninety-seven scholars exclusive of those supported by the town-charity, and who had been assisted in their education from the funds of the society.

About this time the Society for Promoting Christian Knowledge, which had not originally been associated for missionary purposes, finding that they could not enlarge their Indian missions without prejudicing the other designs in which they were engaged, addressed the Court of Directors, for their encouragement and assistance. The arguments used were, that their Indian missions tended so manifestly to the glory of God, at the same time that they were eventually conducing to the good and benefit of the East India Company. For it was urged, that, as the natives became better acquainted with our religion, they will become more united to the British settlers. It was further represented, that the missionaries of the Society were successfully employed in making *converts from popery*, and were thereby contributing in some measure towards the furtherance of the Protestant interest in India; whilst, in the midst of their missionary labours, they were always ready to minister to the spiritual wants of Europeans in the Honourable Company's settlements. These political advantages flowing to the English government from missionary labours in India were duly appreciated by the Court of Directors, who ordered 500 pagodas to be supplied for the purposes of the Society from the treasury at Fort St. George, where the largest expenditure of the mission was incurred.

In the year 1771, twelve adults were added to the mission congregation—viz. three Malays, three natives of Bengal, and six converts from Popery. Besides these, several persons had been awakened to a sense of religion, who, though they had long borne the name of Protestant Christians, had (some of them not for many years, and others never since they were baptized) been in any church, nor had ever received the sacrament of the Lord's Supper, but had now become constant attendants on public worship, and were diligently seeking, through the means of grace thus afforded them, the salvation of their souls. The adult heathens who had been baptized were instructed in the Portuguese language, and through it, advanced in the knowledge of Christian truth, and were in conversation, &c., obedient to the Gospel.

A letter, dated 13th of January, 1772, was transmitted to the Society, giving an account of the reception of another Romish priest and missionary, Francis Joseph Hanson, who, on New Year's Day, had abjured Popery, and was received into the Protestant Church. This person was born at Vienna in 1739, and educated in the Romish Church, in which having taken orders, he, for some time, officiated in Europe, and for the four last years as a missionary of the order of Carmelites at Busora.

Through diligent and prayerful reading of the Scriptures, his mind became emancipated from the thraldom to which it had been long enslaved, and boldness was given him to renounce the dangerous and damning errors of popery, and to embrace the Protestant faith. Accordingly he was, a month after his arrival at Calcutta, in the face of the congregation, enabled to make his abjuration, which he delivered to Mr. Keirnander, who received him into the truly Catholic Church of Christ. After prayer, &c., a sermon was delivered from Rev. xviii. 4, 5; after which, the Sacrament of the Lord's Supper was administered, and Mr. F. J. Hanson partook of it.

There were present on this occasion the Governor, and most of the Council, the Rev. Dr. Burn, and many other gentlemen. A collection was made, which amounted to 313 rupees.

In 1772, the Society received several letters from Mr. Keirnander, containing accounts of the chief circumstances of the mission—his own good health—the partial failure—and restoration to health of the Rev. Mr. Bento da Sauza's, and that gentleman's diligence and usefulness both in the English and Portuguese congregations, the schools, &c.

The congregation had been increased by seven adult heathens, and eleven converts from popery, besides children. The communicants were, in the English congregation 96, and in the Portuguese 104, and in the school there were 94 scholars.

* Detailed accounts of these particulars are contained in the Society's publications. The repeated application of Mr. Kiernander for assistants at length brought the desired help. In July 1772, the Reverend Professor Freylinhausen, Director of the Orphan Institution at Halle, informed the Society, that through the divine blessing he had at length found out a young man, endued not only with sincere and unfeigned piety towards

God, but with such a measure of discretion and learning as might qualify him for the due discharge of the office of a missionary. His name was John Christman Diemer, a native of Alsatia, who at first studied divinity for some years at Strasburg, from whence he removed to Halle, where, besides pursuing his theological studies, he had been employed as a teacher and moderator in the Orphan House. The Society concurred with his suggestion to send this person as a colleague to Mr. Kiernander, whose age and infirmities more urgently called for an assistant, whom he might train up in the duties of the mission, which it was feared would lose ground if no one were at hand to take charge of it in case of Mr. Kiernander's death.

In December of the same year, Mr. Diemer having proceeded to London, was presented to the Society, and the Rev. Mr. Bourdillon being requested to undertake the office, delivered to him the instructions of the board in a Latin oration, which is still preserved in the Society's publications, and affords a delightful specimen of the truly pious principles which actuated the leading men of that venerable body.

During the year 1773, sixteen adult heathens, natives of Bengal, were added to the mission congregation in Calcutta, and six Romanists. About this time Mr. Kiernander was visited with a domestic affliction by the death of his wife. A pleasing circumstance is recorded consequent upon this event, but fully in accordance with the singular liberality of this excellent man. The personal property of Mrs. Kiernander, at her express desire, amounting to 6000 rupees, was appropriated to the building of a school-house, which was much wanted for the mission. It was built on the east side of the church, where what are called the Old Church Rooms now stand, consisting of three large rooms sufficiently spacious to contain 250 children. It was ready for occupation in March 1774. From the assistance afforded by the converted missionaries, an extension of the mission seems to have been contemplated about this time, and the Rev. Mr. Ramalhake was detached to Cossim-Bazar to assist in the Portuguese congregation there; but the sickness of some of the other assistants caused him to be recalled to Calcutta after a short period. A Malabar convert had also been entertained as a catechist, and in the school, three masters and one assistant were employed.

In the course of the year 1774, fifteen adult heathens and two from among the Papists, were added to the congregation. Mention is made in the report for this year of a legacy left by a Mrs. Mary Handel, which had by a year's interest accumulated to 876 current rupees. Besides this legacy a gentleman, (Mr. Edward Stutton,) left by his will the sum of 500 rupees legacy to Beth-Tephillah.

An instance is given of the discouragement which arises to missionaries from the seeming neglect of friends in Europe to the missionary cause, and which if foreseen would often operate to prevent them from giving themselves to a work which must die with them, unless carried on by native agency.

One man who had been a churchwarden, and a great supporter of the Romish communion, since he read the Bible, had absented himself from their service, but was still wavering. This was also the case with many others, some of whom had told Mr. Kiernander, that they could see plainly enough many absurdities and abuses in their religion. They made however a somewhat singular objection to becoming Protestants, viz., that they had seen Mr. Kiernander stand alone and unsupported for fifteen years, no one having come from Europe to assist, and in the event of his death to succeed him; and that in case of his death they would be without protector or a guide.

In 1775 Mr. Keirnander, who beside being far advanced in years and afflicted with a disease in the eye, which rendered an operation necessary, expressed his gratitude and joy at the seasonable aid afforded by the arrival of the Rev. Mr. Diemer in Calcutta. When this gentleman first arrived he was received into Mr.

Keirnander's own house, where he resided till he married a daughter of a Mr. Charles Weston, of whom some account will be given hereafter, who lodged him in one of his own houses.

In the meantime Mr. Keirnander, intent on establishing the mission on the best possible footing, pulled down his old house, and rebuilt it on a plan sufficiently large to accommodate two families, intending to give it to the mission, that the church-school and mission-house might be near each other.

Messrs. Keirnander, Diemer, and the Rev. Mr. Bento, now laboured conjointly. Mr. Diemer giving himself to the acquisition of English, in which he was soon able to minister, occasionally preaching also in German at Chinsurah, and administering the sacraments.

In the course of the year seventeen adults had been received into the Church, two of whom were Mahommedans, and fifteen Hindoos. Among the latter was a man named Ganeswan Dass, who was born at Delhi, where he lived till the death of his father, which happened when he was fifteen years of age. He then repaired to the English army, where he served several offices as Persian interpreter, till he entered into the service of a Major Graham, whom he accompanied to England in 1770, where he was kindly treated, and instructed several persons in the Persian language. In 1774, he returned to Calcutta, and was employed as Persian interpreter, and translator to the supreme court.

Sometime after his return, he occasionally attended church, and in the beginning of May 1774, addressed himself to one of the missionaries, declaring his desire of becoming a Christian, and at length requested baptism. After considerable intercourse with him, and close examination, &c., being persuaded of the sincerity of his profession and desire of embracing Christianity, they complied with his request. On Sunday, May 25, he was baptized, and took the name of Robert. His sponsors were the Hon. Sir Robert Chambers, Mrs. Chambers, senior, and Mr. Naylor.

Twenty-one Papists had renounced the errors of Popery, and joined the little but now increasing flock. One of these proved a happy instance of the effects which with the divine blessing flow from being educated in right principles. He was an inhabitant of Bandel, and came over to the Protestant Church together with his wife, two children, and seven slaves. He had left his house in Bandel, which he intended to dispose of, and was settled in Calcutta. This man some years before had been educated in the mission-school, which being a Papist, he attended merely to learn to read and write English. He now confessed to the missionaries that what he had heard when the other children were catechized, had made an impression on his mind, and had always prompted him to inquire into the reason of the difference between the Romish and Protestant persuasions; and that at length by reading the Bible in the Portuguese language he had fully satisfied himself, and had formed the resolution of becoming a Protestant.

The communicants in the English congregation this year, (1775) were ninety-one, and in the Portuguese seventy-five; some of whom had seldom the opportunity of receiving the sacrament, being hindered by going to sea, or on trading voyages on the river Ganges. Of the congregation ten had died. One of them was an old Portuguese who had formerly been converted from Popery, and received into the Protestant Church by the Rev. Mr. Schultz, missionary at Madras. His circumstances obliged him to leave that place, and go to Calcutta, and there being then no Protestant missionary there to whom he could open his mind, he returned to Popery. As soon however as Mr. Keirnander arrived, he gladly embraced the opportunity of uniting himself with the congregation of the faithful in Christ. Deep and lasting were the sorrows of his heart on account of what he was pleased to call his half-heartedness and backslidings. From this return to his former and best feelings he was diligent in his attention to the means of grace: public worship, study of the scriptures, and attendance at the sacramental opportunities. And not only was he mindful of his own soul's interests, but embraced such opportunities as were given him of communicating what he had received to others. He had a particular felicity of manner in convincing Papists of their errors, and was made a blessing to several persons of that communion. He died in peace, and was gathered to his fathers at the advanced age of 92 years.

We now, for the first time, find mention made of any attempt for the education of girls. In the school, besides twenty boys, who were entirely maintained by the Town charity, seventy-nine out-scholars had been educated. Those who paid for their education received books gratis through the favour of the society. Five orphan girls had been likewise educated under the care of a widow woman, who was indeed a widow, continuing in prayers, &c.; one was maintained by the Town charity, and the four others by Mr. Kiernander.

In 1776, Mr. Diemer writes from Calcutta, that a heathen of the writer cast had been convinced of the absurdities of his own religion, and confessed that the Christian was better. Upon which he was told that if he wished to change his religion, he should be well instructed in the Christian—that it was his duty to prove each, and all, and to hold fast that which was good. He smiled, and said, 'I cannot, and will not change, the old is better for *me*.' He added, 'The common people believe in thirty-three millions of gods, but it is very difficult to know what the Brahmans believe; I had, together with others, a conversation with a Brahman the other day. He asserted that the whole universe is God—that what speaks in me is God—and what animates a dog is God—and when God retires out of the dog he must die immediately.'

The fact is, that they one and all from this notion live as they list. They account God the author of all their immoralities and wicked actions, and so strongly do they adhere to this notion, that they hesitate not to say—'When I have an inclination to steal, I cannot help it—it was so destined.' The Brahman despises all other casts, and the lowest is an object of desecration to all. Such is what is called the Vedant system, or the doctrine of the *Vedas*. These are the most ancient scriptures of the Hindoos, under which the more refined of the present day take refuge, and dignify it with the name of Monotheism.*

* Whatever may have been asserted to the contrary, the Hindu writings recognize nothing of an Almighty, Eternal, Self-existent, all-glorious and Holy Being, who is the sole object of worship and adoration. The intellectual system, as it is called, of the *Veda*, as distinguished from the idolatrous system, is not that of an adoration of a supreme Being, but a fancied *personal identification* of themselves with His all-pervading substance, just as when a vessel of water is sunk in the ocean (to use their own image,) the water mixes inseparably and indistinguishably with the ocean as soon as the vessel is broken, to which the previous delusion is compared. Of the existence of one God, supreme *above*, and of course infinitely *distinct from* all created or extended existence, the Hindu Scriptures know nothing. '*Eko Brahm dutiya Nashta.*' One Spirit and not a second, is the thesis worked out by all the Hindu philosophers. *I* and *thou*, are not in the alphabet of their religion, and *supreme* and *subordinate* are unknown, or at least, unacknowledged terms. Hinduism is in fact pure *Pan-Theism*. An elaborate statement of the *Vedant* system of the Hindus may be seen in Mr. Colebrooke's Essays, vol. i. or Asiat. Res. vol. viii. p. 395, &c. Compare Menu, chap. xii. ver. 1, 2, 3.

This system, which has never wanted its advocates in Europe, is identical with the Egyptian theology. They taught that the soul was a particle of the *divine* æther, which without consciousness animated successively, myriads of sentient beings. And it may well be asked, '*An non disceres Spinozam sua ab hisce Ægyptiis mutuatum esse?*' A daring application of the Pantheistic principle to the theory and historic criticism of the gospel, has of late been made by several German critics, and carried to its highest pitch in the work of Dr. D. F. Strauss, on the 'Life of Jesus.' The following lines of Pope are singularly apt.

'All are but parts of one stupendous whole,
Whose body nature is, and God the soul,
That, changed through all, and yet in all the same;
Great in the earth as in the etherial frame,
Warms in the sun, refreshes in the breeze,
Glows in the stars and blossoms in the trees:
Lives through all life, extends through all extent,
Spreads undivided, operates unspent;
Breathes in our soul, informs our mortal parts,
As full, as perfect, in the hair as heart,
As full, as perfect, in vile man that mourns,
As the rapt seraph that adores and burns.
To Him no high, no low, no great, no small,
He fills, He bounds, connects and equals all.'

In the course of this year, seventy-five persons were baptized in the English and Portuguese congregation. Among these there were fourteen adult Hindus, three Malays, and three Malabareans, six Mohamedans, and one person from the Rohilla country. The communicants in the English congregation were 148, and in the Portuguese 105. Seventy-seven children had been instructed in the school, of whom twenty were the town charity children, and thirty out-scholars, who had partaken of the bounty of the society.

During the year 1778, a Mr. Gerlach arrived in Calcutta. He was sent by the brethren from Tranquebar, to assist in the general duties of the mission. As Mr. Kiernander was now unable to see, and Mr. Diemer was, it appeared, frequently unwell, the arrival of Mr. Gerlach was very opportune.

In 1780, four adult native Hindoos, and one Mohammedan, were admitted to baptism; and four Romanists were received into the Protestant communion. The communicants in the English congregation were 130, and in the Portuguese ninety-three.

For several successive years, things are reported to have continued very much the same; now and then a few additional members being added to the present infant church. In 1781, eight adult natives, besides children, were baptized. The communicants increased to the number of 148 in the English congregation; the Portuguese continuing the same.

In 1782, Mr. Kiernander reported the baptism of six adult natives, and the reception of two Romanists into communion. During this year there was an increase in the number of communicants in the Portuguese congregation of sixteen. The school during the year had educated forty-nine boys, and the Prayer Book was printed and put into circulation.

During 1783, seventeen adults were baptized, and one Romanist added to the congregation. One of the adults who had been baptized was a youth from Cochin China, who having lost his parents, lived with an elder brother, when, a war breaking out, all the family ran into the woods to save themselves. This youth lost himself, and happened to come near the sea-side where an English ship lay at anchor. The captain humanely took the stranger under his care, and after some time recommended him to another English gentleman who sent him to the mission-school to be educated, and paid for his education. Having been four years in the school, he not only learnt English, but wrote a very good hand, and was well versed in arithmetic. He was employed as a writer in the sub-treasurer's office, and continued to attend divine service on a Sunday, &c.

The Rev. Mr. Wulsbrowe Hulse, chaplain to the commander-in-chief, and Sir Eyre Coote, about this time made the mission a present of 500 rupees. Mr. Kiernander likewise presented 1000, and his son Robert William Kiernander 3000, for the use of the mission.

The Rev. Mr. Diemer this year quitted the service of the society as their missionary at Calcutta, and returned to Europe.

The Rev. Mr. Kiernander, in a letter dated Dec. 31, 1785, acknowledges the receipt of books, stationary, and other presents from the society. He mentioned with much pleasure and thanksgiving to God, that his mission under various trying circumstance, not only continued in being, but had been wonderfully supported by the gracious assistance of divine providence. He observed, that though the society had at Calcutta, only one missionary, who had served in the mission upwards of forty-five years, yet the school and the English and Portuguese congregations had been all along regularly served and attended to as far as possible, so that hitherto no part of duty had been set aside. The Rev. Mr. Bento de Sauza, who for many years had faithfully assisted in the care of the Portuguese congregation, after an illness which continued on him from February of this year, died in the month of July. Under these circumstances Mr. Kiernander mentions that he had used the assistance of a Mr. Franzel, whom he represents as an old Candidatus Theologiæ.

In the English and Portuguese congregation had been baptized,

Adult persons, natives of Bengal	14	
Malays	2	
Gentoos . . .	2	
Mahomedans .	1	
	—	19
From the Popish had been received into our church during the same year		10
Communicants in the English congregation		162
In the Portuguese, ditto		136
In the school, were educated children		52

Of these children it is stated that none were boarders, but all out-scholars, of whom about a dozen paid for their instruction from two to four rupees a month; the rest were educated gratis. Mr. Kiernander at this time gratefully acknowledges the goodness of divine providence, in that Colonel Samuel Hampton about the beginning of this year defrayed the charges of some repairs in the church, expenses of a sort which in former years had devolved on Mr. Kiernander himself.

Mr. Kiernander also mentions that the charitable collections made in both the English and Portuguese congregations had been continued through a time of great distress; which circumstance he observes is encouraging, and an evidence of good will to the cause of God.

In a letter bearing date Dec. 31, 1786, Mr. Kiernander signified an intention he entertained of a voyage to London, hoping it might tend to the adjustment of certain matters between the society and himself, observing that he, an old *emeritus*, was not only spared alive, but supported to the age of seventy-four years, in health and strength, and vigour, full as much, if not more than at any former period since the year 1740, when he first arrived in the country. He observed that although the success in the increase of the congregations had not been so great as could have been wished, yet thanks were due to God for the blessing in that degree which had been experienced, nor was he without hopes of better times and greater improvement. The opening prospect promised fair, and was sufficient to encourage a confirmation of the work, with new and united efforts. During the year Mr. Kiernander baptized,

Adult Mahomedans	8	
Natives of Bengal	10	
Caste unknown, but supposed to be of European fathers	2	
	—	20
From the Popish had been received into the Protestant church		15
Communicants in the English congregation	147	
In the Portuguese	119	
		—— 266

In the school had been educated fifty-eight children, &c. At the close of this communication, Mr. Kiernander thanks God that the duties of both congregations had been uninterruptedly attended to. He expressed a belief that the natives were coming to a better understanding and feeling in reference to the European character and the religion of Christians—the comparative good character of the former, and the entire good principles of the latter.

In another letter, bearing date Jan. 20th, 1787, he observes, that notwithstanding his earnest desire to visit England, he could not till help was obtained to take the duties during his absence, and concludes with expressing an opinion, that a glorious prospect was opening in the country for the success of the gospel.

Thus far the Journal of Mr. Kiernander. A cloud of adversity was gathering over his aged head, which, soon after burst, and the ruin of his fortunes followed.

Another missionary came, and entered into Mr. Kiernander's labours. Declining and stricken, he left the scene of his long and arduous labours, now productive of much pain and grief. He went to Chinsurah, and was appointed chaplain to that settlement (a French settlement). On the capture of Chinsurah in 1795, he became a prisoner of war, and in this character received from the English a small subsistence when 86 years of age. At last, pitying his age and misfortunes, he was allowed to go to Calcutta. In the following spring he broke his thigh by a fall, and lingered long in agony. His dwelling contained but few comforts, but divine consolations abounded. In one of his last letters, directed to his native place, Akstad, in Sweden, he writes, 'My heart is full, but my hand is weak. The world is yet the same; there are many cold friends, others like broken reeds, but God makes the heaviest burden light and easy. I rejoice to see the poor mission prosper; this comforts me amidst all.' *

At length he was called hence to be no more seen. His sun set in obscurity to rise in glory.

Before the period to which these events refer, a favourable change had begun to take place in the state of European society in Calcutta, and some persons of influence had shown themselves favourable to the propagation of Christianity among the poor deluded idolatrous and Mahommedan population, but it was thought best to continue the history of Mr. Kiernander's ministry in an unbroken narrative. To him this presidency is indebted for having, during a period of nearly thirty years, and to a considerable degree, by his individual exertions, provided means of instruction for the Christian poor. The fact of there being at the time of his suspension from labour 147 communicants in the English congregation, beside 119 in the congregation called Portuguese, but consisting, in part, of natives of Bengal, and other provinces of itself, shows that his labours

* The cloud of affliction here alluded to, was composed of many drops. It has been stated that he possessed a large property by both his marriages. His munificence was almost unbounded. Twelve thousand pounds, previous to the death of his last wife, had been expended in the erection of a Church and out-buildings. During his blindness he was almost solitary, for few even came to soothe him in his sorrows; his temporal affairs, wholly neglected by himself, were at the mercy of strangers, who were the cause of his ruin.

were extensively blessed; nor can the benefits conferred on them in the supply of the Scriptures and tracts by the Society for Promoting Christian Knowledge at a period when no other means of obtaining them existed, be overrated. In the absence of such information, no correct opinion can of course be offered on the attainment or extent of spirituality of the native congregation. Probably there are unpublished documents containing many interesting particulars, which would exhibit more clearly and satisfactorily the character and state of mind and feeling of persons admitted to baptism from time to time by Mr. Keirnander and his coadjutors. These must be sought for in the communications of the missionary to the Society for Promoting Christian Knowledge. It may, however, be fairly inferred, that the instruction afforded by the missionaries, and the numerous copies of the Scriptures and tracts in various languages put in circulation by them would not be without a measure of those fruits of righteousness which are through Jesus Christ to the glory and praise of God.

A living witness, who was in early life a private pupil of Mr. Diemer's, has supplied the following observations on the character of the mission church congregation at that period.

'Between the years 1774 and 1783, Mr. Kiernander had been assisted with two ministers sent out by the society. The Rev. Mr. Gerlach, I have heard the Rev. Mr. Brown speak of, as a man of true piety and great learning; but he could never attain the accent of the English language so as to preach in it with ease and comfort to himself, and therefore confined himself to the reading of the prayers in English, but preached readily in the Portuguese, and was of great service in assisting all inquirers with his excellent advice and holy conversation. The Rev. Mr. Diemer also assisted several years, and when Mr. Kiernander's infirmities increased, took charge of the school, and established one for private pupils in his own house, which was next door to the public school; and as the public school-room was a large one, his own pupils occupied one end, and the children belonging to the charity the other, with a teacher to attend them, but the whole under his own direction. Mr. Diemer married a daughter of Mr. Charles Weston, who had followed her father's example in abjuring popery and embracing protestantism; she was of a meek and truly Christian temper and deportment, and was greatly beloved by the little flock of the mission church. She was taken off by a lingering disorder at Bundel, the 3rd of June, 1782, in the 23rd year of her age.

'Two years after the death of his wife, Mr. Diemer returned to England with one son, the only survivor by that marriage; but came out again to India as a company's chaplain, about the year 1791. He died a few months after his second arrival. During his stay in England he married a second wife, who left this country shortly after his death. At what time Mr. Kiernander's son (who was born in 1758) returned to India, I cannot say, but he was assisting his father, and officiating in the mission church in 1783. He married a Miss Morris, a young lady of pious deportment and consistent conduct. He generally performed the English service, after his father or Mr. Gerlach had officiated in the Portuguese language.

'The presidency chaplains occasionally assisted Mr. Kiernander, and they continued to do so till he was obliged to leave his charge and retire to Chinsurah. Among several seals to the ministry of these servants of Christ, there were some distinguished persons from among the Portuguese, and even a few from among the British, notwithstanding the general depravity of manners and life then exhibited by them in Calcutta. Amongst the former may be particularly reckoned Mr. Charles Weston. Asiaticus says that he was a son of the Recorder, was born in Calcutta in 1731—was the friend and associate of Holwell, and carried arms as a militia man in 1756. His riches were great, but his poverty of spirit and true Christian humility were still greater, as some now living can perhaps testify. He was a father to the poor, the ready friend of the friendless, wherever he could find them out, and a great promoter of religion, giving largely of his substance, and influencing by his example. To every public institution he was a bountiful contributor ; and in a private way, many tasted largely of his affluence, often without knowing from whom it came : his left hand knew not what his right hand did. A gentleman in Calcutta, who had been in affluent circumstances, became so reduced that he was about to sell his horses, carriages, and household furniture. As soon as Mr. Weston heard of it, he forwarded a sum of money, promising that the same should be continued monthly, with a request that he would continue his usual style of living. His friend afterward found out who it was, that thus befriended him, and Mr. Weston continued the allowance whilst the person lived. This circumstance appeared the more remarkable, as Mr. Weston himself never used any other conveyance than a palkee, had a plain house, as plainly furnished, and his table, at which I was frequently a guest, though plentiful, was never luxurious ; he was very abstemious in his own living, though liberal in giving. This truly honourable man passed the latter years of his life at Chinsurah, amid a group of necessitous people, soothed and supported by his bounty. One hundred gold mohurs a month were regularly distributed to the indigent from a box placed on his table. He died in the month of December 1809, leaving various monies for charitable purposes, and was buried in the Protestant burial ground in Calcutta.

'There were several other converts who also adorned their Christian profession, and the blessed Redeemer was not without witness where his gospel was preached ; but its power and efficacy shone chiefly among the poor, who are generally little known.

'From what I remember of the seriousness and devotion which pervaded the mission congregation, I am persuaded of the truth of that passage in the Memorial Sketches, in which it is said, that Mr. Brown found in Calcutta, in 1786, a small body of pious Christians, and in a course of years had the happiness of discovering that in hidden and unexplored retreats, there were unthought-of individuals who lived the life of faith on the Son of God, and walked in the paths of his commandments; and some who in the utmost privacy, had exerted themselves to stem the torrent of surrounding evil by their religious example in their families, and in maintaining and superintending schools for the instruction of heathen children. Among the rich and great who were not ashamed of the cross of Christ, were Mr. Charles Grant, Sir Robert Chambers, and his brother Mr. W. Chambers, who with their families, were among the constant worshippers or attendants of those days in the mission church, together with some others of respectability. Mrs. Anne Chambers, it may be remarked, had at an advanced period of life accompanied her sons, Sir Robert and Mr. William Chambers to India. She was a constant attendant at the mission church, and died on the 7th of February, 1782, aged 69 years. Here and there we recognize the name of one we have seen and heard of in those days amongst the old epitaphs. Among them that of Mrs. Chapman, who kept a school and brought up children in the nurture and admonition of the Lord—who was a widow indeed, one who trusted in God—her appearance was as venerable as her life was useful and exemplary: no weather, no infirmities kept her from the house of God so long as she could attend, and her place was regularly filled nearly to the end. She departed this life on the 23rd of January 1784, aged sixty-three years.

'I well remember Mr. Diemer weeping after his return from her funeral, and saying, We have lost a Christian indeed, but it is gain to her. The charity-school, supported principally by Mr. Kiernander, has also produced several excellent Christian characters; and some who are now in affluent circumstances have to be thankful to that institution which called forth their latent abilities, and enabled them to become what they now are.'

Mr. Charles Grant was born in the year 1748. He went out to India about the usual age, and returned to his native land after a residence of thirty years in the year 1795, where he continued to devote his great powers for another thirty years to the highest interests of the eastern world.

He had been awakened to a deep sense of serious and personal piety in India, about the year 1778, in the midst of a scene of overwhelming domestic sorrow, by the means of a pupil and friend of the great missionary Swartz,—Mr. Chambers, whose name is mentioned above in connection with Mr. Grant's, and he thenceforth continued till the close of life, a period of nearly half a century, to exhibit both in India and England the genuine fruits of real Christianity. Cautious and wise, perhaps in the eyes of some, slow in making up his mind,—he was conscientious, firm, and honourable in all his proceedings, as well as bold and unhesitating in upholding the sacred cause of Christianity.

As a leading director, and frequently the chairman or deputy-chairman of the honourable court, he gradually acquired by his intuition, his sound judgment, his application to business, his reach of mind, his power of combination and forethought, his transparent disinterestedness, that influence in the councils of the India government which has not often been parallelled.

During the same period he stood forth in the House of Commons, supported by his two fine sons, as a pillar in the midst of the land. There, with the small but mighty band of Christian statesmen, Mr. Wilberforce, Mr. H. Thornton, Mr. Babington, and a few others, he ultimately won almost every cause of humanity and piety in which he was engaged.

In the conduct of our religious institutions, and especially of the British and Foreign Bible, Church Missionary, and Jews' Conversion Societies, Mr. Grant took a leading part.

In one view in particular, India owes a debt to this eminent person which can scarcely be too highly estimated. His labours in increasing the number of chaplains in the Honourable Company's establishment, in improving and regulating their salaries and retiring pensions, and in selecting for chaplains clergymen of undoubted talents, piety, and devotedness to their profession, were unremitting. To secure this last point, the most important of all, he did not rely altogether on his own judgment, but engaged the advice of a thoroughly competent and experienced friend resident at one of the universities; and thus assisted he not unfrequently exchanged other patronage for that of chaplaincies, in order to carry out his great object. It is to this we owe that class of eminently holy men who united the character of the missionary and the chaplain in so high a degree; and of which David Brown, Claudius Buchanan, Henry Martyn, Daniel Corrie, late bishop of Madras, the present bishop of Bombay, Thomason, and a host of others, were conspicuous ornaments.

Some particulars collected from persons who were acquainted with him, may here be introduced respecting one, who was distinguished among the few righteous persons of that day by a remarkable simplicity and godly sincerity of character, and who proved, to a considerable degree, the means of keeping alive that spirit of piety which then began, in a more especial manner, to manifest itself. This person was John Christian Obeck. He was born in 1730, in the city of Magdeburg in Prussia. At a very early age, the truths of the gospel sunk deep into his heart, and held a happy and abiding influence on his life. He used to say 'Before I was fifteen, the Saviour was very precious to me, and was altogether a *Jesus*—a Saviour from sin. His walk through life was consistent with his early profession.

He arrived at Tranquebar, on the coast, in the year 1755, then in his 26th year. We find him acting as clerk and schoolmaster under the Rev. Mr. Hutteman, at Cudalore, in 1762: the following year, 1763, he married Anna Elizabeth Mayer, of Pullicat; after this, he was several years with the venerable and apostolic Swartz, acting as schoolmaster and catechist, and with him he continued until he became known to Mr. William Chambers, with whom he came round to Calcutta in 1777.

In 1782, he accompanied Mr. Charles Grant to Maldah, and continued in that family until Mr. Grant left India. When that liberal friend of good men left the country, he continued to the worthy Obeck a comfortable pension, so that the pious old man was henceforth relieved from the care of earning his daily bread at an advanced stage of life, and had leisure afforded him to enjoy himself in those things in which he most delighted—communion with his God; &c. and as he shone brighter and brighter towards the evening of life, so he endeavoured to allure all over whom he had any influence, to become fellow-partakers with him of the free grace of God in Christ.

In his living he was very temperate, almost abstemious. He had a remarkably healthy frame of body, being rarely indisposed, and then very slightly. He was seldom so ill as to keep his bed or room a whole day, until his last sickness came on, and then he said, '*It is unto death.*'

He had not had the benefit of what is called a liberal education, but with him the fear of the Lord was the beginning of wisdom, and not only the beginning, but a well-spring of life, continually supplying him on every occasion with a word in season. His judgment was so sound that all who had the privilege of being acquainted with him, used to advise on matters prudential as well as spiritual with him, and his influence over a considerable circle was much beyond what falls to the lot of most in his circumstances.

Turning from these brief notices of individual piety, we may now review the improvement in European society, which had already commenced, and which gradually introduced greater facilities for the moral and religious improvement of all classes.

For many years after the East India Company had obtained territory in India; their contest with the native powers, and their unhappy divisions among themselves, occupied the whole attention of the British; but gradually, as their situation became more secure, and the measures of government and commerce better arranged, individuals among them began to give their attention to the languages and literature of the country. With a view principally to supply competent interpreters of Mahomedan law, who should be able to assist the judges of the Zillah courts in their decisions in matters of life and property, the Madrassa, or College for Arabic learning in Calcutta, was founded by Governor Hastings in 1781; and with a view to supply equally competent interpreters of Hindu law, the Sanscrit College at Benares was afterwards founded. These establishments cost the government 20,000 rupees a year each; and, in order to render them efficient, it has been found necessary to add to each an European secretary or superintendent.

Individuals also, at the period already referred to, had begun to cultivate an acquaintance with the literature of the country. Among these, Mr. Halhed was most conspicuous. In 1776, he set himself to study Bengalee and Sanscrit, and in 1778 published a grammar of the Bengalee, to which is added a grammar of the Hindostanee. About the same time, Mr. Wilkins set himself to apply the art of printing to the languages of the East. In this pursuit he was indefatigable. He originated the models, prepared the materials, and shared the manual labour with the native assistants. Among the first specimens of his typographical skill, was Mr. Halhed's Bengalee grammar, and to his font of Bengalee types he afterwards added others in the Nagri and Persian characters.

In the latter end of 1788, Sir William Jones arrived in India. Eminently great in various departments of science, it belongs to this sketch to notice chiefly the influence his character excited on the religious interests of the community. Among the several objects of inquiry which he proposed to himself in India are noted: 'Proofs and illustrations of Scripture—traditions concerning the Deluge—to print and publish the Gospel of St. Luke in Arabic—to print and publish the Psalms of David in Persian verse.'

With those subjects, among others in his mind, he applied himself to the study of the Sanscrit language, and to him we are particularly indebted for overcoming the reluctance of the Brahmins to communicate the knowledge contained in their shasters. He is said to have given his teacher, a pundit of the Vydia, or medical caste, 500 rupees a month. And thus, by a well-directed liberality, opened the means of instruction on more moderate terms to future students.

The growing spirit which thus began to display itself for the cultivation of eastern literature, was further cherished and embodied by the institution of the Asiatic Society in 1784. For this institution also, India is indebted to Sir William Jones. There the kindred minds which then adorned India, collected round the illustrious founder, seconded his labours and began those researches which have so much attracted the learned in Europe, and thrown such light on the languages, literature, and antiquities of India.

It must not be concealed however, that many who engaged in these puruits, were instigated by no love for the literature of the Bible. An idea had become prevalent among learned men in the continent of Europe, excited perhaps by communications from India, that in the long-concealed Brahminical records, evidence would be found to invalidate the truth of the Bible as a revelation from God. It cannot be doubted that some of the most eminent oriental scholars in India at the period we are writing of, entertained the same opinion.

The statements which occur in the writings of Sir William Jones, as to his readiness to reject the Bible should anything be discovered in Eastern records, to invalidate its authority, indicate the state of mind rather of his associates than of his own. To his discerning and pious mind, the invalidating of the truth of the Bible must have appeared impossible, independent of his remarkable testimony to the purity and sublimity of its contents, which has been so often quoted, and so much and justly admired.

Little however as the eastern scholars of that day in India, intended to help on the propagation of Christian knowledge, they were removing those obstacles to the acquisition of those languages of India, and to the printing of the sacred Scriptures in those languages which must otherwise have long impeded the progress of missionary labour; and it is deserving of notice, that one of the very men who had assisted Mr. Wilkins in the preparation of his types, offered his services to the missionaries of Serampore, a few months after their settlement there. His services were accepted, and in the course of a few years he instructed a number of his countrymen in the same art. By these, others have been instructed, till there is no longer any difficulty in obtaining fonts of types in any of the Indian alphabets.

As the means in the course of an all-wise providence were thus provided, both for translating and printing the sacred scriptures, so the desire to employ those means was kindling in the minds of men peculiarly fitted for the arduous work.

Among these Mr. W. Chambers deserves particular mention. He was prothonotary and Persian interpreter to the supreme court. He possessed superior literary talents, and a fine taste, and these were sanctified by sound piety and devotedness to the interests of Christian religion, of which he was a steady and prudent promoter, wherever he could find an opportunity. The giving the sacred Scriptures to his Indian fellow-subjects, was to him a matter of conscientious and earnest desire. With this end in view he addressed himself to translate the New Testament both into Persian and

Hindoostanee. For this work he was eminently qualified, not only by his skill in the languages, but also by the cordial love of divine truth with which his heart now glowed. Opportunity however was not allowed for, his making much progress in the work.

Shortly before this time, the Moravian brethren endeavoured to establish a mission in Bengal, and sent out three missionaries for that purpose: their names were Latrobe, Raabs, and Smith. They took a house in Park Street, but did not succeed, and were soon scattered. Latrobe died at Chinsurah or Serampore, Raabs on the Malay coast, and Smith in Calcutta in August 1783.

It was in this year (1783) Mr. John Thomas, afterwards the colleague of Dr. Carey, arrived in Calcutta as surgeon of the Oxford indiaman. His proceedings as connected with the labours of the Baptist Missionary Society at this presidency, which commenced ten years afterwards, deserve to be noticed particularly, as they also throw a light on the state of society here. In writing to the Baptist Society he informs them—

'I advertised for a Christian; and that I may not be misunderstood, I shall subjoin a copy of the advertisement, from the India Gazette, of Nov. 1, 1783.

'RELIGIOUS SOCIETY.'

'A plan is now forming for more effectually spreading the knowledge of Jesus Christ and his glorious Gospel in and about Bengal. Any serious persons of any denomination, rich or poor, high or low, who would heartily approve of joining in, or gladly forward such an undertaking, are hereby invited to give a small testimony of their inclination, that they may enjoy the satisfaction of forming a communion the most useful, the most comfortable, and the most exalted in the world.'

'Direct A. B. C., to be left with the editor.'

'The two following answers were received the next day. The first is ascribed to Mr. W. Chambers:—

'"If A. B. C. will open a subscription for a translation of the New Testament in the Persian and Hindoostanee languages, (under the direction of proper persons) he will meet with every assistance he can desire, and a competent number of subscribers to defray the expense."

'"The Rev. Mr. —— having read the advertisement of A. B. C. in this day's paper, takes the earliest opportunity of expressing his satisfaction of a proposal, for the more effectually propagating and making known the truth of the Christian religion in this country of superstition, idolatry, and irreligion, and for setting forth the excellency of the holy institution so replete with the means of rendering mankind happy both here and hereafter, most cordially offers his services for promoting and encouraging so laudable an undertaking, and will think himself happy if he can be at all instrumental in bringing it to any degree of success.

'"Mr. —— from the above reasons, therefore, wishes an opportunity of conferring with the advertiser on the occasion."'

The Reverend writer is said by Mr. Thomas to have been a chaplain to the presidency, and is supposed to have been the Rev. Mr. Owen, who, it will be seen hereafter, was a sincere friend and faithful supporter of such measures as were then found practicable, for the promoting of Christian knowledge, among both the British and Indian communities.

We must not here omit to notice the establishment now known as the Military Orphan School. It affords a remarkable attestation to the growing regard to the cause of religion and humanity among the European society of that day; and in its consequences has produced the most valuable effects to society in general.

The institution was planned, and owed much of its success to the humane and comprehensive mind and active exertions of Colonel, then Captain Kirkpatrick. The proposal for its establishment was circulated throughout the army in the latter end of 1782, and met with almost unanimous approbation. The superior officers of the army contributed so largely towards the necessary expenses attending the commencement of operations, that a general appeal to the public was rendered unnecessary.

The general management began to act on the arrangement approved by the army in March 1783. Their first care was to acquaint the government, and the court of directors, with their plans, and to elicit their countenance and support. It was at first intended to send all the orphans of officers to England for education; but till the pleasure of the court of directors on this, and other points connected with the institution, should be ascertained, accommodations were obtained in Calcutta for the orphans in want of immediate care.

In the course of the year it was proposed to government, by the general management, to take under their care, on a fixed allowance for each child, the children also of the Enropean non-commissioned officers and privates in the company's service, stating besides reasons connected with the health of the children, that hitherto little or no pains had been taken to render the numerous offspring of the Europeans belonging to the army of the establishment (whether orphans or the children of soldiers still living) useful to the community: it being a fact but too well known, that not only the cultivation of their natural talents had been totally neglected; but that owing to the habits unavoidably contracted in an European regiment, their morals also had been corrupted in a degree too shocking to be described. To this arrangement the government agreed, and finally, the orphan establishment, consisting of the upper and lower school, was fixed at Howrah.

Respecting the establishment thus formed, one of its

original friends and advocates, a field officer, described its object to be, to give a useful and Christian education to a continued succession of 500 children born of European fathers, and Indian mothers, whose nurture and education had been hitherto so totally neglected, that they had, until now, *been wholly lost to society.*

Though the primary intention of the founders of the institution was to succour the friendless, and render useful to the community, subjects hitherto neglected, yet the officer above alluded to, and no doubt others also, entertained still higher expectations from this work of charity and mercy. Pleading the cause of the Bengal Military Orphan Society, he urged that when the plan of the society should be generally adopted, the happy result would be that more than 1000 hitherto neglected and destitute infants of both sexes would be constantly training up in a course of religious and useful instruction, so as not only to become valuable subjects of the state, but what is of infinitely more consequence, be made the happy instruments of spreading the knowledge of the divine religion of Jesus Christ, and the useful arts of polished society, throughout the benighted and idolatrous nations of Asia. The writer of this sketch can testify that these anticipations have by no means been disappointed. Society has acquired many useful members of both sexes from this institution, and it is worthy of remark, that several individuals of both the upper and lower schools, have of late years been among the most active and zealous in diffusing the knowledge of Christianity among the natives under this presidency.

But this result has not been brought about without the watchful and unremitting care of the successive members of the general management. On the institution being fairly established, masters were sought for from England to take charge of the education of the orphans, and through Colonel Kirkpatrick, who had been obliged to visit England from ill health, the Rev. David Brown was among the first engaged to watch over the infant establishment.

Of him, the author of the preface to 'Memorial Sketches,' who was among his earliest friends, truly says, that Mr. Brown, if not actually the founder of all the great missionary institutions which have been established of late years, and of the plans which have been carried into effect for translating the scriptures into all the languages of the east, laboured in the field as much as any who have followed him, and strove to the utmost of his power to kindle that very flame which has burned, and is now burning in almost every quarter of the globe.

The life of the Rev. David Brown was prolonged through a course of twenty-seven years in Calcutta, and it cannot be denied but that the tone of morals and habits of society experienced great improvement during that period. It is not to be inferred that Mr. Brown alone contributed to this evident improvement. Yet it must be admitted that the influence of his personal character and public ministrations for so long a period cannot but have had a powerful influence and a considerable share in it. It will not then be a vain pursuit if we endeavour to ascertain what it was in Mr. Brown which led to such long and disinterested labours for the benefit of his fellow-creatures, as his life exhibits; this we may gather from the authentic materials supplied in '*Memorial Sketches*,' a work of much interest and of general reference. It appears hence to have been generally *an early experience of the grace of God, raising him from a death in sin to a life of righteousness.*

In a memorandum found among his papers, he gratefully acknowledges—'Thy goodness like the sun dawned on my early days—a godly grandfather who poured out many prayers for me—parents who attended to the instructions given them by the ministers of God—early acquaintance with the Reverends Jesse, Stillingfleet, Milner—mercies all flowing from my God!' And in a short sketch he drew up of the early part of his life, his words are: 'Through a merciful providence I escaped the pollutions of youth—and through the same providence I was disciplined by sickness just before I went to Cambridge. At this time I experienced the gospel to be the power of God unto salvation, in a most sensible manner.' And in another retrospection, he speaks of that sickness 'as a severe illness nigh unto death, before I went to college, which was greatly blessed to my soul.'

With a mind thus brought under a divine influence which strengthened with his years, he *devoted himself to the service of God in the ministry of the Church of England*, and having finished his preparatory studies at the grammar school at Hull, he proceeded to Magdalen College, Cambridge.

The circumstances which led to Mr. Brown's going to India are thus related:—'During his residence at college he corresponded with a friend in London on serious subjects, and related some successful efforts made to do good among the poor and destitute.' He observes—'That friend communicated my letters to a Major of the East India Company's service; the result was, he wished to be acquainted with me—wished to serve me, and introduced himself by letter as follows, before I had even heard of his name, which made the application appear the more wonderful.'

'TO MR. D. BROWN.

'SIR,

* * * * *

'The officers belonging to the army in Bengal have formed themselves into a society for the benevolent purpose of supporting, educating, and introducing into life the orphans of both sexes belonging to indigent deceased officers of that settlement: they have twenty-five male, and twenty-one female children under their care, in Bengal. Their intentions are to send these children to be educated in England, when they arrive at a certain age; but as they propose to have a superintendent of the institution in India, they have authorized a captain of the Bengal army, lately arrived in England, and on the point of re-embarking for India, to look out for a married young gentleman, (a clergyman in preference,) to proceed to India in one of the ships of this season. The prospects are such as, in my estimation, hold out a most flattering view to whatever gentleman may be fixed on; and I presume it would to you be a very great additional inducement, in furnishing you an opportunity of instilling the knowledge of salvation by Jesus Christ into the minds of young persons, most of whom will probably spend their lives among the heathen nations of India. As the gentleman embarks for India in ten days, you must make an immediate choice. I have prevailed on him to wait for your answer until Thursday morning; and if you have thoughts of accepting the offer, it will be necessary for you to come to town without the loss of a moment.

* * * * *

Sir, your's &c.,

A. Mitchell.'

London, Feb. 1785.

'When this letter reached me at college,' writes Mr. B., 'I was just recovering from a long indisposition. Many objections immediately occurred to me; I foresaw them all at a rapid glance, and settled in my mind that I might decline the offer with a good conscience: above all, I was too young for priest's orders, and without ordination I was resolved to accept of no service or situation whatever. I acquainted some of my serious friends with the import of the major's letter, and my sentiments upon it. They differed from me in judgment; they thought it was the voice of providence, and that so unexpected and singular an application, which so fairly promised to advance my usefulness, ought not to be disregarded. I submitted to their counsel, but not before I had besought the wisdom and direction of the Father of light. I must say that from this time I went by the judgment of others rather than my own, and resolved to leave the matter to the decision of three tried friends in the church; and their written opinion I resolved at all events to follow, though in my own mind inclined to sit still and enjoy the tranquillity of college life, and the dear delights of pious and literary friendship there. In this too I was dissented from; and was advised to visit the major, if it was only to return him a proper attention. On the 15th I was introduced to him in town; I found him a gentleman of great resolution and perseverance, and well skilled in the active scenes of life; he feared not to get me through the difficulties of ordination, and all others that might oppose themselves to the plan: the next two days were taken up in seeing Captain Kirkpatrick, the agent and secretary to the Bengal Orphan Society, and in advising with my family. Some difficulties, as expected, arose on the subject of receiving ordination at so short notice, when the late Dr. Watson, Bishop of Llandaff, was at length induced to favour his views, and 'I set off,' writes Mr. B., 'for Cambridge the following day, for the necessary papers which the Bishop directed me to procure, and with these I again waited on him on the 25th; but he appearing now to feel some hesitation on the subject, I caught at it, and said, 'My Lord, I am satisfied, I shall return to college; for my views have been to the ministry, and without ordination I shall not go to India, whatever offers are made me.' After a pause, however, he said he would ordain me, and that he would also have given me priest's orders the day following, if I had been of age to receive them. He appointed the next day for my examination, and ordained me the day after.

'The bishop showed me a truly pastoral regard; he knew my principles, my purposes, and my views; he conducted a long and close examination of me himself, and gave me much valuable advice, which has been a great comfort and support to me. His last words were, 'Go in peace, and may the blessing of God go with you. Do all the good you can, and if it is no better for you in this world, it will be in the world to come.'

Mr. Brown's chief object in accepting the appointment to India was *the furtherance of the Christian religion on the earth.* Riches or personal aggrandizement, says the writer of 'Memorial Sketches,' were not even of secondary moment in his mind. His sole consideration throughout life was whether his labours or possessions could in any way be made subservient to the glory of God in Jesus Christ.

These were the sentiments of one who knew Mr. Brown in the nearest relation of life, and seeing death has long since set the seal of authenticity upon what might otherwise have been suspected of being only the ebullition of a youthful and generous mind, we may refer in confirmation to his own memoranda of his feelings at the period referred to :—

'The Captain (Kirkpatrick) expecting to sail, wished to have the articles of agreement filled up ; but how was the major surprised to find he had misunderstood the offer—that there were no fewer than 500 children on the Orphan Establishment, and that the salary was considerably less than he had first stated to me ; however this unexpected obstacle was easily removed, for since a larger sphere of usefulness was thus opened to my view I regretted not the diminution of salary.'

A time in painful suspense occasioned by disappointment in obtaining a passage occurred it seems after the arrangements with Captain Kirkpatrick were completed. The extracts which follow from a journal kept by Mr. Brown at this time shew with what humble resignation to the divine will he waited the event :—

'"The Lord is with you while ye be with him." I desire to be with the Lord in my intention, and to acknowledge him in all my ways. Let not ambition lead me to mistake his will, nor inglorious depression to desert his cause, then I will not fear ; strength and victory are secured to me by this promise. I will set the Lord against all my fears, inabilities, and wants, and tell the enemies of my soul that He that is for me, is greater than all that are against me.

'We have no cause to fear while we are about the Lord's business. He will enable us to execute whatever he commandeth. Life will soon be over, it signifies little where I am or whither I go, what dangers, perils, or comforts I meet with on my way to a better country—*to heaven my home.* Much less than a hundred years will put an end to sin, the cause of every pain; and provided it shall be found that I have served the Lord Jesus, it will not matter where, at London or Calcutta. I wait to see whether it please the Lord to honour me with a commission to the East, or to give the work to others better and fitter for the discharge of it.'

This was certainly a right spirit, a disciplined, chastened spirit. At length all obstacles being removed, Mr. Brown embarked for India, and reached the place of his destination, and entered on his charge June 8th, 1786, when the following pious and characteristic reflections were entered in his journal:—

'I this day entered upon my solemn charge as chaplain of this foundation, the Military Orphan Establishment. May these souls committed to my care be led to a saving knowledge of the Lord Jesus, and be instructed in all right things to the praise and glory of God! O Lord, my joy will be to see them trained in the way they should go; but give thou them thy Spirit, which alone can direct and keep them in right paths.'

On his arrival in Calcutta, through the influence of the late Mr. Charles Grant, Mr. Brown was appointed chaplain to a brigade: this from very unexpected circumstances led to his becoming presidency chaplain, and finally provost of the college of Fort William on its first establishment. In this way opportunities of accumulating wealth were opened which put his principles to no common trial, out of which however they came pure and uncorrupted. 'My prayer,' said he, in a letter to a friend written in 1802, 'is now principally directed against the root of all evil—the *love* of money. It has cast off from me on the right hand and on the left many of whom I hoped better things. Oh when shall the Lord's people turn not again to folly! There are few who do it not in some way or other; I have compassion, having myself also been tempted; but from what I have seen I dread particularly the consequences of growing rich, not that I am in any danger of being so, but a *very little* money does the business, one thousand or ten thousand a year is the same in operation. 'Give me neither poverty nor riches,' is a safe prayer, it is a prayer against riches, and as such I use it, though in no likelihood of becoming rich; if more come than occasion require, I trust I shall cast my bread upon the waters, the Lord help me so to do!' In 1806 the same sentiment is expressed in even more striking terms:—'The idea of making a competency and returning to England to enjoy it, never occupied my attention for a single moment, because utterly impracticable under present circumstances. I might, it is very true, in the course of years have made some independence if I would have walked in crooked paths, but from which I have been in mercy preserved.'

It not being intended to enter on Mr. Brown's history further than as tending to show the influence he must have exerted on the progress of religion in Calcutta, we will not here notice the sacrifices of a personal nature he made in leaving scenes so agreeable to nature as the prospect of literary distinction and the rewards which usually follow it at college; and especially of one so formed for the enjoyments of friendship in tearing himself away from the society of pious relatives and associates, and the company of many of the excellent of the earth, who cherished the opening appearances of piety and talent in him with paternal fondness. It may be sufficient to observe that the pious and learned Dean Milner gave the highest possible testimonial of his piety and learning to the committee of general management.

Among those to whom the arrival of Mr. Brown in Calcutta was a most welcome event, was Mr. Charles

Grant, so long the able and influential chairman of the court of Directors, and then member of the Board of Trade in Bengal. With reference to the part he took in upholding the mission of the Christian Knowledge Society, ready at this time to fail through various untoward events, it may be observed that previous to that gentleman's residence in Calcutta, he had been commercial president at Maldah. Here his active concern for the interests of religion, manifested itself in various ways. By his influence, men of tried character were placed at the head of different factories in that neighbourhood, who proved inestimable blessings to all around them, the effects of which are still to be seen. Among these may be named as well known, Mr. W. Brown, Mr. W. Grant, Mr. Henry Creighton, and Mr. John Ellerton. In these the natives saw the true Christian character exhibited, and felt its effects in the liberality of their dealings, and the extensive charity exercised towards the poor and afflicted. Schools were established in different villages, in which portions of Scripture and other small books were read. Mr. Ellerton employed his leisure in translating the New Testament into Bengalee, and Dialogues on the book of Genesis, now one of the most popular of books in the Bengalee language, and deservedly valued as an excellent school-book.

It has been stated that Mr. Kiernander found himself in circumstances, at the decline of life, which threatened the total ruin of the mission. The late lamented Bishop Corrie states that he had been informed by persons who had abundant opportunity of knowing the truth, that this calamity was brought upon him by the failure in business of a person for whom he had become surety. From his exceedingly generous habits Mr. Keirnander had made no provision for such an event, and the seal of the sheriff of Calcutta was, in 1787, affixed to the gates of *Beth-Tephillah*, which as part of his own personal property, became subject to the law.

The venerable patriarch was now in the 76th year of

his age, and the 47th of his residence in India, an age at which in any climate he must feel severely the reverse of circumstances. It was in reference to this event, he wrote, that the most sad period of his life was when by old age, fatigue, and other vexations, he was compelled to leave his post when there was no one to take it up and carry it on. But he adds, how wonderfully Divine providence interfered to my great comfort! Three friends were ready, surely by Divine appointment,—the Mission Church was redeemed, and thereby gained kind and careful patrons—Grant, Chambers, and Brown; be their good works never forgotten! Mr. Grant alone paid the sum of ten thousand rupees, at which the Church was valued, and Mr. Brown engaged to officiate in it, which he continued to do for twenty-three years without fee or reward. On the last day of October 1787, the property of the Church was transferred by a deed of trust to Mr. William Chambers, Rev. David Brown, and Mr. Charles Grant, jointly under an engagement on their part, for themselves and their successors, that the building should for ever remain appropriated to the purposes for which it was erected.

Some further particulars recorded in '*Memorial Sketches*,' require to be inserted here, as connected with the progress of religion at this period.

Mr. Brown on accepting the appointment to assist in the education of the children of the Orphan School, had particular regard to the influence the youth of both sexes, so educated, were likely to have in promoting genuine religion generally throughout the country. He had therefore, before he left England, been introduced to the Society for Promoting Christian Knowledge, and elected a corresponding member of that body, under a promise of supplying information respecting their India missions.

During the voyage he employed himself in the study of Hindoostanee, and soon after his arrival at Calçutta, he applied himself strenuously to the acquisition of Bengalee, with a special reference to a translation of the Scriptures into that language for the benighted heathen.

Writing to his parents in 1787, Mr. Brown says, 'My heart's cares and pains are for the ministry, and the real conversion of souls to God among my countrymen in this land: my mind also is perpetually busied about the heathen, whom I long to see members of that Lord whose cross is my hope. Some who fear God in this country have joined in proposing a mission, and I have been busied some time in drawing up papers relative to this business, and hope you will pray that the Lord may prosper this work with His blessing.'

The papers here referred to, about which Mr. Brown speaks of himself as engaged, are thus described in the preface to 'Memorial Sketches.'

'The very year after he went to Calcutta, before the great Missionary Societies or the Bible Society had been thought of, this honoured servant of Christ, in conjunction with two other friends in India, who most gladly co-operated with him, drew up a "Proposal for establishing a Protestant Mission in Bengal and Bahar." In this he urges, with great force and energy, the claims of the natives upon our government, and the duty of imparting to them the privileges which we enjoy, as well in a religious as in a civil point of view. He recommends the measure of translating the Scriptures into the different languages of the East, and the sending forth missionaries to instruct them, fit men, of free minds, disinterested, zealous and patient of labour, who would accept of an invitation, and aspire to the arduous office of a missionary.'

In this document he considers,—what sort of men are to be chosen, in what manner they are to be supported, and what plan is to be pursued by them. Under the first of these heads the description given by Mr. Brown, of the persons whom he wanted to fill the situation of missionaries, shows exactly what he himself was both in heart and life. After assigning his reasons for desiring to have young clergymen of the established

Church, he adds, 'But genuine piety seems to be the grand requisite in a missionary: his work must be his business, his delight and reward. Whoever is greedy of gain, and seeks great things for himself; whoever prefers a life of ease and competence, to a life of toil with an humble subsistence, is not fit for this purpose. But men who are ready to endure hardships and to suffer the loss of all things; who count not their own lives dear to them, and who are willing to do and suffer for the sake of the Gospel; these are the men who are wanted—these are the true missionaries to instruct the heathen successfully in the way of salvation.' To enforce his application to the Honourable East India Company, he sent letters to the then Archbishop of Canterbury, to the late Bishop of Llandaff, to that promoter of every good work, Mr. Wilberforce, and to a great number of distinguished characters in this country, urging and entreating them all to use their utmost efforts, both in and out of Parliament, to draw the attention of the public to this good work, and to gain for it the sanction and assistance of the ruling powers.'

In a letter to a friend, Mr. Brown relates the measures that were pursued here, in order to conciliate the favour of Government, and further developes his plan in a way which must interest the Christian reader. 'The Rev. Mr. —— approved much of the design, and interested others in it; and the Rev. Mr. Blanshard, senior chaplain to the presidency, was very ready to assist in breaking the subject to Lord Cornwallis. We thought it needful in prudence at first to approach his Lordship by very gentle gradations, and therefore pressed the idea of native schools as preparatory to the main business of giving Christian light to this land sitting in heathen darkness. The following letter was written to a friend on the occasion:—

'They had an interview, and pressed the subject of it as closely as they might; but it does not seem that his lordship is disposed to forward our wishes; however, we have the consolation to know that he will not oppose them. He has no faith in such schemes, and thinks they must prove ineffectual; but he has no objection that others should attempt them, and promises not to be inimical.

'This was as much success as we expected, and led to other points. Mr. Grant has had an opportunity of opening his mind to his lordship, who desired him to draw up his thoughts in writing, assuring him that he would pay attention to his opinions. This has been done, and a paper, of which I transmit you a copy, was given in, a few weeks since. It was civilly received, and Lord C. said he would peruse it. But little is to be expected from this effort besides a clear unfolding of the plan. I now hope, that if any propositions arrive from England well recommended, his lordship will not be startled at the idea, but find himself in some measure engaged to give it countenance.

'We think the paper may do good at home, and it is therefore sent to you, and you will use it as occasion may require. Perhaps Mr. Wilberforce may find it useful to combat such objections as he is likely to meet with, and it may assist his views. You will of course submit it to him, and furnish him with a copy if he should wish for it. It has at least made Lord Cornwallis familiar with the subject, and done away many prejudices; so that opposition need not to be feared from that quarter.

'I must also mention that the four bishops named in the chaplains' letter, will be addressed by them, by this dispatch, inclosing to each a copy of their letter to the Governor General.

'It seems most desirable that some attempt toward a mission to the heathen of these countries should now be made at home without delay, either on a public or a private footing. Should it not at present be practicable to effect any thing with the higher powers, and to bring a mission forward on a broad foundation, the zeal of individuals will perhaps avail to the beginning of a good work, which, as the grain of mustard-seed, may spread out into some considerable effect.

'From a conviction of the great advantage that would arise to missionaries from the accurate knowledge of Sanscrit, it is proposed that the acquisition of this language should be made a prime object; as it is the basis of the Bengalee, as well as of several other eastern tongues, and it contains the mythology, laws, history, and literature of the Hindoos. A knowledge of the Sanscrit is necessary for giving a pure translation of the scriptures; and such is the poverty of the Bengalee, that it would be difficult to preach the gospel with the dignity becoming it without the use of Sanscrit. It is therefore proposed, that forthwith two young clergymen be sent as missionaries to India. They will come immediately to Bengal, and remain with us at Calcutta. It will then be advisable that they fix for about three years at that famous seat of Hindoo learning, Benares, which is about six hundred miles journey west from Calcutta, in a higher latitude; a pleasant and healthy situation, where living is cheap. There they may study and furnish themselves with languages. After which they may begin their glorious work, of giving the Gentiles light, with every probability of success.

'A few words are necessary for the qualifications of two persons for engaging in this design. You will be aware that zeal and grace, though essentials, are not the only requisites on this occasion.

'They need be men of general knowledge, and possess such a share of science as may make their conversation interesting to the learned brahmins, who will only be communicative in proportion to the returns made by those with whom they converse. The qualification necessary to a character in which the pious student and prudent missionary are to be united, are obvious enough.

'The young men should obtain some public recommendation through the Bishop of London, or others, to this government, which is essential on every account. You will perhaps have some difficulties at home, but the Lord, if he favours the work, will carry you through them.

'If a mission can be brought forward upon a public foundation, the two gentlemen now invited will consequently be put upon it, and thence derive their provision; but till that takes place, it is agreed they shall be allowed £350. per annum. This will be a subsistence for them, but nothing can be saved from it. If therefore you have found two men of zeal and talents fit for this arduous work, let them come. A sufficiency of bread is offered them, but nothing to excite a spirit of adventure, or to tempt to worldly views. Before you can receive this, I hope some steps have been taken by those in power, toward a mission establishment. But the great move slowly in such matters; and it cannot be otherwise expected, unless they had spiritual as well as political views.

'Perhaps Dr. Watson (Bishop of Llandaff) will be pleased with the idea of two young men coming out to study Sanscrit at Benares. You will probably think proper to communicate this to him, his recommendation of such an undertaking would be a favourable circumstance. His name is known here, and is of great weight.

'I will not conclude without again expressing my hope that all obstacles will be surmounted, and that Providence will open a way through all discouragements for the Gospel to pass into India. If the Society for Promoting Christian Knowledge would give any assistance, how gladly will it be accepted.'

Whilst these measures were pursued for the general extension of missionary efforts, Mr. Brown was not sparing of personal labour or expense in the same cause. He took great pains to inform himself of the actual state of Hindu society. He went occasionally among them in a way not usual with the English; he attended in their domestic circles, their literary and religious entertainments. Writing to a friend a few years after his arrival in Bengal, Mr. Brown says :—'Lately at a Brahmin's house I heard a wonderful man, a Purani, explaining their shasters with astonishing address and elocution. He frequently made the people burst into tears, and weep aloud. Whenever their passions were touched with any pathetic passage, the man obtained several rupees, thrown to him both by Brahmans and Sooders; the latter accompanied their donation with a *pranàm*, or act of worship to the *Purani.*'

The result of these researches was communicated to a friend in the following very correct and discriminating remarks :—'The (Hindu) system is extremely complex, and it is therefore very easy to misrepresent it. The moral state of the people is more palpable, and the grossness of the lower orders more open to attack. It is a great pity so little is yet known of their book-religion: facts would arise out of what is written, that would be the best instruments to overturn their superstition. There is clearly a total difference between the religion of the learned, and that of the common people. The learned are as subtle and ingenious as the most skilful of the Papists, and require similar arguments to subvert their system. All the educated and instructed that I have had the opportunity of seeing, assent to the unity of God, and they possess all the light of natural religion; and I am persuaded, from what I have already seen, that they abound in moral maxims and in more refined sentiments than are to be found in any of the heathen classics known to us, and the insufficiency of natural religion is abundantly evident. I see in them the power of conscience, and that it costs them much effort to quench the light they have; but I see less difference than I expected between the *natural man*, within the pale of the Church, and among the informed heathen. It is not professional Christianity, but Divine grace alone that can produce a real, essential, and *saving* difference.'

'However, when we are possessed of the scattered rays of truth to be found in *Hinduism*, it will be a weapon of some value, for men always feel, and are pricked in their hearts, when they are shown that they live in opposition to the light they have. The Yogees are a wonderful people, purely mystic; they rise above caste, and all other worldly distinctions of Brahminism: they are learned, and, by imaginary excesses, attain heights of enthusiasm that Jacob Behmen never could have conceived. The history of the progression to this state of abstraction and delirium (for there are various degrees) forms a long and curious investigation, and when I am better qualified, I shall wish to trace the whole of it. The *self*-tormentors, who have often been confounded with the Yogees, are illiterate fanatics, and many of them vile and bestial fellows of the baser sort, and in no kind of repute with the well-informed. Besides, it is necessary to distinguish the bookish, secluded Pundits, who are simple, mild, and inoffensive to a great degree, from the heard-of domineering ignorant Brahmins, whose pride, craft, and villany, outdoes the Jew Pharisee, and whose contempt of the Sooders can only be expressed by these words. "This people who knoweth not the law is accursed." However, much guilt is on the head of the best of them for keeping the common people so grossly ignorant, and this may be successfully brought home to them, as well as to the Romanists, for by the invention of images a tenfold blindness is induced. In the Sooder, reason seems wholly unseated, and nothing is left them but the prerogative of the human form.'

Whilst Mr. Brown was thus anxious to obtain correct views of Hindu society, he was equally diligent in applying his knowledge to practical purposes.

'I am now beginning a native school:' he writes, 'composed of Hindu children at the age of about four years, forsaken in a time of dearth by their destitute relations: some are entirely orphans. They will be taught to read English and Bengalee: a translation of the New Testament by an able hand, a pious and learned gentleman, is now being carried on for this purpose, so that I hope they will soon read the Scriptures in their own, and the English language. I mean to support them partly by their own industry; for this purpose I have bought some land, and am laying a foundation which, I trust, God will raise and prosper. The ground, &c., have cost me 1800 rupees (£180).

'The low natives are so sunk in ignorance, that a knowledge of their own language reaches but a short way, to merely a few things around them: they are in sad want of ideas, and scarcely exercise their reason: these truths form a serious barrier to their conversion. They seem first to need improvement of intellect to enlarge the number of their ideas before they have even a capacity for receiving instruction in Christianity. Hence schools are the present favourite purpose in my mind, and I hope many will approve and promote the scheme at home.'

In reference to these proceedings of Mr. Brown, the author of the Preface to 'Memorial Sketches,' observes, 'But the time for Israel's deliverence was not yet come. Moses must wait yet many years before his desires can be carried into effect. The zeal and earnestness which have since that time been called forth into action, were not yet kindled in the public mind, and all the efforts which Mr. Brown then made fell to the ground for want of that support which he in vain solicited. Happily, however, he lived to see his wishes partially realized.

In this year, (1787) St. John's Church (now called the Cathedral) was finished. Ever since 1756, public worship for the Presidency had been celebrated in a thatched Bungalow, situated in the Old Fort. The unsuitableness of this place became at length acknowledged, and measures were taken to erect the present place of worship. The body of this building stands on what was once the burial-ground of Calcutta.

The deed of purchase purports that Warren Hastings, Esq., paid to Raja Neokissen the sum of 10,000 rupees (£1000) for the ground. A committee was appointed as trustees of the property, and afterwards the members of what is now called the select vestry were elected *distinct* from the trustees. From neglect in not noting the death or departure from India of individual trustees, and of not filling up vacancies, the select vestry became in process of time the sole managers of the property, and in defect of claimants as well as from the large sums supplied by government from time to time towards the necessary repairs of the building, the property has fallen to the government who, on the appointment of an ecclesiastical establishment, by virtue of the right so acquired, assigned to the Bishop of Calcutta, an episcopal seat and authority in the same.

About this time the managers of the Orphan Institution communicated with the Rev. David Brown, signifying to that gentleman that they could not allow of his continuing to officiate, at the mission church, and at the same time to hold the mastership of the institution; expressing at the same time their sense of the laudable motives which influenced him. On mature deliberation, and with the advice of friends, Mr. Brown relinquished the Orphan School and devoted himself entirely to the Mission church, &c. He continued at the Orphan house till August 1788. On this occasion Mr. Brown writes to a friend, 'I trust this event will turn to the furtherance of the gospel, which will be a sufficient recompence for the temporal loss I suffer by the change. I am at present chaplain to the garrison at Fort William, where I alternately preach to the whole Bengal army, and I continue to officiate in Calcutta as usual. This is a large field to cultivate.' To the same friend he writes, 'respecting the native school I formerly mentioned as having in contemplation, I commenced, and had made considerable progress in the execution of my plan, but am at present obliged to suspend this design, partly owing to the change in my affairs on quitting the Orphan House, and partly from a want of proper teachers. Among so many Europeans of the lower order it is next to impossible to find a sober person to manage a school. At the Mission School under my direction I have had two masters, but they both proved profligate, so that I am obliged to discharge them, and where to find another I know not.' Such was the then state of things among the European population.

The original idea in Mr. Brown's resignation of the Orphan School, was that of preserving the Mission Church as an open door for the gospel, when under adverse circumstances it was in danger of being shut for ever. It was then hoped that in the course of a year a supply of ministers might be obtained from England. With a view to this the transfer of the Mission property was reported to the Society for Promoting Christian Knowledge, with a request that a missionary might be sent out.

The Rev. Walter Hovenden was afterwards one of the most eminent masters of this institution, and was deservedly beloved by the inmates. It was the privilege of the writer just to know him, and to love him for his work's sake. We were both at the Sand-Heads together for the recovery of our health in 1832. In the month of September, the last day, he died, and his body was committed to the deep in the sure and certain hope that when the sea should give up its dead (and the sea will give up its dead) he should live a bright and blessed star in the firmament of the Redeemer's glory. The following lines were written at the time, as a memorial of him:—

There is no grave prepared by mortal hand,
  To make of thy cold corpse the burial-place;
Nor mourning friends around thy bier could stand,
  To yield thee weeping to the earth's embrace.

What recks it? though the ocean's giant tide
  Rolls in deep waters o'er thy watery rest:
Lives not thy worth through years of labour tried,
  Shrined in the core of memory's faithful breast?

And hallowed there in meditation's hour,
  Shall not thy genial virtue breathe again?
Whilst the fair fruits of many an opening flower,
  Prove that thy culture hath not been in vain.

Ah! who of all that saw and felt the care,
 The tender care with which thy charge was nurst,
Deemed that destroying grief was slumbering there
 So soon from crush'd affection's fount to burst.

Hath it not spoken in the sorrowing tones
 Of honoured age? Of manhood's lustier years,—
Of youth which now no more thy guidance owns?
 Hath it not glistened in the orphan's tears?

Yet not for thee we mourn;—the eternal Sun
 Of righteousness is beaming o'er thee now.
The fight is o'er, the Christian's goal is won,
 The crown of gold is on the angel's brow.

Say would ye call the spirit back to clay,
 That we might cease to mourn its absence here?
To fill our aching void? Away, away,
 The selfish wish! Is not that spirit near?

List to its hallow'd tones—'I may not come
 To you, my friends—but ye may come to me.
And *here* the heavy-laden find their home,
 And peace and joy through all eternity.

Glory to God! in yonder azure sky,
 Another guiding star to man is given;
Praise to the victim Lamb! no more we die,
 But rise a ransom'd fold to light and heaven.

The request above alluded to was duly acknowledged, and the desire complied with in the following letter:—

'TO THE REV. DAVID BROWN, MESSRS. GRANT AND CHAMBERS, CALCUTTA.

'GENTLEMEN,

'The letter under your joint signatures, and dated at Calcutta, March 7th, 1788, I duly received, and agreeably to your wishes, communicated to the East India Mission Committee of the Society for Promoting Christian Knowledge, and afterwards by their direction to the General Board. I have the pleasure to inform you that its contents were received with much satisfaction, and the part you have acted respecting the concerns of the Mission, and the mission church, hath greatly endeared you to the society. * * * The church and premises connected with it, Mr. Kiernander long promised to make over to the society, which promise, it seems, he hath ultimately failed to fulfil, and that you have stepped forward to rescue them from secular uses, and secure them for the sole purposes of religion, is a matter that speaks creditably for you as Englishmen, Christians, and members of our national church. Your act therefore is highly approved by the society, and in the most cordial manner they fall in with your wishes of sending out a new missionary to carry on the sacred purposes they have all along had in view in Calcutta.

'Anxious to accomplish this purpose, the committee looked out for a fit person, who was soon recommended to them for the purpose by the Lord Bishop of Lincoln, in the person of the Rev. Thomas Clarke, a clergyman of his lordship's diocese; * * The society hereby recommend him to your most friendly attention, &c.

'The proposal for establishing a mission on a more extensive scale, in Bengal and Bahar, which you were so good as to transmit to my hands, has been listened to by the Mission Committee and by the General Board with peculiar satisfaction. They approve of its plan, and admire the judgment and piety with which it has been drawn up, and only lament that it is not in their power to give full effect to your wishes. The hope, however, may be encouraged, that a time is shortly coming when efforts for introducing the knowledge of Christ throughout your parts of India, may generally take place; and whereinsoever the society can be aiding to forward such designs, they will not be found wanting.

'I am, &c., &c.,

'GEO. GASKIN, Sec.

'*London, March 7th,* 1789.'

On Mr. Brown's taking charge of the Mission Church he continued Mr. Frenzel, Mr. Kiernander's assistant, as minister of the Portuguese congregation. He officiated to a remnant of that flock for several years, but no account has been preserved as to the result of his labours.

The three chaplains at the Presidency and Garrison, Johnson, Owen, and Blanshard gave Mr. Brown in writing, their friendly testimony to the disinterested piety and zeal which induced him gratuitously to enter on a very laborious ministry, deemed by them of most essential importance to the community, and they, especially Mr. Owen, frequently rendered him assistance, but the weight of responsibility rested solely with himself.

On re-opening the church, the English congregation was inconsiderable in number. St. John's church was opened for divine service in that year, and there the more wealthy found suitable accommodation, whilst opposition, which cannot now be accounted for, seems to have been raised against Mr. Brown's labours in the Mission Church. Seven years after, speaking of the affairs of the mission, he says, 'I shall not carry your views back to the opposition which was made to this work at the beginning, nor to the sacrifices which it occasioned; suffice it to say, that we have passed through evil report and we have passed through good report, and now all men seem clearly to understand that we have no worldly end or interest to serve. The gospel has been preached freely, that is, without income, reward, or any other earthly consideration whatever, and in this respect we glory that it hath been preached as the apostle preached it to the Ephesians, &c., &c. * * * * The dying beds of some who have departed hence in the Lord have been of unspeakable consolation and encouragement to me, and hid repentance from mine eyes, for in death there is no deceit, and that ONE IMMORTAL SOUL should be made wise unto salvation, is worth a life of labour and pains on all that we can lose of a temporal nature.'

At first Mr. Brown officiated in the Mission Church only on Sunday mornings, and met once a week at Mr.

O'Beck's, (who then lived next door to the church in the house Mr. Kiernander had built for his school,) a few persons desirous of religious instruction, with whom he conversed and prayed. These increasing in number, a Sunday evening service was determined on, and also a weekly lecture. Mr. W. Chambers, Mr. Crommelin, Mrs. Hodges, and several others subscribing liberally towards the expense of lighting, servants, &c. The manifest pleasure with which Mr. Brown ministered to this small congregation, and the perseverance with which he pursued what he considered his duty towards the mission, was after a timefollowed with the best consequences. It has been often remarked that a minister, whatever his talents or acquirements may be, preaches more effectually by his life than his sermons, and a remarkable instance of the truth of this remark may be introduced here :—On one occasion when the bell ceased, the number of persons in the church was only six, but Mr. Brown went on as usual. One of the six, a person of high respectability, being the next day in a large company where religion was lightly spoken of, observed, that he was now *sure* that there was some *reality* in it, for he had been the night before at the Mission Church, and the weather threatened to be so stormy that only six persons were assembled, but that Mr. Brown had given them such an excellent discourse that he hoped to remember it to the end of his life, and that he was certain nothing but zeal for God and love to man could have induced him to go on in his duties on such a night. From that time that person became a constant attendant, &c., &c.

In 1789 the Rev. Mr. Clarke arrived in Calcutta on the part of the Society for Promoting Christian Knowledge. The governor of the Free School, which had just then been established and of which we shall say more hereafter, offered him the head-mastership of the school, which he accepted; but a Mr. Clarke having been reported to government by the Court of Directors as appointed a chaplain on their establishment, this gentleman conceiving that some of his friends had procured him the appointment, applied to government and was admitted to the service; and on the mistake being discovered, he did not again return to the mission, nor does he appear to have been well suited for the work.

The institution of the free school is another noble instance of the growing attention of the settlement to the interests of religion. It is the first institution Calcutta can boast of as intended for the benefit of the *Christian public.* The platform was laid in the original charity-school for the maintenance and education of twenty boys, and during the period of Mr. Kiernander's active labour no further provision was felt to be needful; but on the failure of his charity-school the wants of the Christian population became evident, and proposals were issued for the establishment of a new institution. These were so well received by the public that in a few weeks a fund of 26,000 rupees was raised, beside a monthly subscription of above 1,000 rupees.

In the following year the old charity-school became incorporated with the new one, and in 1795 the free-school was finally fixed in its present situation.

In 1791 the Society for Promoting Christian Knowledge again addressed Mr. Brown by their secretary as follows:—

'TO THE REV. J. OWEN AND D. BROWN.

'As there is reason to believe that Mr. Clarke has quitted the service of the mission, I am instructed to communicate to the Rev. Mr. Brown, and to the Rev. Mr. Owen, the particulars of a minute made yesterday at a meeting of the Society's Mission Committee, the Lord Bishop of Salisbury being in the chair.

'*Bartlett's Buildings, London,*
'*Thursday, April 28th,* 1791.

'At a meeting of the East India Mission Committee:

'Agreed in opinion, That letters be written by the

secretary to the Rev. John Owen, and Rev. David Brown, requesting that they will have the goodness to render their utmost assistance in supplying the duties of the Calcutta Mission Church, in case of its being vacated by Mr. Clarke, until such time as the vacancy can be filled up; and that the particular thanks of the Society be returned to the Rev. Mr. Brown for the great attention he has already shown to this good work.'

'GEO. GASKIN, D.D., Sec.'

In a letter to a friend, dated February, 1792, Mr. Brown writes:—

'From the time Mr. Clarke left Calcutta, the Mission has enjoyed the greatest quietness and even prosperity. There has been no abatement of attention in the congregation, nor have the contributions decreased. The prejudices raised are in a great measure laid aside, and we trust several are drawing towards us with a candid ear. The weekly lecture is well attended, and I feel encouraged to continue it. I have besides catechised at the Church on Fridays in the afternoon for some months back. Several poor people send their children, and seem glad to have them instructed. I have many opportunities of speaking to the people, and of attending to various useful calls, and have no reason to repent your advice which fixed me here; yet when I reflect how much I have undertaken, and how deeply I am engaged, I am appalled—I inwardly long for the shade of obscurity. A thousand and a thousand times do my feelings anticipate the joy that the arrival of a missionary or two will give me, for I shall then certainly retire immediately, and never stand forward but when my call is as clear as the sun, that is, when necessity urges me.

'It will give you pleasure to hear that Mr. Owen continues to me the support of his countenance and aid in the mission, and is one of those who stands by it to the utmost of his power. He regularly preaches at the Hospital on Sunday afternoons, where, when I am free from the Mission, I am to take my part with him. He has been of great use, but will, I fear, be thinking of Europe next year. This will be a serious loss to me, for I believe I owe the quietness I have all along enjoyed to his friendship, &c. He is a bold friend, and able to speak with a quashing authority.'

In a letter to the same friend, dated that year, we find some very interesting sketches of character intimately connected with the object of this work, 'Amidst discouragements we have real comforts, several have been attracted, and not a few apparently are changed, they walk at least as becometh the gospel of Christ. There are some of the higher classes who steal behind a pillar and frequently pay us a Nicodemus visit. Whoever comes out to this charge will find us in a prosperous way, and will also find very comfortable accommodations on the mission-premises, rooms are ready and also ready furnished, and nothing will be wanting on our part to strengthen the hands of those who may come; I really wonder so few are prompt to offer for this service! I remember well that even with my poverty of zeal a proposal of the kind when I was in college would have been irresistible. As it was, I left parents, whose first-born I was, and my mother loved me as her own soul, and from whom, for any worldly consideration, I could not have been persuaded to have parted. Mr. E.'s mother, it seems, prevented his coming, and how far he has done right to listen to her dissuasions I will not decide; but these things are in higher hands, perhaps he was not the man, or this impediment would not have been in his way. I hope all who move in this business will admit the necessity of *at least two missionaries together*, to carry on their work with comfort, as I have formerly written. The difficulty of getting fit men to proceed hither must always be great; but God is greater than all difficulties, and he can easily raise up the fittest instruments if he has pleasure in this work, and if not it cannot prosper.

The following extract will give an idea of the existing state of feeling among many of the higher classes at this period, and will be found instructive in a general point of view as descriptive of almost every-day characters as exhibited to the Christian minister under similar circumstances.

'Great changes are taking place almost every day in the situations and offices of men here; and death sudden and unexpected, surprises many, it is feared, in an unprepared state. The death of Mr. D—— when about to embark for Europe, will strike you as an awful event! I saw him lately in the court, displaying wonderful abilities, and very strong passions, not of the benevolent kind. How vain are our agitations! how soon must all our thoughts, except those which relate to a better world, perish! W—— is also gone; I saw him in his last days, and spoke seriously to him, which he seemed to take well, and told me he should be glad to hear me more fully on religious subjects, when he got better. I suggested the fitness of prayer under his present circumstances, and he readily admitted it, and I wished to express in prayer what I found he would not give me leave to do in conversation; for, *with all his moral defects*, he was a pharisee. I prayed that he might see the evil of sin, and feel himself a sinner, and know how to value a Redeemer, and on similar points: he seemed touched a little, but immediately resumed his old strains, and observed, that he did not in general relish extempore devotion, unless a man could hit off an elegant prayer to the Deity, (his own words) then he had no objection. He repeated passages out of several collects, which he professed highly to approve: this gave me a good opportunity, as expressions occurred, denoting a sinful state, and the necessity of forgiveness, to speak to him on these subjects. He still persisted, that he was not an irreligious man, as I might take him to be; that he every night said his prayers, and did his best, &c. &c. Such sights ought to benefit us, when we can do no good: hints for the pulpit arise out of such conversations, that may be of use to other descriptions of character: I therefore never think such visits lost.

'I have lately been called to attend two men capitally convicted, and who were executed within a month of each other; the first was insensible to a degree I never saw any human being; the latter, I hope, obtained mercy. He had been religiously brought up till thirteen years of age, and all his early impressions returned and came upon him with great force and energy. He died calling on the name of the Lord Jesus with a humbled and softened heart. His last words to me were extremely tender and grateful; he begged to pray by himself, wept a silent flood in prayer, then dried his eyes, and finally said to me, that God had done great things for him, and he felt the truest happiness within; "for, Sir," concluded he, "I trust my pardon is sealed." This was all expressed with so little effort, and with such ease and genuine feeling of heart, that I cannot but believe that the hand of God supported him. There is another man convicted, likewise an European, and I shall again attend. But I suffer greatly from these services: during my late visits to the jail, my feelings and imagination were so disturbed, that I could not rest at night.

'This malefactor's pious mother had stored his memory with Dr. Watts's Hymns in childhood, together with several of the Psalms of David, and other portions of Scripture, and when, by Mr. Brown's instrumentality, he was roused by his death-like sleep, his early impressions revived, and the last hours of his life were employed in repeating such of them as were suitable to his melancholy circumstances.'

In 1792, the native hospital was founded. Its object is the relief of natives of all descriptions, who require surgical or medical aid, and it has proved a source of benefit to thousands, who otherwise were liable to perish or to become cripples for life. The project is said to have originated with Dr. Robert Wilson, who was appointed first superintendent, and the scheme was so much indebted to the exertions of the Rev. Mr. Owen, that he was first nominated a governor of the institution.

In the account of the Society for Promoting Christian

Knowledge for this year, it is observed, that 'the endeavours of the Society to procure a supply for their mission at Calcutta, have still proved unsuccessful. The business of the mission, however, hath not been altogether neglected. In a letter from W. Chambers, Esq., and the Rev. David Brown, they observe, that the interest the Society are pleased to take in the affairs of the Calcutta mission, notwithstanding the discouraging incidents which have attended it, cannot but make a sensible impression on their minds, and that they are thereby animated and encouraged to give it such support as they are able, without any abatement either in their present exertions, or their hopes of future success. Mr. Brown, aided by Mr. Owen, and also by the occasional assistance of Mr. Blanshard, the two chaplains of that Presidency, had been enabled, and they trusted would still be able, to keep the mission-church open, and they hoped that Divine providence would continue to prosper the Society's endeavours for the diffusion of religious knowledge in Bengal. They also observe, that at the expense of a few hundred rupees, out of a considerable sum, generously contributed by Mr. Charles Grant and Mr. Udney, toward the accomplishment of a plan of building that had been suggested, they had made comfortable accommodations for two missionaries, should so many be sent out, who, they hope, in that case, would also find a well-disposed congregation, and the resources of the mission equal at least to its present exigencies. Messrs. Brown and Owen give similar assurances of aid. Mr. Owen observes, that it was with justice the Society returned their thanks to Mr. Brown, who had exerted himself in behalf of the mission with equal good sense and zeal.

The year 1793 may be justly considered as the commencement of a new era in the religious history of India. A long period had elapsed since the mission at Tranquebar had been taken under the patronage of the Society for Promoting Christian Knowledge, and no other attempt of the kind had been entered upon by any class of Christians in England. The recommendations of Sir William Jones to translate and circulate among the Hindus, portions of our sacred scriptures, and the more direct efforts of Mr. Brown and the friends who joined with him in submitting to some of the leading men in the Established Church, the proposal for a mission on an extended scale in Bengal and Bahar, whatever effect they might produce on *individual* minds, had excited no *general* interest. The Society for Promoting Christian Knowledge answered respecting the 'proposal,' that they approved its plan, admired the judgment and piety with which it was drawn up, but lamented it was not in their power to give full effect to it. The public mind in England, however, had been training, by various means, to works of Christian love, and the effect of it as far as it concerns missions, appeared first among the Dissenters. From small beginnings the Baptist Missionary Society had been established in 1792. To Mr. (afterwards Dr.) Carey, belongs the honour of having given a body to the spirit of missions, and to Mr. Thomas perhaps Bengal is indebted for having led the Baptist Missionary Society to fix on India as the future scene of their labours. That gentleman, on his return to England, advertised for subscriptions for carrying on the work, which he represented as greatly favoured by several persons of influence in Calcutta, of translating the Scriptures into Bengalee. The Baptist Society forthwith invited him to return under their patronage. This invitation he accepted, and the progress by which his mind was led to this determination is thus related in the statement he made to the Society :—'I sailed the second time to Bengal in 1786, with the same captain and officers, and in the same ship as before. That very season the Rev. D. Brown, who now preaches in Calcutta, went over and took charge of the *Orphan School*, where all the children of European soldiers are educated and provided for. On my arrival there I found a Mr. Udney, and a Mr. Chambers, and two or three more who were connected with Mr. Grant's family, all serious people, and we used to go together to hear Mr. Brown on the Lord's-day, who preached to the children under his charge; and after a little while, we had a prayer-meeting, and sometimes a word of exhortation was given. Mr. Grant removed from Maldah to Calcutta; on his coming to us we were increased and strengthened, and I preached at his house every Lord's-day evening. One day as Mr. Udney and I were walking out, he gave me to understand that Mr. Grant wished me to stay in the country, to learn the language, and preach the Gospel to the Hindoos; but I was averse to the climate, dreaded a longer separation from my family, and had no particular bent of mind to the work. Having also the charge of a ship's company as their surgeon, without any probability of the Captain giving me leave to stay, or of another surgeon being found to supply my place, I could not accede to the proposal, yet it would often return to my mind, and after a few weeks I became greatly concerned at heart for the condition of the perishing multitudes of Pagans in utter darkness, and was inflamed with fervent desires to go and declare the glory of Christ among them. Waters enough have risen since to damp, but will never extinguish what was lighted up at that time. After much prayer and many tears, I gave myself up to this work, and the Lord removed difficulties out of the way, confirmed the mission, and comforted me by adding two souls (both European) to my first labours, who continue my hope and joy, and, I trust, will be my crown at the day of Christ's appearing.'

In 1793, Mr. Thomas embarked the third time for India, with his family, accompanied by Dr. Carey and his family. Circumstances not favouring their settlement in or near Calcutta, at first they were led to accept secular employment in the neighbourhood of Maldah, where they could at the same time pursue the objects of their mission. Nothing is recorded in their early journal that belongs to this sketch, except a remark of Dr. Carey's, that hundreds of the Portuguese

Christians were reported to be desirous of religious instruction; which remark affords an individual evidence as to the effect produced by the missionaries of the Society for Promoting Christian Knowledge, in behalf of that class of the population of Calcutta.

During this year (1793) the increased attendance at the Mission Church, rendered the enlargement of the building necessary. When it first devolved to Mr. Brown's care, as the 'Bethtiphla' of the aged Zacharias Kiernander, it was in a very different style to the elegant structure now presented to the eye, as one of the ornaments of the '*city of palaces*.'

From its original appearance it was designated by the natives *Làl Girja*, (*làl*, red; and *girja*, church;) by which appellation it is still best known, though now presenting the appearance of a massy stone edifice. Those who remember the old building describe its internal fittings-up and furniture, as consisting of a brick pulpit built against the wall, its aisle rough uncovered tiling, a few rude benches and pews of unpainted plank, formed the general seats, with a small number of chairs without pews for the gentry, and it did not accommodate at that time more than two hundred persons; yet was it strongly built of good masonry, and very lofty, so as to be an object of attraction.

Encouraged and assisted by the fine taste and scientific abilities of his friend Mr. W. Chambers, Mr. Brown was not long in making a beginning, to enlarge and improve the building. The inner east wall which then divided the chancel was removed, and some beautiful highly finished Corinthian pillars were substituted, to support the roof, or break the ill-proportioned length. The increasing congregation soon required the space these pillars occupied. They were first decreased in number, and then reluctantly removed altogether, and other means of preserving the proportion as well as enlarging the space were resorted to, by extensive bows thrown out in the centre, and galleries erected at the extremities. It also was gradually fitted up in a manner suitable to the climate, abundantly lighted, supplied with an excellent organ and handsome pulpit and desks, to correspond with the general neatness of the whole.

On the 29th of December 1793, the improvements being finished, Mr. Kiernander was invited to open the new chancel, when he administered the sacrament, and expressed himself extremely happy at seeing the church so much improved, and greatly increased in attendance. Mr. Kiernander's attendance on this occasion was communicated to the Society for Promoting Christian Knowledge. In the report of the Society, containing an account of these proceedings, considerable regret is expressed, that the Society still is under the necessity of mentioning, that no opportunity has occurred of sending to Calcutta another missionary, notwithstanding the pains that have been taken to find out a person for that station.' It is added, 'The providence of God it is hoped will yet raise up labourers for his vineyard.'

Mr. Chambers did not live to see the improvements of the church finished ; his death was deplored by the settlement as a public loss. In the Report of the Society for Promoting Christian Knowledge, he is said to have been 'the great friend and ornament of the mission ; to whose zeal, prudence, and upright character in the settlement, it owed its best support.'

We may here add, though it has been in some degree anticipated, the character of this eminent man and Christian, as given in Lord Teignmouth's Life of Sir William Jones :—

'The loss of Mr. Chambers must be particularly lamented by all who feel an interest in communicating a knowledge of the doctrines of salvation to the natives of India. In an early period of life, he saw and felt the truth and importance of the Christian religion ; and while his own conduct exhibited the strength of his conviction, he thought it a duty to employ his talents and acquirements in disseminating amongst the untaught natives a knowledge of that faith, which he regarded of supreme and universal importance. In this view he determined to undertake a translation of the New Testament into Persian, and devoted all his leisure to the performance of this task, with the most zealous solicitude to make it accurate, but he had not completed half the Gospel of St. Matthew, when it pleased Providence to call him out of this life.' This brief notice of so eminent a man and Christian philanthropist, seemed due to the conspicuous part he acted in every thing relating to the good of India.

To return to Mr. Brown. His health sunk under his various and accumulated exertions: at length he consented to go out to sea, as the only remaining means from which his restoration could be expected. But never more was this devoted servant of Christ to resume his work of faith and labour which proceeded of love. The Indiaman on which he embarked struck on a sand, and the disadvantageous circumstances under which he was afterwards placed, greatly increased his weakness. It pleased God however that he should be brought back to the bosom of his family, and that when surrounded by the objects of his tenderest love, his spirit should be called home to partake in the joys of the blessed. His last morning on earth was particularly calm, collected, and resigned, and his last breath spoke thankfulness for the merciful consolations he enjoyed, the great kindness that had been shown him, and his confidence in the gracious promises of God. While in the act of thus expressing his gratitude, he closed his eyes, raised his feeble hands, and still moved his lips in inward worship, but his voice was heard no more! He fell asleep in Jesus! It is worthy of remark, that in giving direction respecting any inscription by which the remembrance of him might be perpetuated to posterity, he desired it to be recorded, not that he had filled high and important stations in the Church of our East India settlement,—not that he had been distinguished by the confidence, respect, and friendship of each successive administration of the supreme government,—not that he had been placed at the head, and assisted to form a splendid and most important establishment as Provost of the College of Fort William,—but that in the Mission Church at Calcutta for twenty-five years, he preached the Gospel to the poor. A slab to this effect has been inscribed by the congregation, and placed within the walls of the Old Mission Church.

After the death of Mr. Brown, a memorandum was found among his papers, bearing date this year, respecting one of the earliest testimonies to his ministry after his labours became wholly confined to Calcutta. About three years ago Mr. Brown's sister arrived in India, and having a religious sense of the goodness of providence in preserving her through a dangerous voyage, expressed a wish to attend church where she might offer up her grateful thanks for mercies received. Mr. R. who had not been in a church for many years, escorted his sister on this occasion. They attended the evening service at the mission-church; both were impressed with the sermon which they heard, and he said immediately after, 'Sister, I shall never forget this sermon: I shall come again to this church.'

Ever after he was constant in his attendance, and grew daily in knowledge and in grace. He was faithful to his convictions, and acted up to the light which he received. At length his mind became fully settled in belief of the truths of the Gospel. He then made an open profession of his faith in a crucified Saviour, and met the scorn and derision of his worldly connections with the courage of a good soldier of Christ. He was not forward to declare his sentiments, or to obtrude religious discussion on others, but he never hesitated to explain his views when called upon to do so, for he was "ready to give an answer to every man that asked him a reason of the hope that was in him, with meekness."

His religion proved itself to be a reality, by the effects produced on his life and temper. He lived once without God and religion; he was naturally of a hasty temper, and subject to violent gusts of passion ; in these respects, he became visibly a "new creature." Few men had more self-command than he acquired. His family are witnesses to his concern for their salvation and his own ; his retirement witnessed how he poured out his heart to God in prayer, and obtained answers of peace at the throne of grace. His acquaintance and dependants witnessed how much his temper was improved, softened, and subdued by religion. His Christian profession was uniform and consistent ; and his death proved to all around him the felicity of those who have hope in God. How calm and resigned was he to the stroke of death ! How tenderly affectionate to his family ! How confident in the goodness of God his Saviour, and that He, into whose hands he had committed his soul, would provide for his widow and children ! This, no doubt, is Christianity—true religion—and the very effect which the gospel ought to produce on all who hear it. Two days before his death, his sister wrote me as follows :—' My brother has just called me to him and inquired for Mr. Brown ; he said that you were the dear friend who had helped him to approach a merciful God who would never forsake him, and that with you he wished to pour forth his heart to Him in thanksgiving and praise.'

The year 1794 was marked by the death of Sir William Jones. How much the taste he cultivated and imparted to others for literary pursuits, tended to improve the manners of Calcutta society, cannot easily be decided. But love of science alone would not have produced the solidity and refinement of character exhibited by this distinguished man. The author of his life justly observes :—' If we sometimes suffer the humiliation of seeing great talents and extensive erudition prostituted to infidelity, and employed in propagating misery, by endeavouring to subvert the basis of our temporal and eternal welfare, we cannot but feel a more than common gratification at the salutary union of true genius and piety. Learning that wantons in irreligion may, like the Sirius of Homer, flash its strong light upon us; but though brilliant it is baneful, and while it dazzles, makes us tremble for its safety. Science therefore, without piety, whatever admiration it may excite, will never be entitled to an equal degree of respect and esteem with the humble knowledge which makes us wise unto salvation. The belief of Sir William Jones in revelation, is openly and distinctly declared in his works; but the unostentatious effusion of sequestered adoration, while they prove the sincerity of his conviction, give an additional weight to his avowed opinions.'—Again, 'the mind of Sir William Jones was never tainted with infidelity, but there was a period, as I have already observed, before his judgment was matured, and before he had studied the sciptures with close attention, when his belief in the truth of revelation was tinged with doubt. But these were the transient clouds which for a while obscure the dawn, and disperse with the rising sun. His heart and his judgment told him that religion was a subject of supreme importance, and the evidence of its truth worthy his most serious investigation. He sat down to it without prejudice, and rose from the inquiry with a conviction which the studies of his future life invigorated and confirmed. The accomplishment of the prophecies relating to our Saviour had impressed upon his youthful mind this invaluable truth, that the language of Isaiah and of the prophets was inspired, and in this belief, to which fresh proof were progressively added, he closed his life. He has, I trust, received through the merits of his REDEEMER, the reward of his faith.'

Whilst such were his settled principles, he cherished an habitual feeling of piety in his mind:—'His thoughts and attentions were not confined to the perishable concerns of this world only, and what was the subject of his meditations in health, was more forcibly impressed upon his mind during illness. He knew the duty of resignation to the will of his Maker, and of dependence on the merits of a Redeemer, and I find these sentiments expressed in a short prayer which he composed during his indisposition in September 1784, and which I here insert.

'O thou bestower of all good, if it please thee to continue my easy tasks in this life, grant me strength to perform them as a faithful servant; but if thy wisdom hath willed to end them by this thy visitation, admit me, not weighing my unworthiness, but through thy mercy declared in Christ, into thy heavenly mansions, that I may continually advance in happiness, by advancing in true knowledge and awful love of thee. *Thy will be done!*

'I quote with particular satisfaction this short but decisive testimony of the religious principles of Sir William Jones. Among many additional proofs which might be given of them, is the following short prayer composed on waking, July 27, 1783, at sea, also copied from his own writing:

'Graciously accept our thanks, Thou giver of all good, for having preserved us another night, and bestowed on us another day. O grant, that on this day, we may meditate on Thy law with joyful veneration, and keep it in all our actions with firm obedience.'

Minute circumstances frequently tend to mark and develope character as a further instance of this observation, however trifling it may appear, the application of Sir William Jones to himself of two lines of Milton, in his own writing, under a card, with his printed name in addition to more substantial proofs, may be quoted in evidence of his habitual frame of mind:

'Not wandering poor, but trusting all his wealth
With God, who called him to a world unknown.'

On another scrap of paper the following lines appear; they were written by him in India, but at what period is not known, nor indeed of any consequence:

SIR EDWARD COKE.

'Six hours in sleep, in law's grave study six,
Four spent in prayer, the rest on nature fix.'

RATHER

'Seven hours to law, to soothing slumber seven,
Ten to the world allot, and ALL to heaven.'

The remarks which follow approve themselves to the reflecting mind, and are earnestly recommended to the consideration of the youthful reader.

'In matters of eternal concern, the authority of the highest *human* opinion has no claim to be admitted as a ground of belief, but it may with the strictest propriety be opposed to that of men of inferior learning and penetration; and whilst the pious derive satisfaction from the perusal of sentiments according with their own, those who doubt or disbelieve should be induced to weigh with candour and impartiality, arguments which have produced conviction in the minds of the best, the wisest, and most learned of mankind.

Among such as have professed a steady belief in the doctrines of Christianity, where shall greater names be found than those of Bacon and Newton? Of the former, and of Locke, it may be observed, that they were both innovators in science; disdaining to follow the sages of antiquity through the beaten paths of error. They broke through prejudices which had long obstructed the progress of sound knowledge, and laid the foundation of science on solid ground, whilst the genius of Newton carried him *extra flammantia mœnia mundi.*

These men, to their great praise, and we may hope to their eternal happiness, devoted much of their time to the study of the scriptures. If the evidence of revelation had been weak, who were better qualified to expose its unsoundness? if our national faith were a mere fable, a political superstition, why were minds which boldly destroyed prejudices in science blind to those in religion. They read, examined, weighed, and believed, and the same vigorous intellects that dispersed the mists which concealed the temple of human knowledge, was itself illuminated with the radiant truths of Divine revelation.

Such authorities,—and let me now add to them the name of Sir William Jones,—are deservedly entitled to great weight: let those who superciliously reject them, compare their intellectual powers, their scientific attainments, and vigour of application with those of the men whom I have named; the comparison may perhaps lead them to suspect that their incredulity (to adopt the idea of a profound scholar) may be the result of a little smattering in learning, and great self-conceit, and that by harder study, and a humbled mind, they may regain the religion which they have lost. 'I shall not apologize,' continues his biographer, 'for the extracts which I have introduced from the works of Sir William Jones, nor for the reflections to which they have naturally led. The former display that part of his character which alone is now important to his happiness; and I am authorized to add not only from what appears in his printed works and private memoranda, in more than one of which, containing a delineation of his daily occupations, I find a portion of time allotted to the perusal of the scriptures, but from principle and satisfactory testimony, that the writings of our best divines engaged a large share of his attention, and that private devotion was not neglected by him. The following lines which afford a proof both of his taste and piety, were written by him after a perusal of the eighth sermon of Barrow, in his retirement at *Krishan-Nagar*, in 1786; and with these I shall conclude my observations on his religious opinions.

'As meadows parched, brown groves, and withering flowers,
Imbibe the sparkling dew and genial showers:
As chill dark air inhales the morning beam,
As thirsty harts enjoy the gelid stream;
Thus to man's grateful soul from heaven descends,
The mercies of his Father, Lord, and Friend.

In "Memorial Sketches" we find an account of the last hours of this great man, which possess a melancholy interest both as indicating the insufficiency of earthly superiority to comfort in the trying hour, and also the consolation attending his religious principles, which those who cultivate only his literary acquisitions will in vain seek in them: 'Sir William was at his old garden-house, and all the entreaties of his friends could not prevail on him to come into town or to suffer any besides his native servants to attend him. A day or two previous to his death, this resistance abated, and he had consented that a medical attendant should be in the house with him; this was however only finally agreed to the evening before he expired; when Dr. Hare is very sure he had a serious impression and apprehension of his approaching end, and he then said, that he had suffered so much the last ten days, that he would rather be told that he should die next morning, than to be assured of life by enduring the same a fortnight longer. He lamented frequently his not having gone to England, and said he had no object on earth to keep him here, that he had more money than he could use, and that his studies could be as well carried on in England as in India. In short he had brought his plans nearly to a close. His moulvis and pundits had been dismissed some months, and he wanted no more that they could furnish. I have reason to believe that he had little faith in any help that the physician could bring him, and he even intimated that the will of God must be done, although he submitted to take whatever was prescribed. He had no idea that his liver was affected, but thought that his stomach was disordered. However, he assuredly felt himself drawing to his end, and was very indifferent to what was done. The abscess, the doctor supposes, broke towards morning, and produced instant death. His servants say he was restless, and was taken with vomiting, and nature made other efforts. He got up, ordered some tea, and dressed himself. Having taken a little tea he ordered the servants to withdraw. I really believe he then resigned himself to God, and committed his soul into the hands of that Redeemer he confessed before men. I am led to hope this from some anecdotes which I heard of his religious sentiments several months before he died, and which gave me much satisfaction. He was very sincere in his opinions, and avowed them; but he was cautious not to divulge how much his heart was affected. He knew the world, and his habits led him to conceal what he was apprehensive would not be understood, but placed to the account of religious ostentation; he thought every one must stand or fall to his own master, and having made up his own mind, he left others to themselves; and let me not say that he erred in so doing. He is gone! and no one in this country has followed him with more reflections and sighs than I have done. He died on Sunday morning the 27th of April, and was interred the following morning. I went very early and found only Enius by his body, who shed many tears. I took a candle and dwelt for some minutes on every feature. His face was infinitely beautiful in death; his nose had an exquisite delicacy, a fineness and variety I cannot describe, though the idea is fixed clear and deep in my own mind; his mouth was speaking; his forehead impressive of awe, and strongly characteristic of the laborious and unremitting attention he devoted to the acquisition of knowledge. My feelings perhaps carried me away, but since the death of that good, enlightened and dear friend, Mr. William Chambers, I have not felt anything like the death of Sir William Jones.'

About this period a proposal was made to the late Mr. Thomason by Mr. Grant, to fill the mission church at Calcutta. His mind was for some time absorbed in the thought of being thus employed in his divine master's service, and every thing that could be done was done to enable him to accept the proposal, but two things concurred to determine his relinquishment of it. The appointment was then offered to Mr. Buchanan, of Queen's College, and by him accepted.

Upon this decision it was remarked by Mr. Thomason's most intimate friend and colleague,—'Here we cannot but notice the wisdom and goodness of divine providence in so overruling events, as to bring about the best final results. Had Mr. Thomason accepted the chaplaincy, he would have been a very faithful and efficient minister of the Gospel, and have done much good. But I question whether at that time it would have extended much beyond the immediate sphere of his labours. He was young, decidedly pious, devoted and active, and must have been a blessing wherever stationed. He had an extraordinary facility in learning languages, and would have become an eminent oriental scholar, and in all probability India would have been eminently benefited by his translations of the Scriptures into more than one of their vernacular tongues. But I do not think he would have exercised a commanding influence, nor formed any very comprehensive plans for the benefit of that vast continent, nor have entered at all into that almost boundless field in which Dr. Buchanan rendered himself so eminently conspicuous, and which he cultivated with such great advantage to the millions of India.

Of all the literary and pious men which Cambridge at that time possessed, few, perhaps none, had the peculiarly appropriate qualifications of Dr. Buchanan for that important station. His mind was calm, intellectual, and comprehensive. His manners reserved, dignified, and commanding. His literary attainments were considerable, and gave promise of great increase. He sought, acquired, and effectually sustained a place in the society of the most learned men in the university; even whilst an undergraduate, there was an elevation about him which left younger men of inferior talents and attainments but ill at ease in his presence. His very appearance conveyed the idea of a person destined to do things at which others would never aim, and to adopt measures on a scale of magnitude, to which few would find themselves equal, or dream of accomplishing. When it is added, that Dr. Buchanan was as eminent for his piety, as distinguished for his talents; as simple in his manners, as he was dignified in his appearance;

as single in heart, as comprehensive in mind; as attentive in the discharge of very humble duties as he was active in planning, and vigorous in executing schemes for Christianizing the immense population of India,—no doubt will be felt, that the loss of Mr. Thomason's labours *at that particular crisis*, was more than compensated by those of Dr. Buchanan.

The first specific intimation of the important sphere of labour to which the providence of God was conducting this afterward distinguished servant of God is contained in a letter to the Rev. J. Newton, 1792, 'Mr. and Mrs. Grant passed through Cambridge lately; Mr. Simeon and I dined and supped with them. I hope the conversation of that evening was useful to me, from hearing various accounts of the apostolic spirit of some missionaries to the Indies, and of the extensive field for preaching the gospel there. I was led to desire that I might be well qualified for such a department, in case God should intend me for it. Hence the origin of my three *desidera before-mentioned*—Scripture knowledge, some zeal, and good health.' This was a good beginning, and is a remarkable instance among many of God's secret workings in the heart of particular individuals, while the way is being prepared by his more general workings in the vast kingdom of providence and grace, the world and the church.

Early in the year 1794 Mr. Newton made the first direct proposal to Mr. Buchanan of a voyage to India. His reply was, 'I request you to accept my thanks for the affectionate letter which I have just now read; I have only time to say, that with respect to my going to India I must decline giving my opinion. It would argue a mind ill instructed in the school of Christ to pretend to decide on an event so important and unexpected, an event which will doubtless give a complexion to the happiness and usefulness of every hour of my future life.

'It is with great pleasure I submit this matter to the determination of yourself, Mr. Thornton, and Mr.

Grant, all I wish to ascertain is the will of God. I hope that the result of your deliberations will prove to be his will; were I required to say something I should observe that I feel myself very ill-qualified for the arduous situation in question. My intimate friends know that my plan of college study was to attend more immediately to academical learning the two first years, and to preparation for the ministry in the third and last, upon which I am now entering. I think that our regard for the glory of God requires us to endeavour to find a person of acknowledged ability in things both human and divine, who has already approved himself such an one as might successfully resist gainsayers and prosecute his mission with energy. A beginner, particularly if he be of slender capacity and attainments, will naturally shrink from such a situation, fearing lest he should tarnish the honour of his embassy by an unskilful or ungraceful negotiation.

'On the contrary, if the Lord does with me as with Jeremiah, and bids a child go and teach a great nation, it would be vain to plead my incapacity, since if he sends me he will certainly touch my mouth. Only I would observe that in the present state of Christianity it would appear that as strict attention ought to be paid to human means in our endeavours to promote the success of the gospel as if it were merely a human dispensation.

'I trust that every word of the above is dictated by a regard for God's honour and not my own.

'That his honour may be greatly promoted by the result of your deliberations is the prayer of C. B.'

The judgment as well as the piety of Mr. Buchanan's reply to this proposal deserves to be noticed, and affords a satisfactory indication of his qualifications for the important station to which it refers. The following sentiments expressed in a subsequent letter are equally pleasing.

'With respect to my going to India, I am still in a strait between two. Some considerations incline me to stay, others persuade me to go, as being far better. Being unable to judge for myself I submit it to the divine direction with perfect resignation. So gracious is he who careth for me, in this respect, that your determination whether for or against my going will be alike agreeable to me, I am equally ready to preach the gospel in the next village, or at the end of the earth.'

Such was the elevated spirit of piety which actuated Mr. Buchanan early in this year; as it advanced, he wrote as follows to Mr. Newton:—

'We have had Mrs. Udney and Mr. Cecil's family at Cambridge for a few days. It gives me great pleasure to see piety gladden with its presence our learned walls. Pride and superstition have doubtless built most of our colleges; but I am inclined to think that genuine piety built some of them. A solitary walk in such places has a tendency to incite elevated thoughts of God and of his goodness to man through successive ages.

'My purpose in troubling you with this letter was to say that I bear that affection for you a child beareth to his father, a desire to conceal his faults (if he has any) and to magnify his virtues, that I hope to be preserved from the snares and cares of this world, and thereby enabled to adorn that gospel which you first wished me to profess.'

Dr. Buchanan was ordained at Fulham by the late Bishop Porteus, on Sunday, the 20th September, 1795. Immediately after his admittance into holy orders he entered upon his engagement as curate to Mr. Newton. Early, however, in the year 1796, the friends, by whose Christian kindness and liberality he had been introduced into the church, conceiving that his talents might be more advantageously employed abroad, recurred to the plan which had for some time been more or less in their view, and resolved to endeavour to obtain for him the appointment of a chaplain in the service of the East India Company. Application was accordingly made to a distinguished director, the late Charles Grant, Esq., accompanied by such testimonials as amply certified the qualifications of Mr. Buchanan for the office to which he had been recommended.

In consequence of the various and uncommon character of the testimonials both from the university and the excellent bishop, by whom he had been ordained, as well as others of a private nature, Mr. Buchanan was appointed one of the chaplains to the East India Company on Wednesday, March 30th, 1796. When introduced to the Court of Directors, &c., he was addressed by the late Sir Stephen Lushington on the importance of his office, and on the duties imposed on ministers of religion in India. Mr. Buchanan thus mentions the address of the honourable chairman many years after it had been delivered.

'The venerable baronet observed that French principles were sapping the foundations of Christianity and of social order; and he earnestly inculcated on me the duty of defending and promoting the principles of the Christian religion by every proper means. I was much affected by the solemnity of the occasion, and by the energy and feeling with which the address was delivered, and the subject of the charge itself made a great impression on my mind, particularly when meditating on it afterwards during my voyage.'

On the 3rd of July he preached for Mr. Newton at St. Mary Woolnoth, and terminated by a pious and affectionate farewell, his short connection with the congregation of his dear and venerable friend.

The extract in which reference is made to Sir S. Lushington's speech will shew to the reader what was the then state of opinion in Calcutta among the company's servants; and as licentious principles are always followed by licentious practices, we may infer that even external morality, not to say Christian practice, was at a very low ebb.

Mr. Buchanan landed at Calcutta on the 10th of March, two days before the completion of the 31st year of his age. On his arrival he was hospitably received by the Rev. Mr. Brown, and resided for a short time in his family. He then took a house in Dhurum Tollah, where however, he continued but two months, being at the end of that time appointed chaplain at Barrackpore, a military station about sixteen miles above Calcutta. This was to him a great disappointment, as it afforded few opportunities for the exercise of his ministry, and fewer for that which he had most at heart. There was no place for public worship, and divine service was never required by the military staff to which he was attached.

After a short residence he thus describes the station of Barrackpore: 'The station where I now am, has been called the Montpelier of India. Here I enjoy every thing that can minister to comfort or elegance, except society. We have society, too, but it is only polite society. There are not many here, I fear, whose hearts are awakened to the love of virtue and truth. Nevertheless, I possess two companions of inestimable value, I mean those two books which are written by the finger of God: the book of God's *word*, and the book of God's *works*. These are treasures which are inexhaustible, and which afford me in my retirement, pleasure, company, and comfort.'

The following picturesque description will serve to place the reader down on the spot above alluded to:

'I am situated on the banks of the Ganges. The country is champaign, but covered with trees: the most numerons are mangoe, cocoa-nut, banyan (the Indian fig) and plantain-trees. The river is covered with boats passing and repassing. There are two elephants amusing themselves at the water-side. One of them is eating plaintain leaves, which are his ordinary food. He takes hold of the leaves with his trunk, and puts them into his mouth. The other is washing himself: he fills his trunk with water, and then throws it round him, so that he is covered with the spray. A little boy is now going to mount one of them in order to lead them home. As he is not very heavy he sits upon the point of the trunk, and thus the elephant lifts him on his back. An elephant has no bridle. How then is he directed? The boy has a rod of iron, sharp at one end, and with this he pricks his head when he goes wrong.

'When the elephant wishes to set down the ladies, who frequently ride upon him, he falls upon his knees, and when they have dismounted, he rises. He is altogether a wonderful animal.

'On the other side of the river I see a flock of vultures, they are hovering over a dead body which is floating down the stream. Many of the Hindoos cast their dead bodies into the Ganges, that they may be conveyed to paradise! About a mile up the river a funeral pile is just lighted. It is now near evening when this rite is usually performed. The relatives accompany the corpse to the water-side, where a pile of dry wood is raised about the body, and the *nearest relative* applies the torch. The jackalls, allured by the smell, will presently come down from the woods and prowl about. They live on carrion of all kinds, and are generally inoffensive.

'The air is frequently thronged with kites, hawks, and crows, who are looking for snakes and other noxious creatures, and they are so successful in their search that we are seldom annoyed by these animals. So attentive is providence to the comfort of man!

'A woman burnt herself with her dead husband about three days ago, a few miles up the river. This happens very frequently.

'My servants bring me a glass of wine and water. Two are concerned in the operation, one of them will not touch the glass though he will pour the wine into it! So strange are the superstitions of this people. Another will wipe my shoes, but he will not wash my feet. A third will bathe me, but he will not fan me. You see, Miss E——, what strange things we travellers behold!'

'Have I told you all? or shall I mention a north-wester. This is a violent tornado from the north-west, which makes a regular and magnificent progress through the heaven: violent wind, thunder and lightning, roll on in a kind of collected body. This short-lived tempest is very awful, and very grand. It is always a welcome visitor, for it cools the heated air, and refreshes all nature around.

'I am now so familiarized to violent thunder, that I scarcely ever notice it, except when I go out purposely to contemplate the grandeur of a northwester.'

Such are the scenes presented to the Christian in his every-day walks, and even while sitting in his retirement. Truly "the dark parts of the earth are the habitations of cruelty." And oh, how appalling to the disciple of Jesus, and how awakening in reference to the obligations which we, as Christians, in possession of the light and truth of God, are under to these dark parts of the earth.

When Mr. Buchanan arrived at Calcutta, Mr. Brown was one of the two chaplains of the Presidency. He held also the chaplaincy of the garrison. Some of Mr. Buchanan's friends in England conceived that the latter appointment might have been transferred to him, or that he might have officiated at the Mission church. As to the garrison, motives of delicacy and kindness towards Mr. Brown, with whom he lived from the first on the most friendly and affectionate terms, prevented him from soliciting such an arrangement, and the Mission church was then occupied by the Rev. Mr. Ringaltaube, a clergyman of the Lutheran church, who had been sent to India under the patronage of the Society for Promoting Christian Knowledge. No sooner however, had Mr. Ringaltaube abandoned this post, as he shortly afterwards did, than Mr. Buchanan participated with Mr. Brown in the gratuitous labour of the Mission church. He occasionally also performed divine service in his house at Barrackpore, probably as often as he could obtain an audience. The following letter to Mr. Brown, shows not only the nature of their intercourse and friendship, but also the tendency of a want of success in the ministry to depression of spirits, connected as it necessarily is in India with similar effects produced by the climate.

'I think you speak of yourself with more diffidence, or rather despondency, than you ought. How do you know that your Thursday evening lecture is not the most useful of all your ministrations; and with respect to industry, have you not much reason to be thankful that you have been preserved from seeking great things for yourself? I think you very happy indeed that you have nothing to do with this world; but that your *chief* work is to make proof of your ministry, as the Lord shall prosper it. As splendid a crown awaits him who shall do a *little* in *this* country, as him who shall do much at home.'

'It is not probable that you or I shall live long. What seek we then? There is no fame for us here. There is some reproach, whether we be *faithful* or not; so that we lose nothing by being faithful. I am so young in these things that I do not know anything about them. I have only entered the wilderness, but I apprehend *much*. I would gladly enter Canaan, without "encountering the greatness of the way," were it the will of God; and were he to give me faith and strength for it, I would *to-morrow*, with great joy, leave this world with all it offers. Were I sure it would not entangle and destroy me at last, I would rather stay and do something for God; but I am not sure of that. . . . . I sigh much for singleness of mind, and purity of heart, and love to God, which distinguish the disciple of Christ, and I often wonder whether it is to be effected by keen affliction in body and spirit, or by the power of the word of God dividing asunder like a two-edged sword, or by long-fighting and sorrowful experience slowly teaching and ending with a doubt whether I am taught.

'Amidst the multitude of my thoughts, "the Lamb that was slain," is my only hope!'

Thus, for the present, was Mr. Buchanan almost a silent witness, in this Patmos, for the word of God. Who can avoid perceiving in it a generous, spiritual and heavenly mind, a blessed preparation for that which was before him, and to which he was afterward called, and so it was; and, though Mr. Buchanan's sequestration at Barrackpore debarred him from very active employment in the duties of his ministry, it afforded him a valuable opportunity for private study, which he diligently and successfully improved.

At this time he writes to Mr. Henry Thornton:—'I am now proceeding in a work which I began when I last enjoyed retirement—viz. a serious and, I may say, laborious examination of the Scriptures in the original tongues. My inquiries are not so much philological as practical. The meaning of the Holy Spirit in Scripture is the "one thing needful," for the student, and I hope it will be the subject of many a joyful ἕυρηκα to me. This severity of investigation reminds me of my mathematical vigils.

'This, Sir, is a climate which tries the mind like a furnace. Deterioration seems inherent in Indian existence: were God to grant me a peculiar blessing, it would be a habit of industry in this country.

'I have a Moonshee in the house to instruct me in the Hindostanee and Persian languages. Not knowing what may be the purpose of God concerning me, I have thought it my duty to attend early to the languages of the country; and to the constitution, civil and religious, of the mixed people in it.'

Early in the ensuing year he wrote to Mr. Grant in the following terms:—

'I have now been near a year in the country. I wish to know what you think of my voyage to the East. I seem to have come out under rather unfavourable auspices. No feature of my mission is very agreeable, but I view the whole as the counsel of the Almighty, and I know that in His plan there is great beauty, though I may not perceive it. I suffered a long struggle before I could resign myself passively to my unexpected destination, but the struggle is now over, and I view myself as one who has run his race, to whom little more is left to do.'

These lines are here introduced, in the hope, that they may be of use to some who may be brought into similar circumstances, in enabling them to rise above them, and this brief memorial of Mr. Buchanan's first appointment in India, will not be given in vain, if it serve to check in any who may be similarly situated, either abroad or at home, the too natural disposition to despondency and haste, and to lead them in the conscientious improvement of present opportunities, to wait patiently for further openings, and in the meantime to "hope in God;" and if it tend to abate in those who may be observing them any impatience of their backwardness in fulfilling even just expectations, and to teach them that charity which, concerning the substantially pious and sincere, "hopeth all things."

The following letter, written to Mr. Grant about this period, will throw further light on the state of things in reference to religion.

'Lord Mornington has been here near six weeks. As yet he maintains much dignity in his government. He goes regularly to Church, and professes a regard for religion. He has been at Barrackpore for ten days past. He was surprised when I told him that we never had Divine service there, or at any other station. He was still more surprised when he heard there were horse-races here on *Sunday* morning.'

A character is here introduced, of whom much of interest is to be told :—

'The apostolic Obeck is well, and affectionately remembers all your family. He succeeds to Swartz in the title to our reverence and esteem.'

Mr. Obeck was a native of Germany. He was for many years employed as steward in Mr. Grant's family during his residence in India. The piety and fidelity of this good man were rewarded by the liberal support and friendly regard of his patron to the day of his death.

Mr. Buchanan adds :—'Remember me to Mrs. B; she alone opposed my coming to India. Tell her not to triumph. She has not seen to the *end*.'

In a letter to Mr. Newton, written about three months months after this dispatch, he mentions another circumstance, which shows strongly the then state of feeling on the subject of religion.

Before Sir John Shore, afterwards Lord Teignmouth, left India, Mr. Brown procured an order of Council, that the military in the garrison should attend at the Presidency Church every Sunday morning at six o'clock, there being no chapel or service in the garrison itself. Strong opposition was made to this order, on the ground that the troops would suffer in their health by marching in the sun. They attended a few Sundays, but at last the clamour became so violent, that the order was revoked, and the triumph over religion considered complete. What an awful state of a professing Christian people! Christians triumphing over Christianity —treading it under foot—doubtless because it interrupted them, and made them uneasy in the indulgence of the evil passions of a fallen nature.

It was not long after this, that in another letter addressed to Mr. Grant, (1799) Mr. Buchanan acknowledged the good resulting from an order of the Honourable Company against Sunday horse-racing, and the erection of chapels at some of the military stations. 'Your moral regulations of May last are come, and not before they were wanted. They have been just published and are *well received*. I ought not to say published. Lord Mornington's delicacy induced him to communicate them by circular letter. They ought to have been proclaimed from the house-top.'

About this period, adverting to the Baptist Missionaries at Serampore, Mr. Buchanan ventures an opinion on the then Missionary prospects in India. Of Mr. afterwards Dr. Carey, he remarks, that he was then chiefly employed in laying the foundations of future usefulness. He is translating the bible into the Bengalee tongue. 'This, like Wickliff's first translation, may prove the father of many versions. But,' continues Mr. Buchanan, 'a rapid spread of the Gospel is not to be expected in India; zeal and labour, and the lapse of years, will no doubt produce the usual fruit. In the revolution of this century, the 'dawn' of the Gospel has appeared in India. After many centuries have revolved, there may be a general light. This, it must be admitted, was a gloomy view of the subject, but all was gloom around him. Speaking again of the faithful Obeck, he says, 'Mr. Obeck in Calcutta is like Lot in Sodom. I asked him one day if he could produce ten righteous to save the city. He replied, 'I am not sure I could produce ten, but I think I might five.' What a state of things, at the close of a century of rule in India!'

In a letter to a young friend at College, he writes, 'Infidelity raged here with great violence formerly, but it is rather on the defensive now. It was fashionable for a time to allege, that oriental research was unfavourable to the truth of Christianity; but the contrary is found to be the case. As far as my own inquiries have gone I can truly say,—I have seen the star, and worshipped in the East. In the study of eastern history and learning, there is endless proof of the truth of both the Old and New Testament.'

It is not the object of the present sketch to notice the manners of society; and yet an occasional touch to show their bearing on the Christian character and *morals* may not be wholly irrevelant. The following occurs in this letter. 'I suppose you have heard of the grandeur of English life in India. To live in the first circle in India is to live at court. There is nearly the same dignity of etiquette, elegance of equipage, and variety of entertainment. Every lady is handed to table according to her rank; and no grace is said!'

Of the natives he says—'Their general character is imbecility of body and mind. Their moral powers are, and have been for ages, in a profound stupor; and there is seldom an instance of their being awakened. A partial attempt or rather *experiment* is now being made by some Christian teachers. The Hindoo mind seems at present bound by a *satanic* spell; and it will require the co-operation of a more than human power to break it. But Divine co-operation implies human endeavour. Many ages must then elapse before the conversion of India is accomplished.

'With respect to moral action the Hindoos pay as little attention to their own religion, as a rule of life, as the *English do to their's*. Your profession of the Christian religion is a proverbial jest throughout the world. . . The Hindoo is born blind, but you put out your own eyes. Loose principles and sensual indulgence first dim them, and then the 'drop serene' of the new philosophy quenches the orb!

'A residence in this country adds much to the *dignity* of the European. Here the labour of a multitude is demanded for the comfort of one: and it is not so much demanded as voluntarily given. In no other country can we so well see the homage matter pays to mind. Generally however, it is but the homage which black pays to white. This is the grand argument for keeping the Hindoos in a state of mental depression.

'You know the character of the Hindoo superstition. It is lascivious and bloody. I know no epithet that embraces so much of it as either of these two. Of the first I shall say nothing, their caprine orgies in the interior of their temples, and the emblems engraved on the exterior, &c.

'Their scenes of blood are not less revolting to the human mind. Human sacrifice is not quite abolished. The burning of women alive is common. This power of self-sacrifice arises from insensibility of mind, and from that alone; just as a child may be persuaded to plunge into danger, which infant reason cannot see. So the Hindoo of childish capacity, is persuaded to destroy his existence; he views neither death or life in their true light.' Inference: all comparison therefore between the *fortitude* of the Christian martyr, and the *madness* of the Hindoo, is nugatory and absurd.*

* One Sabbath morning a peculiar duty called me into the heart of the native town, early in the forenoon. Many poor heathen were

Mr. Buchanan was appointed to a vacant chaplaincy at the Presidency, by Lord Mornington, in Feb. 1800, and an occasion soon occurred to call forth the energies

passing to and fro, one to his farm, another to his merchandise; knowing neither the privilege of the Christian Sabbath, nor Him who is its Lord. As I returned on my way to church, I had to pass a large temple, dedicated to Kali, which I had often noticed with much interest, from its rural situation and striking appearance. A flight of steps led up to the room in which the hideous idol was placed, represented as holding in one hand a human head by the hair, and trampling a man under her feet. At the foot of the steps a crowd of people was congregated, and some ceremony of more than usual import appeared to be going on:—I endeavoured to discover what it was which attracted so much attention: a moment's glance informed me,—it was *the* SACRIFICE OF A SOUL!

In front of the temple, stood a beautiful native child, a boy of about six years of age, richly attired: a hoary brahmin stood on each side of him, and in their turn, poured into his ear the various muntras he was to repeat, the prayers he was to utter, and the manner in which he was to approach his idol god: within the temple stood the officiating brahmins, also occupied in worship. It was evident from the splendid dress of the child, and his numerous attendants, that he was the son of parents rich in this world's goods, but poor, alas *how* poor, in heavenly treasure. They thought this public display of devotion was the best they could do for their boy; but the god of this world had blinded their eyes, and they knew not when they sent their child to offer to Kali, that the precious offering he made, was to be his immortal soul.

But my story ends not here: this temple is commended to my remembrance by a more pleasing circumstance. A fine brahmin boy, about eight years old, who for a year previous had been under instruction in a school under a Christian Society in this city, paid me a visit at my house; and in course of conversation, alluding to this same spot, he said, 'Sir, as I was coming to your house, while we were passing Kali's temple, my brother and the sircar, who were with me, made salaam to the 'Thakoor,' (idol) but *I did not do so.* Sir! it is very bad—it has hands, but it cannot lift up anything—it has eyes, but it cannot see—it is only a piece of mud! The *true* God is *up*; Sir!'

There is great hope and great encouragement to the persevering labourer, and the missionary and the teacher may hold on their way, expecting a blessing. Place the ark of God near Dagon, and Dagon *must* fall. How important it is to begin *early* in sowing good seed in the heart! This will prove an antidote to all the follies of idolatry, and will enable even a little child to strip it of its mask, and to see it as it is.—"In the *morning* sow thy seed"—

'Thou canst not toil in vain;
Cold, heat, and moist, and dry,
Shall foster and mature the grain
For garners in the sky.' M.

of his powerful mind in the exercise of his ministry. He was appointed to preach a sermon before Lord Mornington and the principal officers of the government, on the day appointed for a general thanksgiving for the late signal successes obtained by the naval and military forces of his majesty, and of his allies ; and for the ultimate and happy establishment of the tranquillity and security of the British possessions in India.

This sermon was so generally approved, that Mr. Buchanan received the thanks of the Governor General in Council, with a direction that it should be printed. It was founded on Psalm xxi. 11.

Its subject-matter was, principally, the character, the progress, and the effects of the new French philosophy, to which he justly attributed the awful struggle in which this country was then engaged.

Copies of Mr. Buchanan's thanksgiving sermon were distributed by order of Government, in every part of the British empire, and produced an uncommon sensation, and tended to a considerable extent to change the *tone*, to say the least, of feeling and expression on subjects of which it so luminarily and impressively treated. 'You may easily conceive,' he observes, writing to a friend in England, well acquainted with the prevalence of sceptical principles at that period in India, 'the astonishment of men at these religious proceedings. However all was *silence* and decent acquiescence. It became fashionable to say, that religion was a very proper thing, that no civilized state could exist without it ; and it was reckoned much the same thing to praise the French, as to praise infidelity.'

The importance of this public recognition of Christianity as the only basis of civil prosperity, was soon perceived in the increasing attention to personal religion. This is therefore an important era in the history of the progress of Christianity in India. Christian society was soon observed to increase and flourish. Merit was patronized, immoral characters were marked and young men of good inclinations were encouraged and distinguished.

The following observations of the good Mr. Brown at this time are confirmative of the above statement :—

'These solemn acts,' observes that excellent man, and the public thanksgiving which took place for the the first time under Marquis Wellesley's government, awakened a *religious sense* in many, and led to an open and general acknowledgment of the divine providence, which has been highly beneficial to the interests of true religion and virtue.'

Mr. Buchanan now received frequent communications from different parts of India, on religious subjects, and questions on infidelity. He observes, 'This subject is often forced upon me, but I have seldom permitted myself to *defend* Christianity.* I have usually acted on the offensive, and attacked infidelity.† This is a very unpleasant mode to the infidel. 'During the last year,' he adds, 'I have received many anonymous letters on polemical divinity, but the correspondence has generally ended in real names.'

The following is from another hand :—

'There is an evident change in the face of society ever since I have been here. Lord Wellesley seems inclined to support the Christian religion by *every* means. Vital religion is also increasing. It seems to be fostered under the wing of that general sanction to Christianity which has lately been given. This is the only place in India where religion has been countenanced. We have now many families here in which piety meets with real encouragement.'

On the 18th of August, 1800, the College of Fort William, which had been virtually in operation since the 4th of May, was formally established by a minute in council. The important bearing of this institution

* When Dr. Watson's Apology for the Bible was put into the hands of George the Third, he repeated the word several times,—apology—apology—'I did not know the Bible needed any apology.'

† See Faber on the Difficulties of Infidelity.

on the interests of Christianity will justify more than a reference to it in these pages. Mr. Buchanan in a letter to Mr. Grant thus briefly alludes to this important measure, 'Lord Wellesley is at present engaged in founding a college for the instruction of young civil servants in eastern literature and general learning.*

The Rev. Mr. Brown was appointed to the office of provost, and Mr. Buchanan to that of vice-provost. The duties devolving on each are thus described in the College statutes :—

'It shall be the peculiar province and sacred duty of the provost, &c., governing the College of Fort William, to guard the moral and religious interests of the institution, and vigilantly to superintend the conduct and principles of all its members.' Divine service was directed to be regularly performed in chapel at such times as the provost should appoint. By this institution two hundred students, the whole generation of English India, were placed under the care of these two excellent men and profound scholars.

With the commencement of the year 1801, the important duties of each were entered upon and cheerfully sustained. Early in this year Mr. Buchanan wrote to his friend Mr. Grant, 'The greater part of the students promise to distinguish themselves. There are as remarkable instances of application here as I have known at Cambridge. Both the churches are generally full.' A little after he writes, 'No impropriety of conduct is known ; all is silence, study, and decorum ; all dine in the college hall in the presence of the professors. There are some instances of a serious spirit of religious inquiry among the students. No such field is anywhere to be found for learning and piety, as that which Calcutta at this time exhibits. Our church continues in much the same state in which I described it to be in my last. We have had an addition of some communicants, chiefly from college.

* 'The College of Fort William in Bengal,' published by Mr. Buchanan, 1805.

'The chief labour of the churches is fast devolving upon me. My religious correspondence in India is greater than at any former time. The congregations at the New Church are more numerous than ever.' He subsequently writes, 'Our churches are more crowded than ever. Even on Wednesday evening there is a great number, and good is done. Some of the students attend on that evening; their presence warms the heart of old Mr. Obeck; they know and visit him. How would Mr. Grant rejoice,' he sometimes says, 'to see these things!' The pillars are removed, and a number of additional seats made to accommodate the many who come.'

While the members of the College of Fort William were zealously employed in the prosecution of their labours, the Governor General in Council, on the 15th of June, 1802, received with the utmost concern the commands of the Court of Directors for the immediate abolition of the important institution. On the 22nd following, Lord Wellesley communicated this dispatch to Mr. Buchanan, who, in common with every other friend of the College, deeply lamented this unexpected determination. In this document instructions were given to supersede that institution by the revival of a seminary which had existed previously to the establishment of the College; but no modification or extension of that plan could, as the Governor-General contended, embrace the objects proposed to be secured by the collegiate establishment of Fort William. Lord Wellesley therefore expressed his decided conviction that the present establishment was necessary to secure proper order and discipline together with good morals and religion.

But the orders of the court were imperative, and seemed to require their immediate execution. To this therefore, his lordship accordingly proceeded, but in fulfilling this painful duty, a most serious and difficult question arose with regard to the time when the abolition of the college should take effect. The determination of this question involved principles so deeply affecting the welfare, future prospects, and just expectations of the students, professors, &c. that Lord Wellesley felt himself compelled to declare that the abolition of the college of Fort William, must be gradual, and that the institution should not terminate before the 31st of Dec. 1803, when the great body of the students then attached to the college, would have completed the course which they had so successfully commenced. His lordship also expressed a hope that his memorial would induce the directors to alter their determination.

Early in the year 1803, Marquis Wellesley presided at the second annual disputation of the students. The result was most satisfactory. The following extract from a letter of Mr. Buchanan to his wife in England, well describes his own feeling on the subject. 'You say that you hear the college is abolished. It has been long abolished in London, but it still exists here in greater spirit and utility than ever, and it must continue to exist (though perhaps under a different name) as long as the British empire reigns in India.' The directors wish the institution to be called a *seminary*, and then they will support it. I have no objection to the name, provided the young men are taught, and they must be taught in future. Much has been effected by the institution of the college. Of the students who have just left college, only eight out of thirty have contracted any debt. Many of them have saved money, a thing unheard-of in India, and by the old civil servants accounted impossible. The reign of native money-lenders is now at an end. Satisfied, however, with the good that *has* been done by the institution, we wait submissively for the period of its dissolution, which will be in December next.'

The following extract is peculiarly interesting, as shewing the exalted state of Christian feeling relative to the great work to which Mr. Buchanan was so sacredly devoted. 'My heart seeks to be disengaged from collegiate labours, and to find rest and refreshment in the one spiritual work of the everlasting gospel. Fortune or fame cannot add an hour's happiness to my present existence, but they may interrupt it. I feel a secret pleasure in the purpose of the directors to abolish the college as it respects *myself;* but I feel at the same time that its continuance under other men would be favourable to my evangelical labours in this country.

'In perfect confidence therefore that God will order all things aright in time, manner, and event, I implore direction of His Spirit to improve the passing day. My chief source of despondency at times is want of fellow-labourers, of learned and serious men in this vineyard, where there is so numerous a body of well-educated young men. I would willingly at this moment give 50,000 rupees, £5000, for two respectable and religious young men established at the church in Calcutta, and capable of conducting the studies of the college.'

The bad effect produced on the minds of dissipated and ill-disposed young men by the abolition, is thus briefly stated :—'On the arrival of the order of the court of directors abolishing the college, the students found that religion and morality formed no part of the plan substituted, and so absolutely did they consider the court's opinion to be favourable to the old system of relaxed morals, and contracting debt, that they circulated a placard in college, containing a parody of Henry the Fourth's speech to his son, beginning with these lines :

> 'Pluck down my officers ; break my decrees,
> For now a time is come to mock at form.
>
> 'Have you a ruffian, (a writer,) that will swear, drink, dance,
> England (the court) shall double-gild his treble guilt,' &c. &c.

The religious part of the community perceived the evil that would necessarily follow immediately. Good old Obeck sighed from his heart, and exclaimed, 'Cruel, cruel!' while the *banyans* (money-lenders) and the old leaven in the service grinned their ghastly exultation. The wound inflicted by that letter on religion and exemplary morals is not healed to this day. The first symptoms appeared in the gradual secession of the students from the mission church, &c.

'In the midst of all "the Lord reigneth." His gracious providence hath ordered all things aright—hath produced the good already done, and will overrule the evil past and to come, to His own glory and the good of His faithful Church on earth. If God were pleased to give me my heart's desire, he would give me more grace and a greater sense of the value of souls; with a measure of greater health and more undisturbed leisure to make known the glory of the Gospel among the people here, during the short period that may be allotted to my ministry.'

During this exciting period, Mr. Brown's health was fast failing him, and he was in a fluctuating state of mind, whether to go to England or remain longer in India.

It is with pleasure we turn from this account of the establishment and results of the College, to notice the general effects of Mr. Buchanan's and Mr. Brown's ministry. Among the individual instances, is a Major Sandys, who, in a season of affliction, had been led to attend the faithful preaching of these devoted men of God. Their ministry was eminently blessed to the bringing him to the knowledge and open profession of the Gospel, from the proud holds of philosophical infidelity. To this gentleman, with whom Mr. Buchanan afterwards maintained an uninterrupted and affectionate intercourse, he wrote, after his return to Europe on account of ill-health, as follows :—

'I suppose you will have seen all your friends by this time, and settled your plans, &c. We do as usual in Calcutta. Serious religion appears to increase. Mr. Obeck is still alive, but declining fast. He begs his blessing on you, whom he calls "a young man," and wishes you a long Christian life. You are quite forgotten by the gay world here, even by those who used to feast with you sometimes. Those who are always asking me about you, are the poor people who knew you but half-a-year. —— is sick. He has had many attacks. *She* seeks comfort at church, and *he* begins to think that perhaps he can obtain it nowhere else.' Subsequently, in reply to a letter received from this gentleman, Mr. Buchanan writes :—

'I am rejoiced to find by your letters that the Gospel is still glorious in your view, and that the world and its vanities has not obscured the heavenly vision. May this happy state be ever yours, without alloy or reverse, but such as may be necessary to confirm, and strengthen, and perfect you in the inner man, &c.'

The following is an affecting, but interesting, and consolatory account of the death of an individual in whom Mr. Buchanan had taken the most lively interest, the son of Mr. Elliot, who, on account of his distinguished proficiency in oriental learning, had been appointed by the Marquis Wellesley to an embassy to Arabia, but who, after having fulfilled with great ability the duties of his mission, fell a victim to a fever in that country; and, as a mark of distinguished honour, was interred in the garden of the *Imam* of Senna.

At this period the amiable and most decidedly Christian Obeck finished his earthly career. The following notice of the closing scene of his distinguished life, as well as some farther particulars of his character, will be read with interest. Mr. Buchanan writes :—

'The departure of the aged Obeck appears to be at hand. At least he thinks so, and bids me impart to you his blessing, while his understanding remains. He was carried into church last night, and was so much revived by the service and view of his brethren, that he walked out with assistance. His only food at present is bread dipped in wine.

'Under this decay of body, his mind is more vigorous than ever. He has, within this last year, assumed a very intrepid tone in rebuking sin, and remonstrating with the lukewarm, and in defining a holy life in India. But he has great joy among the true disciples, and his spiritual comforts have of late been abundant.'

In a subsequent letter to the same friend, he writes:

'The good Obeck is still alive, but his loins are girt for the heavenly journey. He is confined to his room, and cannot attend church, but the church attends him. He listens with delight to the voice of praise in the adjoining building on the Sunday and Thursday evenings. We have arranged all his temporal affairs to his satisfaction. He has given us his text for his funeral sermon, in preaching which I fear my spirits will fail me. It is difficult to speak of the deceased father to the surviving children.'

This venerable man was now very fast approaching his end. Early in September he felt a presentiment that he should not live to the close of that month; and, accordingly, Mr. Buchanan thus announced his death to his respected friend and benefactor :—

'The aged Obeck has at last departed. For some weeks before he almost daily expected his dismission. He had no spiritual conflict at his last hour; but manifested constantly peace, and joy, and high assurance. He was sensible to the last; and when he could not speak, he testified his exultation of soul by pressing ardently to his breast his fellow-saints. He left to you and your family his solemn blessing. I send you a paper containing some notice of his death.

'Just before his death, I preached his dying sermon in the Mission Church from these words :—" The time of my departure is at hand, &c." Mr. Brown will preach his funeral sermon next Sunday-evening.'

The following account is given of the honourable career of this good man :—

'He has ever been distinguished for his genuine piety —for his ardent faith in the Gospel—for his singular benevolence—and for his unremitted labours of love among the poor and needy. He has been long known in the place as one who was always " going about doing good ;" exhibiting an affecting and amiable example of that " pure and undefiled religion taught by the precepts and doctrines of the Saviour."

'But his chief labour was in inculcating the sacred

truths of the gospel whenever he had opportunity, and such opportunities he often enjoyed. Many persons have for some years attended his prayers in his family, which was indeed a church in his own house, where they enjoyed the inestimable advantage of hearing his spiritual instruction, and listening to the counsels of age and experience.

'His temperate and pure life has now carried him to his seventy-third year. And from his fifteenth year (as I think he once mentioned) he has endeavoured to serve God. Since that period he has had a sense of religion in his heart, and has been enabled to "keep himself unspotted from the world."

'All persons who knew him had reason to expect that God would honour the death of so faithful a servant; and this honour hath been conferred on him in an abundant manner. During the two last months of his illness, the praise of his Redeemer has been his constant theme. Surrounded daily by his numerous family, his pleasure has been to talk of the things of God, and of the glories of the kingdom to which he is hastening. And his ability has been as great as his pleasure. For, even at this time, when it is doubtful whether he will survive another day, and when his bodily frame is in the last stage of debility; even now his understanding is clear and unclouded; his perception of divine truths is undoubtedly stronger than at a former period of his illness; his soul seems to swell with exultation when he recounts the past mercies of God; and his admonitions and exhortations to others have an earnestness and emphasis, united with a force of reasoning and firmness of persuasion, which is nowhere to be seen but on the deathbed of a Christian, and which nothing can inspire but a power from on high. He does not speak of manifestations and visions of glory, which have sometimes attended the death of good men, but he manifests a calm, rational, and placid spirit, founded on the basis of an immoveable faith, yet accompanied by such ardour of expression, and by such an assurance of hope as would abash philosophy itself.

'He has none of those doubts which are often found on a death-bed. He has not those fears and misgivings of conscience which the unstable and careless Christian experiences. He has none of those fearful forebodings which harass the soul of the despiser of religion in his last hour. He is a stranger to that gloomy despair, which often haunts the soul of the man who hath passed through life the slave of ambition, or the votary of pleasure. No, *his* last moments are the happiest of his life. *His* ambition through life has been to obtain "that honour which cometh from God;" and *his* pleasure has been in serving God with his whole heart; in loving his neighbour as himself; in forgiving his enemies; and in praying for those who persecute and despitefully use the professor of the Gospel of Christ.'

His own dying confession was as follows:—

'I am a sinner saved by the mercy of God in Christ. By nature I am impure, and unholy. Nothing in me, no merit of mine, could make me the object of God's distinguishing grace. But I believed the word of God, and was enabled to offer up my prayers at an early age, that he would open my understanding, and lead me to a knowledge of his truth. And his promise was fulfilled to me, (as it is to every serious inquirer,) "Ask, and it shall be given unto you; seek, and ye shall find." By degrees the mysteries of the Gospel were opened to my view. I beheld myself a lost and condemned soul, lying with a multitude in a world of wickedness; subject to the just wrath of God. But I at the same time heard of the offer made to a perishing world by the Saviour Christ. I beheld the whole world overwhelmed by a flood of sin and misery, and the ark of redemption floating on the waters. Every page of the Gospel showed me that there was no salvation but by the Ark, Christ; that his atonement on the cross was the only atonement for my past and future sins; that his gracious Spirit influencing my soul, was the only preservative from my evil passions, and from an ensnaring world, and that his mediation alone procures access to God, and warrants an answer to our prayers.'

'Thus,' said he, 'the perusal of the word of God was blessed to my soul. I received it in its plain and obvious meaning, and I have had a constant experience of its truth through my past life. It has been a light to my steps, and a lantern to my paths. Its peculiarities appear now all light and glory in my soul. I know that the denunciations of God against the despisers of his Gospel, will be expressly executed, and I know that his promises of glory to the righteous will be fulfilled in a way that eye hath not seen, or ear heard, or hath entered into the heart of man to conceive; and the anticipation of this glory is to me *unutterable.* My prayer at my last moment is, that this power of the Gospel may be felt more and more at this place; that the blessing of God may rest on this Church; that the ministers may labour in the word with zeal and faithfulness, and that the hearers may receive the word preached with meekness and affection, that so the testimony of the Gospel may prevail, and the Church of Christ may begin to flourish in this dark corner of the world.'

'I leave,' he added, 'my blessing on this Church. As to my numerous family, I leave them with scarcely the means of subsistence; but I leave them dependent on that gracious providence, which has supported me from my youth to age, in a state of apparent poverty, and yet possessing abundance. I leave my children to God as to a surviving father, who will care for them as he hath cared for me, and will I trust bless my instructions to the salvation of their souls.

'As to *myself*, my hope is in heaven. The promises of God are in a manner wholly fulfilled to me. His truth and faithfulness are demonstrated to my soul. By his mercy "I have fought the good fight, I have finished my course, I have kept the faith. Henceforth," &c.

Such are the sentiments, the expressions, and the heavenly hope of this good man.

In the same month, another deeply interesting character is noticed by a valued brother, as follows:—

'My dear ——

'I am returned from hearing a most affecting and impressive discourse from Mr. Buchanan, with a degree of feeling that does honour to his heart, on the occurrence of the last week. I am anxious that Mr. Buchanan should know how grateful I feel for this high tribute of respect to the memory and virtues of a beloved brother, and I therefore entreat you to express to Mr. Buchanan my sincere gratitude for this distinguished mark of regard for him. Tell him that he has afforded to my mind a real consolation, and that I trust I shall ever after be the better, for the affecting and forcible manner in which he has held forth to imitation, the example of a life of true piety.

'Never while I live will the memory of Mr. Buchanan's solemn discourse on this melancholy occasion be obliterated from my mind.

'Your ever affectionate,

'N. B. EDMONSTONE.'

The person thus alluded to was Mr. Archibald Edmonstone of the Board of Trade. His life was uniformly marked by a deep tone of consistent profession, of the purifying religion of Christ. His last words were, "Blessed be the God and Father of our Lord Jesus Christ, who through his abundant mercy hath begotten us again to a lively hope," &c. 1 Pet. i. 3.; which words were engraven on his tomb.

These are a few names in that then Sardis, of which a better state of things remains to be told.

In the month of November, 1803, Mr. Buchanan first communicated his thoughts on the expediency of an ecclesiastical establishment for British India, in letters to the Archbishop of Canterbury, and to the rest of the episcopal bench, having previously submitted them to the Marquis Wellesley. The reply which he received from the late Bishop Porteus confirmed and encouraged him in his determination to bring that important subject before the public. His object was to point out the expediency of such a measure, 'both as the means of perpetuating the Christian religion among our own countrymen, and as a foundation for the civilization of the natives. The inadequate state of the clerical establishment in India at that period, for the great purposes of the instruction and religious communion of our resident countrymen, formed the first part of the Memorial. In the second part he supposed such an establishment to have been given to India, and proceeded to consider the result with respect to the native population. After describing in just and forcible terms their actual condition, the pride, immorality, and bigotry of the Mahommedans; and the vices, enormities, and barbarities of Hindoo superstition and idolatry, Mr. Buchanan argued out the policy of attempting to civilize and improve their condition. He writes—'Their apathy is extreme, their prejudices daily weakening in every European settlement, divided in an opinion political and religious, more tenacious of custom than of opinion, and thus to disseminate new principles among them is by no means so difficult as it is frequently represented.'

The third part of the Memoir strongly confirmed the practicability of the proposed plan of ultimately evangelizing the nations of Hindostan. Many interesting facts were stated relative to the existence of Christianity in India from the earliest ages, and particularly respecting the native Christians, on the coast of Malabar.

The Memoir was with great propriety, and in a strain of dignified and impressive eloquence, dedicated to His Grace the then Archbishop of Canterbury.

In an appendix to the Memoir there is a variety of very important information on the superstitions of the Hindoos, tending powerfully to correct the erroneous opinion so commonly entertained of them at that period as a mild, humane, and inoffensive race.

To return to the subject of the College of Fort William. According to the regulation of Lord Wellesley, in obedience to the decision of the Court of Directors, it was to close on the 31st of December, 1803. It was, however, a very gratifying circumstance to the friends of that institution that on the 3rd of January, 1804, a dispatch announced to the Governor-General the determination of the Court, that the College should for the present continue on its original footing.

In the course of the year 1804, several circumstances occurred, connected with the College, which were particularly interesting, as showing the state of feeling then existing both among Europeans and natives. The following is an extract from a letter to Major Sandys in the month of February :—

'We are much the same in church, state, and college, as when you left us, only that I am literally alone in many matters of a public nature, particularly in a battle now fighting (the worst that I have yet had) with Mussulman and Hindoo prejudices against translations of the Scripture. Their clamour has assailed the government. Lord Wellesley and Mr. Barlow are neuter ; but the old civil servants fan the flame. A folio volume would not detail the particulars, but I trust you will soon hear of the good effects. In the meantime I am growing infirm in body, and long for more holy employment than that of hewing of wood and drawing of water only for our future sanctuary in India. I know that what is doing is useful ; but spiritual comforts do not accompany the occupation in the degree I desire, and look forward to, when I have peace from public conflict.'

So early as the year after the present period of these memoirs a commencement had been made in the translation of the Scriptures into several languages. The first version of any of the gospels in Persian and Hindoostanee, which were printed in India, issued from the press of the College of Fort William. The Persian was superintended by Lieut.-Col. Colebrooke, and the Hindoostanee by William Hunter, Esq. The gospels were translated into the Malay by Thomas Jarrett, Esq., of the civil service.

Of these and other translations of the Scriptures then projected and undertaken, only a very inconsiderable part was executed at the public expence. The sole charge incurred by the College in the department of sacred translation was for the Gospel of St. Matthew in Persian and Hindoostanee. With this exception the extensive biblical works successively announced from this institution were carried on at the private expence of those members of the College, amongst whom the Provost and Vice-Provost held the first rank, and others who deemed it to be of the highest importance to promote the diffusion of sacred literature in India.

It had long been an object of anxiety to these excellent men to obtain a version of the Scriptures in the Chinese language. After many fruitless inquiries, they in this year succeeded in procuring the assistance of Mr. Lassar, a native of China, and an Armenian Christian, whose name is well known as a learned professor of that language. Mr. Lassar arrived in Calcutta in the capacity of a merchant, &c., and having met with some difficulties, he became known to Mr. Buchanan, who, appreciating his talents, generously liberated him from his embarrassment, and engaged him at a stipend of three hundred rupees per mensem (£30) to devote himself to the translation of the Scriptures and to the instruction of a Chinese class, formed of one of the elder, and three of the junior members of the missionary establishment at Serampore. The expected reduction of the College rendering it inexpedient that Mr. Lassar should be attached to that institution, this stipend was afforded for about three years at the sole expence of Mr. Buchanan. Another occurrence this year marked an improved state of moral feeling in Calcutta, and particularly illustrates the salutary influence of the College of Fort William. This was the institution of a civil fund for widows and orphans. Considerable discussion took place. The old leaven of the service wished to include black illegitimate children. The junior servants who had gone from the college, as well as those then in, almost with one voice exclaimed against a measure which they conceived would have a tendency to sanction vice and to countenance an illicit connection with native women. A letter was addressed to the service by a young man formerly of the college, and then in the Governor-General's office, in which he complained of their violation of the divine law, &c. This attempt to bring back the service to principles of honour and chastity received the sanction of the Governor-General and all the friends of revealed religion. Caricature prints exhibiting the mover of the subject with a black child in his arms, pleading its cause in full assembly, while a black dye (nurse) behind urged him forward; and various other devices marked the popular question and tended to brand the immoral practice with deserved contempt. The shame of the old service was intense, and they execrated the college and its fruits. The contest was maintained for a considerable time by printed correspondence, and the fund was at length established *without* the approbrious clause, and was certainly a remarkable triumph over a state of things that had so long existed almost without a disapproving voice. Had any man but a few years before have ventured to resist such a measure on the ground of religion or moral propriety, he would have become the jest of the whole service. In reference to this Mr. Buchanan writes, 'He must be an entire stranger to what is passing in Bengal who does not perceive that the College of Fort William is sensibly promoting an amelioration of the European character as well as the civilization of India.

Upon the general subject of religion in Calcutta, Mr. Buchanan gave the following encouraging accounts to a friend:—

'The Mission Church is now becoming too small for the auditory. Many families go away every Sunday morning, seats being in general occupied an hour before service. You will be glad to hear that —— still perseveres in listening to sacred things; as do many other young political servants, &c. The demand for religious books, particularly of evangelical principles, has been very great these two last years. Messrs. Dring told me they had sold an investment of fifty octavo bibles in the course of three months, &c. And, subsequently, he writes: 'On account of the increase of our congregations, we are about to have two morning-services on Sunday—the first at seven o'clock in the old church, and the second at the usual hour of ten in the new. We have some of all sects in our congregations—Presbyterians, Independants, Baptists, Armenians, Greeks, Nestorians, and some of these are part of my audience at the English Church. But a *name* or *sect* is never mentioned from the pulpit, and thus the word preached becomes profitable to all.'

Passing over a period in which Mr. Buchanan notices a series of opposition to the pure principles of Christianity, a letter addressed to His Grace the Archbishop of Canterbury will be read with interest as bearing on a subject deeply connected with the best interests of Christianity in India.

'Permit me, my Lord, in the name of the few representatives of the English Church in Asia, to offer to your Grace the tribute of affectionate congratulation, and to express our hope that the glory of Messiah's kingdom may be manifested to all nations of the earth during the period of your administration.

'Our hope of evangelizing Asia was once founded on the College of Fort William. But a rude hand hath already touched it, and unless the Imperial Parliament interpose, it will soon be said of this great and useful institution, which enlightened a hemisphere of the globe, '*Fuit illium et ingens gloria.*' Its name, however, will remain, for its record is in many languages, and the good it hath done will never die, for it hath taught many the way to heaven. Had the College of Fort

William been cherished at home with the same ardour with which it was opposed, it might in the period of ten years have produced translations of the Scriptures into all the languages, from the borders of the Caspian to the sea of Japan.

'An idea seems to have gone forth in England, that Lord Wellesley founded his College merely to instruct the Company's writers. Lord Wellesley founded the College of Fort William to enlighten the Oriental world, to give science, religion, and pure morals to Asia, and to confirm it in the British power and dominion.

'It is the opinion of intelligent men in India, that the formation of an extensive ecclesiastical establishment is a measure which, during the present revolutions of Europe, will tend greatly to confirm our dominion. It is certain that nothing could more alarm the portentous invader of nations than our taking a religious possession of Hindostan. Five hundred respectable clergy of the English Church established in our Gentu cities, would more perplex his views of conquest than an army of fifty thousand British soldiers. The army of fifty thousand would melt away in seven years; but the influence of an upright clergyman among the natives of his district would be permanent. He would be to them in time their mouth and mind, and speak for them peace or war. Friendly, admonitory, social intercourse, is what is wanting to enchain the hearts of the people of Hindostan, and to make them *our* people.

'The toleration of all religions, and the zealous extension of our own, is the way to rule, and to preserve a conquered kingdom. It is certain that men are ruled virtually by the Church, though ostensibly by the State in every country. The seeds of moral obedience and social order are all in the Church.

'One observation I would make on the proposed ecclesiastical establishment. A partial, or half-measure, will have no useful effect. A few additional chaplains can do nothing towards the attainment of the great object in view. An archbishop is wanted for India; a sacred and exalted character, surrounded by his bishops—a venerable personage, whose name shall be greater than that of the transitory governors of the land; and whose fame for piety, and for the will and power to do good may pass throughout every region.

'We want something royal in a spiritual or temporal sense, for the abject subjects of this great eastern empire to look up to. They cannot conceive themselves in a settled state without a Sultan or Maha Raja. They are incapable of freedom, for superstition keeps men in childhood. And yet they have neither king nor emperor. They have neither national temple, nor high priest. They are a mixed multitude, who have no common sentiment of truth or falsehood, of right or wrong. Every man contradicts his neighbour, and the Europeans tell them they are all right.

'Spiritual power, with means of instruction, is wanting to awaken to life this sluggish and inert life. Vegetating in ignorance and passive misery, they want a sacred guide, who shall take them by the hand, and lift them up, and look them in the face, and express some interest in their happiness. The success of the solitary missionary demonstrates what would be the powerful effect of the whole Church.

'It will be a satisfaction to your Grace to know, that the translation of the Scriptures into the oriental languages still proceeds with spirit, though many do not smile on our labours. A few individuals have devoted their slender means to the furtherance of this good work, but these private resources will soon fail. A *commencement*, however in the translations, is of vast importance. They are begun "in faith," and leave to the Divine author, to bring to a happy termination (though not perhaps in our time) his own most holy word.

'We have it in contemplation to bring the great question of giving the Scriptures to the heathen before the public in a few weeks, and to move the subject at all the presidencies in India at the same time. The Protestant mission here must be used as the engine to effect this design (wielded by the power of the College) seeing we have no church of our own as a corporate body, and the duration of the College is uncertain. If the public voice shall favour the proposal, an immense sum will be subscribed, and the translations will be carried on under happy auspices. I consider that the success which has hitherto attended the translation of the Scriptures, is a token for good, and the best "sign" we have at present that Providence means to preserve to us this country.'

The disapprobation with which the extensive nature of the College of Fort William, had been viewed by the Court of Directors, had long prepared its superintendents to expect a reduction of its establishment. Anticipating, therefore, the suspension of that department in it, which had hitherto been instrumental in the translations of the Scriptures into the oriental languages, they were anxious to make some provision for the continuation of that important work. With this view they encouraged individuals to proceed with versions of the Scriptures, by such means as they could command; purposing, at the same time, not to confine this encouragement to Bengal, but to extend it to every part of the East where fit instruments could be found. Mr. Buchanan particularly devoted his influence as Vice-Provost of the College, in aid of the translations then in the hands of the missionaries at Serampore, and to endeavour to excite the public interest in their favour. For this purpose, early in the year 1806, he drew up 'Proposals for a Subscription for Translating the Scriptures into Fifteen Oriental Languages,' containing a prospectus of Indian versions and observations on the practicability of the general design. To these proposals, thus composed by Mr. Buchanan from materials partly furnished by the missionaries, their names were subscribed; and in the month of March copies were distributed liberally in India and England, in this country to the Court of Directors, to the bench of Bishops, to the Universities, to Lord Teignmouth, as President of the British and Foreign Bible Society, and to some other public bodies, as well as to many private gentlemen. In India, copies were transmitted to nearly the whole of the principal civil, and to many of the military officers in the Company's service, from Delhi to Travancore, to many of whom the mission at Serampore was previously unknown. Mr. Buchanan obtained permission at the same time to send the proposals in his official character as Vice-Provost of the College, free of expense to all parts of the empire; and, he accompanied them, in most instances, with letters, which amounted to about one hundred from himself.

In two of these letters to friends in England Mr. Buchanan informed them it had been at first intended that they should issue from the college under the sanction of government. It appears that he communicated the manuscript to the Governor-General; but although he was personally disposed to favour the undertaking, he declined authorizing a measure which might appear to identify the government too closely and prominently with an extensive plan for promoting Christianity among our native subjects. Whatever may be conceded as to the cautious policy of this conduct, it cannot but be regretted that the noble and extensive work thus projected could not have been placed under the immediate superintendance and controul of the College of Fort William, possessing as it did, in the assemblage of Oriental scholars collected around it, such superior facilities for its execution, connected as it was with the Church of England, and consequently affording a pledge both as to soundness of principle and unity of design, which could be expected from no other quarter.

It was, however, plainly implied in the proposals, that the undertaking would enjoy the countenance and support of the College; and it was doubtless on this ground that the concurrence of the public was principally obtained. That expectation was accordingly expressed in the following terms:—

'Our hope of success in this glorious undertaking depends chiefly on the patronage of the College of Fort William. To that institution we are much indebted for the progress we have already made. Oriental translation has been comparatively easy in consequence of our having the aid of those learned men from distant provinces in Asia, who have assembled during the period of the last six years at that great emporium of eastern letters. These intelligent strangers voluntarily engaged with us in translating the Scriptures into their respective languages, and they do not conceal their admiration of the sublime doctrine, pure precept, and divine eloquence of the word of God. The plan of these translations was sanctioned at an early period by the Most Noble the Marquis Wellesley, the great pattern of useful learning. To give the Christian Scriptures to the inhabitants of Asia is indeed a work which every man who believes these Scriptures to be from God will approve. In Hindoostan alone there is a great variety of religions, and there are some tribes which have no certain cast or religion at all. To render the revealed religion accessible to men who desire it; to open its eternal sanctions, and display its pure morals to those who seek a religion, is to fulfil the sacred duty of a Christian people, and accords well with the humane and generous spirit of the English nation.'

Another passage of the document from which the preceding extract is taken, announced to India the formation and the proffered friendship of the British and Foreign Bible Society, as furnishing material encouragement to the proposed undertaking. Thus accredited and patronized, the address from the missionaries at Serampore was advertized in the government gazettes and published throughout India, and such was the approbation with which it was received, that in a short time the sum of sixteen hundred pounds was subscribed in aid of the intended translations.

Thus a gradual but satisfactory change in the state of things in reference to Christianity in India had worked its way to the glory and praise of God, who raised up the instrument and worked effectually by the means employed.

It was in this year, 1806, that the Rev. Henry Martyn and the Rev. Daniel Corrie, who was afterwards raised to the episcopate of Madras, arrived in Calcutta. The life and writings of Henry Martyn are too well known to need any detailed account either of himself or of his labours. Not so of that eminent servant of God, the late Bishop Corrie. It was the privilege of the writer of this sketch to know him intimately, and to have the advantage of his fatherly counsel throughout the course of his own ministry. The following brief memorial may suffice, as a memoir is on the eve of publication:—

The name of Corrie is associated with the best benefactors of India. Buchanan, who laboured till he made the woes and wants of India pierce the ear of England, was his friend. The humble, laborious, and spiritual minded Brown loved him tenderly. Henry Martyn, who laid all his splendid talents at the foot of the cross, devoting them to the Lord, who redeemed him with his own most precious blood, loved Corrie as an only brother. And Thomason, amiable, talented, and pure in heart, the friend, companion, and fellow-labourer of these devoted men, felt a holy joy, in the success of Corrie's labours, and entertained for him a brother's tenderness and regard.

Bishop Heber, whose name will live, loved Corrie, and thought he promoted his Saviour's cause in promoting his faithful servant. Bishop Turner, a profound theologian, an elegant scholar, of enlarged mind and most spiritual in his affections, and possessing, in a high degree, discrimination of character, entertained for Archdeacon Corrie a warm attachment and a brother's love, which was most cordially returned by Corrie's tender heart and devoted spirit. Brown and Turner were his first and last and most beloved friends.

The Rev. Daniel Corrie, having been nominated a

chaplain on the Bengal establishment, arrived in India towards the close of the year 1806, in the 29th year of his age, full of love to his Saviour, and of devotedness to his ministerial duties. His college friend, Henry Martyn, was then in Calcutta, burning with zeal, and bright with sanctified knowledge and Christian love. By Brown and Martyn he was warmly welcomed, and most affectionately did these friends regard each other, and earnestly seek India's real welfare from the sole giver of every good and perfect gift.

For a few months after Mr. Corrie's arrival in India he continued in Calcutta, rejoicing many hearts by the evangelical plainness and purity of his preaching, and by the fervour of his zeal and holiness. His first station in the *Muffusil* (up the country) was Chunar, where he soon was able to speak to the natives in Hindoostanee, of which he had acquired the rudiments during his voyage out. He engaged a native Christian to teach and catechize, and established schools to instruct native children in the truths of the gospel. Benares, about twenty miles distant, had also the benefit of his visits and ministrations. He loved his Saviour ardently, and for his Saviour's sake he loved the people among whom the Lord had placed him. This love he manifested by preaching the gospel, establishing schools, and erecting churches. By the assistance of his friends, of whom one of the foremost was Dr. J. Robinson, brother of the late Archdeacon, he raised a small church at Secrol, soon after another at Benares, and in 1818 the beautiful church at Chunar, after a model of the one he served in England, together with a small chapel at Buxar, for the poor invalid soldiers and their wives, who were chiefly native women. At this place he located a native catechist, by whom a native school was formed in which Christian principles were fully and successfully taught. Mr. Corrie left Chunar in 1810, to join his friend Henry Martyn, and to unite with him in ministerial labours at Cawnpore. Here he continued not much more than one year, being forced by a severe attack on the liver to relinquish his duties for a season and proceed to Calcutta, and thence as soon as possible to sea. Mr. David Brown went with him in the same ship in a dying state. Tempestuous weather drove the ship back almost a wreck, and about a fortnight after Mr. Brown's spirit was relieved from the troubles of life and entered into glory. Mr. Corrie soon after embarked in a ship bound to the Mauritius; but again a storm arose and the vessel was obliged to put in at Vizagapatam. His health having improved he prosecuted his voyage no farther, but returned to Calcutta before the close of the year.

This was an important period of his life. In Nov. 1812, he married Miss Myers, who proved to him a help-meet from the Lord. Her mind was strong, her judgment excellent; her natural talents cultivated with great care, and her affections purified and regulated by the word and Spirit of God. After twenty-four years of happy union, Mrs. Corrie died in Dec. 1836, to be followed, alas! in six short weeks by her husband.

Mr. Corrie being appointed to Agra in 1813, took with him that venerable servant of Christ, Abdul Messeh, who had been brought to the knowledge of the truth as it is in Jesus, by Henry Martyn, and baptized the year before by David Brown. Abdul was indeed a convert, and being converted, he strengthened his brethren, and brought souls to the Saviour. A native congregation was soon formed at Agra, and soon counted fifty members. The word of the Lord grew and prospered, but within two years a dangerous attack on the liver drove Mr. Corrie from India for a season to visit his native land. During a stay of about two years in England, he was much engaged in preaching for the Church Missionary Society, and in turning the hearts of British Christians to the spiritual destitution of their fellow men in Hindoostan. On his return from India with Mrs. Corrie, and an infant daughter, in the middle of 1817, Benares became the scene of his ministrations and devoted labours. It was while here that he raised through the help of friends, the fine and beautiful church at Chunar, (his first station) and the chapel at Buxar. At this time he devoted much of his care and thoughts to the Church Missionary Society, by establishing schools in connection with the Society for the Christian education of Hindoos and Mahommedans.

In 1819, he became presidency chaplain. While filling this important office he pursued his plans and exertions in the cause of education, and with great cordiality welcomed and aided that excellent and indefatigable lady, Mrs. Wilson, in her arduous efforts to promote native female education.

The gifted Bishop Heber conferred on Mr. Corrie the appointment of Archdeacon of Calcutta, in the year 1823, on the death of Dr. Loring; an appointment which reflected high credit on that amiable prelate's judgment, and associated the weight of responsibility and high office, with the meekness, humility, experience, fervent piety, and talent of Corrie—thus making them all more influential for the promotion of true religion, and the good of the church.

His appointment to the Archdeaconry did not entirely prevent him from doing something personally for the native congregations so dear to him. Besides the addresses which he never failed to address to them whenever opportunity offered, he translated, at the desire of Bishop Middleton, Sellon's Abridgment of Scripture—the Prayer Book, and many of the Homilies, into Hindostanee. He likewise drew up Outlines of Ancient History in English, for the benefit of native youth. The third edition of that simple and excellent work was considerably enlarged, and was translated by another hand. Its great value consists in the tone of pure Christian principle which pervades it, making all history prove that "sin is the reproach of any people," and that "righteousness," and righteousness alone, "exalteth a nation;" that all good cometh of God, and all evil from the corrupt heart of man.

The deep interest which Archdeacon Corrie took in

the cause of sceiptural education, led him to project a classical and English school, denominated the 'Calcutta High School,' which valuable institution was organized and finally established by the judicious and holy Bishop Turner, the successor of Bishop Heber.

In 1834, after a sojourn of nearly twenty-eight years in India, Archdeacon Corrie was called to England to be raised to that high station in the church for which the grace of God had so eminently qualified him. His natural powers and qualifications, a humble view of himself, simplicity of heart and purpose, unbounded benevolence, and a calm sound judgment, being so sanctified by the Divine Spirit, and so turned into the channel of holiness, rendered him the object on which all eyes looked, and many hopes rested, when Madras was erected into a bishopric. His striking humility, his eminent zeal, his devoted fidelity to the cause of simple evangelical truth, his transparent purity of character, and spirituality of mind; his calm judgment, his firmness in essentials, and his liberal views, were the religious and intellectual endowments which raised high hopes of his being a truly eminent bishop. Nor did his exceeding urbanity and gentleness, his condescension to all, his affectionate attention to the young, and his extraordinary winning voice and look, fail to be reckoned up amongst those characteristics which drew towards him the hearts and hopes of thousands.

On Trinity Sunday, 14th of June, 1835, Arcddeacon Corrie was consecrated Bishop of Madras by the Archbishop of Canterbury and the Bishops of Lichfield, Carlisle, and Bangor. The University of Cambridge conferred upon him the degree of L.L.D. On the 24th of October, his lordship landed at Madras, and on the 28th of the same month, was installed in the cathedral church of St. George's. He preached his first sermon on the following Sunday, from Gal. vi. 14. "God forbid," &c.

The choice to be the first Bishop of Madras, fell on this venerable servant of God; and never was choice wiser, and never were fond hopes more fully realized. Every chaplain and missionary rejoiced, thanked God, and took courage. Time was daily ripening and mellowing every Christian grace, and developing every talent. Our venerated bishop brought the Christian experience and the fruits of a thirty years ministry in India, to bear upon all that came before him. Never did kindness and gentleness, patience and forbearance, and consideration for the opinions of others, shine more conspicuously than in Bishop Corrie. And never were the necessary qualifications of firmness, dignity, and wisdom, more separated and purified from every base alloy, than in the beloved subject of this imperfect and unworthy tribute.

Unworthy as every sketch must be of an original so preeminent, it is given as a testimony from one who knew and loved him. His was indeed a bright example, and as such it is thus presented to the reader. To God be the glory! The brightness exhibited was a ray reflected from Him who is the brightness of his Father's glory. He shone as a light, but it was because the Spirit of glory and of God rested on him! Let us follow him as he followed his divine Lord and Master, Christ.

The following sketch of the lamented wife of Bishop Corrie will not be without its interest, as one of the last employments of his hand and pen:—

'Mrs. Corrie's parents were among the first fruits of the ministry of the late Rev. David Brown, many years senior chaplain in Calcutta. She was brought up with great care, and had the privilege of being much in Mr. Brown's family. Her mother took great pains to preserve her from the influence of native servants, and herself instructed her in the various branches of female education at an early age. Mr. Brown perceiving her aptness to learn, took also great pleasure in teaching her the elements of Hebrew and Syriac; and the scriptures in the original Hebrew soon became familiar to her. It may be mentioned that she acquired in early life a correct knowledge of both French and Italian, and had read some of the best authors in those languages. Such was her aversion to any thing approaching to display, that only those who were in habits of familiar intercourse could conceive of her mind and acquirements. The instructions of her mother had impressed Mrs. Corrie's mind with a reverence for religion in childhood, and when about thirteen years old, during a course of catechizing by Mr. Brown in his family, she began to receive religion as a personal concern. From that time to her death, it held the first place in her affections, and was the mainspring of all that activity in duty, and that cheerful piety which distinguished her,' &c. &c.

The writer of these memorial sketches of Christianity knew Mrs. Corrie intimately, and on many and repeated occasions had the privilege of her society both at home and in travelling. Her conversation was always instructive, never trifling. The amount of her labours and efforts for the public good of India is scarcely credible. On committees of management her influence for good was very great, and her personal sacrifices not a few. Her record is on high.

Her end was peace. She lived in faith and died in hope. She laboured here, and peacefully entered into her rest. She finally took to her bed in November 1835. Her Bible, which had been her daily companion through life, was kept by her side, and was her chief solace. She spoke with deep feeling of her own unworthiness, and want of improvement of former mercies, &c. She had been brutish (she said) under chastisements, and careless in prosperity; she had no hope but in Christ, adding—

'Jesus! thy blood and righteousness,' &c.

with more to that effect.

On another occasion she said to the bishop: 'Am I safe?' To which he replied, 'You know as well as I that "If any man sin, we have an advocate with the Father,"' &c. 'But,' said the sufferer, 'will he receive me?' The bishop answered—'Does He not say, "Come unto me,"' &c. and also reminded her of the passage which her early friend and pastor, the Rev. D. Brown, when on his death-bed, pointed out as the most surprising passage in all the Bible, Jer. iii. 1, &c. The passage was read to her, and after a pause she said, 'Yes; I feel that I *am* a child, though a naughty one' —adding, 'though some were further off from the brazen serpent than others, yet as many as looked lived.' She also said, 'When one comes into these circumstances we cannot but see our unprofitableness.' Once when she seemed, a little easy, the bishop said to her, 'Can you repose in the arms of your heavenly Father?' She added, 'And in Jesus the Mediator.' At another time she said, 'I dare not doubt his power or his willingness.' At another time, 'Whom he loveth he loveth to the end.' Soon after she said, 'There I shall see our dear ones—we have two in heaven and two on the way.' Then to her daughter she said, 'See that you follow, and tell Laura the same, that none of our family be wanting.' The bishop said, 'You will see your dear father too.' She added, 'And my grandmother,'—with more on the subject of seeing as we are seen, and knowing the Saviour as we are known of him. After the family had breakfasted she received the Lord's Supper, when she desired her daughter, and also Miss Hutchins to attend. Her breathing was so difficult, that after receiving the elements, the service was for a time interrupted, but was at length brought to a conclusion; she joined with evident fervour, and at the close added an impressive *Amen*. While suffering most she repeated in broken accents, or by repeating a word or two suggested to the bishop to take up the subject:

'I'll speak the honour of his name,
With my last lab'ring breath,' &c.

repeating several times at intervals,

'Dying, clasp him in my arms.'

During the forenoon of Wednesday, among the verses repeated was :

'Beneath thy cross I fall,
My Lord, my life, my sacrifice,
My Saviour and my all.'

dwelling on the words—'*my sacrifice.*'

At another time :—

'Lo, glad I come, and Thou, blest Lamb,
Shall take me to Thee as I am,
Nothing but sin have I to give
Nothing but love shall I receive.'

When alone with her daughter, soon after the bishop had retired to get a little repose with a view to the approaching night, she brought the subject before her in the following manner as recorded by herself. After speaking of the near approach of her death, she blessed me with deep affection, and afterwards said, 'I have two angels in heaven, I am blessed indeed ; and dear Laura too ; give her my love,' &c. with much more. The same evening, after a pause she said, 'I have been too fond of the world, and its love and admiration, but God has weaned me from it by this long illness.' Almost the last words she spoke were—'What is that?—"I looked and there was no deliverer,"' &c. Violent spasms came on, and she "*entered into rest.*"

How oft we see the dearest plans we form,
Fade in the sun, or perish in the storm !
How oft the brightest hopes their pinions wave,
Then cease to soar, and find an earthly grave.
Weep, India, weep ! a Father's loss deplore ;
For he who sought thy welfare is no more.
And he whom Martyn loved, is called away
To meet his friend in realms of cloudless day.
Quenched is that light which once so brightly shone,
And all the mildness of its radiance gone ;
For India has received another blow,
In that true shepherd of Christ's sheep laid low.
A watchman's voice in Israel has been hush'd,
And many a hope in Corrie's grave been crush'd.

He who so meekly all his honours bore,
Shall wear his crown upon a happier shore.

Though Hindostan has lost a heaven-lit gem.
'Tis gone to deck a Saviour's diadem.
Though here no more his light shall shed its flame,
The fountain of that light is still the same.
The church has lost a tender pastor's care,
But still to Jesus may that church repair.
The pillar rent from Zion's earthly fame,
Shall in the temple of our God remain,
And though a faithful watchman we deplore,
The word he preached shall live for evermore.

It was in 1806, that Mr. Buchanan entered upon his long-projected journey to the south of the Peninsula; but as his researches in that part of India have been long before the public, and extensively read,—any further notice of them here is unnecessary, besides which, the present sketch is only intended to embrace North India.

In March 1807, Mr. then Dr. Buchanan, returned to Calcutta, having accomplished an arduous and most interesting journey of more than five thousand miles. It was with deep regret that he found that the college of Fort William, which had flourished and produced such important results, had been reduced and crippled in its operations.

In the progress of this extensive journey it was, that Dr. Buchanan conceived the design of a Christian Institution, which was afterwards established in Calcutta, and must now be noticed, but only briefly, as Dr. Buchanan himself published his reflections on viewing the distant towers of Juggernaut from an eminence on the banks of the Chilka Lake, and the design which he then conceived of some Christian institution, which might gradually undermine the frightful idolatry he had been contemplating, and blot out its memory for ever.* The historian of the decline and fall of the Roman Empire informs us, that he first conceived the thought of his elaborate and eloquent work amidst the ruins of the Capitol. It was an association of a more sublime and sacred nature, which suggested to Dr. Buchanan

* Christian Researches. p. 31.

the design of the institution, the general plan of which he then briefly described.

Soon after his return to Calcutta, he employed himself in digesting and arranging its form and constitution; and on the 28th of May he thus adverts to the subject, at the close of a letter to Colonel Macaulay:—

'By the Indus I send home a small work for publication, not in relation to Malabar, but to Juggernaut; nor to him directly, but to a Literary Institution, whose object shall be to promote Christian knowledge in Asia by means of books; which institution shall be exclusively literary, and shall have no connection with any missionary society. The institution already exists, and is in extensive operation.'

The work alluded to was printed, but afterwards deemed not expedient to publish. The title was as follows:—'The Christian Institution in the East; or the College for translating the Holy Scriptures into the oriental tongues.' The origin and object of the institution were described nearly in the terms of the preceding letter. It was dedicated to all good men, to be an instrument in their hands of extending the knowledge of revealed religion, by the translation of the Holy Scriptures, and was placed under the immediate patronage of the Archbishop of Canterbury, as President of the Society for Promoting Christian Knowledge. One of its subordinate objects was, to print small tracts on certain branches of art and science, fitted for popular use and improvement.

The various instruments of the institution were next enumerated, comprizing the venerable Bishop of the Syrian Church in Malayala—the British and Danish missionaries throughout India,—Judah Misrahi, a learned Jew of Cochin, engaged by Dr. Buchanan as a translator of the New Testament into Hebrew,—Professor Lassar, for the Chinese language,—and the late Rev. Henry Martyn, with two learned coadjutors, natives of the East, for the Persian, Arabic, and Hindostanee languages. With the exception of Mr. Martyn, who arrived at Calcutta during the absence of Dr. Buchanan, he stated that he had visited all the before-named persons at their respective residences, and had informed himself as to their abilities and principles. It was not intended to form an expensive establishment; but that a professor should be stationed as a literary agent of the college in each of the principal provinces of the East, to study a particular language, to collect information, to correspond with the Society at home, to compose and to print books, and to instruct the natives in printing, &c.

Such is a partial outline of the college thus proposed for oriental translation. The intention in short was to establish a British Propaganda, which in proportion to the extent of its object, should be superior to that of Rome, the fame of which still survives in Asia. Upon its original formation, Dr. Buchanan proposed to the Baptist missionaries at Serampore, being then extensively engaged in translating the Scriptures, that they should associate, merely in that character, with other fellow-labourers in different parts of India; which proposal was however declined by them, and the name of the 'Christian Institution' was in consequence but partially assumed, and but imperfectly carried into execution.

With respect to the main design of the 'Christian Institution,' as a college of acknowledged responsibility, embracing the associated learning and piety of the East, for the grand purpose of sacred translation, and possessing commanding patronage, effective support, and enlarged superintendence and control, the failure of its establishment can scarcely be considered but a subject of regret.

We may now return to a further notice of Dr. Buchanan's proposal of an ecclesiastical Establishment. In reply to Dr. Buchanan's memoir, he received a valuable letter from the then Bishop of Llandaff, which is inserted at the close of the Christian Researches, and to which the reader is referred. Subsequently in a letter to Col. Macaulay, Dr. Buchanan writes,—'I have had a letter from the Bishop of London, dated 1st of September last, in which he says, that it was too late last session to bring forward the proposition for an Ecclesiastical Establishment for British India, but that the Archbishop of Canterbury intends to move his Majesty's ministers on the subject next session.'

It appears that the necessity of such an establishment had occurred to Dr. Kerr, of the Madras residency, almost simultaneously, and a memorial was addressed by him to Lord William Bentinck on the subject. He soon after entered into his rest.*

Dr. Buchanan's Memoir produced, as might be expected, a considerable sensation on the public mind. The subject was not only highly important, but it was new. The world had indeed heard much of Eastern commerce, policy, and conquests, but of East-Indian religion, little or nothing. Now and then the name of a chaplain to the Company had been mentioned, and still more rarely, that of a missionary to the Hindoos. But, generally speaking, the whole subject of the religion of India was little known, and still less regarded. Its European population was presumed, without thought or inquiry, to be sufficiently provided with the means of Christian instruction ; and as to the natives, they were considered as a race so completely separated from ourselves, and at the same time so religious and even moral in their own way, that with the exception of those who had heard something of the Danish missionaries on the coast of Coromandel, the idea of converting any considerable number of the Hindoos was either treated as altogether unnecessary, and even unjust, or deemed in the highest degree visionary and impracticable.

A flame was kindled. The religious hailed this production as presenting facts and arguments of a most

* See Christian Observer, vol. xi. p. 80.

important nature, and as opening a boundless sphere of exertion to the newly-awakened and expanding energies of the Christian benevolence and zeal; while others, and these a numerous and respectable class, considered it, as at best, a rash and unauthorized publication, and even deprecated it as tending to excite dissatisfaction at home and disturbance abroad. The growing extent and influence of the British and Foreign Bible Society, and the anxiety which it evinced to promote the translation of the Scriptures into the oriental languages, added materially to the displeasure and alarm of the persons last alluded to. These different sentiments upon this important subject, were, at the time, publicly expressed, and the controversy is doubtless in the recollection of many. On the one side was a pamphlet, published in October 1807, under the title of 'A Letter to the Chairman of the East India Company, on the Danger of Interfering in the Religious Opinions of the Natives of India, and on the views of the British and Foreign Bible Society, as directed to India.' The author is now well known to have been Thomas Twining, Esq., Senior Merchant on the Bengal Establishment. And early in the year 1808, the controversy was renewed by the publication of a pamphlet, entitled, 'A Vindication of the Hindoo, from the Aspersions of the Rev. C. Buchanan, M.A., with a Refutation of his Arguments for an Ecclesiastical Establishment in British India,' by a Bengal Officer. With respect to the British and Foreign Bible Society, a reply was published by the Rév. Mr. Owen, Secretary, &c. And amongst others, the venerable Bishop Porteus wrote some remarks on Mr. Twining's pamphlet, which were published anonymously, and which, in a strain of well-directed irony, defended the measures of the British and Foreign Bible Society, and what His Lordship termed, 'Dr. Buchanan's invaluable Memoir.' At the same time appeared Mr. J. W. Cunningham's 'Essay on the Duty, Means, and Consequences of Introducing the Christian Religion among the Native Inhabitants of the British Dominions in the

East.' Mr. Cunningham's Essay was followed by the Prize Dissertation of the Rev. Hugh Pearson. One other work of singular excellence and authority, and of which it may be justly remarked, that had it appeared in an earlier stage of the controversy, it would have superseded every other, was that of Lord Teignmouth, 'Considerations on the Practicability, Policy, and Obligation of Communicating to the Natives of India the Knowledge of Christianity.' This has been pronounced an incomparable and unanswerable work, and is well worth the perusal even at the present day. The *Christian Observer* also wrote largely and ably upon the subject, till, at length, the storm became a calm.

It is not extraordinary that the same elements should be at work in India also. The train was first indeed laid there, and strenuous and persevering efforts were made to arrest, or, at least, to impede the progress of Scriptural translation, and to restrain the efforts of Christian missionaries. In a letter dated Sept. 1807, Dr. Buchanan writes to Colonel Macaulay :—

'I am on the eve, I fear, of a rupture with the Government. The cause is the Gospel. They are endeavouring to restrain the exertions of the missionaries in Bengal. I have not yet interfered; and, I trust, it will not be necessary, for I love peace, and not war; particularly at the moment of my leaving the country. But I shall do my duty, and leave the event to God!' In another letter, dated Oct. 12, he writes: 'The attack I announced to you in my last, has not been yet made. I wish you were at my side during the storm. I have friends, but they are not soldiers. I am the forlorn hope, and yet I have not twelve men. Nay, more, my friends tell me I must be killed. The assault, however, must be made, but whether by silent escalade at the midnight watch, or by heavy and hot battery at noonday, I have not yet determined. I think the latter.'

The rupture with the supreme Government to which Dr. Buchanan here refers, was of a very serious and unpleasant nature. The occasion was a course of sermons preached in the presidency church on the Christian prophecies, which proved so acceptable to some of the congregation, that they expressed a wish he would permit them to be printed. To this request he acceded, and preparations were made accordingly. On transmitting however an advertisement to the Government Gazette, announcing the intended publication of his discourses, he was surprised to find that the insertion of it was refused, that an order had been issued to the other printers forbidding them to publish the *obnoxious* notice. Shortly afterwards he received a letter from the Chief Secretary to the Presidency, desiring that he would transmit the manuscript of his sermons on the prophecies for the inspection of Government. To this unexpected demand Dr. Buchanan gave no immediate answer. It had long been the subject of painful observation to him, that on the departure of the Marquis Wellesley, during whose administration the spirit of promoting learning and religion in India, had been general and ardent, a directly contrary disposition was manifested; as if it had been previously restrained by his pretence. This first appeared under the administration of Sir George Barlow, and had been acquiring strength ever since.

Lord Minto had now assumed the supreme Government; and as several measures were adopted which appeared to Dr. Buchanan to operate very unfavourably for the interests both of learning and religion, he deemed it his duty, before he quitted Bengal, to address a memorial to his Lordship, in which he particularly directed his attention to the character and tendency of those measures; and in so doing explained his reasons for declining to comply with the wishes of Government respecting the sermons on the prophecies.

The Memorial was published some years afterwards by Dr. Buchanan * in his own vindication and defence, and evinced, as it has been well observed, 'the tem-

* See his Apology for Promoting Christianity in India.

perate firmness of a man, who knowing that the Gospel is the power of God unto salvation, is neither ashamed to profess, nor afraid to defend it.' The Memorial states the four following facts: first, the withdrawal of the patronage of Government from the translation of the Holy Scriptures into the oriental tongues. Second, attempting to suppress the translation of the Holy Scriptures. Third, suppressing the encomium of the Honourable the Court of Directors, on the Venerable Missionary Swartz. And fourth, restraining the *Protestant* missionaries in Bengal from the exercise of their functions, and establishing an imprimatur for theological works. Not a word of reply was vouchsafed, but the Memorial sent home with unfavourable animadversions, &c.

The painful transaction which has been thus detailed was nearly the last of a public nature in which Dr. Buchanan was engaged in Calcutta. The time was now approaching for his second and final departure from that city. Accordingly in the month of November he preached his farewell sermon to the congregation at the Mission Church from the words of St. Paul to the Philippians, chap. i. 27. "Only let your conversation be as becometh the gospel of Christ."

In a confidential letter to a brother, the venerable Brown thus writes of this man of God:

'You ask me if Dr. Buchanan is my friend? I answer, I know no man in the world who excels him in useful purpose or deserves my friendship more. Perhaps there is no man in the world who loves him so much as I do; because no man knows him so well. Further, no man in the world I believe, would do me service like him. We have lived together in the closest intimacy ten years, without a shade of difference in sentiment, political or religious. It is needless to add, without a jar, in word or deed. He is the man to do good in the earth, and worthy of being metropolitan of the East.'

About the close of 1806, this excellent man and attached friend of Buchanan, who thus bears testimony to his worth, had the happiness of forming an association for correspondence with a small band of fellow-chaplains, his friends, who to strengthen each other's hands, and encourage one another, agreed on mutually communicating such observations and facts as they gleaned in their respective labours. Among these, Mr. Brown had generally the greatest share of intelligence to impart; being placed in what had become, through the blessing of God, the most fruitful field of the Eastern harvest.

The first communication was made according to agreement by this venerable man, as follows;—

'*Calcutta*, Jan. 5th, 1807.

'At our last meeting at the pagoda, (for prayer and consultation,) on the 9th of December, I was requested to transmit to my dear brethren copies of the paper No. 1.* It was written under a painful retrospection of past unprofitableness in the ministry, depressed and opposed, from the beginning, my hopes at the end of fourteen years were nearly broken. I have now cause to bless the Lord that he put it into my heart to propose a union for secret prayer.

'Since the year 1802 we have been enabled to go on from strength to strength. The cloud of embarrassment which for several years hung over the mission-church, was, in July 1805, removed by government, who paid 12,064 rupees on its account, and gave a monthly allowance of 234 rupees for its support. I ought perhaps to communicate the paper proposing the establishment of an evangelical fund. Our success has been great; the property is now valued at forty thousand rupees. This may serve to shew that small beginnings should be no impediment to the commencement of useful plans. Let us call to mind Professor Franke, and the foundation of the orphan-house at Halle, in Saxony. In outward

* The document here referred to I cannot find.

as well as in other respects, we have been raised from a low estate. The prospects now opening are most cheering to our hopes.

'A BIBLE SOCIETY.—A TRANSLATION FUND.—AN ACCESSION OF MINISTERS OF THE GOSPEL.—I was led to notice some of these matters in my sermon on the morning of new-year's day.

'On Christmas-day I was called to bear a testimony before our governors. I preached from Isaiah xxv. 9. As texts, sermons, &c. are to form part of our quarterly correspondence, I trust my brethren will not be sparing of their communications under this head. I send extracts from mine—No. 1, 2, 3. A good outline will often be useful and edifying.

'You will recollect that one of our last conversations when we parted with our friend Martyn, was on the *right mode of preaching*. I have by me some thoughts of the venerable Joseph Milner on the subject—copy of which I inclose, No. 4. You will observe that this letter is eighteen years old. They were written to a young military chaplain, placed precisely in your circumstances.

'The most material communication which I have to make on the subject of events since our dispersion, is the sickness of Mr. ——. On Saturday the 20th of December, he was seized with fever and bowel-affection. His physicians thought him to be in danger. I called frequently at his quarters, but did not see him till yesterday se'ennight. He presently began to speak freely on the subject of preaching the gospel. He observed there were various shades or sorts of preaching which could not be called preaching the gospel; that some left out religion entirely, and kept to morality alone, and that such preaching would suit an heathen as well as a Christian. Others again preached piously, but the piety was of a description that would suit an Arminian or Calvinist, or even a Socinian equally well;—but that neither was the gospel of Christ. He then noticed with expressions of deep humility, and with tears, the defectiveness of his own ministry. He said he had always held the fundamentals of Christianity, but that it had been the error of his whole life, till lately, not to bring them sufficiently forward. He now perceived that the peculiar doctrines of the gospel were the vital principles which gave it all its power and influence.

'I could not but speak warmly of the faithful testimony which we had heard him bear to the truth as it is in Jesus; he replied with melting and broken accents,—"If I have contributed but a mite to such a cause, I shall deem it the happiest circumstance of my life; but I fear I have done nothing towards it."

'The unfeigned humility and contrite confession of an elder brother affected me much. He considered his change of views as a happy change, and seemed fully satisfied there was no rest, hope, peace, or comfort, for a sinner, from any other doctrine than Christ alone. He spoke of each of you with the overflowing affection of a grateful heart. Has your ministry, my brethren, done no good? Have you destroyed the souls for whom Christ died? (as you have been charged by some)—Is not such a tribute worth all the scorn you have met with from unreasonable and wicked men?

'In noticing events I ought not to pass over in silence the change in my own circumstances by the abolition * of the offices of Provost and Vice-Provost of the College of Fort William, which took place on the 31st ultimo. This did not however prevent me from enjoying the happiest new year's day I have known in India. The vessel is somewhat lightened—a load of envy, responsibility, and anxiety is removed. I have long been satisfied of the truth of that divine aphorism which saith—"A man's life consisteth not in the abundance of the things which he possesseth." Abundance adds nothing to the support of life—nothing to the enjoyment of life—nothing to the protection of life.

* Mr. B. proffered his gratuitous services to the Governor-General, on the abolition of the offices; but they were not accepted.

'This has been a season of uncommon *spiritual* comfort to us, and we have been enabled to say—

> 'When all created streams are dried,
> Thy fulness is the same;
> May I with this be satisfied
> And glory in thy name.'

'On Wednesday evening, 31st Dec. I preached a retrospective sermon on 1 Cor. ii. 1—4. I noticed the apostle's plainness of speech: verse 1, subject-matter of preaching: verse 2, and circumstances of infirmity: verse 3, I appealed to the congregation that I had endeavoured to follow the apostle in the two first particulars, and that I had resembled him in the third.

'The first time I preached at the mission-church was on Good Friday, 1787, and my subject was taken from the 2nd verse of the above text. On the 1st of Jan. I met some of the friends belonging to our prayer-union, and proposed to form a prayer-meeting under my own direction, on the plan adopted by Mr. Simeon. It will commence in the course of next month, when the mission-house will be ready. We shall make mention of you always in our prayers.

'On the 3rd of January, eleven ministers of the gospel met Mr. ——, previous to his departure for the coast, at the Pagoda, to commend him to the grace of God. It was an occasion much to be remembered unto the Lord for his gracious presence, and our uncommon mutual edification. The 150th Psalm is a proper finish to this my first report, "Praise ye the Lord."

D. BROWN.'

At the end of the first quarter, Mr. Brown again addressed his friend as follows:—

'*Aldeen*, *April* 6, 1807.

'You are already acquainted with the circumstances under which we commenced the new year. Mr. —— continued to bear his testimony among us until the beginning of February. At the Presidency Church, he was heard with uncommon attention and acceptance. In his last sermon on "*The way of salvation*," he concluded his discourse in the following words: 'Thus they preached who have lately passed through this place to their respective stations in this Presidency, and to them I desire in the most solemn manner to add this my parting testimony also. We commend ourselves, and the gospel we preach, to your consciences in the sight of God. We call you not to subjects of doubtful disputation, but to things in which all are agreed who worship God in the Spirit, and rejoice in Christ Jesus, and have no confidence in the flesh. We preach not for party or contention's sake. We seek not to entangle or encumber the conscience of the weakest Christian. We seek, my brethren, but to lead you to happiness by the way in which we have found peace to our own souls.'

'When Dr. Buchanan returned to Calcutta he naturally enquired what conversions had taken place from such uncommon opportunities of hearing the gospel. If we cannot point out particular instances we can state that there has been a general effect produced, which cannot fail to be favourable to the progress of true religion. Those who know the Lord have been excited to give more earnest heed to divine things, and have been quickened to greater diligence in the path of duty and greater zeal for the cause of Christ, and to a more fervent spirit of prayer and thankfulness, and to take a more particular interest in the spread of the gospel and for the support of missionary efforts. Again, several who were heretofore but half-enlightened have received more light. Some who halted between two opinions are become decided, and promise to adorn their Christian profession. Lieutenant-Colonel ——— has shown much seriousness for some years past, but I always suspected that his religion was buried under a rubbish of self-righteousness. He lately stated his views to a friend in reference to the discussion of doctrines in Calcutta, and they now appear to be clear, decided, and consistent. As I have known many persons sit long under the faithful preaching of the gospel in a purblind state, never understanding whether God justifies the sinner, or the sinner justifies himself, I am rejoiced to find that so much good has arisen to a class of hearers whom I always considered as the most hopeless part of the flock.

'The attention of some of the inconsiderate, I think, has also been awakened, and we may hope that a good work is beginning to be wrought upon them. On Easter-day Dr. Buchanan preached from 1 Peter i. 3, "Who hath begotten us again to a lively hope through the resurrection of Jesus Christ from the dead." A most weighty and powerful discourse. It was a word in season, very awful and affecting. Thus has the same gospel been preached at this presidency by seven chaplains in the course of a few months:—surely he who sent it will prosper it.

'On the 31st of January we had a prayer-meeting in the Pagoda, previous to the departure of Mr. and Mrs. —— for the coast. We had a party of near thirty. It was a season very comforting and refreshing to our spirits. On the preceding Sunday we heard of the safe arrival of Messrs. —— at Rangoon, and of the very favourable reception they had met with there. On *Monday* arrived Dr. Buchanan with all his boxes of MSS. safe. He had sent some of them in the *Rahim-Shah*, which in the course of his voyage he overtook and found in distress; the passengers wished to leave the ship and to come to Bengal in the Danesberg. Dr. Buchanan thought he might as well remove his boxes. The passengers, more anxious for their own trunks than his MSS., filled the boat; and the boat upset before Buchanan's boxes were on board. A large boat was then sent to fetch the passengers, and with them the MSS. arrived safe on board the Danesberg. At our meeting on the 17th, we had abundant cause for many thanksgivings to God. Every man from Chunar to Rangoon was at his station. Mrs. ——, whose life had been despaired of, was restored, and I had additional motives for thankfulness in my own late family mercies. We mentioned by name all who had before assembled with us at that place, and every station to which they had gone forth, viz., Bombay, Madras, Vizagapatam, Rangoon. We made mention of the mercies vouchsafed to Bengal, at Calcutta, Serampore, Cutnar, Dinapore, Barampore, and Chunar, nor did we forget any who are engaged in missionary labours or other labours for the spread of the gospel.

'Mr. —— sailed with Captain —— for St. Helena in February. He seemed to increase every day in humility and zeal, and I hope he will live to preach Christ at St. Helena and the Cape where he means to go. The temper of his mind will best appear from the following extract of a letter he wrote me from on board the Harriet:—

'"A letter from you was, next after those which I received from my dear family, one of the greatest gratifications which my present situation admits of. The kind remembrance also of those revered and esteemed friends who are my brother-clergy, but whom I look up to as examples in their labours in the teaching of the truths of the gospel, must needs be highly grateful to me. In your correspondence with them, remember me with the utmost kindness and affection to them. With respect to the sermons you speak of, I shall find no trouble in copying them legibly at your desire. I anticipate some disappointment you will meet with in them. If it has pleased God to enable me to speak one word of truth, you will see too plainly that we are not to think to be altogether secured against the weakness of him by whom it is delivered, &c.

'"Many thanks for your cordial wishes and your prayers for me, which I value as the prayers of one whose prayer I believe 'availeth much.' We had on board for a short time a Mr. ——, who appears to me a true Christian, and who had exerted himself in that first of our duties, the enlightening the heathen, and who moreover comes much recommended to me as a friend of yours. If you see him after this arrives, I will beg you to make my best compliments to him. His children are quite well. May God bless you, my dear Sir, and be with you and yours, &c.

'"*Saugar, 24th February,* 1807."

'Our worthy friend, Captain ——, is quite well, and received your letter together with the one to me.

'Captain —— was at the Mission-church on the Sunday evening before he sailed: after service he came into the vestry and requested me to visit a sick friend of his, a Captain —— (one of the Company's captains). I found him in great distress of soul, overwhelmed and trembling under a sense of sins, he said, "All the Scriptures are against me." I asked him, what scripture? He replied, "Woe unto you when all men speak well of you." He went on to say, "I have lived upon this plan, and I have succeeded. I have been that good moral man the world approves and applauds; but now I see myself in another glass. I perceive my life to have been wicked, selfish, deceitful. My most honourable transactions, and those for which I am most commended by the world, were dishonest and vile, having a bad principle at the bottom. Now my sins come to my remembrance, and lay heavy on my heart, and I am so oppressed I cannot pray, &c. &c."

'I told him his complaints were like sweet music to my ears, I wished I could hear such from all the human race, for then the Gospel would be acceptable tidings. I told him, that much as he seemed to know and feel of his case, he did not know a thousandth part of the evil of it, yet I trusted that he knew enough to make help welcome. We then turned to the Psalms, which expressed similar complainings — then to the prophet offering consolation, "Ho, every one that thirsteth, &c.," then to the holy evangelists, "Let not your heart be troubled, &c." Then we prayed, and parted perhaps to meet no more in this world. His spirit seemed refreshed. Next day I sent him a list of texts from the whole book of Psalms suited to his distress, and a tract called, 'A Remedy of God's own providing, &c.,' which had once been blessed to myself under distress of mind. I also sent him Watts's fine translation of the fifty-first Psalm. He returned the following answer :—

'*Feb.* 6, 1807.

'DEAR SIR,

'After being sometime asleep last night, towards morning I got up, and had some comfortable hours after continuing in prayer for some considerable time ; but alas, I am clouded again—however I will strive to the last, and oh, that I may find acceptance, for my case is heavy indeed. I thank you sincerely for your precious little book. Oh that I could find comfort from it ?—However, I will struggle to the last.

'I remain, dear Sir, your obliged,

'(Signed) P. ——

'The wish of my heart will be to write you of peace and acceptance from Bencoolen.'

'On the day following, Capt. —— and he went down to their ships at Diamond Harbour.'

These precious relics appear to the writer of this sketch of more value than the most elaborate record of mightiest deeds of mightiest men. They are the simple annals of passing occurrences, entirely of a religious character, and showing to the life what was the religion of the day.

Mr. Brown continues, 'In what remains I shall confine myself to "signs of the times." What is going on in our own confined spheres of action, is but as the dust of the balance. I suppose we are each looking forward to the evangelizing of the whole earth, and that we shall think nothing done while any people or nation remain unconquered by the cross.

'All our Governments of India have opposed the diffusion of the knowledge of Christianity among the natives. This opposition, however, is the effect of mere panic, which is vanishing fast away like smoke. Dr. Buchanan has consulted me on the expediency of his returning by the route of Antioch at the end of this year. I have entirely acquiesced.'

Among the communications addressed to the Rev. Mr. Brown by the friends engaged in this correspondence, the following, from the Rev. Henry Martyn, will be read with interest :—

'I begin my first communication to my dear and honoured brethren, with thankfully accepting their proposal of becoming a member of their Society, and bless the God and Father of our Lord Jesus Christ for this new instance of his mercy to his unworthy creature. May His grace and favour be vouchsafed to us, and His Holy Spirit direct all our proceedings, and sanctify our communications to the purposes for which we are united!

'On a review of the state of my mind since my arrival at Dinapore, I observe, that the graces of joy and love have been at a low ebb. Faith has been chiefly called into exercise, and without simple dependence on the Divine promises, I should still every day sink in fatal despondency: self-love and unbelief have been suggesting many foolish fears respecting the difficulties of my future work among the heathen. The thought of interrupting a crowd of busy people like those at Patna,* whose everyday is a market-day, with a message about eternity, without command of language, sufficient to explain and defend myself, and so of becoming the scorn of the rabble, without doing them good, was offensive to my pride. The manifest disregard of the people, and the contempt with which they eyed me, confirmed my dread. "Sufficient for the day is the evil thereof;" "As thy days, so shall thy strength be," were passages continually brought to my remembrance, and with these at last my mind grew quiet. Our country-

* About twelve miles from Dinapore.

men, when speaking of the natives, said, as they usually do, "they cannot be converted," and, "if they could, they would be *worse* than they are!" Though I have observed before now that the English are not in the way of knowing much about the natives, yet the number of difficulties they mentioned proved another source of discouragement to me. It is surprising how positively they are apt to speak on this subject through their never acknowledging God in anything. "Thy judgments are far above out of their sight." If we labour to the end of our days without seeing one convert, it shall not be worse for us in time, and our reward is the same in eternity.

'The cause in which we are engaged is the cause of mercy and truth, and, therefore, independently of revelation and seeming impossibilities, it must eventually prevail.

'I have been also even occasionally troubled with infidel thoughts, which originated perhaps from the cavillings of the Mahomedans about the person of Christ, but these have been graciously never suffered to be more than momentary; at such times, the awful holiness of the word of God, and the deep seriousness pervading it, were more refreshing to my heart than the most encouraging promises in it. How despicable must the Koran appear with its mock majesty and paltry precepts, to those who can read the word of God. It must presently sink into contempt when the Scriptures are known.

'Sometimes when those fiery darts penetrated more deeply, I found safety only in cleaving to God as a child clings to his mother's neck. These things teach me the melancholy truth, that the grace of a covenant God can alone keep me from apostasy and ruin.'

What a beautiful picture is this part of the letter of Martyn's mind!

'The European society here consists of the military at the cantonment, and the civil servants at Bankipoor. The latter neither come here to church, nor have accepted my offer of going to them to officiate. There is, however, no contempt shown, but rather respect. Of the military servants, very few officers attend, and, of late, scarcely any of the married families, but the number of privates and the families of the merchants, always make up a respectable congregation. They have, as yet, heard very little of the doctrines of the Gospel. I have, in general, endeavoured to follow the directions contained in Mr. Milner's letter on this subject, as given in Mr. Brown's paper, No. 4.

'At the Hospital I have read 'Doddridge's Rise and Progress,' and the 'Pilgrim's Progress.' As the people objected to extempore preaching at church, I have in compliance with their desires, continued to use a book, but on this subject I should be glad of some advice from my brethren. I think it needless to communicate the plans or heads of any of my sermons, as they have been chiefly on the parables. It is of more importance to observe that the word hath not gone forth in vain,—blessed be God! as it has hitherto seemed to do in most places where I have been called to minister, and this I feel to be an animating testimony of His presence and blessing. I think the commanding officer of the native regiment, and his lady here, are seeking their salvation in earnest. They now refuse all invitations on the Lord's Day, and pass most of that day at least in reading the word, and at all times discover an inclination to religious conversation. Among the privates, one I have little doubt is truly converted to God, and is a great refreshment to me. He parted at once with his native woman, and allows her a separate maintenance. His conversion has excited much notice and conversation about religion among the rest, and three join him in coming twice a week to my quarters, for exposition, singing, and prayer.

'I visit the English very little, and yet have had sufficient experience of the difficulty of knowing how a minister should converse with his people.

'How repeatedly has guilt been brought upon my

conscience. Oh how will the lost souls with whom I have trifled the hours away, look at me in the day of judgment. I hope I am more convinced of the wickedness and folly of assuming any other character than that of a minister. I ought to consider that my proper business with the flock over which the Holy Ghost hath made me overseer, is the business of another world, and if they will not consider it in the same light, I do not think that I am bound to visit them.

'About the middle of last month, the church service being read in Hindostanee, I submitted to the commanding officer of the European regiment a proposal, to perform divine service regularly for the native women of his regiment, to which he cordially assented. The whole number of women, about two hundred, attended with great readiness, and have continued to do so. Instead of a sermon, the psalms, and the appointed lessons, which were not translated, I read in two portions, the Gospel of St. Matthew regularly forward, and occasionally make some small attempts at expounding. The conversion of any of such despised people is never likely perhaps to be of any extensive use in regard to the natives at large, but they are a people committed to me by God, and as dear to him as others, and next in order after the English, they come within the expanding circle of action.

'After much trouble and delay three schools have been established for the native children on Mr. Creighton's plan; one at Dinapore, one at Bankipoor, and one at Patna: in the last of which the Persian character is taught as well as the Nagree; the one in use among the Mahomedans, the other among the Hindoos. The number of children is about 60. The other schoolmasters, not liking the introduction of these free schools, spread the report that my intention was to make them Christians, and send them to Europe, in consequence of which the Zemindars retracted their promises of land, and the parents refused to send their children; but my schoolmasters very sensibly went to the people, and told them, 'We are men well known among you, and when you are made Christians, then do you begin to fear.' So their apprehensions are subsided, but when the book of parables, which is just finished, is put into their hands, I expect a revival of their fears. My hope is that I shall be able to ingratiate myself a little with the people before that time, but chiefly that a gracious God will not suffer Satan to keep his ground any longer, now that the appointed means are used to dislodge him. But though these plans should fail, I hope to be strengthened to fight against him all my days, for from what I feel within, and see without, I know enough of him to vow with my brethren, eternal enmity against him and his cause.

'Respecting the state of the natives hereabout, I believe that the Hindoos are lax, for the rich men being few or none, there are few Brahmins, and few *tamashas* (exhibitions,) and without these, idolatry droops. The Mahometans are numerous and ignorant, but from the best of them I cannot learn that more than three arguments can be offered for the truth of their religion; which are, the miracles wrought by Mahomed; those still wrought by his followers, and his challenge, in the second chapter of the Koran, about producing a chapter like it, all of which are immediately answered.

'If my brethren have any others brought forward to them, they will I hope mention them; and if they have observed any remark or statement that will apparently affect a native's mind, they will notice it.

'Above all things, *seriousness* in an argument, which seems above all things necessary, for without it they laugh away the clearest proofs. Zeal for making proselytes they are used to, and generally attribute to false motives; but a tender concern manifested for their souls is certainly *new* to them; and seemingly produces corresponding seriousness in their minds.

'From an officer who had been in the Mahratta service, I learned some time ago that there were large bodies of Christians at Warwa in the Mahratta dominions, Sardana, Delhi, Agra, Bettea, Baglipoor. To obtain more information respecting them I sent a circular letter to the missionaries residing at the three latter places, and have received two letters in reply. The Padre at Baglipoor is a young man just arrived, and his letter contains no information. From the letter of the Padre at Agra, I subjoin some extracts, premising that my questions were, 1st, By whom were you sent? 2nd, How long has a mission been established in the place of your residence? 3rd, Do you itinerate, and to what distance? 4th, Have you any portion of the Scriptures translated, or do you distribute tracts? 5th, Do you allow any remains of caste to the baptized? 6th, Have you schools, and are the masters heathen or Christian? 7th, Is there any native teacher or catechist? 8th, Number of converts.

'In concluding my report, I take the liberty of proposing two questions on which I should be thankful for communications from my brethren at our next quarterly report.

'1st. On the manner in which a minister should observe the Sabbath—whether he should make it a point of duty to leave no part of his discourses to prepare on that day—whether our particular situation in this country, requiring redoubled exertion, in those of us at least who are called to the heathen, will justify the introduction of a secular work into the Sabbath, such as translating the Scriptures, &c.

'2nd. In the commencement of our labours among the heathen, to which model should our preaching be conformed; to that of John the Baptist and our Saviour, or that of the Apostles? The first mode seems more natural, and if necessary for the Jews, comparatively so enlightened, how much more for the heathen, who have scarcely any notions of morality. On the other hand, the preaching of the cross has in all ages won the most ignorant savages, and the apostles preached it at once to heathens as ignorant perhaps as these.

(Signed) H. MARTYN.

'*Dinapore, April 6th*, 1807.'

The following letter contains an account of the last days of two of the early members of the Prayer Union:—

'On Friday morning last, about half-past nine o'clock, died at my house, after a sickness of about a month, Mr. —— of Goamalty. "He came here," he said, "from the midst of business, and less prepared to die than he had often known himself." But at that time his disease was not judged mortal. It was thought necessary only that he should go home, where he ought to have been, the surgeon said, two years ago. In the prospect of this he came to experience great joy. It struck him that he was going to England on a mission. He had a relation in London, a bookseller and circulating librarian, who very unwisely dealt in any work that brought profit. It was not his father's way, who was far happier than the son. Mr. —— hoped to rectify this wrong, if not altogether, at least so as to supply India with abundance of religious books. This, with the consideration of watching the education of his children, brought him to view his sickness as a blessing. Mr. Brown, he said, had twice sent him off with a blessing, and now it seemed I was to do the same. But it pleased the Lord to appoint another issue to his affliction. On Monday morning he was declared in imminent danger, and at night desperate. It then seemed he would not survive many hours, and I did not think it right to let him remain in ignorance of his condition. He received the information that he was dying with entire composure. After speaking of Mrs. —— and Mr. Grant, he said he could have liked to see his children, but he committed them to Christ. He had had a long stand in the hope of the gospel, and comforted himself that he was a Christian twenty years ago, without which comfort his case must have been hopeless now; he could not have settled the matters of everlasting life upon his death-bed. To a religious soldier who came to watch with me, he said, "Let me shake hands with you, brother, you are a soldier of

Christ. Ah! Obeck! Obeck! Faithful Obeck!" During the three days and nights he lingered, his mind was not at all disordered, though he was not able, he said, to fix it upon spiritual things. He seemed continually conscious that he was dying. He called me once, to say, "I shall go soon." "*What, die?*" "Yes," he replied. Again he said, "My colour is changed!" It was a shadow, I believe, which fell over him. I asked him whether he felt departing. "I feel nothing," he answered. In his last afternoon he called me to repeat a request he had made, saying, "You will not find me sensible after to-day." He had afterwards a restless night, but in the morning died so quietly that, though sitting in a chair touching his cot, and expecting his departure, I did not perceive it. There was not a motion or a sigh. The end of this man, I hope, was peace.'

Extract of a letter received from Mr. ——, Berhampore:—

'My beloved Sir,

'Gloomy days seem gathering over us. All quarters seem full of change. It is an occasion for much faith and watchfulness, and perseverance.

'Yesterday three weeks, I believe, died in my house Mr. ——. Yesterday died there Mr. Grant. He arrived on Wednesday night sick of a bilious fever, which had gone too far, and could not now be mastered. Nevertheless, the surgeon was not desperate till Friday morning, then he declared Mr. Grant dying, and die he did about one o'clock.

'I have nothing spiritual to record respecting him. When he came I was in bed full of pain and medicine. On Thursday we lay each upon a cot in the same room, but were neither of us well enough to converse. On Friday I do not recollect that he spoke, except yes and no, to the surgeon. When his case was declared desperate, he was senseless. I tried him often, but he shewed no sense of anything. I could only pray, and that weakly, that God through Christ would accept him.'

The following letter, bearing date the 7th July, 1807, is from the Rev. D. Brown to his brethren, according to engagement, and is valuable in the present sketch, as throwing light upon the "Christian Institution," already alluded to in Dr. Buchanan's correspondence :—

'My dear Brethren,

'The day of dispatch is arrived, and behold I who exhort others to promptness have nothing prepared, and now I could easily persuade myself to say nothing, upon the supposition that I had nothing worth communicating ; yet I know if I had put down a few hints before this day came round, I should have had more than enough in quantity at least. We seem to go round in a circle and have nothing new to observe, yet it is not so. Something is passing in and about us every day worthy of notice, and from which instruction may be gathered and improvement made for the benefit of ourselves and others. We have all a great deal to say if we would. The discussion of the important questions suggested by our dear friend Martyn, respecting "the manner in which a minister shall observe the Christian Sabbath, and the mode to be adopted in addressing the heathen," will be useful. I trust they have occupied your attention, and that you will favour me with your sentiments upon them. The mere suggestion of such topics is attended with practical good, as they furnish matter of self-reflection, and lead the mind to that most useful of all duties, self-examination.

'I shall now try to give you a page on each of the following heads :—*The Christian Institution—Native Schools—Public Ministrations—Register of Events.* I begin with the "*Christian Institution,*" as being the most important article of this quarter's communications. Before Dr. Buchanan left Cochin, I suggested to him an idea of a college for translations ; and, during his passage to Calcutta, he prepared a sketch, under the name of the "British Propaganda," which, on his arrival here, we fully discussed. We then thought of making Serampore the centre of action, as the place for carrying on our operations, intending to engage the missionaries (who had been active and useful to us) as the principal agents. I fully expected their concurrence but when the plan was laid before them, they stumbled *in limine;* they could not submit to the preliminary article, "that a clergyman of the Church of England should be the superintendent of the institution." This gave a new and nobler turn to the design, which freed it at once from localities, personalities, and all peculiarities of religious denomination: this gave birth to the Christian Institution, which is calculated to do good to all, without interfering with any; which has for its object to engage all the talents of all good men in India, without mixing with their peculiarities, or passions. I own I am much delighted with the contemplation of this plan, and augur so well of it, that I have ventured to give it a glorious title, of which, I trust, it will be found more worthy than the great king to whom it was originally applied. (Ezek. xxviii.)

'I have written to Mr. —— on the subject of the Christian Institution thus:—

'By the Indus, Dr. Buchanan sends home a book, which, I hope, will please you. I have no doubt that you will highly approve; there is now placed before you in the Christian Institution a mean by which you may promote the interests of Christianity, without being involved in ecclesiastical plans, or in doubtful measures. I take it for granted no serious person will oppose the "Christian Institution." I, therefore, beg leave to submit to you the propriety of asking the East India Company to give it liberal support; two or three thousand rupees *per mensem* (the wages of a single servant) would greatly promote the objects of it; and it is hard it should be left to the generosity of a few individuals here, or to private subscription at home. I trust you will exert yourself in this cause, and put forth all your strength.

'You are aware of the temper of the times: —— at first approved the translations, and promised to subscribe privately, but, from the moment the change in his views took place, the translations were discountenanced, and all but quashed.

'Overwhelmed on every side as we are, we go on prophecying in sackcloth, without strength and without means. —— has occasioned about ten thousand rupees (already subscribed) to be withdrawn, and by withholding his support, has deprived us of at least a LAC; this, however, you may remedy by an order for a monthly sum of your treasury, which, I am confident, you will not fail to do.

'In the sequel, I tell Mr. —— that I shall not live to see the prosperity of Zion; yet she will prosper, and all those that love her, &c.

'The next subject is "*Native Schools,*" on which I need not say much at this time. I applied to Mr. —— for information, as proposed at the Pagoda meeting on the 29th of November, 1806, and enclose his correspondence on the subject. The chief thing, I think, to be attended to at the outset, is to avoid expensive undertakings of any kind. It would have been well for me if I had been cautioned in this respect; from the first I began a costly native school, adopting children, and taking upon myself their support and provision, but it came to nothing. Mr. Creighton's expenditure should be kept in view as the best and safest guide. I own I do not see it to be the duty of chaplains in their present pilgrim state, to engage deeply in the plan of native schools; though, I think, they will be required on an extended scale in the course of a few years. The most that I would advise, under present circumstances, where there is zeal for such a work, would be to commence a single school of the cheapest sort, by way of gaining experience, and to allow it to increase by degrees. I would not suffer more than twenty boys to be taught, nor would I increase the first expense for a year or two. We are always doing too much, or rather overdoing everything; at least, I fear, it has been my case. I have had zeal, without knowledge—have run, before I was sent—preached the Gospel, when I ought to have preached the law—given, when I should have withheld, and thus defeated all my purposes of usefulness. May my brethren profit by my unhappy errors. In one sense your strength is to sit still; for there is a tide for which we must wait, and with which we must work, if we would do good. We are always at contraries (I mean to say that *I* am); when we have the will, we want the power, and when we have the power, we want the will.

'I beg a report of the native school commenced may always form an item in your quarterly correspondence, for a few experiments are worth a world of speculations. Though I seem to discourage your effort in this way, I have your success in it much at heart, and would say to you, work while it is day, and let others enter into your labours.

'*Public ministrations*—of my own I can say but little. I am too uniform in my preaching—sin and grace are my constant subjects: the plague of my own heart, and the blood of Christ, are the topics on which I dwell. Indeed, I know not what to say, or in what manner, and am as much—nay, more, at a loss than I was twenty years ago. I go on more by feeling than by system at present. I am, indeed, an old song. Mr. Buchanan, though old too, has come forth since his return to Calcutta, with new energy, preaching to the heart and conscience with greater force and ability than he ever did before; but he has the worst opinion of the Calcutta hearers. He says nothing will do them good, but an earthquake, a massacre, or fire from heaven. In my opinion, good is progressing with us, except in the higher classes, among whom there has been a falling off.

'In January last I signified to some persons of the mission congregation, my intention of discontinuing the Wednesday-evening Lecture, on account of its encroaching too much on my time. While the college continued I was obliged to be almost daily in Calcutta, and the Evening Lecture made no great difference; but now that the cares of the college had ceased, and the calls of duty were at home, I thought five days in the week too much to sacrifice (for so many broken days are at least made by the Wednesday and Thursday being partly occupied); I told them I would wait six months and consult with Dr. Buchanan. He decided for giving up the lecture. But when it came to the point, I found an host rise up against my determination; so, for peace and love sake, I go on as usual, and the discussion is put off *sine die*.

'*Events.*—Some late sudden deaths have spread a gloom over Calcutta.

'1. Mr. ——, visited his Indigo works at Russapaglah, one morning, and returned home rather indisposed. No danger was apprehended till about eight or nine o'clock in the evening. By two o'clock he was dead. He had some knowledge of the gospel, but he who lives according to "the course of this world," whatever may be his knowledge, will die in uncertainty, and so it ought to be, that presumption may not be encouraged in any, yet Mr. —— left a *sort* of testimony in writing. I desired Dr. Buchanan to send Mrs. ——, Mr. Cecil's little book—'A Friendly Visit to the House of Mourning.'

'2. Colonel —— was a great man with his master, and a great infidel. "How are the mighty fallen!" They depart and no sign of salvation is found in them.

'3. Mr. ——, a young man of considerable talent, an active magistrate, adored by the world, the intimate of Mr. ——, and his acting executor, burst a blood-vessel and expired suddenly.

'4. During the last quarter, we have lost several members of the mission congregation. Mrs. Hutteman left a bright testimony, and had an entrance administered to her abundantly into the everlasting kingdom of our Lord and Saviour Jesus Christ. To preach the funeral sermons of departed saints is delightful work. May my dear brethren have much of it! It has been one of my best supports. Now and then one going off triumphantly to glory, is a sweet refreshing consolation. And when I stand by the death-beds of such dear children, I forget the labours and sorrows I have had by the way.

'5. A lady who attends the mission-church, told her husband about a month ago, that it had pleased God greatly to change her mind on some points, and had brought her to a patient acquiescence in the divine will; that she had formerly considered the loss of a child as more than she could bear, and that she should certainly become distracted; 'but now,' said she, 'if it should please the Lord to take away a child, I hope I could submit.' Within the month, a child was taken away, and suddenly, after some slight indisposition; the mother found it one morning black with mortification, from the knee to the foot, and from the elbow to the finger-ends, and it presently expired. The mother kneeled down before all present, and gave thanks to God with a loud voice, kissing the rod, and adoring his hand. I found her in great peace, and rejoicing in divine support. Is not this the finger of God?

'6. An old lady lately afflicted with sickness, and yet very ill, has by deed of gift made over to the evangelical fund, in Company's paper, sixteen thousand rupees. Is not this an event! The fund (now forty-three thousand rupees in cash, and a house) is valued at half a lac of rupees. Thus has God prospered an undertaking which began (in Dec. 1802) as a grain of mustard-seed.

'7. Pagoda Prayer-meetings, this year:—1st. On the 3rd of January.—2nd. On the 31st.—3rd. On the 17th of March; a thanksgiving.—4th. On the 2nd of June; to be henceforth held monthly, on first Thursday, for the success of the gospel.—5th. On the 7th of July; (this day). At each of the last meetings six missionaries and Sabat were present.

'I must now conclude (sermon fashion) with a word

on family and personal mercies; but who can count the sum of them? or how shall I in a page mention more than one or two instances: the increase of my family by another added soul, is a mercy to be mentioned with grateful recollection. We have now eight children whom we wish to educate for God, and for whom we ask not for long life, for riches, or honour, except that which cometh from above!

'My hand tires—I must yet add a few words: I trust we are growing in family religion. We have more of the spirit of prayer among us, and more power in our religious exercises. I find greater facility in expounding to the children, and gain more attention, and though I have sad cause to complain of the plague of my own heart (who has not?) yet I am fighting for victory in his name, who has overcome, and who makes more than conquerors all who fight under him.

'I shall conclude by adding, that no thought ever fills my mind with so many pleasing reflections as your advent to the East Indies. When I think you all over, and pray for you by name, I feel unexpressible satisfaction; and rejoice with exceeding joy in the hope of seeing the beginning of a more glorious gospel-day. Mr. Thomason in a letter just received says, he has been sickly, but adds, 'My mind however, I thank God, is the same as ever, wholly bent upon India, and full of hope almost against hope!' Is it not a marvellous thing to see so many of you at your posts fighting the battles of the Lord! I do, and will rejoice, and shall never cease to pray for you, while I have my being, nor to praise God for you with increasing esteem and affection.

'Dearest brethren,
'Your faithful friend and brother,
(Signed) 'D. Brown.'

The following extract from a farewell sermon preached by Dr. Buchanan on occasion of his departure from Calcutta, will give a tolerably correct view of the state of the religious community of Calcutta at that time. The subject chosen was the epistle to the church of Philadelphia, from which he took occasion to illustrate the then existing state of religion in Calcutta. He observed after some preliminary observations :—

'You will naturally advert to your own state and circumstances as a church, &c. and will now expect that we should illustrate them more fully.

'In our Lord's address to the churches, he generally uses the same words as a preface,—"I know thy works," —as if he had said, all of you make a profession of religion, but I know thy works; I know whether the voice of prayer be ever heard in thy family, or the voice of secret prayer in thy closet. I know the *motives* of thy conduct, whether thou supportest religion from conscience' sake, or from motives of convenience, interest, or reputation. I know whether thou art a "whited sepulchre," walking about with my people, or whether thou art "pure in heart," worthy to see God.

'Our Lord having asserted his own omniscience, in the perfect knowledge of our works, proceeds to declare what our state and circumstances are.

'"I have set before thee an *open door*, and no man can shut it." In the application of these words to the Church he was addressing,' Dr. Buchanan observes, 'a short time ago, the door was shut even in regard to ourselves, and we dwelt in the region of darkness and in the shadow of death. Held captive by infidelity or blinded by prejudice, we appeared to be as insensible to the call of Christ as the ignorant heathen around us. The very acknowledgment of the religion of Christ was in those days accounted an act of fortitude; but that his religion ought to be given to the heathen world, was what scarcely any man had fortitude to declare. But the door is now opened, the door of utterance to his ministers, a door of entrance into the hearts of hearers, a door of admission to the Gentile nations. "And this door," saith our Lord, "no man can shut." Many attempts will be made to shut it. If the work be from

God, it will be resisted by evil men. If Satan's kingdom be in danger, the design will be opposed by infidelity and superstition. But the door is opened, and our Lord has declared for our encouragement, that no man can *shut it*. And he speaks a *prophecy* in the text, in those very remarkable words, far more applicable to us and to our day, than to the Church of Philadelphia,—"Behold! I will make them of the synagogue of Satan to come and to worship before thy feet." They who are now bound in the chains of Satan and enslaved by a senseless idolatry, they will come unto thee and seek communion with thee. The truth shall be declared, and the gates of hell shall not prevail against it. For the fulness of time is come, for the appointed season is at hand, and from this time and from this place the Gospel of the Son of God will run and be glorified through the countries, the kindreds and tongues of the eastern world.

'Little of this great work can be seen in our time, little more than the "loosening of the bonds," and the "shaking of the nations,"—we all who are now alive must pass away almost in the beginning of the conflict. But it is much to have seen the day of glory dawn. It confirms our faith in the true word of God, and when we thus see his dispensation accomplishing in regard to nations, we are led to look to ourselves to see whether his dispensation in regard to us be also accomplishing, whether the "day-star hath yet risen in our hearts," and we have a good hope of entering into his glory as forerunners of them that are to come after.'

How far the anticipations of the preacher have been realized will be seen in the subsequent pages of this brief sketch.

We are next led to notice the appointment and subsequent career of that venerable servant of Christ, the Rev. Mr. Thomason. It will be recollected that his earlier appointment was overruled in favour of Mr. Buchanan, respecting which their mutual friend Mr.

Jerram at that time observed, that nothing could be more evident than that the hand of God was in it, and pertinently remarked on the different and varied qualifications of each. It was on this occasion that the following letter was written to his mother.

'Yesterday evening Mr. Simeon communicated the result of his correspondence with Mr. Grant. The inference is so decisive in his mind and mine, that I do not lose a moment in informing you of it. It appears evident that a minister who is not calculated for usefulness at home, will never become useful abroad, and that change of place or employment cannot of itself quicken the soul, which for eight years has been sleeping over its labours. I feel the truth of this more deeply than I can express, but not a thousandth part so deeply as I should. Having now dismissed all thoughts of foreign service, I hope to give myself wholly to the work that is before me. May God enable me to live more to Him, "lest after having preached to others, I myself should be a cast-away!"'

The humility and genuine Christian spirit generally pervading this letter is strikingly characteristic of the man. However Mr. Simeon concurred with Mr. Thomason in the interpretation of God's providence at the present juncture; the reader need not be told that he differed wholly from his self-condemnatory reflections and inferences. Notwithstanding that the door of missionary labour was closed upon Mr. Thomason for the present, it is not long before we are called on to contemplate him under another aspect,—'waiting like one of those angels who at God's bidding post over sea and land, listening to the first intimation from on high to go wherever he might be sent.' If the chains of local attachment had bound him too strongly to Shelford, they were soon to be snapped asunder: if his affections had wound themselves too closely round anything earthly, the roots were soon to be loosened and removed to another soil. In this waiting, willing spirit, Mr. Thomason had not long to remain. It was put to the test at the end of 1806, but it was not till the spring of 1808, that Mr. Thomason's long-meditated design of consecrating his powers through life to his God and Saviour in a distant land, was brought to maturity. He thus imparted the state of things, and that of his own feelings, to his mother.

'*March* 4th, 1808.

'My acceptance of the appointment has not yet come before the court of directors, yet I cannot help feeling that the event will assuredly be brought about. I own that the more I consider the various leadings of divine providence, and reflect on the unweaned tenor of my former wishes and plans, comparing them with what I now feel, the more am I convinced, that such a change of my situation will be accomplished. And I think, my dear mother, when you reflect on the course of my life from the beginning,—on the singular manner in which I was led to devote myself to the ministerial work,—on the course of providence by which the matter was brought about,—and above all, on the earnest and repeated desire I have felt again and again for this particular destination,—especially when you think, that the work of my heart has been uniformly prevented by one great obstacle, and that this is now entirely removed, I think that you will conclude that the time appears to be come. The same person who was once decidedly adverse, so as not to hear of it without tears, is now happy in the thought of it. She no longer thinks of the sea nor of the climate; but counts it a privilege and an honour to be exposed in such a cause. * * * * *I consider that what others expose themselves to for lucre and worldly honours, ministers ought to endure for nobler ends.*

'All this I am sure meets with corresponding feelings in your own heart, my dear mother; you have again and again given me up to God, &c. What an honour and happiness there is in making sacrifices for Christ. I am sure the more we are enabled to do this, the more solid peace shall we enjoy, and the more shall we know him to be a good Master. I trust that you will be fitted for every trial, and strengthened to do and suffer the whole will of God.'

Filial affection of the intensity of Mr. Thomason's, subordinated, as we behold it in this letter, to the love of an unseen Saviour, and to a concern for the souls of his fellow-creatures far off and unknown, is a spectacle for angels, observes the author of his incomparable memoir.

In little more than a month after he had written it, he was studying Persian under a Moonshee, at Hertford; having received his appointment to the mission church of Calcutta, he was making use of every effort to acquire a language so important in India, and panted to be at his post.

He writes:—'I have commenced the laborious and important work; laborious indeed it will be, but I set about it with unspeakable pleasure, and I trust that God will help me in it. The prospect of spending my strength and my life in the work of the ministry, where help is so much wanted, and the field of labour extensive, is indeed delightful.'

When the ship was actually under weigh, and England was beginning to 'lessen in the lingering eye,' he wrote the following parting lines to his affectionate mother:—

'*Travers, under weigh, June* 10, 1808.

'This morning we were summoned on board. The wind has become fair, and we are proceeding out to sea. Our dear and honoured friend Mr. Simeon accompanied us to the vessel, and is now with us. We all retired to our cabin, and united in prayer, desiring to consecrate this spot to God, and to commit ourselves and all the ship's company to his gracious care, &c.'

A full account of his voyage, and the circumstances of it, are recorded in the Memoir by Mr. Sargent. Suffice it to say here, that he suffered shipwreck.

To Mr. Simeon from Calcutta, Mr. Thomason wrote on the all-absorbing subject of his providential escape as follows :—

'*Dec.* 5, 1808.

'Here we are, by the good providence of our God, at the wished-for haven. June 10th, we left Portsmouth. Nov. 19th, we arrived at Calcutta ; but we have arrived in a way we did not expect, not only *over* the waters, but *through* them. On the morning of Nov. 7, the Travers struck upon a rock, and in a short time was a complete wreck. The ships in company escaped in all haste from the scene of danger, and were soon out of sight. We were left, *not to the mercy of the winds and waves*, but *to the mercy of God*, who marvellously interposed and brought us off in safety, &c.'

Mr. Simeon's comment on his friend's preservation, is too appropriate and characteristic to be omitted :—

'How deep and mysterious are the ways of God! that you should be made willing to transport yourself and family, and all you had, to the shores of India, and then be landed on these shores, glad to escape with your lives! You review the calamity in its true light, I adore my God for giving you so just a view of it. God has said to you as to the first-born of Egypt: "I have spared your lives, and you shall be mine." I trust it is not the wish of either of you that a commutation of the Levites should ever take place. You are well contented and happy that His *service* should be your *one* employment, *himself* your *only* portion. . . . I am persuaded that God has designs of good towards you and the people of Calcutta. The exercises of love to which your necessities have called them, will, I hope, be matured to a habit, and such an attachment be formed as shall endure to all eternity.'

Mr. Thomason's arrival at Calcutta gladdened the hearts of many in that city, who received him as from the dead, especially that of Mr. Brown, who welcomed him as he had done Mr. Martyn before, with all the cordiality of Christian love. His first interview with that eminent servant of the Redeemer, he thus touchingly narrates: 'We both sat down, but it was long before my tears suffered me to speak. They were tears, as I told him, not of sorrow, but of joy and thankfulness, wonder and praise. He told us to look around the walls—the furniture and the house were ours. It was a house built in faith and prayer, as the residence of a missionary, out of the contributions of a number of poor persons, who many years past had subscribed towards a fund for the support of the gospel, and united their prayers, that God would send them a minister. Need I say that every chair and table spoke to us with a voice that thrilled through our hearts, and overwhelmed us? Truly we could then praise God for our shipwreck! We could see a good reason for the dispensation. It was plain that God had thrown us upon his praying people, that he had cast us from the rest of the world, and laid us under the obligations of Christian love, in order that we may be devoted to the sacred charge of feeding his sheep. He has placed us in circumstances where every thing is actually the fruit of faith and love, in order to teach us that we have but one thing to do.

'Mr. Brown next introduced us into the vestry and church, where many had assembled the evening before to thank God for our deliverance, and pray for a blessing on the minister preserved to them.

'The second Sunday after landing at Calcutta, Mr. Thomason commenced his ministry from the text, "Knowing the terrors of the law, we persuade men." Mr. Brown also, the same day, preached a thanksgiving sermon for the greater part of the crew of the *Travers*, few of whom, however, attended the sermon, and fewer still the Sacrament administered the following Sunday by Mr. Thomason, with express reference to their signal deliverance.' In the same letter he says, 'If it please God to spare my life, I hope to give some efficient aid in translations. At present, of course, I can do nothing.

but *others* are doing wonders. Honoured and beloved Martyn, whose face we are not likely to see for a long time, is doing, as always, great things.'

The following is an account of distribution of labour. On Sunday two services; one at eight in the morning, and another at eight in the evening. On Thursday evenings he had a service, and on Saturday evenings he assembled the children in the church, accompanied by their parents and friends. Another evening of the week was allotted to visiting those who were decidedly religious; they met together at different houses for the purpose of hearing the Scriptures expounded, &c., but the state of society was adverse; he wrote to Mr. Simeon, as to the progress of the gospel. 'In addition to the common difficulties, arising from the character of the *heart*, there are obstacles here which are tremendous. The civil servants of the Company hold the highest rank, you may call them the nobility: then come the merchants, the shopkeepers, the half-cast. These form so many circles of distinction, and so many sorts of pride, which have had a sad effect in checking a free intercourse among the people. With certain unavoidable exceptions, these do not mix together, and will hardly be seen together. The religious people I have seen in Calcutta have retained these prejudices. The bringing them to worship God in the same room has been a strange thing among them. Our regular congregation at the old church is much smaller than you would expect—not more than 250 on an average; on the week-day 100; but you are to recollect there are no servants in this number. The church would contain 450.

'You have no idea in England (he writes after a somewhat longer residence in India) of the peculiar difficulties which oppose the progress of the gospel in this place. They are prodigious, and in the greatest degree discouraging; arising partly from the nature of the climate, and partly from the nature of the society, and chiefly from the close intercourse with the wretched natives, who are more degraded than you can imagine, and who have the entire charge of the children, and management of household matters. The natives swarm around us, and corrupt the minds of children from the earliest years. To an Englishman the effect of their example, and the contagion of their language cannot be adequately represented. The natives become mothers of a progeny, notorious for bad morals and weak minds. There are some favourable exceptions, but only a few can be mentioned. Religion alone raises them : this gives a solidity of character ; they become trusty and well-behaved. These form a great majority of our congregations. The number of rich people and Company's servants, who come to Church, is comparatively small ; the better sort of people send their children home at five or six : until then, they are under the charge of native servants, and their minds are poisoned, as far as they can be, at that tender age. The parting from them is heart-breaking. They part with them, very often never to see them more. This produces a sad derangement in society. *There is no such thing as a domestic circle.* The olive-branches round the table, so delightful in England, are unknown. The children cannot even speak their mother-tongue. They have to learn English on their way home. There is a dissolution of all the tender, amiable, cheering household virtues. These observations apply to the far greater number among us. Some there are who diligently labour against these disadvantages, &c. It is a fixed rule with us that the children are always in the presence of one among us. We never suffer them, not for a moment, to have any intercourse with the servants alone.'

In less than half a year Mr. Thomason's congregation increased, and considerable interest in religion was excited, and instances of decided impression came to the knowledge of the minister. 'Not even in Cambridge,' he testified, 'have I witnessed such deep and solemn attention to the word of God.'

Having made considerable progress in Persian during

the voyage, Mr. Thomason gave himself, in addition to his ministerial employments, to the study of Hindostanee and Arabic. He writes, 'We rise very early, and return from our morning ride by six. At half-past six we have family prayer; at seven we breakfast. Between that and two I am in the study! at two we dine. At three I am in my study again till five: then we have family prayer, and, from six till nine or ten is occupied in riding, and visiting friends, in private parties and public duties. I have found it necessary to decline all invitations to dinner, without exception. This has enabled me to be regular, and very retired, without giving offence. Our week-day meetings in private houses would rejoice your heart.'

That such devotedness of time, talent, and whatever endowments he possessed, should be owned and blessed of Him, from whom cometh all holy desires, all good counsels, and all just works, who gives the single eye and the heart unfeigned, is only to expect the fulfilment of the divine promise. 1 Cor. xv. 58. So favourably had Mr. Thomason's labours been received, that before the lapse of six months, it was necessary to enlarge his church; and though the days, as they rolled on, were scarcely distinguished from each other, in the prosecution of the work of each day, he had the most perfect enjoyment. One comfort was wanting to him, and the want was felt,—a minister of congenial sentiments stationed near him, with whom he might have unreserved intercourse, &c.* 'At this time' he writes, 'the word of God does not appear to be *very rapidly* advancing, yet we hear of much that encourages us. The work of catechizing seems to promise good, but we want the outpouring of the Spirit, and until the Spirit be poured upon us from on high, no *very great* good can take place among us; we are praying for this; without this we may toil all night and catch nothing. Oh that the preacher may

* The Rev. D. Brown was at this time living at Aldeen, at some distance from Calcutta.

catch the sacred fire, and the people rejoice and be glad.

'I find our Thursday evenings profitable times; we are going through the gospel of St. John; the congregation does not much exceed one hundred and fifty people, but they come to hear plain truths, and we often find the Lord is with us indeed.'

In what spirit he was thus doing his master's work at this time, the following remarks tell us. 'We are in the sixth chapter, "The bread of life." My subject this evening includes these two verses, "He that eateth my flesh, &c. As the living Father hath sent me, *so* he that *eateth me*, even he shall live by me." What can a poor empty creature say of the fulness there is in Jesus. What can I say of Jesus dwelling in me, and my dwelling in Jesus? *O how we fritter away these passages, if we are not living nigh to God*, and enjoying the glorious knowledge of the gospel in daily dependence on the Redeemer! This I want very much, nay, lamentably, and my people will be meagrely fed. That word "dwelleth in me, and I in them," fills my soul with wonder, and abases me in the dust. I would know it and feel it, but know not how I would speak of it; and recommend it, but have no heart for the marvellous theme. Will God in very deed dwell in this diseased polluted heart? Does he dwell there? And can I, a vile and wretched sinner, be said to dwell in him? Though I scarcely dare say yes, yet I feign would come and cast myself upon the Saviour. It is my only refuge and hope, and if this reposing of the soul in Jesus, be indeed to eat his flesh and drink his blood, I would now do it, yea, I must do it. Still I cannot lay hold on that word, "dwelleth in me and I in Him."

'I feel very remote from this,—it is too high, I cannot reach it. I feel like a blind man leading the blind. My comfort lies in the freeness and sovereignty of God's grace; for while it gives strong meat to those who are full-grown, it administers milk to the babe.

'My dear and honoured brother, you know not how

very far I am from being a minister of the Gospel. I am no Gospel minister, for I know it not. I sit down and pen some miserable thoughts on Scripture, and occupy a certain portion of time in talking about the love of God, and the sufficiency of Jesus, and the work of the Spirit, but it is sad trifling with myself and my hearers.

'Martyn tells me he has begun to preach to the natives at his new station. The poor and maimed come to him on Sunday for relief. When collected he knows not how to dismiss them without speaking a word about the bread of life. But he gives a poor account of them. The discouragements are greater than you can imagine. It seems as if the line of duty consisted in waiting and watching, in a prepared state for opportunities that may offer, than in going forth and talking to them as missionaries; when and how such opportunities may be expected, I know not. The Lord send them, and give us grace to improve them! If the tide flows, the ship will sail.'

It was previous to this that Mr. Martyn had ministered to the women at Dinapore. At that time he wrote to his friend and brother Mr. Corrie, thus, on the subject of going among the natives with the Gospel, &c.

'Oh that the time were come, that I should be able to carry the war into the enemy's territory. It will be a severe trial to the flesh, my dear brother, for us both; but it is sufficient for the disciple that he be as his master, and the servant as his Lord. We shall be accounted as the filth of the world, and the offscouring of all things. But glory be to God, if we shall be accounted worthy to suffer shame for the name of the Lord Jesus!'

If on my face, for thy dear name,
Shame and reproach should be,
All hail reproach, and welcome shame,
If Thou remember me.

From this extract it is evident that had he given way at once to the strong and full-flowing tide of his zeal and love, it would immediately have carried him, with the bible in his hands, into the streets of Patna, though to have commenced his ministry in that idolatrous city, would have cost him much. Of all his fellow-labourers and correspondents at this time, no one was, perhaps, in all respects, so congenial, and like-minded as Mr. Corrie,—especially on all points regarding the heathen; he was of one heart with himself; and to that unrestrained intercourse by letter which Mr. Martyn held weekly with Mr. Corric, he was indebted for much of the purest felicity of his life.

Besides preaching to the women, Mr. Martyn had established several native schools, in which considerable progress had been made in reading, &c.; and he became anxious cautiously to introduce Christian books into them, on which subject in a letter to Mr. Corrie, he says, 'I bless God that you are brought to act with me on a broad and cautious plan; but I trust our motto will be, 'Constant though cautious;' never ceasing to keep our attention steadily fixed on the state of things; and being swift to embrace every opportunity.'

But Martyn's chief work was the translation of the Scriptures. To this he was earnestly urged, as being that work for which, in reference to the natives, he was best fitted. A new stimulus was given in this year by a proposal from the Rev. D. Brown, that he would engage manfully and directly in that work, in which he had already made a commencement, and translate the New Testament into the Hindostanee and Persian languages. This proposal he eagerly, yet diffidently, accepted; and animated by the expectation of beholding his labours brought to a successful termination, he prosecuted them with a delight commensurate with his ardent diligence. These expectations were realized; Martyn lived to complete both, and also a translation of the Psalms into Persian.

The Hindostanee translation was finished in India in the month of March 1808; nor if we consider how much time he had spent upon it from his arrival in Calcutta, and how laboriously he prosecuted it, after

Mr. Brown had summoned him to direct his efforts to that end, can it be affirmed that it was hurried to a conclusion with a heedless and blameable precipitancy.

> 'Twas not the hasty product of a day,
> But the well-ripened fruit of wise delay.

'It is a real refreshment to my spirit,' Mr. Martyn writes to Mr. Corrie, 'just at the moment of sending off the first page of the Testament to Calcutta, to take up my pen to write to you. Such a week of labour, I believe, I never passed, not excepting even the last week before going into the Senate House. I have read and corrected the manuscript copies so often that my eyes ache,' &c.

Concerning this great work, Mr. Thomason thus speaks :—

'The slip of paper inserted in one of your letters, concerning an observation of Dr. ——'s on Martyn's nicety of style, surprised me much. It is not like the judgment of a scholar and a critic. Would not the Professor be ashamed of a false concord or bad idiom in addressing the University? How can we be too attentive to these proprieties? How can we hope that any translation of the Scriptures shall survive the lapse of ages, unless the style be carefully attended to? Bad style is like bad poetry, soon forgotten and despised. *Accuracy and elegance* combine to form a standard which is itself a great means of preserving languages from decay. Martyn is justified by experience. He has in his Hindostanee translation of the New Testament, finished a work which will last; for it is a model of elegant writing as well as of faithful translation. It is so faithful as to represent with scrupulous accuracy the whole meaning, yet not so elegant but that any one acquainted with the language, can read it with ease.'

To return to the subject of schools before making any further observations on Mr. Martyn's ministration among the natives. One fruit of his prayers and result of his prudence, above alluded to, was the successful introduction into his schools, very shortly after the sermon on the Mount; and on the 21st of September he had the exquisite joy of hearing the poor heathen boys reading the words of the Preacher, "A wise man's heart deviseth both time and judgment." It was in this spirit of patient and dependent wisdom, that Mr. Martyn had acted respecting the schools, and it was the same rare temper of mind which prevailed on him to abstain for a while from preaching to the natives publicly. Again and again did he burn to begin his ministry in Patna; but again and again did he feel deeply the importance of not being precipitate. It was not, however, without much difficulty that he checked the ardour of his zeal.

Connected with Mr. Martyn's labours in India the name of Sabat is but too well known by his rejection of that faith which he then appeared to profess in sincerity and truth. In him Mr. Martyn confidently trusted that he had found a Christian brother, nor were these hopes respecting Sabat's religious character more sanguine than both in reason and charity he might fairly have entertained. Of his abilities a most favourable report had been made by Dr. Kerr of Madras, who represented him as a man of good family in Arabia; as having been employed as an expounder of Mahomedan law at Masulipitam; and as being well skilled in the literature of his country. With respect to his belief of Christianity, although Mr. Martyn soon discovered in him an unsubdued Arab spirit, and witnessed with pain many deflections from that temper and conduct which he himself so eminently exemplified, yet he could not but believe all things and hope all things, even while he continued to suffer much from him, and for a length of time with unparalleled forbearance and kindness. How could he allow himself to cherish any doubt, when he beheld the tears he shed in prayer, and listened to the confessions he made of his sinfulness, and to the professions he uttered of his willingness to whatever was reprehensible in his behaviour. No sooner had he arrived at Dinapore than he opened to Mr. Martyn the state of his mind, declaring, with seeming contrition, that the constant sin he found in his heart filled him with fear, 'If the Spirit of Christ is given to believers, why,' said he, 'am I thus after three years of believing? I determined every day to keep Christ crucified in sight, but soon I forgot to think of Him! I can rejoice when I think of God's love in Christ; but then I am like a sheep that feeds happily, whilst he looks only at the pasturage before him, but when he looks behind and sees the lion, he cannot eat.' His life, he avowed, was of no value to him, the experience he had had of the instability of the world had weaned him from it. His heart was like a looking-glass fit for nothing except to be given to the glass-maker to be moulded anew. Can we wonder concerning one who uttered, with apparent sincerity and much earnestness, sentiments such as these, that Mr. Martyn should observe to Mr. Brown, who had sent him from Calcutta to Dinapore, that 'Not to esteem him a monument of grace, and not to love him, is impossible.'

A striking contrast to Sabat is the meek and holy character of Abdul Messeh, another convert, over whom Martyn had only to rejoice. He was the keeper of the jewels of the King of Oude. Having listened to Mr. Martyn's public preaching in the open air at Cawnpore, whither Mr. Martyn went from Dinapore, he discovered the pearl of great price, and was afterwards baptized at Calcutta on Whit-Sunday. On this occasion Mr. Thomason wrote with gladness of heart, 'Last Sunday was a happy day, Mr. Brown baptized in my church an adult Musulman. The man had long given evidence of his conversion. His heart was touched under the ministry of dear Martyn. Hearing that a sermon was preached in Hindoostanee, Sheikh Saleh (his Mahomedan name) thought he would attend. He went and was caught in the net. The preacher began with reproof and ended with the consolation of the gospel. The holy strain of the former part of the discourse filled him with a solemn awe, and the gracious promises of the latter, with a longing desire to become acquainted with Christ. He went away serious. In reading over, and writing out the Persian translations of the gospels, his understanding became more fully informed, and his heart more touched with the truths of God. He chose them, renouncing all his former errors, and determined at all events to be a servant of Jesus. Without any solicitation from others, he soon discovered that it was necessary he should be baptized, and accordingly made application to Martyn. *After proper instruction and a full trial*, at the end of fifteen months from his first hearing Martyn, he was baptized. We gave notice to those who were likely to be interested in the matter, and a goodly number were assembled. We shall not soon forget the day. We are full of joy and hope. The work has been entirely of God. Our new brother, now called Abdul-Messeh (the servant of Christ) is humble, and grave, and quiet in his behaviour, and there seems every reason to hope he will adorn his profession. May such scenes become frequent among us!'

He again writes, 'We have never yet seen Martyn, but hope to be gratified in the course of a few months. He has, at length, determined to try the sea air. He has been brought very low.' The meeting thus earnestly desired,—as Mr. Martyn's health declined rapidly—took place sooner than was expected. Nov. 3. Mrs. Thomason writes, "Dear, dear Martyn arrived, and we had the unspeakable delight of seeing his face. The agitation I felt through the whole morning was such as I never experienced in India. Joy and sorrow alternately—joy to see him, sorrow for the occasion. In three or four weeks he leaves us to go to sea for his health. He is much altered, is thin and sallow, but he has the same loving heart. No tongue can tell what a refreshment the sight of him has been to us. I should be thankful to be his nurse if he could remain with us; but one would wish him to try every means, hoping that God may yet spare him for a few years.'

'Martyn and I am both writing under the same roof.' —her husband adds,—'This bright and lovely jewel first gratified our eyes on Saturday last. He is on his way to Arabia, in pursuit of health and knowledge. You know his genius, and what gigantic strides he takes in everything. He has some great plan in his mind, of which I am no competent judge. But, as far as I do understand, the object is far too grand for our short life, and much beyond his feeble and exhausted frame. Feeble indeed it is. How altered and changed! His complaint lies in the lungs, and appears to be incipient consumption. In all other respects he is exactly the same as he was. He shines in all the dignity of love, and seems to carry about him such a heavenly majesty, as impresses the mind beyond all description.'

Mr. Martyn's visit to Calcutta, thus described, was as ointment and perfume, that rejoice the heart, in the family of Mr. Thomason and of Mr. Brown. The Church of God in Calcutta also derived lasting benefit from his residence among them, transient as it was. His sermon on behalf of the Bible Society was of eminent service. His labours revived all! Mr. Thomason says, 'Our assemblies at church are greater than was ever known. On Christmas-day, there were above 1,200. The hearts of many have been made glad.' In a few hours after this was written, Mr. Martyn had sailed for Persia. To spare the feelings of his brethren, as well as his own, he departed suddenly, without bidding them farewell. As an angel of love and mercy he had appeared among them; as an angel, he may be said to have vanished out of their sight.'

The formation of the Bible Society in Calcutta, may not inaptly be introduced here. In reference to it, Mr. Thomason writes, 'Those who know not with what ill-ominous forebodings, and with what a torpid touch, every attempt to lift up the torch of revelation in India, had been invariably met, can but inadequately conceive the joy of those who love the Bible, when, as was the case this year (1810), the foundation of a Society was laid in Calcutta for the dispersion of the Word of Life through the length and breadth of the land. On this occasion, Mr. Thomason was not backward, either to rejoice, or to contribute, or to act.

'Some members of council, the Commander-in-Chief, and the Judges, as well as other influential men, engaged to promote this holy cause. By ignorance adopting the semblance and tone of oracular wisdom, all attempts of this nature had been denounced as fraught with extreme peril to our Indian empire. But the darkness was beginning to pass away, and with it all the phantoms of the night. That noble Institution, in its commencement and progress, has awakened a most salutary interest in many a bosom, and as to native prejudices, they have slept on tranquilly, or if roused for a moment, it has been to relapse into slumber still more profound. So will it be with respect to the immolation of widows; so will it be also when the hand of power shall be lifted up to crush the abominations of Juggernaut,' &c.

DESCRIPTION OF AN INDIAN YEAR.

April is the middle of the hot season—fiery days and stormy nights. Thus it has pleased a gracious Providence to temper the severities of the climate. Were the hot days to continue long, man, beast, and vegetable nature, must all perish. When the refreshing winds fail, the sultriness is almost insupportable. Then comes a storm that cools the air: then the heat returns, then the lull, then again the storm for several days successively. We rise to go forth, and inhale the cool of the morning, and rejoice. About June, comes the rainy season for two months. This refreshes us. From the middle of August, to the middle of October, the clouds having poured forth their contents, the country is soaked. The winter having left us, the heat of the sun draws forth the moisture, and we live almost in a hot bath. All nature seems to droop. Were this season to be prolonged, few could endure it. About the middle of October, we have sharp mornings and bracing airs. Thus the years go round.

The Calcutta Bible Society, which, in the previous year, had been framed and prepared, this year commenced its navigation of charity. Well might the friends of Christianity in the East, call on all that is within them to bless God's holy name. When the first Committee met, Mr. Harrington, the Chief Judge of the Native Court, being President, and Mr. Brown, Secretary, the day of their assembling, the first of February, 1811, was a day far more worthy of record than any of those which shine on political considerations, in the annals of Hindostan.'

'We begin to see,' Mr. Thomason writes, the following month, 'effects of the operations of the institution:—An interest about the Bible is excited—questions are asked—remarks are made—misrepresentations abound—and the thing is discussed—where all was a dead calm. Men are attacked—they repel the blow. This leads them to look into the Bible and its evidences. It is delightful to observe the reaction and its effects. Could you but spend one month and examine the characters of our Committee, you would adore the providence of God, who fashioneth all hearts. You cannot conceive how tremblingly alive we have been during the organization of this good work; there was so much to be apprehended from the fears, indifference, and prejudices of men. Great and marvellous are the works of God, let us rejoice and be glad. It is impossible to describe the joy I feel in contemplating the probable harvest of knowledge, piety, and happiness which will arise from this institution, in this quarter of the globe. It gives greater stability to our proceedings than the most splendid conquests.'

How far these observations are justified, and to what extent realized, it might be sufficient to refer to the Bible Society's last year's Report. But the following testimony of the late lamented Bishop Corrie, cannot but be interesting:—

1831.

'At the period of the formation of this society, I was sent, in the course of providence, to the chief presidency of India. The scriptures, even in the English language, were extremely scarce, and only to be purchased at an enormous price. Pocket Bibles of the plainest sort, cost £1. sterling. The scriptures therefore were not very plentiful amongst the military, to whom my labours were at first more particularly directed. With what thankful joy they received the supplies sent out to that country by this society, I cannot express. No sooner did they hear of its existence than they applied for supplies from it, &c. This thirst for the word of God led to the formation of an Auxiliary Society in Calcutta. The ladies parted with their ornaments and the expensive portions of their dress, and in a *few days*—*one thousand pounds* sterling was realized. The scriptures have since been translated and extensively circulated. Not only are they eagerly sought after, but extensively read, and been the means of the conversion of many. Many instances might be given. The following was noticed: 'A youth of sixteen while reading in the New Testament in one of the schools, a chapter in St. Matthew, suddenly rose up and said to the missionary—'I wish to be baptized.' On being questioned as to his motive, he laid his hand upon his heart, and said, 'I am sure that is the word of God.' The *most* efficient native missionaries were school-masters, who in teaching the scriptures had themselves received the truth in the love of it, and felt its saving power.' A son of a Brahman, nineteen years of age, who was in a consumption, was taken to the banks of the Ganges, and while lying there was heard to call upon the name of the Lord Jesus. His friends rebuked him, and desired him to call upon the name of *Harri*, chief of the fairies. He replied, 'You may call on whom you please, but Jesus is the name that brings peace to my soul.' A schoolmaster was heard uttering this dying prayer :—'O thou Son of God, thou knowest that I have believed thy gospel, and that I have taught it faithfully to the children!' He almost immediately expired. I firmly believe that many are in this way obtaining a saving knowledge of God in Christ, and silently passing on to heaven without any profession before men.'

Very many instances of a similar nature are known to the writer of this sketch, which may hereafter be noticed. For the present the reader is referred to the last deeply interesting report of the Calcutta Auxiliary Bible Society, and also to the last Report of the Parent Society, in which he will find detailed the number of versions printed and circulated by the society up to the present time. I cannot have distributed less than 20,000 portions of entire copies in the Persian, and Hindostanee, and Hindoo languages during my residence in India, over a district in extent as large as all Ireland.

It was in this year that Mr. Thomason had the unspeakable satisfaction of seeing his own labours crowned with a large blessing. The vineyard from his first entrance upon its labours, had given a pleasant smell, and the fig-tree had put forth its buds; fruit also was visible, but now, to the vivid satisfaction of the patient labourer, it was abundant. 'It would fill your heart (he writes to Mr. Simeon,) with joy to see us here. Whatever reason we have had heretofore to see the hand of God in our coming to India, has been greatly increased of late. New scenes of usefulness open—my hands are now quite full, and through mercy I see the gradual operation of a gospel ministry. Some persons of late have been brought to a serious concern for their souls. Those who were once scoffers, hear, and weep, and promote the cause they formerly despised, and our own people, which is a great mercy, and received as an answer to prayer, are more united amongst each other.' And now, my dear brother, go on to write to me. I never needed so much the kind communications of a Christian friend and brother. The state of society here, and the state of the climate, oppose difficulties which you can hardly appreciate if described. The climate has influence upon one's natural sloth in a thousand ways; and society is so constituted, that we are opposed at every step by the pride of rank and office and colour, to a degree surpassing all conception. Had I chosen to live here in the state and dignity of chaplain, my path would have been easy, but in the attempt at *a parochial line of labour*, the difficulties are prodigious.'

I have several original letters of Henry Martyn's in my possession, relating to this period, which might here be introduced, but for fear of extending the work beyond what is thought desirable, they are withheld. A few extracts may hereafter be given. In the lately published letters, edited by the Rev. S. Wilberforce, will be found very many written during the period of his residence at Dinapore, from Nov. 1806 to April 1809, the longest period he remained at one place in India, and are deeply interesting. They exhibit in a bright and continually increasing light, his elevated spirituality, his extreme tenderness of conscience, his deep conviction of the value of souls, and his overwhelming sense of the responsibility of his office as a minister of Christ. Of the tenderness and sensibility of his character, his journal, as well as his letters, bear the strongest marks. A more tender plant was never reared in the garden of the Lord, and never was one perhaps more severely tried. It is astonishing to witness the various and opposing winds of adversity which a plant so tender and so frail was able to withstand. Alone in a foreign land, with frequently no one but his God to be near him,—in delicate health, and evidently overtaxing in the studies and labours of his ministry, the powers of a weak and enfeebled frame, with a companion, whose arrogance, self-conceit and petulance, would have exhausted, as Mr. Martyn unconsciously records to his own praise, the patience of any human being; generally without a friend with whom to take sweet counsel, and in whose society he might have experienced, that "as iron sharpeneth iron, so doth the countenance of a man his friend;"—blown upon by such adverse winds from every quarter, is it to be wondered at, that this tender plant shook sometimes even to its roots. Rather is it not to be wondered at, how he withstood such agitating storms at all; how with grief, solitude, bodily indisposition and those sorrows which are peculiar to the Christian, and which Mr. Martyn eminently felt all at once expending their force upon him, his harp was so often attuned to joy, and his accents those of one who had his songs in the night; and how he was enabled to withstand such, and not only withstand but to grow under the apparently adverse influence of such a tempest of trial. In the end it was too much for him; but the orchards of Tocat, which witnessed the last blast that blew, witnessed also his last and highest gain; the tempest which spent its fury in carrying him out of existence, transported him to the garden of God, and there for ever secure, and for ever blessed, without a storm to ruffle its leaves, or a wind to molest its blossoms, this plant of the heavenly Father's planting, now rears its head and blooms serene in calm, undisturbed, and ever-enduring repose.

Blest is the memory of the just,
When to their rest they go,
And dear the place where now their dust
In Jesus sleeps below.
A heavenly light shines bright amid the gloom,
And points to Calvary and Joseph's tomb.

Yes, the Redeemer, through the shade
Of death's dark valley passed,
The ransom for his people paid,
He loved them to the last.
And death can now no more one soul retain
That hopes in Him who burst its cords in twain.

If precious to us be the spot,
Where rest the holy dead:

That land will not be unforgot,
Whence Martyn's spirit fled.
TOCAT! beneath thy hills his ashes lie,
But HE has reached the eternal hills on high!

In May 1809, it was, that Mr. Martyn was removed to Cawnpore. The following are a few extracts from letters written at that period.

'Respecting my heart, about which you ask, I must acknowledge that Henry Martyn's heart at Cawnpore is the same as Henry Martyn's heart at Cambridge. The tenour of my prayer is nearly the same, except on one subject—the conversion of the heathen. At a distance from the scene of action, and trusting too much to the too highly-coloured descriptions of missionaries, my heart used to expand with rapture at the hope of seeing thousands of the natives melting under the word as soon as it should be preached to them. Here I am called to exercise faith—that so it shall one day be. My former feelings on this subject were more agreeable, and the same time more according with the truth; for, if we believe the prophets, the scenes that time shall unfold, though surpassing fable, are yet true. While I write, hope and joy spring up in my mind. Yes, it shall be. Yonder stream of Ganges shall one day roll through tracts adorned with Christian churches, and cultivated by Christian husbandmen, and the holy hymn be heard beneath the shade of the tamarind. All things are working together to bring about that day; and my part in the blessed plan, though not at the first exactly consonant with my wishes, is I believe appointed me by God. *To translate the word of God is a work of more lasting benefit than my preaching would be.* Besides, I am sorry to say, my strength for preaching is almost gone.'

'*Cawnpore, Nov.* 6, 1809.

'DEAREST BROTHER,

'This must I think find you at Pertabghur, though the last did not. I have had another summons to Culpee, which I shall attend to, as I may kill two birds with one stone. There is some force in what you say about our refusing to go on these expeditions. It did not occur to me before. I have had Europe letters, one from Godfrey, another from Col. Sandys. Godfrey mentions his removal from Wellington to London, Hensman's marriage, his visit to Dr. Buchanan, Cecil, &c. Cecil is dying, full of love and humility. Col. S. gives a delightful account of my former acquaintances in Cornwall—old and young are turning to the Lord. His accounts have filled me with wonder and joy. England will take the lead in bringing on the Millennium. His mother (80 years old) whom I and every body else thought incorrigible, has voluntarily given up her cards and gaiety in order to live with her pious son, and she now says she was never so happy in her life. Lydia Grenfell's brother, a most amiable man, and one of my prime favourites at school, is become a truly converted man. Though he is a merchant in London, he exerts himself like a minister, warning all around him to flee from the wrath to come. Her mother also, once so hostile, contemplates the change in her children with satisfaction, and observes, 'Of what use are worldly riches without the Gospel in the heart?' The old Mr. Hitchens, whose two sons are evangelical ministers, lately died, having a good hope that he was received at the eleventh hour. He sent for his sons, confessed his own ignorance, formality, coldness, and indifference to the ministerial office. Thus the Redeemer goes on conquering and to conquer. The old man was one of the wise men of this world, a great astronomer: nothing afforded him so much amusement as to ridicule his sons, and he used to distort and exaggerate their Calvinistic opinions in such a way, that one would have thought that he wished to be the reputed father of two lunatics. His elder brother was brought to the truth a short time ago by the piety of his children also. When will the Spirit thus poured out on England be vouchsafed to India. Let us never cease to expect it, pray for it, talk and write about it. I have sent home to Godfrey a sharp rebuke, for not having so much as mentioned the subject in his whole letter. Sabat and myself have had many quarrels this week also, but good has come of it I think. Last evening he went to visit a Christian of Aleppo, and found a Christian Turk of Constantinople, but this man must be a Greek I suppose, for I never heard of a Turk converted to Christianity. What he heard seemed to rouse him, for he came back full of desire to get on in his glorious work. Mr. Brown has sent me a letter from Mahommed Rasheed, a Calcutta Moonshee, containing his opinion of Sabat's work. It appears to me almost scurrilous, insomuch that I have not yet dared to show it to Sabat. Accompanying it came fifteen chapters in Persian by the hand of the same genius. Such stuff as I never saw from the pen of a Hindoo Kaith. This he has sent as a model for Sabat. Mr. Brown has been strangely perverted by Mr. Harrington (whose Moonshee this luminary is) if he really wishes that Sabat should alter his work to make it more like Mahommed Rasheed's. Sabat is going to Lucknow again. It will be high triumph to him to be able to exhibit the Hindoostanee's learned production to the literati there. But I shall not give it him till he goes. It would turn his head and our work would stop. We hope to finish the revisal of the Romans in Arabic to-day. Yesterday at sunrise I preached to the dragoons: at 10 at head-quarters; several ladies were present, and but few else. On account of the cold weather the sepoy guards are changed for Europeans, so that I had not half my men of the 53rd last night. The Padre Julio is come to Cawnpore, and will call I suppose to-day. My compliments to Major and Mrs. Maxwell and all enquiring friends. Do not cheat me of a letter on pretence of being on a journey, nor fear that I shall cheat you of your rupees, for I am overflowing.

'Your's, ever affectionately,

'H. MARTYN.'

'*Dinapore, Nov.* 23, 1809.

'DEAREST BROTHER,

'Mirza wants to go to bring his wife, and I am not willing to let him till he has finished correcting the Parables and we have done with the Epistles. So he works like a man in earnest, and keeps me so employed that I have hardly time to set pen to paper for you. Col. and Mrs. P. passed on Friday. We dined on board their budgerow. Sabat was delighted with the Colonel, not having often met with a faithful man, as he said, among the gentlemen of the sword, and I was also much gratified and comforted in him. Mr. and Mrs. Robinson from Allahabad have sent me a letter. The disputes this week with Mirza and Moorad Ali have been more than usually interesting: there seems a real interest in Mirza to know whether Mahommetanism is founded on any rational evidence or no. Though he is always for identifying the two religions, yet I can often prove to him, of course, that if he is a strict Mahommedan he will perish, according to our word. One day when he confessed it, he said in great earnestness, Sir, why wont you try to save me? On my asking what I should do for him, he wished me to go to Phoolwaree to discuss the subject with the learned men there. I told him I was willing to go, but did not see why he might not ask for himself. Mirza said to Moorad Ali one day, 'It is absolutely impossible that the Scriptures could have been changed,' and I believe that Mirza thinks so, hence the passages he meets with in the Epistles and those which I read to him from the Prophets, strike him very forcibly. Still the divinity of Christ and the Trinity are stumbling-blocks to him. For Moorad Ali also is staggered. He confessed with seeming earnestness that they had received Mohammedanism only on a blind faith, and that if some great Shekhool-Islam, whom he mentioned, could not give satisfactory evidence for their religion, he should embrace the Gospel. All this is since the coming of Sabat. He is a precious acquisition to me as well as to the Church, and grows, I think, in grace. He opened his heart to me very fully a few days ago, and confessed that for the three years he had been a Christian, he had not enjoyed peace of mind and freedom from fear, because of his indwelling sin. As his fears, I perceived, arose partly from ignorance of the Gospel plan of salvation, I endeavoured to unfold it to him. On the same occasion he said many things on his weanedness from the world, and related some interesting anecdotes respecting the vicissitudes he had met with in life which had tended to show him its vanity. He said that now his heart was like a broken glass, fit only to be given to the glass-maker. Respecting our going to Persia, he argues thus: If in this room there are but six chairs, which are not enough for it, and none in the other, we must take one or two and carry them thither. What answer have you for this? Thus my letter is despatched with great rapidity.

'Thanks for the ——'s alteration: send more.

'Your's with unchangeable affection,

'H. Martyn.'

'*Cawnpore, Dec.* 5, 1809.

'Dearest Brother,

'The youth Ramsley has been with me the whole morning, allowing me no time to converse with you or do any other work. He is good-natured and entertaining, but sadly given to lounging, and there is no sporting doors out of Cambridge. He has been telling me a great deal about P——. Poor P——. *Labitur infelix.* He is spoken against everywhere in a way that sometimes gives me pain and offends me, but what can be said in reply? He has given too much cause for it. You do not seem to have conversed with Mrs. D——: she professes great humility and simplicity, but no real seriousness I believe. We shall have more and more reason every day to rejoice in our fee-refusing determination. Last Monday night I set out, and at the end of the first stage was obliged to stop, as the bearers there had only been sent from Cawnpore that day. I had a wretched night, and next morning on the way had much ado to keep myself from fainting. I called to the bearer for water, but there was none to be had; however the mercy of God saved me from a swoon which might have lasted to death. I reached the Jumna in the afternoon, and found the party encamped on the opposite side, not at Culpee, but a long way below. The ladies were the two eldest Miss Macans: very modest well-behaved young women. Mr. Richardson made two warm attempts to induce me to accept some Company's paper, said he should be much flattered, that he was not a poor man like the military. But I was inexorable: *flecti nescius.* By Mr. Cecil's advice after the example of Cato, I have learned to say *no.* Parson has subscribed 800 rupees to the Bible Society: you and I are to pay 100, according to Mr. Brown. I have given directions to have as much given for me as for you, and not more. I am now out of debt and overflowing with rupees. I wish I could meet with an opportunity of sending my debt to you. But I shall see you I hope face to face. If you cannot get to Meerut, I think it is better you should take half my duty than vegetate at Futtyghur. On Sunday I preached to the dragoons, my chief and only congregation now. The artillery are encamped without the station: my audience at head quarters consists almost entirely of ladies. On Sunday evening I was requested to baptize Colonel Wood's daughter. I consented, but told them I would not stay to dinner. Mrs. L—— said there would be only themselves and one lady, so I promised to stay, as I had no company at home. But I bitterly repented, for soon a crowd of dragoon officers came in, and instead of having an opportunity of introducing conversation suitable to the Lord's day, I was obliged to sit and hear nothing but nonsense. I lifted up my heart in prayer continually, that this might not be sin to me, and I thought with longing affection of those dear societies of saints then engaged in prayer and praise. The General is very rough and uncivil, not more so to me than to others; but he treats us all like upper servants; so, as I have nothing to gain by fawning, I keep aloof from him perhaps more than I ought. To-night there is a huge party at his house to meet Shumsheer Bahadoor, Nawab of Bundlecund: the particulars of this you may expect next week. Sabat is returned from Lucknow, but returns to spend his Christmas with Baillie. He brought testimonies from the true heir of the Persian throne and a variety of other Persians, that he is no learner, as the Bengalee Moonshee called him; but what is better, he is willing to revise his work and make it more easy. I have had a long letter from Mr. Brown, but only about the translations. Have you got the Missionaries' Hindee Gospel? I think it is tolerable. A letter from —— says he is going to Agra. There are some serious reflections in his letter. After professions of friendship, he adds, What a heart-breaking thing if we should not meet in heaven, and then goes on to say that the danger is on *his* side, and says, that he prays constantly for grace to declare all God's truths, though indeed they are but one.

'Your's ever affectionately,

'H. MARTYN.'

'*March* 5, 1810.

'Yesterday I had to preach to two very small congregations—their aggregate not fifty—you I suppose were laid up, and P. perhaps on a sandbank, so that little was done in Hindostan Proper yesterday. But such fruitless days shall not continue much longer. If it cannot be said that the day has broke, let us hope that we see the morning star.

Let the glorious day approaching,
  On their grossest darkness dawn;
And the everlasting gospel,
  Spread abroad thy glorious name!

'I was not very well pleased with my discourse to the

beggars, yesterday, (about 500,) because I fear *I hurt* their prejudices without *removing* them. On God's grant of flesh to Noah, I said,—Therefore we kill and eat. If God had considered one animal more holy than another, why did he not say so? If, for instance, the cow had been excepted, why did he not say so? There was a dead silence, and nothing said after it.'

'*Jan.* 1st, 1810.

'At church we have from twelve to sixteen,—at the balls Satan gets a hundred, though one regiment is gone. Every night almost they are at it. Yesterday, at the General's request, the sacrament was administered; no one attended but himself and the ladies. It was a cold season. Yesterday, after the sacrament, on observing to the General that I wished the young men had followed his example, He said, 'Why yes; though it is a very serious thing, we ought not on that account to be deterred from it.' The first speech I ever heard from his lips that ever tended to seriousness. His iron heart will perhaps melt, but he could not bring himself to kneel at the sacrament.

'Now for my congregation of the poor and the blind, the lame, the maimed. I went without fear, trusting to myself and not to the Lord, and accordingly I was put to shame,—that is, I did not succeed half so well as on the preceeding days. I shuffled and stammered, and indeed I am persuaded that there were many sentences the poor things did not understand at all. I spoke of the dry land, rivers, &c. Here I mentioned Ganga, good river, but others as good,—God loves Hindoos, but does he not love others too? All are alike before God. He hath made of one blood all nations of men. Some applauses—some hisses. Number about 550.'

Such is Mr. Martyn's account of his labours and the state of things at Cawnpore, more fully detailed in his journal and letters, &c. Mrs. Sherwood, who also lived at Cawnpore, and was in constant intercourse with him, writes thus respecting these labours of love, which so much tried and so little satisfied him.

'It was in the end of the year 1809, Mr. Martyn commenced his singular labour of preaching to the Faqeers: about 500 met every Sunday evening at his residence. He used to stand on his *chabuta* while they filled the grass-plat round it. It is scarcely possible to describe these objects; no dreams nor visions excited in the delirium of a raging fever could surpass these realities. They were young and old, male and female, tall and short, athletic and feeble, bloated and wizened, some clothed with abominable rags and matted uncombed hair, locks streaming down to their heels, every countenance being hard and fixed as it were by the continual indulgence of bad passions. Such was the congregation which assembled every Sunday evening in Mr. Martyn's domain. The plan which he adopted in his instructions to these poor wretches was to urge the moral duties, as summed up in the ten commandments, and the course was not finished when he left Cawnpore. The writer can also assert from her own recollections that Mr. Martyn in these discourses constantly endeavoured to prove the need of a Saviour. This was at times sufficient to call forth frequent bursts of anger, with shouts and curses, and deep and lengthened groans, passing from those most near to those furthest off, with hissings and threatening gestures, &c.

'This service was often carried on when the air was hot as from the mouth of an oven, when the red glare of the setting sun showed through a dry hot haze which parched the skin as with fever, and when the disease in his chest rendered it painful to that child of God even to speak at all. Mr. Martyn was not aware to the very last Sunday of his residence in Cawnpore, that any fruit whatever had sprung from this particular portion of his labour; and yet it was there, from those addresses to the Faqeers, that the most fruitful blossom of all the various branches of his ministry in India was to appear.

'It happened one Sunday evening in the spring of the year 1810, that a party of young Mussulmen were regaling themselves with their houkahs and sherbat in a *kiosh* which overlooked Mr. Martyn's garden whilst he was haranguing the mendicants below. If they called him a fool for his pains it was nothing more than what his countrymen at Cawnpore were in the habit of constantly doing; presently however they felt inclined to have a nearer view of the assembly, and down they came and placed themselves before the front of the Bungalow with their arms folded, their turbans on one side, and their lips drawn up in contempt.

'Forming one of this light and vicious group was a man afterwards well known in the missionary world, the Sheikh Salah, *alias* Abdul-Messeh. He was thus brought to hear Mr. Martyn's address to the *Faqeers*, in which it pleased God to enable him to see that truth which was concealed from other eyes. It was then and there brought to his mind, that as the purity of the law is such, that man can never fulfil its demands, such a Saviour would be needful, who was not only able, but willing to do for him that which he could never do for himself. When Mr. Martyn had finished his translation of the New Testament, the book was given to this same Sheikh Salah to bind. He availed himself of this opportunity of reading the divine word, and this decided him in favour of Christianity. He afterwards became a burning and shining light to his people, and as he lived so he died in the faith of Jesus.'

'The time was approaching when Mr. Martyn was to leave Cawnpore; the last Sunday was come. In the morning he opened the Bungalow which had been prepared for a place of worship, the first Christian temple which probably had ever existed at Cawnpore. The occasion was an affecting one, and those who beheld the touching aspect of that man of God on that occasion never can forget it. His usually pale face was flushed with the excitement, and the fire of hope and holy love seemed as it were to shine forth, and to express themselves in his address to the congregation with a force too strong for his feeble frame. All the usual party accompanied him back to his own bungalow, and being arrived there he sunk almost fainting on a sofa. Soon, however, he recovered, and asked some one to sing a very favourite hymn—

> 'O God our help in ages past,
> Our hope for years to come;
> Our shelter from the stormy blast,
> And our eternal home.'

'The whole party met again in the evening on the *chabuta* from whence Mr. Martyn was addressing the *Faqeers*, for the last time. The last evening of his ministry was intensely hot. The audience was turbulent, grossly insulting, groaning and hissing, moving to and fro, and exhibiting human nature in its most frightful aspect. The murmur sometimes arose so loud as wholly to interrupt the discourse; but as soon as silence was restored, Mr. Martyn's voice was again heard, sweetly, calmly, yet powerfully proceeding from the point in which he had been compelled to break off. Again the holy man was nigh to fainting when this exercise was concluded. That same evening the separation took place, but never can those who then parted forget the expression of his pale countenance, or the lovely yet mournful smile which then rested on his features.'

The years 1812 and 1813 were marked by judgment and mercy. Sorrow upon sorrow rolled in as the year rolled round. The year 1812 was ushered in by an earthquake. It was preceded by a loud noise; the houses shook; the oil in the lamps on the walls was thrown out; the birds made a frightful noise; the natives ran from their houses, calling on their gods; the sensation most awful, &c. This fearful prodigy was followed by that desolating disaster, the Serampore fire. Mr. Thomason thus describes the sad and saddening scene, 'I could scarcely believe the report, it was like a blow on the head which stupifies; I flew to witness the desolation, the scene was indeed affecting. The immense printing-office, two hundred feet long, and fifty broad, reduced to a mere shell; the yard covered with burnt quires of paper, the loss in which article was immense. Carey walked with me over the smoking ruins, the tears stood in his eyes. "In one short evening," said he, "the labours of years are consumed. How unsearchable are the ways of God! I had lately brought some things to the utmost perfection of which they seemed capable, and contemplated the missionary establishment with perhaps too much self-congratulation! *The Lord has laid me low, that I may look more simply to him.*" Who could stand in such a place, at such a time, with such a man, without feelings of sharp regret and solemn exercise of mind? A few hours ago and all was smiling and flourishing, and now all is vanished into smoke and covered with rubbish! Paper, on which the words of life were to be printed, covered the ground half-consumed, beautiful founts of metal types, all consecrated to the service of the sanctuary, melted into misshapen masses, &c., &c."'

Another severe affliction was the rapidly declining health and subsequent death of that eminent servant of God, Mr. Brown, who for the space of seven-and-twenty years had preached the pure unadulterated gospel of his Redeemer, and had been an ornament, intellectually and spiritually, to the Church of England. He was the father of the Bible Society in India, and to him it was owing that H. Martyn, who venerated and loved him, brought the Hindoostanee version to a successful termination. He began to sicken in the spring, and before the hot season had expended its strength and fury, he was where the sun could not light on him by day, nor any heat, &c.

About two months before his death he wrote in pencil some recollections which contain an account of his feelings in the prospect of his departure.

'March 22nd.—I feel myself to be sinking fast, I

said, 'My times are in thy hand. I ascended into the chamber of the divine attributes, and had a pleasing assurance that Jehovah is good, that great is the Lord and of great power. His understanding is infinite, and I rejoiced in his sovereignty. He made me sensible that for aught I know that very day was the best for my dissolution, best for my soul which I could commit to Christ, best for my family, dark and very stormy as the dispensation must appear within and awfully afflictive, best in all respects, thus my view of God in Christ delivered me from depression of mind, from all fear that hath torment, and from apprehension of evil of every kind with respect to mind, body, or estate. I could trust all confidently with God. Nor was the adversary permitted to assault me for a moment. Isaiah lv. 9 assures me of mercy infinite, "As the heavens, &c."

'My crimes are great but not surpass,' &c.

'The glory of Christ and his kingdom occupied my thoughts. My heart prayed, "Thy kingdom come," thou art worthy, O Lord, to receive all glory, and honour, and power, &c.

'The Saviour's progress through the week of his passion was the comforting subject of my meditations.

'The Hebrew Psalter has been very precious to me.' *

The following is from a lady now living who was one of his most intimate friends :—

'He performed the duties of the Mission Church from 1786 to 1808, without any regular assistance, but was occasionally helped by the Presidency chaplain. After Mr. Thomason arrived, he still continued in turn with him till he died in June, 1812. He gave his labour gratis, and not only his time and labour but also his money. At one time he enlarged the church at his *own* expence. He paid five thousand rupees for the ground on which the parsonage-house is built; the building of the house was paid for by the trustees of

* See Memoir of Rev. T. T. Thomason.

the "Evangelical Fund," a fund which David Brown began in 1802, and which has ever since proved very useful to the Old Church.* He also furnished it with lustres, &c. At one time he had a handsome income, but he spent all his money in the Old Church and other acts of generosity, for he died *poor* and left a widow and eight children to the *sole* care of the God whom he had loved and served all his life; but the children of the righteous are not neglected, nor his widow left to pine in hopeless poverty. She died ten years after her excellent partner, and all the children living in affluence and devoted to the God of their Father.'†

The government about this time became suspicious of the missionaries, and the result of a long correspondence was the dismissing of some from the country, which, however, was afterwards overruled. These were the first American missionaries, Messrs. Judson and Newel, &c. They had turned their backs upon their native country, they had passed through many a peril, and endured many a pang, to impart the gospel to our benighted fellow subjects; but after a short residence in India, and after a conduct, against which nothing could be excepted, they were summarily ordered to depart. While the priests of the foul and debasing rites of Juggernaut were countenanced, the revenue being increased by their abominations, these self-denying, devoted servants of the Redeemer, were driven from those shores to which love alone of the most exalted order, and of the purest description, had carried them. Not long, however, after the shameful dismissal of the Christian ministers, the friends of true religion in England rose up as one man, to claim permission of the government to make known the Saviour's name in those dark and

* A new Church has lately been erected out of its proceeds, and a converted native ordained and appointed to it.

† The sons, civil servants of the Hon. East India Company, and the daughters married to the same, the "seed of the Righteous are indeed blessed."

neglected territories. On the renewal of the East India Company's charter, the tables of the two houses of Parliament were loaded with petitions to that effect. Testimonies also were given at the bar of the House of Commons, most favourable to the petitioners. On the opposite side, ideal phantasmagoric figures, were exhibited to alarm and deter; but these disappeared gradually, as the light was let in on that darkened part of the stage. Lord Teignmouth, formerly Governor-General of India; shewing on the one hand England's incontestible obligations, and on the other, the security in which they might be fulfilled. The Marquis of Wellesley also, in the House of Lords, advocated all prudent attempts to promote Christianity in the East. His speech was calculated to convince all who were not steeled against conviction, with regard to missionaries, he never knew of any danger arising from them. Some of them were learned men, and were employed in the college of Bengal. He had always considered them as a quiet, discreet, and learned body; and he had employed them in the education of youth and translations; more particularly in translating *the Scriptures into the Eastern languages.*'

While all this was going on, Mr. Thomason, who was engaged in revising the Arabic version of the scriptures with Sabat, and in conducting through the press H. Martyn's Hindoostanee New Testament, wrote to the Church Missionary Society, inviting them to place two missionaries in his house, whom he undertook to instruct gratuitously in oriental literature. But the project that lay nearest his heart, was evidently the establishment of native schools; and as a preparatory step, a school for school-masters. Of the plan of native schoolmasters, Mr. Thomason says with warmth and energy, but with the coolness of considerate wisdom: 'This school would be a noble establishment; I despair of seeing any good done in a place where the objects of ignorance and vice are innumerable, until some institution has been formed. But I fear it would not suit the adventurous, and grand, and dashing spirit of the age. The good people of England would suppose, that a free school containing one thousand children, must be tenfold more productive than one containing twenty-four children; not considering the great importance of having one school-master, they would suppose the money almost wasted. School-masters must be made *here*, not in England. . . . The benefit would be distant, at present scarcely perceptible; but future generations would arise and call us blessed.'

In the year 1813, thirteen of the most respectable people in Calcutta signed a public address to government, petitioning for the Bible in behalf of the Malays: to the surprise of all, this thing so novel and so bold, met with a favourable reply. The government acknowledged that the thing was laudable and important, and promised 10,000 rupees, about £1250. in aid of printing an edition of the Malay Bible. To be very earnest in spiritual subjects, and to wait patiently, is no common attainment, but how important!

The late Bishop Corrie was at this time stationed at Agra, having with him Abdul Messeh, as a fellow-labourer. Their united labours were not in vain in the Lord, but were stamped with marked success. They are thus alluded to by Mr. Thomason:—'Corrie wins all hearts, European as well as native. My soul greatly rejoiceth in the good that is doing there; and when I look around and see the comparatively barren fields of Calcutta, I rejoice in the waving crops of Agra. You have scarcely an idea of his valuable qualities and fitness for Indian labour. He is patient, humble, mild, full of love, always alive to his work, apt to teach, ever on the look-out, richly furnished with argument, and exhortation, and holy unction. Having seen much of him lately, the remembrance of him is sweet. His very image does me good. Abdul is another Corrie, with a prodigious store of eloquence and practical wisdom.

'The appearance of a new Governor-General in India,

has a sensible effect on the still surface of an Indian life. Nor is the excitement it occasions of short continuance. It requires time, before things can subside into their ordinary quiescence. Like steel filings, when the magnet is introduced ; at such a moment all is motion and attraction ; multitudes are considering the aspect it may have on their own private interests ; others are inquiring—their affections being set on things above—what will be its bearing on questions of everlasting moment. In the middle of October, 1813, the Earl of Moira arrived at Fort William, and whilst the guns were announcing that he was in the midst of those he was to govern, a little band of Christians were met together, revolving in their minds whether a revocation of that cruel edict, which had expelled some missionaries, and driven others to the outskirts of the empire, might be obtained. A memorial was prepared and presented, but was ineffectual. Messrs. Nott and Hall were compelled to leave India, and whilst withdrawing from a land, to the good of which they had devoted their lives, they put forth a strong and memorable vindication of their character and principles. .It was addressed to Sir Evan Nepean. He was their friend, and would have befriended them, but could not, of course, resist authority.'

Early in 1814, the new Governor-General, who often attended the Mission Church, notwithstanding its unfashionable character, and appointed its minister to perform stated service at Barrackpore, his own country residence, fixed upon him also to accompany him as chaplain in a journey of state through the provinces. He soon after commissioned him to draw up and submit to the government a plan for the education of the Indian population.

It was at this time, that intelligence was received of Dr. Middleton's appointment to be the first Bishop of Calcutta. Mr. Thomason's heart was cheered by the intelligence, and he gives us the effusions of that heart at the moment—'His work on the Greek Article is of the first order: surely the author of such a work will be an episcopal man in the true sense of the word.'

While on his tour up the country, this excellent man's feelings were deeply exercised about the moral and religious condition of the country through which he travelled. At almost every reach of the river, (the Ganges,) and at every resting-place at night, an increase of that compassionate zeal, which had led him before he left Calcutta to draw up and present to the Governor-General a plan for the instruction of the Hindoos, kindled afresh in his bosom. 'In ascending the Ganges,' he writes, 'and visiting the towns and villages on its banks, we see an enormous population of degraded beings with our eyes. The first place of importance was Murshedebād, the once famous metropolis of Bengal. It is an immense city, swarming with inhabitants, but exhibiting the sad marks of decayed greatness. Oh, it was an affecting sight to look around at the countless throngs, and observe moral, political, and religious degradation, without one symptom of improvement. We have annihilated the political importance of the natives, stripped them of their power, and laid them prostrate, without giving them anything in return. They possess neither learning, nor emulation, nor power. Every spring of action seems deadened. They wallow in the filth of a senseless and impure religion, without any prospect of deliverance. You can conceive of nothing more wretched than Hindoo towns and villages. Nothing like architecture, except in their temples, the streets are narrow and dirty, the house inexpressibly mean, teeming with inhabitants, whose appearance is disgusting in the extreme. At Benares, I ventured to visit the shrine held so sacred. It was an oppressive sight. The avenues to it are narrow, crowded with Brahmins and bulls! the symbols of their impure religion meet the eye in every corner, and the horrid din of the Brahmins, and Faqeers, and bulls, and beggars, and bells, was too much to be endured. I hastened from the place, as from Pandemonium, and thanked God for in durance for some time, on occasion of a large fair annually held near to the Honourable Company's territory.

His account of it is as follows:—

'On reaching the Nipal, I was seized by the soldiery. The Jammadar (commander) put me under a guard and threatened my life, upon which I opened my New Testament and read, "I am also a man under authority, my Lord and Master is the Almighty God and Saviour of the world. No man hath sent me hither. My guru (spiritual guide) forbade me and told me you would seize me. I am come in the name of God, an ambassador of the Lord of armies. My commission is from him, and my message to you. You threaten to take away my life. In the name of God and his Son Jesus Christ, I offer you life eternal. And as though God did beseech you by me, I pray you in Christ's stead be ye reconciled to God. Repent and believe the gospel, and do not so wickedly." All cried out, "He is a good man. He brings good tidings. He is not a man of war, but of peace. Let us do him no harm, but send him away, we dare not let him proceed, &c." The door is thus far still shut, they however frequently come down into the plains to the company's boundaries to trade, when opportunities of intercourse and giving the scriptures, &c., which have been translated into their language, occur. On one occasion, about a dozen Pundits and some of their courtiers, resided with me on the most friendly terms, and were entertained for a month. Every day intercourse was thus afforded and embraced of making known the gospel to them; and on leaving, each received and took away with him a copy of the New Testament.'

It was at this period that Dr. Middleton, the first bishop of India, arrived, to the rejoicing of the hearts of many. Mr. Thomason thus notices this auspicious event,—'In the midst of war and distraction, here is a man of peace come among us for works of peace. Even in troublous times our Jerusalem may be built. All the accounts have been favourable. He has commenced with a noble confession of his principles and motives for coming to India. Our friends have been made glad and have gladdened us by their accounts. I hope to know him soon. Oh, that it may please God to regard us with compassion, and incline the hearts of his servants to come over and help us! We want *learning* as well as *piety*. It would make your heart ache to go through this land. Whoever comes must make up his mind to labour and prepare for discouragements. I cannot use flattering speeches to allure my brethren. They must be prepared to fight battles, and must expect disappointments. India is a scene of peculiar trial. Our hopes are often blasted; if we are very sanguine and impatient we must smart for it. We must learn to *plough* in hope, wait, pray, and believe. Adversaries abound, whose mouths are ever open, and who have many grounds of offence in the fickleness of professors and instability of the native converts. The trial is sharp, and such as the gospel only can carry us through. We have had a fresh cause of grief in the relapse of Sabat. I never thought well of him. He left me at Mongyr after completing the New Testament. On his return to Calcutta, he published a book against the Christian religion, he calls it Sabatean proofs of the truth of Islamism and falsehood of Christianity. Many rejoiced; the bishop is grieved. I have learned some useful lessons, to be backward in praising; above all to be careful how we publish the tidings of our operations.'* Of Abdul Messeh he adds, 'I pray that he may be kept in humility and in active labour until our brother return to us. Abdul needs Corrie, and so does the church at large. A fitter instrument for leading on the native converts, for winning the affections of the people, and carrying on missionary labours, can hardly be found. They speak of him at Agra with tears; his *love* has won them all. He was, humanly speaking, their stay and centre of union.'

* Sabat, see Thomason's Life. p. 243.

It was in this year that the Rev. Henry Fisher, now Presidency chaplain at Calcutta, arrived. Of the devotedness and labours of this good man, and oldest friend of Bishop Corrie's, much of interest could be detailed; but he still lives. Hereafter some deeply interesting accounts of death-bed scenes may be introduced, as also an account of several native conversions.

It was not long after Mr. Thomason's return to Calcutta, that he set about establishing an asylum for the female orphans of European soldiers. This is now one of the noblest charitable institutions in the presidency of Calcutta, and has been a source of blessing to thousands. The destitute condition of the female orphans of European soldiers belonging to the king's regiment, attracted his notice during his voyage, and deeply affected his heart. Deprived of their natural protectors, and left to the casual mercy of successive individuals, if they escaped the dangers of infancy they were exposed to the corrupting influence of scenes of profligacy. To preserve such from contamination, Mr. Thomason proposed to the community the establishment of the Female Orphan Asylum, July 1st, 1815. *

That days of new and unwonted lustre were about to dawn on India, the least sanguine might anticipate, when in two successive years the Christian youth of Calcutta, were seen preparing to receive confirmation from their bishop, and the Hindoo population of the same age, were assembled for instruction in English literature, in an institution originated and maintained by wealthy and learned natives. Such an establishment, without having any direct bearing on the promotion of Christianity, could not but be conducive to it.

In reference to the first confirmation by an English bishop on the plains of idolatrous India, a minute and detailed account was then given.

The formation of the Hindoo College was sudden and

* See last Report for 1842.

unexpected. The plan of the College was submitted and finally adopted by a general Committee, formed principally from among the rich natives, on an application from them to Sir E. East, entreating him to assist them. Secretaries were chosen; Sir Edward was desired to be president, and Mr. Harrington to be vice president. They accepted the offer. The Governor General fearing that this was a movement towards Christianity, requested that the latter would withdraw. He did so; and Sir E. East withdrew also, to the surprise and regret of those who had embarked in the work.

Notwithstanding this unpropitious circumstance, the matter went on, subscriptions to the amount of £10,000 were spontaneously raised, and more soon flowed in. Such was the origin and commencement of the present Hindoo College, which has been so productive of infidels, some of whom have been caught in the missionary-net spread for them on the other side of the tank, in front of its College, and elsewhere, and entered the Christian Church, through the laver of baptism, we trust, to be finally saved. An account of some may hereafter be given. One is episcopally ordained, and now preaching in a beautiful and substantially-built church in Calcutta.

The literary union of Hindoos led soon to a combination amongst Christians in the Institution now existing under the name of 'The School-Book Society;' its object being to furnish the natives with heathen writings; everything bordering upon Christianity being most scrupulously and systematically rejected. Good however, has come out of it; books of a moral tendency at least have of late years been admitted, printed, and circulated, and more recently some with just the *smell* of Christianity upon them.

It was in 1816, Mr., now the Rev. William Bowley, was settled at Chunar, by the late Bishop Corrie. In 1817, the Church Missionary Society gained a firm position, and presented an extended and bold front in

Calcutta. Mr. Thomason became its secretary in the commencement of that year, and towards its conclusion he speaks with animation and joy of missionary meetings in his church, and among his congregation. He writes, 'We have begun our missionary operations in print; for the first time two of our highest civilians show their faces to the Indian public, in connection with a professedly missionary institution. The Lord be praised! The secretaryship has just devolved on me, and more than employs me. I cannot get through all my work.' In the month of October of the same year,—'We have established a monthly missionary prayer-meeting at my church. Missionary communications are read, and prayer is offered up for missionary prosperity. Ten years ago such an event would have thrown the settlement into an uproar.' At this time among other things, Mr. Thomason was engaged on a version of the Psalms in the Persian language,—the revision of the Arabic Old Testament, and in carrying a revised edition of the Arabic New Testament, and Henry Martyn's Persian New Testament, through the press. Under this pressure, superadded to his pastoral employments. he writes,—'I am filled with astonishment at the opening scenes of usefulness,—*send us labourers—faithful and laborious labourers.* Being obliged to undertake so many departments, renders me sadly deficient. Preaching, translating, writing letters, attending committees, all is feebly and unprofitably done.'

The first ordained missionary sent out by the Church Missionary Society to Calcutta, was the Rev. William Greenwood. His first place of residence was Kidderpore, where he had no employment as an ordained minister, and was after a short residence appointed to Chunar. His labours there during the whole period of his residence, was confined to the European invalid soldiers and the few other residents.

At the commencement of 1818, the late Bishop Corrie wrote to the corresponding committee in Calcutta—'The usual number of Europeans who attend divine service is about forty ; and that of native Christians, who attend worship in Hindoostanee, about *seventy or eighty*. The number of both congregations has been gradually and regularly increasing, and testifies to the diligence and devotedness of Mr. Bowley, and of the blessing attending his labours. I conversed with ten Hindoos, who appear to be fully convinced of the truth of Christianity, though not yet prepared to encounter the consequences of an open confession of Christ. Some of them even join Mr. Bowley occasionally in prayers. One of them on being asked what he considered the great peculiarity of the Christian religion, answered, that in every other religion *works* were made a condition of justification, but that in Christianity, only faith in Christ is required,—while wonderful to say, it produces more holiness than any other system. The whole congregation almost were in tears during an address in which Mr. ——— set before them the Saviour's sufferings, and during the communion the greater number appeared deeply affected, and all of them exceedingly serious and attentive.'

A convenient spot of ground for the erection of a church having been fixed on, Mr. Turnbull, the proprietor, on being requested to dispose of it, generously offered it as a gift for the purpose intended ; and the Marquis of Hastings was pleased to aid the collection by the very liberal donation of £100. The church having been commenced, various reasons urging the measure—the Rev. Mr. Greenwood, was appointed to minister to the European congregation ; leaving Mr.Bowley wholly at liberty for ministering to the natives, &c. Mr. Greenwood arrived at Chunar, Jan. 13, 1819.

In the month of July 1818, a Hindoo Brahman and a Mohammedan Munshee (teacher or scribe) were baptized. After divine service and address by Mr. Bowley, they both came forward. The Brahman then addressed the hearers : 'Behold! I declare before all, and let Hindoos and Mussulmans pay attention to my words. I have been on pilgrimage to Jugga-nauth—to Dwakanauth—to Badri-nauth, and to other places of pilgrimage—but, behold! in all my travels, I found not the true way of salvation, till I came to this place, and heard the gospel, which by God's grace, I am convinced is the only way to happiness; and I truly believe and declare before Hindoos and Mahomedans, that if they do not embrace the gospel, the wrath of God will abide upon them, and they shall be cast into hell.' On saying this, he drew out his brahminical thread, and broke it asunder before the people, saying, 'Behold here—the sign of my delusion,' and then delivered it to Mr. Corrie.

After him Muni Alli, the munshee, thus addressed the people: 'Attend, brethren, and hearken unto me! I was a Mussalman, and had spent much of my time in the company of learned men of the same profession. I have studied the meaning of the Koran, and I have paid adoration to the tombs of *Pirs* (spiritual guides.) In those days, whenever I saw a Christian, my spirit was stirred up within me to slay him; but on hearing the holy gospel, light has sprung up in my mind, which has increased; and I have been more confirmed in this faith since I saw the Pentateuch and Psalms. To receive Christian baptism I have come from Delhi. My mind has moreover been strengthened and established by the instructions which I have received from the Rev. Mr. Corrie; and now, before all my brethren present, I embrace this true way of salvation.' After this Mr. Corrie delivered a discourse on Matt. xxviii. 19. and then baptized the two candidates, the Brahmin by the name of *Kewil Massih,* (only Christ) and the Mussulman by that of *Munif Massih* (eminent in Christ.)

Mr. Bowley continued his wise and zealous efforts, assisted by Nicholas, one of the natives educated by the Rev. D. Corrie. The place of divine worship was usually crowded on Sundays by native Christians, and the heathen were occasionally drawn to attend and listen to the words of eternal life, among whom some instances of saving conversion occurred. In addition to his other labours, Mr. Bowley was at this time employed in a revision of H. Martyn's Hindoostanee translation of the New Testament. Two of the gospels had been printed by the Calcutta Auxiliary Bible Society, and from these he derived essential help in his labours of love among the natives. In the following year, Mr. Bowley, wishing to superintend the press, visited Calcutta, and was there solemnly set apart to the sacred ministry by the imposition of hands, according to the usage of the German Lutheran Church,* by the Rev. Messrs. Jetter and Deer, who had just arrived under the auspices of the Church Missionary Society. The following testimony is from a gentleman in the Company's Service visiting Chunar. 'It was delightful to visit the native Christians, to behold especially the beautiful order and decorum of the females. At church, the first sight of a congregation of sable worshippers is of course very striking. In my walks I was reminded of a country village in England, on the Sabbath day; some were sitting at the doors, and others in the veranda,† reading, and all were so quiet, that one

* Afterwards admitted to Episcopal Ordination, by Bishop Heber.

† THE VERANDA.

On nature's face once more I gaze,
Once more her charms I view,
With what delight my eyes I raise
To that pure vault of blue!

The kids are sporting on the green,
And all around is fair;
Oh! how enlivening is the scene!
How cool the evening air!

The foliage of the trees how light!
Of brightest green their dye;
While I from the veranda's height,
Delighted cast my eye.

Raised from a couch of pain and death
By Him who reigns above;
May I until my latest breath,
Ne'er cease my God to love!

could not but be sure that the gospel of peace was known there. I have not seen anything like it in India before: heathen testimony to the change is very strong. Hawkers and venders of goods, never now venture within their precincts, as they only meet with reproof or advice, instead of selling any thing. And the very coolies of the place have learned something of Jesus Christ and his gospel. The after-records of this most interesting mission are in the Church Missionary Society's publications, and familiar to missionary readers, and may hereafter be concisely given, if the limits of the publication admit, but its principal object is to give to the public what is less known. The conversion, lives, &c. of some converts eminent among the many, will in this case be mentioned, and with the greater satisfaction, as they were personally known to myself. The Rev. Messrs. Friend and Eteson, were in the years 1828—30, successively appointed to this mission. Mr. Friend soon sickened and died. An interesting memoir of

Oh! if my heart with joy can leap
To view a world like this;
How glorious to fall asleep,
And wake in realms of bliss!

Though fair this beauteous world below,
Yet fairer is the place
Where Jesus to his saints shall shew
The brightness of His face.

There shall the tree of life abide,
To heal God's chosen sons;
And *there* the stream of life shall glide,
As crystal clear it runs.

No need for sun to shine by day,
Nor moon to gild the night;
God's glory shines with endless ray,
The lamb shall be their light.

Oh! when on Jordan's banks I stand,
May I my Saviour see,
And catch a glimpse of that bright land
Where still I hope to be!

him appeared at the time in the Church Missionary Record. Mr. Eteson confined his labours to the European congregation, for which he was best calculated, and among whom he laboured with considerable success. Mr. Eteson was at the same time a diligent student of the native languages, and has an extensive and critical acquaintance with them, which I believe is usefully exercised in reviewing present translations. He is at this time the Company's chaplain. The following is an unpublished letter from the Rev. Mr. Bowley to myself:

'What shall I say of our Chunar mission. When I first came here, and for many years afterwards, a convert was a prodigy. In fact, to renounce heathenism was the blackest crime a man could commit. Now we have between twenty and thirty Christian families—about fifty orphans, all under Christian instruction, and worshiping God in Christ. In a village opposite Chunar, there are three families, with two lads, all agriculturists. A native reader is placed there, who conducts worship with them twice a day, and during the day visits the villages around, reading the scriptures, and distributing tracts, &c. 'At another village, fourteen miles from Chunar, on the banks of the river Ganges, we have Matthew Ranjit, an old experienced Catechist, and three families, agriculturists, &c.

'At the home mission at Chunar, we have David Thakur, and two married young men from among our orphans, all engaged in the work.

'Karam Massih, one of our oldest converts, is again fixed as native catechist at Buxar, where he before laboured for many years. He assembles, as heretofore, morning and evening, the native Christian congregation, and reads the scriptures, and distributes them among the heathen and Mohammedan population.

'My own duties at the station are at present both English and Hindostanee, regular services at church on Sunday and week-days. Daily worship in my own residence, open to all.—Superintending orphan asylums, &c.—Translations, &c.

'During the rainy and cold seasons, I itinerate as usual; visit the badre-fair, preaching at the villages, and distributing books on the banks of the Ganges, spend a fortnight or three weeks at Juanpore, Azemgurh, &c. Some weeks are spent in visiting villages and towns south-east of Chunar. Scarcely a year but some die in Christ. Of this description, four already this year. One pious old widow ten years ago, gave me 1000 rupees for missionary purposes, and a week before her death, 2100 for the same purpose. These are the fruits of prayer, pains, and faith in Christ—*the increase given of God*.*

At the close of the year 1816, the corresponding committee at Calcutta, received a communication from Lieutenant Stewart, stationed at Burdwan,† proposing an extensive plan of native schools at and near that place. Three schools were accordingly established under the Society's care. With the concurrence of the committee, the plan was afterwards extended, and additional schools opened. Of the state of these schools an impartial observer says, August 28th, 1817, 'If every missionary did as much as Lieutenant Stewart has done and is doing for the cause of civilization and religion, he needs be in no fear as to his reputation with those who employ him. He has done wonders in this neighbourhood in regard to education.' The number of schools was soon afterwards increased to ten, in which about one thousand children were taught the Bengalee language, by the new method so successfully adopted in Europe, with some improvements. Though Lieutenant Stewart did not formally and regularly teach the Scriptures in the

* The Rev. Mr. B. has translated the whole Bible into Hindoo.

† Burdwan is situated about twenty miles north north-west of Calcutta. The Mission Establishment is about two miles from the city, by the side of the great Benares road, but is surrounded by a considerable village population. It now comprises within its enclosure about twenty-one acres of land, and contains a church, two houses of residence for the Missionaries, an Infant School, a Boys' and Girl's School, a village consisting of about twenty houses in which Christian families are settled, and where they find a peaceful asylum amidst the degrading idolatry which surrounds them.

schools, he was in the habit of distributing copies of the gospels and religious tracts, &c., which were eagerly sought after by the young people when they had learned to read.

Receiving an impulse, and borrowing light, from the plans and operations of the active and excellent Mr. May,* of Chinsurah, he still further improved his system, and of its efficacy Mr. Thomason writes, 'It was very pleasing to hear a simple and good account of the English government, the two houses of parliament, the army and navy, and universities of England, with its chief towns, cities, and rivers, from a company of poor Bengalee boys; who, unless they had been brought under instruction, must have remained in entire ignorance and stupid indifference to improvement.'

The Rev. Messrs. Jetter and Deer were settled at Burdwan, on their arrival in India, in Nov. 1819. Lieutenant Stewart having purchased a piece of ground and built a house for the accommodation of the missionary family; the former took charge of the central school, recently erected, in which the English language was taught; and Mr. Deer superintended the Bengalee schools. In 1820 there were about twenty scholars in the central English school, and 1050 in thirteen Bengalee schools. Their attendance was interrupted by the frequent recurrence of heathen festivals, and by occasional delays in the field. Mr. Jetter writes, on occasion of a visit paid them by a kind friend:—'We were much grieved that he could not see much of the schools, as the natives had just then two holy-days, (if indeed we may call them so) when all the schools were shut up. They worshipped during those two days paper, pens, and ink! By doing so, they say they become wise.'†

* A devoted and exemplary missionary connected with the London Missionary Society.

† The writer caste, to whom the above reference is made, worship the things mentioned as peculiar to their profession. Every profession, and every trade, and every grade, &c. do the same annually. Tradesmen—their account books: Mechanics—their tools: a Farrier—not only his tools, but the horses' hoofs.

In 1821, the Rev. John Perowne proceeded to this station. His reception by the residents was most cordial; a subscription was set on foot for the erection of a suitable place of worship, and on application to government, by the local authorities, an eligible spot of ground was assigned for the site of a church, and an order issued to supply the sum wanted to complete the estimate out of the public treasury. The success of the schools was demonstrated by an interesting and extensive examination. Mr. Deer, in addition to his ordinary engagements, took five boys into his house at his own expence, to whom he gave religious instruction, &c. 'I am sometimes delighted,' he says, 'with the answers which I obtain when I ask these boys the meaning of passages of scriptures, v. g., when I asked, What did our Lord mean when he said, "Whosoever seeth me, seeth the Father?" One, who is of the Brahmin caste, answered, "I think it may be understood that, As the Father, the Son, and the Holy Ghost are one, therefore, whoever seeth the Son seeth the Father also." At another time when I asked why David called Christ his LORD, though he was also called the Son of David, the same boy said, "David had become acquainted, through the prophets, with that great Redeemer who was to come, and in that respect he called him his Lord, and because he became incarnate in the family of David he is called his son."'

The first converts in this mission were baptized on the 5th of May, 1822. An adult native received on this interesting occasion the name of Daniel, and a youth of thirteen years of age, that of John. Another candidate for baptism was a very promising youth, in whom Mr. Perowne had been much interested and of whom he had formed considerable expectations.

Mrs. Perowne, after many unsuccessful attempts, succeeded in forming a Bengalee school for girls. Mr. Perowne observes, 'the remarks and questions of the children in the schools evince that a foundation is laid for much future good. There is abundant reason to bless God for what has been done. Who would have expected, a year ago, to see *one thousand* Hindoo children reading the gospel? Nay, so greatly are the prejudices of the natives removed, that those very boys, who a few months since disliked, or refused to read any book which contained the *name of Jesus*, are now willing to read a history of his life and doctrine, &c., and what is more, in some cases they have solicited the gospel in preference to every other book.'

The operations of the missionaries were continued with much energy in all the departments of their labours, until interrupted by an awful inundation in 1823. All the houses of the poor Bengalees fell in, and the people were obliged to climb up the trees in order to save their lives. 'There they sat, without sustenance, for four days,' says Mr. Reichardt, then on a visit at Burdwan, 'crying to their god, "Hari, Hari, save us, we are lost!" Brethren Deer, Marsch, and myself, were in one house, and if the water had risen but one inch higher it would have entered our rooms, and we should have been obliged to flee to the roof, for which purpose we kept a ladder ready; however we were spared this danger by the water decreasing. Many idols, and particularly those which they had prepared to celebrate the Pujā of the goddess Durga, (vilest of the vile,) were broken to pieces or floated away. I saw a heap of them, about six in number, lying broken to pieces or floating away. The impotency of these idols were greatly exposed, and many of the Bengalees began to ridicule them, saying, 'Our gods are dead, they could not prevent the flood.' I am sorry to say this impression of the nothingness of idols, which they, during this awful catastrophe, received, is already worn off. For soon after the flood had subsided, instead of the image of Durga, they worshipped a waterpot into which they had cited her spirit.'

The history of this mission is also detailed in the Church Missionary Society's reports, and must be well known to the supporters of the society. It is decidedly one of the most interesting of the Society's stations.

The Revs. J. J. Weitbrecht, and J. T. Linke have for some years past, up to the present time, had charge of it together with Bancurah, &c. In the month of October last the bishop, with his chaplain, the Rev. J. H. Pratt, visited Burdwan, examined the various schools, and held a confirmation, of which a very interesting account is given in the Church Missionary Record for April, 1842.

The number of native Christian families residing on the mission premises, are twenty, consisting of seventy-five souls; an increase of eleven is spoken of in Mr. Linke's last report. Preaching to the heathen in that immense city, and in the surrounding villages, is now regularly kept up with considerable interest, which the journals of the missionaries testify. The English school, which has given such general satisfaction at the annual examinations, now consists of seventy scholars. The number of Bengalee day-schools is five. The Report of 1839 states, in reference to the indigenous vernacular schools, that having through their means extended through the district a general knowledge of the Holy Scriptures, they would be gradually discontinued.

The ORPHAN BOYS AND GIRLS SCHOOL promise, under God, the greatest probable results. The number of boys is thirty; the girls thirty-eight, varying in age from three to sixteen years.

ACCOUNT OF A CONVERTED BRAHMIN.

He had, at the age of eleven, been initiated into the ceremonies and rites of Brahminical superstition: he travelled to different places of celebrity in heathen mythology, and underwent austerities of various kinds, and performed prescribed penances. During his travels, he several times heard the Gospel; at length, he received a tract, called, '*Which is the true Shaster?*' It arrested his attention, and excited his curiosity. He afterwards obtained a copy of St. Matthew's Gospel, which he also read. On passing through Burdwan, he attended the chapel, conversed with the missionary, received instruction, and was baptized.

SKETCH OF THE HISTORY OF JAMES, A NATIVE CATECHIST.

It must be deeply interesting to every friend of missions to hear of converts brought into the fold of Christ, and enabled through a number of years, not only to walk consistently with their holy profession, but by their zeal, energy, and stedfastness, becoming a blessing to many others.

The individual, of whose life a brief outline is here offered to the reader, was a man of this description. During the space of eighteen years, which intervened between his baptism and his death, he was a useful, humble, and faithful servant of his Lord, who evidently felt a deep interest in the spiritual welfare of his brethren, and laboured to promote it.

James was first brought under the notice of Christians, by attending as a pupil in a Bengalee school, under the superintendance of a pious officer in the neighbourhood of Burdwan. He was from thence removed into a boarding-school, situated in the same gentleman's compound, where English and Persian were taught, in addition to Bengalee. After three years instruction, his mind appeared deeply influenced by the truths he had heard and read, and he expressed a wish for Christian baptism. He was accordingly baptized in the year 1820, at the age of fourteen, the first convert to Christianity at Burdwan. He continued in the school some time longer, till appointed as an assistant-teacher. After this, he became, under the direction of the missionary, a superintendent of a number of Bengalee schools, and about the same period he began to preach the gospel to his countrymen.

His relations were at first exceedingly distressed at

his conversion, uncommon as such an event then was; but they, nevertheless, visited him occasionally at the mission premises. The missionary spoke kindly to them, and explained the doctrines of the Christian religion, in which he was warmly seconded by the young convert. He soon perceived with joy that their prejudices were decreasing, and, in the course of three years, his father, uncle, and two brothers, were drawn by the constraining love of Christ, to confess Him as their only Saviour, and were baptized in His name. These individuals are still living, and have maintained, on the whole, a humble consistency.

During the last five years James was stationed at Bancurrah as catechist, and superintendent of four Bengalee schools, containing 400 scholars; and though, during the greater part of that time, the station was only occasionally visited by a missionary, yet he fulfilled the trust committed to him very satisfactorily, not only maintaining the schools in a most effective state, with the assistance of a few sircars (native teachers), but also using every effort by preaching to promote the conversion of souls. In his leisure hours he composed a number of sermons *in English*, of which language he had a correct and somewhat extensive knowledge. These sermons evidently showed his mind to be under the influence of divine grace, and that he was in the habit of studying the word of God with care and diligence.

In his family, his conduct was most exemplary, both as a husband and a father. He instructed his children himself, as well as his wife; had regular family-worship, at which those who felt interested in religion were frequently present, and he enjoyed the high esteem of his neighbours, and of the most respectable natives of the station, which is one of the strongest proofs, that an upright and blameless conduct was uniformly maintained by him.

This good man was carried off in the midst of his days, and the fulness of health, at the early age of thirty-two, during the month of March 1837, by that dreadful scourge of India, the Cholera Morbus.

On Easter Sunday he had attended at the place where the small community of Christians at Bancoorah, read the Church prayers and a sermon. The following morning he rose unwell, medical assistance was called in, but it was too late. In twelve hours from the commencement of the attack, his course was finished. He was much in prayer during the forenoon, and confessed his sins with contrition, but after twelve his consciousness returned only at intervals. During one of these lucid moments, he said to his afflicted wife, 'I am going to leave you: we have been mutual companions for many years—trust in God—live near to your Saviour, and we shall be reunited again.' These were his last words. He was visited in the evening by some kind European gentlemen, who knew him, but he was too far gone to enter into conversation. The following day his remains were interred, the commander of the regiment at the station kindly undertaking to read the burial service, and there he rests till the trumpet shall sound, and the dead shall arise, and this mortal put on immortality.

On one occasion the Rev. Mr. Weitbrecht writes :—

'My little flock of native Christians look more like a flock of Christ than ever before. I have lately had the joy to see that the Spirit is at work, particularly among the young. . . . Our moonlight visits appear to be greatly blessed to them, young and old. A greater mutual attachment has been formed between the pastor and the flock ; their hearts are more open for spiritual conversation, and family devotion is encouraged and appreciated. One English school in the town has greatly increased. The Acts of the Apostles, the Epistle to the Romans, Prophecies of Isaiah, have been read and explained during the last year, and I have reason to believe with considerable advantage to several of the boys.'

THE CALCUTTA MISSION.*

The Calcutta mission was commenced by the Rev. Mr. Jetter, and has been continued by the Rev. Messrs. Reichardt, Wilson, and Sandys, and the present missionaries. On my arrival in India, in 1823, there were some half-dozen converts; there are now several hundreds connected with it in and about Calcutta; but Calcutta has always been a much-neglected field of missionary effort, as far as the Church of England is concerned. Instead of fifty, seldom more than one missionary has been labouring there at the same time. Other societies have occupied and still occupy this most important sphere of missionary effort. Herein I do rejoice and will rejoice, and thank God, but my heart longs to see our own branch of Christ's Church putting forth its energies more vigorously. I confess I am ashamed of both our universities. They have given us bishops, but not *one* missionary. Men of missionary spirit have gone forth to this part of India, as we have seen, in the devotedness of a Brown and a Buchanan, and a Corrie and a Martyn, but they were not left at liberty to full missionary labour. In the language of one of these, what is wanting is men,—that precious commodity,—who shall be *wholly* devoted to the work. The same individuals are too much divided in their attention. Meanwhile our Dissenting brethren are accumulating around us. At this time we had ten dissenting ministers of different kinds constantly labouring in Calcutta, (since increased to more than twenty,) their presses are at work, their legs, their lungs, all are engaged in the great and good cause.

Of the importance of Calcutta as a missionary field of labour, a very interesting letter from the missionary now stationed there, was published in the March number of the 'Missionary Record,' for 1843. The present standing of the mission and its varied depart-

* Note,—See Appendix.

ments of labour are well described in late communications published by the Society in the April and May numbers, to which the reader is referred.

Surely we may hope that great things are in store for India. We cannot think of what God has done already, without carrying the thought forward to the future. Who can think of the noble army of martyrs now in heaven, and their labours of love on earth, and not rejoice in the thought that this is only as the dropping before the shower, or the first-fruits of a glorious harvest. The names of Middleton, Heber, Turner, Wilson, and Corrie as bishops; and Brown, Buchanan, Martyn, Fisher; together with those now in the field, warrant the hope that greater things are in reserve for our Indian Empire.

As the Indian sojourner passes along the banks of the dark-flowing Ganges, whose waters as they roll their course towards the vast ocean, wash one line of provinces immersed in superstition, and cities wholly given to idolatry, and whose stream from its source in the great mountains to its junction with the mighty deep, is one testimony to the demoralized condition of the land through which it runs; it is something to be able to pause at one place, and to say, 'Here those holy men of God prayed,' and to another and say, there they preached, &c. And to know that a few are humbly and unostentatiously treading in their foot-steps. Blessed be God!

The Rev. Mr. Deer was removed from Burdwan, to Culna, after the arrival of the Rev. Mr. Perowne, and afterwards to Nuddiya, *Krishn Nagar*. The result of his labours are too well known to the Christian public to need any minute detail,—a mere reference to the Church Missionary Society's publications may suffice.

The principal people from among whom this almost unexampled success has arisen, are a sect among the thousand sects of Hindoos, bearing the name *Kurta Buja*, i.e. worshipper of the Creator, as distinguishing them from idolators. The sect was founded by the famous Jai Nairain Ghosal, founder of the far and long reputed English School at Benares, by whom also it was endowed. They have spread over various parts of Bengal, and are supposed to amount in all to about 100,000. They do not generally make themselves known, as they are abhorred by the orthodox Hindoos on account of their anti-Hindoo sentiments. Other accounts have been given of the origin of this sect, as the following:—'They are derived from the sect of the Dervesh amongst the Mahommedans, but have adopted in addition some articles of faith resembling the Christian. They worship only one God, have nothing to do with idols, and believe that God will come into the world in a human form.' Mr. Deer thinks they are of recent origin. I do not at all agree with the opinion of their being of Mahommedan origin; they seem to have, on the contrary, the strongest marks of Hindoo origin.

In July last the whole district was divided into five, each of which was placed under European missionaries. There are more than 100 villages in the whole district in which there are baptized converts, in some a greater, in some a less number.

There are about 500 families already brought into the Christian fold, numbering 2000 souls or more. Besides these, there are nearly 3000 inquirers under Christian instruction. There are in all six missionaries, five catechists, and twenty-three readers. Sixteen mud-built chapels, one pukkah-built; (i.e. of solid masonry) but it is sufficient in reference to this important and interesting sphere of labour, to refer to the testimonies of the Bishop and Archdeacon of Calcutta, together with that of the Rev. Mr. Weitbrecht, upon which latter, the writer of this sketch places the most unhesitating confidence, as also that of the Rev. Mr. Innes, secretary to the corresponding committee.*

* See Society's Report for 1840—1842, and Missionary Record for May 1842.

It is with deep grief of heart that I pass over the space of 500 miles—to describe the station next occupied by the Church Missionary Society.

THE BENARES MISSION.

Benares is a city of great renown, and perhaps better known in England by name, at least, than any other part of North India. It is the Oxford of the East. The city is seen to best advantage from the river. Its streets are so narrow, that a good jumper might go over the whole city from parapet to parapet. The houses are lofty; some of them six stories high, but they are not grand. It is a place of immense trade. It manufactures silks and brocades, &c. very showy and very expensive. According to Hindoo belief, or rather credulity, the city was once paved of gold, but for the sins of the people it has degenerated into stone. Though scarcely above a mile in diameter, it is said to contain 650,000 inhabitants. It is, in all India's estimation, the most holy city, and it is even said, that if a Christian (the vilest of the vile) die there, he will go to heaven.

As a missionary station, it was first occupied by the Rev. Mr. Morris and Mr. Adlington, successively, schoolmaster, catechist, and ordained missionary, but little is recorded of their labours. Schools were chiefly attended to by these gentlemen, and preaching to the natives was only occasional. Their labours were however, in their measure, doubtless blessed, and were, preparatory to the labours of succeeding missionaries. The schools were scattered over the city, and were decidedly Christian schools as to the nature of the instruction given, and were efficiently superintended. These gentlemen were succeeded by the Rev. Mr. Eteson, who continued there only a short time, and was, after the death of the Rev. Mr. Friend, removed to Chunar. Mr. Eteson's labours were chiefly confined to the superintendence of Jai Nairain school, a particular account of which will hereafter be given in this sketch. The Rev. Mr. Krukerberg followed, but was shortly removed to Burdwan. Thus has this mighty city been trifled with in reference to missionary work. The Rev. Mr. Smith was next appointed to, and still continues at this station. He has been successively assisted by the Rev. Messrs. Knorrp, Leupolt, Schnider, &c.

The mission-premises are situated about a mile and a half south-east of the cantonments at a village called Sigra, near to the native town. The enclosure contains about fifteen bigahs of ground, equal to about five English acres. The situation is very well adapted for the purposes of a mission, being in an airy and healthy place, quiet and retired, removed both from the vicinity of the cantonments, and the noise and bustle of the city, without being inconveniently distant from either.

The compound, or enclosure, surrounded by a wall, contains three larger, and one small Bungalow (house), the former designed for the residence of ordained missionaries, and the smaller for the European schoolmaster. There is, besides, another building, devoted to the use of the Christian orphan boys, who form so interesting a part of the mission, and was, together with the Bungalow, occupied by the Rev. Mr. Leupolt, having been built by local subscriptions, raised for the purpose. Close to the mission compound, separated only by a road, is the school for the native girls' establishment.

In connection with the mission, there is also in the city a large school for native boys, founded by a wealthy native, named Jai Nairain, who left at his death two Bungalows in the cantonments, the rent of which was to be applied to its support, and to the assistance of *poor* native youths during their attendance at it. He bequeathed also a large and commodious building to be used as a school-house and residence. Government liberally added a monthly donation of 250 rupees, and it was placed in the hands, and committed to the management of the Church Missionary Society; Hindoos, Mahomedans, and Christians, are eligible. The English and native languages are taught. In the former, and partially in the latter, geography, astronomy, mathematics, history, &c. &c., are taught. The average daily attendance is 150. The Scriptures are also daily taught. The scriptural knowledge of the pupils especially surprises every one who visits it. In all respects it vies with the General Assembly's school in Calcutta. This department of labour, till lately, devolved wholly on the Rev. Mr. Leupolt.

The Rev. Mr. Smith's time and talents are chiefly devoted to translations and preaching. There are several chapels and other appropriate places for this purpose in various parts of this immense city. At one or other of these places there is preaching twice every day, sometimes from the verandah to the people in the street, and frequently in the inside of the chapels. These places, fitted up in every respect after the manner of similar places of worship in India, present a remarkable spectacle, and what a few years ago would have been considered incredible in this city, so wholly given to idolatry; that they are tolerated, much less frequented, is next to a miracle. The number of these chapels is four.

It is well occasionally to look back, and trace the march of events. But thirty years ago, and a missionary could not, without risk of life, have ventured into Benares. Now "wisdom crieth aloud, and uttereth her voice in the streets, she crieth in the chief place of concourse, in the openings of the gates, in the city she uttereth her words."

The knowledge of salvation through a crucified Redeemer, as revealed in the Gospel, is very extensively, if not generally known, and when we consider the countless thousands that daily come in and go out of this far-famed place of pilgrimage, the metropolis of Hindoo superstition,—who can calculate the moral effect produced by this constant preaching of the cross! "Faith cometh by hearing, and hearing by the Word of God." Add to this, the almost numberless copies of the Scriptures and tracts, that are distributed from time to time, and a wide and vast field is presented to the faith of the missionary, and of those who rejoice to contribute to the support of their labours of love. The chapels are calculated to contain about 150 or 200 persons each, and are generally filled. The congregation gradually collects, first one, two, and three, then more successively till the place is filled. They listen attentively to the words of eternal life; some assent, and others dispute, as occasion and the state of their minds lead them. It is pleasing to remark on these interesting occasions, how 'by manifestation of the truth, the word of God appears to *commend* itself to every man's conscience in the sight of God,' and deeply interesting is it to notice the different effects produced on the hearers, some assenting, some mocking, and others saying, "We will hear thee again of this matter." It is, in fact, the repetition of what is recorded throughout the missionary record of the Apostles, and we might stake the veracity of the Scriptures on the identity of the reception and rejection of the Gospel, as preached in the first and the nineteenth century of the Christian era.

LINES ON VIEWING ONE OF THESE MISSIONARY CHAPELS.

O thou, whose eyes have lighted on this pile,
Built in a place where large and numerous,
The fanes to superstition rise, think not
That this is one more temple vainly reared
To the false gods, whom this dark land adores,
And for their service meant and set apart.
No! here the *living* God is worshipped! here
The King, the Lord of Hosts, holds his high court;
Here peace and mercy to a guilty world,
His messengers proclaim: here in his name,
Publish salvation through a Saviour's blood.
O Reader! art thou one of those who love
And care for Zion, then rejoice that God,
In this benighted place has found a shrine.
And would'st thou hasten that event desir'd

> And long'd for, when this world in all its coasts,
> Shall be one temple to IMMANUEL's praise;
> Pray for the peace of Zion, for who love
> And seek her welfare shall themselves be blest.

The orphan establishment is one of the most prominent features of this mission. Since its establishment, it has been eminently blest of God, accounts of which have for time to time been published in the Society's Record, &c.

Converts, as might be expected in such a place, are few, but they are rare ones. Among them was a man named Ram Rutan, of whose uncommon talent, strength of mind, and devotedness of heart to Christ, from his conversion to his death, I myself, and all who knew him, can testify. He was baptized by the Rev. Mr. Smith, and frequently accompanied him to the bazar and other preaching places; on one occasion to Delhi, which proved to be the last journey in this life. His conduct and conversation on that occasion delighted the heart of Mr. Smith. He was a star of the first magnitude, and bright and brilliant was his course to that world, where they that have instructed others shall shine as the brightness of the firmament, &c. Dan. xii. 3.

Others are following after, though with more feeble step, yet firmly and steadily, and very usefully; and all walk so as more or less to cast the light they have received upon those in the midst of whom they live;—they live in love and fellowship with each other—bear a good report in the city of most, if not of all men; and may be safely said to be outwardly harmless and blameless, the sons of God, without rebuke, in the midst of a crooked and perverse nation. It is impossible to look on their families without seeing that the gospel is "the power of God unto salvation" among all people. And that it produces its blessed effects in domestic as well as in every other department of life—the husbands *love* their wives, and the wives *reverence* their husbands, and they feel themselves and show to others that they are "heirs together of the grace of life, by being called into that one body where there is neither male nor female, but all are one in Christ Jesus."

On a Sunday, divine service is performed at a chapel erected many years ago by Bishop Corrie, on the road-side leading to the cantonment. Here the native Christians assemble together in the name of Him who said,—"Where two or three are gathered together in my name, there am I," &c. and their number is increased by the attendance of Christian drummers and others from the lines. A week-day service is also held at the same place every Thursday evening. The Rev. Mr. Leupolt generally has two full services with the orphan and other children, in the chapel attached to his own house.

Besides the institutions, which are strictly Church of England in their construction and operation, there is at Benares a School-Book and Religious Tract Association, in which all the missionaries are associated. There is also a printing-press in full operation at Mirzapore, connected with, and supported by these institutions, and a weekly paper in the native language is well sustained by the contribution of useful articles and information by the different missionaries, and is sold and circulated principally among the native congregations, and to some extent among the heathen population.

The whole work is advancing under the evident and distinctly marked sanction of the great Head of the Church. God's presence and blessing are so visible that there is no mistaking it, and we are warranted in the hope that as in a spiritual sense, gold dust is every day thus being sown with unsparing hand, the streets of this far-famed city will be changed from stone into gold again, so that in a degree, that description in the Revelation shall be true of it, "And the street of the city was pure gold, as it were transparent glass." *

In passing along the Ganges upwards, from Benares and Chunar, the next important station of the com-

* See further interesting accounts in the numbers of the Church Missionary Record for March, April, and May.

pany, and celebrated for Hindoo superstition, is the city of Allahabad. There is a Baptist missionary here, and also one or two American missionaries, but no grand attack has ever been made upon the strong-holds of idolatry by which millions of inhabitants are enslaved. The Church Missionary and Propagation Societies have wholly overlooked it, though next to Benares in importance. The Rev. Mr. Crawford, formerly chaplain at the station, established a school, and daily preached in the native language, while residing there, and the Rev. Mr. Bowley of Chunar, for many years has visited it on its annual festivals, when thousands of pilgrims throng the city and its environs.

Cawnpore is the next large civil and military station. It has generally three or four European and native regiments in cantonments, except when required for active service. Here the Propagation Society has one missionary. Schools have been established, a Christian Translation Society formed, and a few books and tracts have been translated and put into circulation, &c.*

* *Christian Translation Society for Upper India*, in connection with the Society for Promoting Christian Knowledge, instituted at Cawnpore, Feb. 4, 1837. President—the Right Rev. the Lord Bishop of Calcutta. Board—Major General Oglander, William Mair, Esq. C. S. the Rev. R. P. Brooke, B.A. (Ex-off.) the Rev. M. J. Jennings, M.A. [Ex.off.] the Rev. J. J. Carshore, A. B. Treasurer—James Wemyss, Esq. C.S. Secretary and Superintendent of Translations—The Rev. J. J. Carshore. A.B. Corresponding Secretary of Calcutta—The Rev. J. T. Pratt, M. A. Corresponding Secretary at Lucknow—Capt. James Paton.

Report—The season for the publication of a report of their proceedings, and the exhibition of a statement of their receipts and disbursements having arrived, the board of Management of the 'Christian Translation Society for Upper India,' in connection with the 'Society for Promoting Christian Knowledge,' feel pleasure in presenting the same to the Donors and Subscribers to the Society.

The works which have been undertaken and completed by the Society's translators, are Persian, Oordoo, Sanscrit, and Hindooee Versions of Bishop Porteus's 'Summary of the Principal Evidences for the truth and divine origin of the Christian Revelation,' and an Oordoo translation of the 'Sinner's Friend:' and those which are being prepared, are Oordoo, Sanscrit, and Hindooee Versions of the 'Concise History of our Lord Jesus Christ,' and an Oordoo Translation of

But there is no preaching missionary to the heathen population; zealous chaplains have at times done what they could in superintending and otherwise contributing to the support of schools, &c. and perhaps more than any other station aided the Church Missionary funds without receiving aught in return. Among the schools there is an infant and an orphan establishment,* under the management of a Committee.

Bishop Taylor's 'Moral Demonstration, or a Conjugation of Probabilities proving that the religion of Jesus Christ is from God.' After the completion of the works in hand, the board intend to have that portion of Archdeacon Paley's Evidences, in which the authenticity of the historical books of the New Testament is proved, and Bishop Wilson's 'Knowledge and Practice of Christianity,' rendered into the Persian, Oordoo and Hindooee languages.

* *Cawnpore Native Female Orphan Asylum.* We have seen the First Report of this Institution, and have been much interested by its details. It gives us sincere pleasure to witness every endeavour made to ameliorate the condition of the Female Natives of this country, to raise them to their proper level in the scale of intelligent beings, and to see them above all delivered from their spiritual bondage, and included in the blessed number of those "whom the truth makes free." We wish that all success may attend the efforts of the Committee in their present undertaking, and that it may receive the blessing of Him, "in whom there is neither Jew nor Greek, there is neither bond nor free, there is neither male nor female."

The Report informs us that 'On the 10th of July 1834, a Committee of Ladies assembled at Cawnpore, to consider how the proceeds of a contemplated fancy sale might be most charitably appropriated. The perishing state of a number of children rendered orphans by a grievous famine then prevailing in the provinces west of the Jumna, most forcibly arrested their notice, and awakened their sympathy. They resolved therefore, to devote the proceeds of the sale to the relief of these little sufferers; and to render their charitable intentions permanent, they resolved also to put forth the plan of an asylum, and to appeal to a generous public for support before they commenced an experiment which involved so much responsibility. The answer to their appeal was most noble, exceeding their most sanguine hopes; and accordingly about the 20th of October, a mistress was provided, and the doors of the asylum thrown open for the reception of the children. In the original plan it was proposed to lodge the children for the present in the Rev. Edward White's compound, and they are now there: when however funds and ground for a site are obtained, the proposed scheme of raising a suitable building will be carried into execution.'

All the children are orphans, and with the exception of one, are natives of Bundlekund. Several of them were rescued from the most atrocious barbarity.

Meerut has already been noticed as having had two catechists employed by the chaplain, the Rev. H. Fisher, whose name is so intimately associated with those of

From the opening of the Asylum in October 1834 till June 1835, sixty-four children were admitted; of these, two ran away under the influence of fear immediately after their admission. One was deaf and dumb, another a helpless little cripple,—both these died. Five others have also been carried off by diseases supposed to have been introduced into their constitution by their former nauseous and unwholesome fare. Several of them were rescued from the most miserable state of slavery, and bore marks of horrible barbarity on their persons—the nose of one having been cut off, and the use of her limbs almost taken away by long confinement. In short, the existence of the Institution for the space of only nine months, has brought to light cases of the most dreadful cruelty, and such as could never have been conceived by Europeans as existing so near their own doors.

As to the mode of instruction adopted by the Committee, their chief object has been to induce the minds of the children to habits of reflection, and to store them with what is most useful. The Pestalozzian method has been adopted as far as it has been found practicable.

A great portion of the time of the children is devoted to various useful descriptions of needle-work, knitting, making bread, &c. After all expences have been paid, a balance will be found in favour of the institution, of Sonat Rupees 8,932 : 7 : 2, of which the sum of Sonat Rupees 7,144 : 4 : 5, is lodged in government securities, and the remainder is in the hands of the Treasurer for current expenses. With this balance, the proposed buildings for the reception of the children are to be erected as soon as a judicious plan has been formed; and as scarcely a month passes without adding new members to the institution, the average number of admissions having been nine per month, it will be necessary to commence operations speedily.

The greater part of the children are precluded at present, either by their short residence in the asylum, or by their extreme youth, from affording material assistance for their own support, but it is hoped that ere long the proceeds of their work will contribute considerably to the funds of the institution.

We subjoin the concluding words of the Report—

'The Committee having fulfilled their duty in laying before the friends of the institution these particulars, now close their report by offering to the Almighty disposer of events their tribute of gratitude, that they have been selected as instruments for the relief of so much distress and misery. Next to God, they would also express their thankfulness to the generous patrons of the Institution for having listened to their appeal, and having come forward so liberally to raise the structure of Christian benevolence. The little that has transpired of heathen wretchedness and profligacy in connection with the few children who have come into their hands at present, assures them how much remains behind the screen as yet unexplored; and they feel convinced never was a plan proposed capable of rendering

Brown, Corrie, and Martyn, but has not till lately had an ordained missionary. It was in 1815 that this gentleman first arrived as military chaplain to this station, and soon acquiring the spoken language, he was enabled to assist and superintend the Catechists, and otherwise administer to the heathen by whom he was surrounded. His ministrations were eminently blessed of God, and a congregation of natives was, ere long, gathered together, to which Mr. F. regularly ministered, assisted by the Catechists.

At the close of 1826, this gentleman wrote to friends in Calcutta,—'Our missionary establishment this year affords not much to communicate. My own more immediate personal occupations are extensive and laborious. The church, the hospital, and other occasional duties, entirely engage the chaplain's time, in a place like this, and a faithful labourer would be a blessing. Behadur

more benefit to human beings than that of an Asylum under Christian management in a heathen country. To body and soul is the benefit conveyed. The body is saved from misery and wretchedness in this world, and the soul has the means afforded of being made wise unto salvation by the knowledge of a Saviour! The effects already produced on the children are very great. They came into the school poor little helpless persecuted children, the victims, many of them, of horrid barbarity, and their souls blighted under a moral pestilence, and exhibiting no trace of truth, honesty, or the fear of God, for how should they fear Him of whom they were ignorant, and whose name they had only learned to swear by? Now, although the time of their residence in the Asylum has been so short, how great the contrast! The poor little persecuted child looks happy and contented, the helplessness of misery in its appearance is gone. The mind, which was a wilderness, is now being trained into a garden, the soul, which was the seat of corruption, is being purified by the introduction of pure principles and motives of action; and though it would be too much to attribute to the Asylum the working of changes in morals beyond what is reasonable and according to the ordinary course of things, yet by the grace of God, its work had not been in vain in this respect, and the Committee can thankfully contemplate the cessation of the evil practices of lying, swearing, stealing, among the children, with the belief that it is in the heart that the change has commenced. The Committee feel assured that it is only necessary for the public to make themselves acquainted with these interesting facts by personal experience and observation, when all existing prejudices will vanish like a cloud before the force of truth.'

Massih (catechist) as usual, resides on my compound. I think him sincere, faithful, and diligent. He still acts as my clerk among my native flock, and instructs the catechumens. One of these men is in a very interesting state, and I hope ere long to have it in my power to communicate his story, when his name shall be enrolled among the other converts. The converted naick, (corporal) Matthew Prabu Din, is still with us, he is a steady, pious, and consistent Christian. The young professor, Jacob Jai-phul, has absented himself, and we know nothing of him. Munif too is said to have returned to his brother, and of course to his former profession, (Mahommedanism) though I have no particulars.'

Anund Musseeh was the other catechist. The history of his early conversion to Christianity, and subsequent exemplary life, are well known to the readers of the Church Missionary Society's publications. Mr. Fisher writes on this occasion,—

"On a visit of Anund to Delhi, he heard that a number of strangers from several villages of the west were assembled together, nobody knew why, near the imperial city, and were busily employed in friendly conversation, and in reading some books in their possession, which had induced them to renounce their caste, to bind themselves to love and associate with one another, and to lead a strict and holy life. He instantly set off to their place of rendezvous, and found about 500 people, men, women, and children, seated under the shade of the trees, and employed in reading and conversation. On accosting an aged man among them, the following conversation passed :—

"'Who are all this people, and whence come they?' 'We are poor, and lowly, and we read and love this book.' 'What is that book?' 'The book of God.' 'Let me look at it?'

"It was the Gospel. Many copies were possessed by the party, some were printed and others written by themselves from the printed copies. Anund pointed to the name of Jesus, and asked, 'Who is that?' 'That is God. He gave us this book.' 'Where did you obtain it?' 'An angel from heaven gave it to us at Hardwar fair.' 'An angel!' 'Yes, to us he was God's angel: but he was a man, a learned pundit.' 'These books,' said Anund, 'contain the religion of the European *sahibs*, (gentry.) It is their book, and they printed it in our language for our use.' 'No, no,' replied the aged man, 'that cannot be, for they eat flesh.' 'Jesus Christ,' said Anund, 'teaches that it does not signify what a man eats and drinks. Eating is nothing in God's sight. "Every creature of God is good," &c. "Not that which proceedeth out of the mouth," &c. The kingdom of God is not in meat," &c. 'That is true, but how can it be the Europeans' book, when we believe that it is God's gift to us.' 'He sent it to us at Hardwar.' 'No! God sent it long ago to the Sahibs, and they have translated it and given it to us.'

'These Testaments were circulated at *Hardwar*, by Mr. Chamberlain, a Baptist missionary, five or six years before, and fell into the hands of several persons residing in different, but neighbouring villages. A public reader seems to have been selected in each of them; great interest was excited; they determined to separate from the rest of the Hindoos, and to establish themselves a distinct sect; and as their numbers daily and rapidly increased, the idea was at last suggested of convoking a public meeting of all their congenial associates, to ascertain how many accepted this new doctrine. The large grove of trees near *Delhi*, seemed a convenient spot; and this interesting group was assembled for this very purpose when *Anund's* visit took place. He afterwards revisited them at their respective villages, and his instructions were most gratefully received.'

The naick before alluded to was the first convert to Christianity from among the soldiery of India.

The following account of him is from Mr. Fisher's own hand, and has never I believe been published in England.

A BRIEF AND SUMMARY NARRATIVE OF THE CONVERSION OF MATTHEW PRABU DIN NAICK.

1837.

MY DEAR FRIEND,

There is nothing in my humble opinion more remarkable than the present tone of public feeling in India upon the subject of evangelizing the Natives of the land, when compared with what I well remember it to have been two and three and twenty years ago. On my first arrival in this country, I was astonished, as I believe all strangers usually are under similar circumstances, to behold the reality, the living demonstration before my eyes, of the degraded state to which ignorance and superstition can and do reduce the human mind and morals. Most of us indeed have read awful, heart-rending, accounts of the state of the unevangelized portions of the world, and perhaps we have with some difficulty persuaded ourselves to believe them; imagining that such accounts must be partial and exaggerated. But when such men as Dr. Claudius Buchanan and Henry Martyn published their testimony to what their eyes had seen and their ears had heard—(most minutely and eloquently described by the former of these two distinguished characters in his Christian researches)—it was impossible to withhold our implicit credence. I did myself believe! I read and inquired into many interesting particulars, and 'the Groans of India'* induced in my heart corresponding feelings of pity! I was deeply impressed. The melancholy records came over my soul with affecting power. It was as if I had "lifted up mine eyes to behold" the dark visions of Ezekiel unfolding the abominations which were so provoking to the Lord, or (as the angel said unto the prophet,) "*greater* abominations than these" in the chambers of imagery, and which brought down at last

* The *Groans of India.* I allude to a small Tract published, I believe, by the late Rev. Mr. Thomason, and which I read in England.

the execution of the curse of God on apostate Jerusalem. People at home would hardly believe what we may see, almost every day, at our very doors, "every form of creeping things and of abominable beasts and all the idols (of the house of Israel) pourtrayed upon the walls round about"—"the places wherein the nations which we possess, serve their Gods under every green tree." It so happened in the providence of God that Buchanan himself was frequently one of my home congregation, and I was therefore privileged to see much of him, and hear affecting confirmation of the authenticity of the accounts published by him from his own lips. I readily believed in such authority, and yielded to the anxiety, which our frequent conversations induced, to visit this land of darkness, and to lend a helping hand (God enabling me so to do) to rescue from spiritual bondage and death these unhappy people. And now after visiting and settling in the land, I am able to speak that I have known, and testify that which I have seen.

Amongst the wonderful things which, on my arrival, first challenged my observation and amazement, I cannot forbear to mention *one* which I certainly was quite unprepared to behold. Of course I saw quite enough of the cruelty and the blood.* "The dark places of the earth are full of the habitations of cruelty," and I heard more than enough of the abominations, and the filth, and the disgusting habits of the people; but I was not prepared to hear of educated and polished Christian gentlemen manifesting the most perfect indifference to the scenes around them, nay, even adverse to all attempts to bring about a change; and, apparently

* Soon after my arrival, there happened to be one of the Hindoo processions marching through the streets of Calcutta. A Devotee was at their head, crowned with garlands of flowers, with an iron spike thrust through his tongue, and an iron rod sharpened to a point, with which the poor wretch had pierced the fleshy part of his arm, and as he danced along, he kept sawing the iron backwards and forwards, the blood spouting from the wound profusely. I did not follow the crowd, but doubtless he must have soon fainted or probably died.

intimidated themselves, actually striving to intimidate others from all interference with the degrading system which prevailed. And yet so it was. There was either this unaccountable indifference and apathy in beholding the whole scene, or there was the ominous warning, 'You had better not *meddle with the prejudices of the natives;*' and if you cannot join in the cry, "Great is Diana of the Ephesians," at least be silent! or you 'will be called in question for the uproar,' that your interference will excite. There was evidently a feeling prevailing even on the minds of some of the enlightened rulers in the land, that a more dangerous means for alienating the affections of the people, could scarcely be imagined, or one more likely to shake the stability of our rule, than to attempt to interfere with their religion, however wisely it might be done. A man, therefore, will be considered an enemy to Cæsar who shall dare to think or act for himself in this matter. So beware! I thank God heartily that those days are gone by, and, we trust, never to return. The childish and unreasonable apprehensions which were once allowed to enfeeble and nearly paralyse every effort to do good are now at rest. It is no longer considered perilous, and the dark forebodings are scarcely of any weight. We now may go fearlessly forward and proclaim our Eternal King, and yet not implicate our characters as enemies to the powers that be. We no longer apprehend, to use the strong language of Buchanan, 'that the poor infatuated wretches who come to lay their bones within the precincts of Juggernaut, will mutiny and take away our dominion. The consequence is far more likely to be, that the blessing of Him that was ready to perish, will rest upon us.' I believe that nearly all candid and liberal men are now convinced that they might as successfully attempt to restrain the flow of some mighty river to the ocean, or to arrest the spreading beams of the rising sun in the diffusion of day-light, as to stop the progress of evangelical truth through the world. The leaven has begun to work. The healing waters have begun to flow, already " are the waters risen, waters to swim in, a river that cannot be passed over." (Ezek. xlvii). Who shall say to the sun, " stand thou still'—who shall say to the sea, " hitherto only shall they come, and here shall thy proud waves be stayed."

I offer these few remarks in order to introduce to your notice and that of your readers a narrative of some interest, from the peculiar circumstances attending it, and which is not, I believe, very generally known, as I think it ought to be. At the time of its occurrence (now above seventeen years ago) there were still found some few alarmists who anticipated that rebellion, and civil war, and misery, were likely to follow forthwith all efforts to convert the people; and when a *high caste* Sepahee had embraced the Christian faith, the consequent discomfiture of our armies and the overthrow of the British power in India, were prophetically foretold, as the sure consequences of so 'singular and unprecedented a circumstance.' The following narrative will illustrate the nature of these apprehensions, and I should hope will also tend to show how visionary and unfounded they are.

'In the month of December 1819, I was much surprised by the receipt of a letter, of which the following is an extract, from the Bishop of Calcutta, Dr. Middleton:

'Rev. and Dear Sir,

'You are, by this time, probably aware, that some measure of public attention has been drawn to the subject of the conversion of a Brahmin, belonging to one of the regiments quartered at your station. It may be of importance that I should be fully acquainted with the particulars, and I cannot so properly apply to any one in such a case as to yourself. I shall therefore be glad to receive your statement as early as you can conveniently send it to me, &c.

'I am, Rev. & dear Sir,
'Yours very faithfully,
T. F. Calcutta.'

'*29th Nov.* 1819.'

'A few days after the receipt of this letter, which I acknowledge, surprised me not a little, as I had never (previous to the Bishop's letter) heard a syllable upon the subject, I received through the Brigade Major (1st) a copy of a letter which had been written to Colonel Nicol (then the Adjutant General), in order that the same should be reported to the Marquis of Hastings, as Commander-in-Chief, and also (2d) copy of the orders which were issued in consequence of the Major's report, to the following effect :—

No. 1.

To the Adjutant General of the Army.

'May I request you will do me the honour to report to his excellency the Commander in Chief, a most singular and unprecedented circumstance that has lately occurred in the corps under my command, viz. the conversion of a Naick named Prabhu Din Pundah, from the Hindoo to the Christian religion. He was baptized by the Rev. Mr. F——, on the evening of the 20th, and that without my privity or consent. As the 1st battalion of the 25th regiment N. I. is composed chiefly of the highest caste of Brahmins, this event has filled them with the greatest consternation; and in its consequences may prove injurious to the corps, particularly in its recruiting department, the prejudices of the natives being such, that men of high caste will be averse to enter it, under a supposition that means were to be employed to convert them. The Naick Prabhu Din Pundah, was a high caste Brahmin, and much esteemed in the corps until the late event.

'I have the honour, &c.

'M. B. *Comg.* 1*st Bat.* 25*th N. I.*'

With the above was received No. 2.

To the Adjutant General of the Army.

'SIR,—I am directed by the most noble the Governor General in Council to acknowledge the receipt of your letter of the 12th instant, transmitting a copy of a letter from, &c., respecting the conversion of Prabhu Din, a high caste Brahmin and Naick in that corps, to the Christian religion, and his baptism by the Rev. Mr. F——, a regular military chaplain on this establishment, without any previous information having been afforded to the battalion.

'2. With reference to the feeling of consternation which Major B—— describes to have been created by this occurrence among the men under his command, and to the very dangerous consequences which might be experienced were this procedure of Mr. F——'s supposed to be coupled with the official duties of the situation to which he has been appointed by government, his lordship in council is disposed to view the matter in the most serious light, and feels extremely anxious to be satisfied in regard to the means which have been used to induce the individual in question to embrace the Christian faith.

'3. In order that all the circumstances of the case may be brought fully to the knowledge of the government, the Governor General in Council has desired me to request that His Excellency the Commander in Chief will cause a special committee to be convened at Meerut to investigate and report most fully upon all the circumstances referred to in Major B——'s letter, which may tend to throw light either upon the origin or progress of the conversion of Prabhu Din Pundah to Christianity.

'4. His lordship in council considers it also necessary that the committee should be particularly instructed to enquire and report whether any and what measures have been adopted in that cantonment, which may in any way be considered to interfere with the religious prejudices of the native soldiery, in view to their conversion by the employment of native or other emissaries, in frequenting the lines of corps, or residing for such purposes within the limits of the military cantonments.

'5. In conclusion I am instructed to request that his

excellency the Commander in Chief will direct the removal of Naick Pradhu Din Pundah from the 1st battalion of the 25th N. I. causing a promotion to be made in his room, his pay and allowances to be drawn for by the Brigade Major at M——, where he is to remain until the pleasure of government, after the proceedings of the committee, now ordered, shall be made known on this singular and unprecedented case.

'I am, &c.

'W. C.

(True copy.) *Sec. to Gov. Mil. Dept.*

The following is my reply to the bishop :—

'My Lord,—Having had the honour to receive your lordship's communication respecting the conversion and subsequent baptism of Matthew Prabhu Din, Naick, in the 25th regiment N. I., I beg leave, in cheerful compliance with your lordship's request for full information upon the subject, to state the following particulars :— Could I however have imagined it possible that Major B. had written so intemperate a record of this open transaction, I must have felt it an incumbent duty to address your lordship long ago, but as that gentleman assured me, in reply to a note of mine, written in consequence of your lordship's letter—thus 'he had merely "related the fact" in compliance with what he felt to be his duty,' and gave me no intimation of his having proffered any alarming prophetic conjectures of his own, I could not anticipate consequences of an unpleasant nature, and therefore did not think it necessary to trouble you upon the subject.

'I believe your lordship is already fully aware, that since my residence at M—, I have had abundant occasion to observe a strong spirit of enquiry prevalent amongst many of the natives as to the nature of the Christian religion. Unsolicited, and I may say, wholly unsought on my part (as my time was fully occupied by my large European flock) numbers both of Mahomedans and Hindoos frequently visit my house for the purpose of begging, if they cannot afford to purchase, our Scriptures in the native languages; or to enquire into the meaning of the different passages which awaken their curiosity or excite their feelings. The interesting result has been a certain degree of intimacy between us, and, in some instances, the ultimate conversion, baptism and consistent Christian deportment of those who have joined themselves to our Church. One of these men, whose uprightness and abilities qualify him for the office, is employed by me to conduct this little Church under my own eye and direction, which he does with zeal and considerable talent. His name is Anund Musseeh.* During his absence on occasional missionary labour amongst the Saadhs (to whom he is particularly acceptable) my Moonshee Mooneef,† who is also one of our Christian congregation, takes his place.

'Part of the daily occupations of this little party of native converts is to read the Scriptures in their own apartments, which is an old convenient upper room over one of the gateways of the city of M——. Of course this room is free of access to every voluntary visitor. Their congregation of hearers varies much in numerical strength, sometimes six or seven, old and young men, at other times twice the number. Among the occasional visitors at this place, the soldier in question frequently made his appearance, and ultimately requested to be introduced to me. His visits to me, in consequence, were very frequent, and the decided change of his opinions, and, I trust, of his heart, marked and satisfactory. I found he had been long labouring under deep conviction of the worthlessness and wickedness of his heathen

* Lately ordained a Church Missionary by the present Lord Bishop.

† Mooneef was baptised by Mr. Corrie. I grieve to say that some years after this he awfully apostatized. Yet he was a man of *apparently* great heart-experience as well as head knowledge, if an opinion could have been grounded upon his remarkable capability to talk well and scripturally. But "wine and strong drink" were his ruin. He was one of the *innumerable* instances I have met with of the *almost* hopeless professions of penitence. Mooneef died miserably, soon after his leaving me, a *drunkard*.

ignorance and idolatry, even for nine years. He kept these thoughts much to himself, preferring to wait " the convenient opportunity," but the convictions of his heart became stronger and stronger until he went with his regiment to the Isle of France. There he used to watch for opportunities to steal into the Christian Church, and comfort himself by thinking to worship the Christian's God in spirit, though ignorant of the meaning of the language, or of the terms of devotion which were in use, and could only comfort his sorrowful heart with the conscious reflection that '*the Christian's God* knew his heart.' He earnestly longed to meet with some one who should be competent to instruct him what he must do to be saved. Yet many depressing fears of consequences, both of a temporal and spiritual nature, frequently discouraged him. At last, he made up his mind, that if ever opportunity should offer itself to speak to a Christian clergyman, he would unfold the state of his soul, let the consequences be what they might. He gave a very affecting account of his state of mind during the remainder of his stay at the Mauritius, and in his voyage back to Calcutta. A furlough being granted to the soldiers who had distinguished themselves, *Pradu Din* went to his native village, and after spending a little time with his relations there, he was not contented merely to display the medal upon his breast, but unfolded his whole mind and his fixed resolution to embrace Christianity. At first they endeavoured to dissuade him, but finding him immoveable, desisted, and parted from him with *many* tears. His mother exclaiming, as he left her, 'You have changed your faith and lost your caste, and say you have found the true God. Beware, you *never change again!*' He rejoined his regiment at Cawnpore, which happened almost immediately to be moved to the station of M——. His first inquiry was, 'Who is the chaplain, and does he teach my brethren?' He was told of the little upper chamber where the native Christians met together, and went to see them. 'I felt at once,' said he, 'when I saw the nature of their employment, and heard their words, I said, *Jesus Christ has heard my prayer! God's mercy has brought me here.*' His frequent visits were soon observed by the Brahmins of his corps, and when they became apprised of his intention to become a Christian, they manifested extreme sorrow to him, and strove to convince him of what they thought his folly, and by kind remonstrances to shake his purpose. They enlarged on the perilous consequences which would surely follow, the irremediable loss of his high and honourable caste, the rejection of all intercourse in future with his numerous and dear friends, *the certain displeasure of the Government*, who would assuredly disgrace and dismiss him for becoming a Christian; thus that he would lose everything dear to him in life, and finally life itself, for who would give him *khana peena*.* His reply was uniformly the same: 'Jesus Christ will be my friend, He is the friend of all who trust him, and as to caste, there is none so high as the Christian caste. It is more honourable than all, for Christians are the people of the true God, He is their *Father*. My becoming a Christian cannot make me a bad soldier, and I see no reason to believe that Government will cast me off any more than any other of the non-commissioned officers, for instance the serjeant-major, or the quarter-master serjeant, or the drummers, all of whom are Christians: and why should they punish me unless I commit some fault?'

The Brahmins now finding him so resolved, tried to shake his stedfastness by the offer of money, and proposed to subscribe and settle upon him a monthly sum of twenty rupees for his life. This he instantly rejected, saying, that he believed Jesus Christ would provide for him much better than they could, and with this advantage, that it would be *for ever*. Finding him resolute, they endeavoured to vilify his character, represented him to be a drunkard and a glutton, nay, at last, insisted upon

* Maintenance.

it that he was insane. Some of these scandals appear to have been believed by some of his superiors, for a regimental court of inquiry was instituted into his conduct; the result of which however was, that the most satisfactory evidence was brought forward, not only that he had always conducted himself remarkably well, but that he was a particularly smart, intelligent, and active soldier.

'He was baptized by me at his own request (which I beg your Lordship will have the goodness particularly to observe) on the 10th of October, just before his departure on some regimental duty, and there was an end of the matter. The Brahmin soldiers ceased to trouble him, and the only symptom of "consternation," which the Major in the plenitude of his zeal so pathetically laments, is that the Naick cooks and eats his meals by himself, barred from admission within the magic circle by which the Brahmin surrounds his Choola. In every other immaterial respect he remains just as he was before, to use the military phrase, "a steady soldier and a good man." The only mark upon him is that he reads his Bible, and prays to the one eternal God, through Jesus Christ his Saviour.

'I trust this plain unvarnished statement to your Lordship will place the matter in its proper light, and be a sufficient proof that the intemperate and irritating representation which it has been thought proper to transmit for the information of Government, was not warranted by the circumstances of the case, if only it had been properly understood.

'I have the honour to be, &c.'

To this letter I received a brief reply from the Bishop, thanking me for my prompt compliance with his wish. 'I have read your narrative,' said he, 'with intense interest, and think it exceedingly affecting. You must however prepare yourself for the official inquiry which will be instituted, but I cannot see that you can have any thing to apprehend from this faithful and prudent discharge of your duty as an ordained minister of God, or as a chaplain upon the establishment,' &c.

A Court of Inquiry was called at Meerut on the 6th of January, 1820, in obedience to the orders of government, and the following contains the copy of the proceedings as recorded by the President:—

'Proceedings of a special Court of Inquiry, held by order of Sir G. Martindell, commanding the 2nd division of the field army, to inquire into all the circumstances attending the conversion of Prabhu Din Naick, of the 1st battalion 25th regiment, to the Christian faith.

'*President.*—Captain S. Arden, 1st battalion, 27th regiment.

'*Members.*—Captain H. D. Showers, Major of the Brigade; Captain W. Reding, 1st battalion, 27th regiment.

'Prabhu Din being called into court is desired to state what were his motives for embracing the Christian faith, to which he replies:

'I frequently observed the conduct of Christians. In various particulars, their superiority and strictness of behaviour and love of truth were visible, and it induced me to inquire into their religion, and believing it to be true, I embraced it.

'Q. How long is it since you made your first inquiries into the Christian faith?

'A. About nine years since, when I went as a volunteer to the Isle of France. My attention was particularly attracted by the regular observance of the Sabbath, and by seeing the Europeans going to church to worship. I from thence determined to make diligent inquiry when I could. But neither on my return to Calcutta or afterwards at Cawnpore did I find what I thought a convenient opportunity, or leisure, for I had heavy duty to do; so it is only since I came to Meerut that I have had leisure or means of information.

'Q. When you arrived at Meerut did you yourself first make inquiries, or did any body come to you in the lines?

'A. I made my own inquiries myself from these two men now standing here, and who live near the Sudder Bazar. (Mooneef, Mr. F.'s Moonshee, and Bahadur Musseeh, a native convert baptized by Mr. F.)

'Q. Did you go to Mr. F. of your own accord, or did Mr. F. send for you?

'A. I went of my own accord to Mr. F.'s house. Indeed I went to every body of whom I thought it wise to inquire.

'Q. Did you know or did you ever hear of any person visiting your lines to instruct any of the Sipahees in the Christian faith?

'A. Never! I neither knew nor ever heard of such a thing.

'Q. How were you received after your baptism by your corps and company?

'A. They said nothing to me upon the subject, I did not receive any unkind treatment from any of them except one Sipahee of the left Grenadiers, who was always an enemy of mine. He reviled me, and frequently said I was become a sweeper. I quietly remonstrated with him. I felt angry, and so I left him.

'Q. Did ever any of the Sipahees offer you any money not to become a Christian?

'A. Yes. Two of the men called after me and said, We suppose it is money that you want, and if so, we will give it you, provided you will not become a Christian. I replied, My mind is resolute, I shall not change. I am determined to seek God, the only true God, in whose sight rupees are nothing.

'Q. How much did they offer you?

'A. Twenty rupees a month for my life.

'Q. Indeed! how could you refuse that offer?

'A. (Accompanying his reply with a very expressive look and action indicative of contempt) '*Rupeia muttee hain,*' * *I wanted the salvation of my soul, which money will not buy.*

* Gold is sordid dust.

'Q. In your daily intercourse with the men, after baptism, did they ever show you any ill will?

'A. No! none at all.

'Q. By the Court to Major B——. Did you ever know of any emissaries coming into the lines of your Regiment with the design or attempt to convert any of the men to the Christian Faith?

'A. No, never. If there had been any I certainly should have been informed of it.

'Q. To Prabu Din—Did you ever hear if any soldier in your corps, commissioned officer, non-commissioned or private assert, that now you were become a Christian Brahmin, recruits would not come to enlist?

'A. No, I never heard any such words.

'Q. Proposed to Major B. by Mr. F——. Will Major B—— have the goodness to inform the Court in what way the 'consternation' which he described having been evinced, (in his letter to the Adjutant General) betrayed itself after the baptism of Prabu Din.

'A. By Major B——. The men seemed to be dissatisfied with the Naick's conversion. They exceedingly *wished that it had not taken place,* for he was a man of very high caste, and much respected in the corps. Major B—— does not know of any improprieties in the man's conduct since his baptism, but the Major would rather offer to the Court this summary statement (presenting it) of his information first received of the proceedings in the affair in consequence. This statement was accordingly received, entered in the proceedings of the Court, and the original, according to standing orders, forwarded with them to Head Quarters.

'STATEMENT.—On the 21st of October, I received a note from Lieut. S——, the Adjutant of the Corps, intimating that there were rumours in the lines, of a Naick in the 2nd Grenadiers, named Prabu Din, having been baptized, but as the Naick was on the Judge of Circuit's guard, he could not ascertain the fact, and requesting to know if the circumstance had been reported to me. I replied that his note was the first intimation which I had received upon the subject, and requested that he would be particular in his inquiries and let me know the result. He called on me in the evening, and said that he had not a doubt, but that the Naick had been converted. Upon this I wrote to Captain Showers, the Brigade Major, on the subject, who called on me the following morning, and said, that the Naick had been baptized on the 20th, by the Rev. Mr. F——.

'Shortly after this the Adjutant called for orders, and then stated to me that the men of the corps appeared very much dissatisfied at the Naick's conduct. I therefore thought it advisable to order such of the native officers as were Hindoos, as also Lieutenant Smith, the interpreter, to attend me at the Adjutant's quarters at ten o'clock the following morning, when their apparent consternation at the conversion of the Naick, induced me to add the second paragraph in my letter to the Adjutant General of the army, respecting this singular occurrence.

Signed 'M. B.
'*Comg. 1st Bat. 27th Reg.*

'The proceedings of the Court here closed.

Signed 'S. ARDEN, Capt.
'*President.*

'For the result of this inquiry I somewhat anxiously waited, expecting that Prabu Din would be of course restored to his forfeited rank and situation in his corps, but it was deemed advisable to abide by the directions already given respecting him, and he has remained at Meerut ever since, living on his pay. Better than all, he continues to live consistently with his profession, a sincere and faithful Christian believer.

'When Sir Edward Paget was Commander in Chief, and was passing on his tour of inspection through Meerut, I stated in conversation all the above particulars to him. He expressed a most lively interest in the situation and circumstances of such a man, and authorized Colonel Nicol to propose to Matthew Prabhu

Din to appoint him to a higher rank in some one or other of the local corps. Matthew expressed himself very grateful for such condescension, but said with great emotion, although respectfully, I cannot accept this ; I have done nothing that should involve dismissal from my own corps, in which I am now a degraded man. Send me back to my regiment, and I shall have the disgrace washed out, and I will thankfully go back. As this request however could not be complied with (though I know not why) Matthew remained on his pension pay. I ought not to withhold one circumstance, which I think highly creditable to his character. At the commencement of the Burmese war, Matthew Prabhu Din requested me to communicate to Major General Sir Thomas Reynell his wish to be allowed to volunteer and join any of the native corps that were going on the service. 'I have long eaten their salt, said he, and men are wanted, I am ready!' Sir Thomas highly appreciated his military feeling, and admired the man. He is a fine tall athletic soldier, and his spirit is of a noble order, but it seems there were some insurmountable difficulties in the way, and he was courteously told it could not be. I am not acquainted with the reasons.

'Some few years too after these events his old corps marched through Meerut. The non-commissioned officers and men of his company came to visit Matthew and greeted him with *much cordiality* and kindness. Many of them exclaimed, 'Why don't you come back to us, what harm have we done? Our officers, the Saheb log, are Christians. Our Serjeant Major and Quarter Master Serjeant are Christians. The drummers also are Christians, why cannot you remain?' What could he reply? 'It is the Company's will and pleasure.'

'I believe this feeling now widely prevails, for I have learned from authority which I cannot doubt, that many Sipahees have expressed their conviction that however our British law of toleration warrants the free exercise of his own faith to the Mahommedan or to the Hindoo, yet that in embracing Christianity, the doom of Matthew Prabhu Din most inevitably awaits them. They would be dismissed from their regiment as unfit to be employed, and disqualified for any association with their equals and for the confidence of their superiors. The Rev. Anund Mussih assured me that several Sipahees had expressly told him, 'We are heartily disposed to embrace the truth, but these *consequences* are too painful for us to endure.'

'Surely however we may venture to indulge the hope that such consequences will *not* follow,—but that we may yet live to see the day, when a similar reply may be made respecting the *Christian* Sipahees, as once was given to the late Gen. H—— respecting the pious soldiers of H. M.'s 14th Foot. 'What sort of fellows are these,' said the General to the officer who then commanded them, 'for whom the chaplain is pleading to build them a private reading-room—he calls them "*his men?*"' 'The best men,' said the Major, 'in the whole regiment. I only wish they were all "his men."' 'Then,' exclaimed the General, 'they shall have their room.'

'H. F.'

The Rev. R. Richards now labours perseveringly at this station. The congregation assembling at the mission chapel built by the late Begum Samru,* consists of

* In 1833 the *Begum Samru*, now well known in England, made the munificent bequest of 150,000 rupees in trust to the Bishop and Archdeacon of Calcutta, for missionary and charitable purposes. The money was invested in Government paper for the purposes specified. Some discussion arose as to the most desirable mode of employing the interest so as best to meet the wishes of the donor, it being deemed necessary that the trust should not be left vague and uncertain as to its object. The preparation and employment of Christian missionaries suggested itself as the most desirable course, and in the correspondence which ensued it was finally determined that the interest of one lac of rupees should be appropriated to this direct object, and fifty thousand in other works of charity amongst prisoners and debtors.

150 persons, of whom 50 are communicants. Mr. Richards writes on the present state of the native mind in reference to Christianity. 'I have obtained so much favour in the eyes of the natives of Meerut, that they now invite me to their most private apartments, and willingly listen, with their wives, to the preaching of the word of God. There is indeed a wonderful change in this respect, &c.' And again, subsequently, 'I am happy to say that the people hear the word without disputing, and often come to the chapel during divine service, listening with much attention; they likewise begin to testify respect for the Christians, and on the other hand exhibit coldness towards their Brahmins, all which circumstances are of an encouraging character.

AGRA is another scene of missionary labour, already mentioned in connection with Bishop Corrie and Abdul Messeh. No missionary was placed here, notwithstanding the happy commencement of Bishop Corrie's labours, until the year 1837, when the Rev. J. J. Moore, was appointed by the Church Missionary Society's corresponding committee, to proceed thither to endeavour to restore that which had been lost, and to strengthen that which might remain, but was ready to die; and to extend the knowledge of the Redeemer throughout that immense, and now more than ever before, important field of labour. Agra having become a seat of government for the upper provinces, to which, therefore, persons from all parts would be called on business with the board.

The following is an extract from a letter written by the late Bishop Corrie, when living at Agra as chaplain: To provide for some sincere souls, who have not otherwise the means of subsistence, we have taken forty bigahs of ground, &c. Three Faquers, among others, are now employed to keep and dress it, no small proof of their sincerity.

'Last week a Byragi came, who resided twelve years in a jungle, surrounded part of the time with fire, expecting his god (deota) would appear to him. He is a sensible man, and appears to be sincere. Do not suspect, I beg you, that your letters can possibly give me trouble, I receive pleasure and profit from them, and pray that my soul may be kept alive to the success of the gospel. We must not only sow the seed, but harrow it in by prayer to Him who alone can give an increase. I am thirsting for missionary news, to refresh my spirit, drooping, alas, in the midst of scenes which should kindle to missionary exertion! O how does familiarity with the vices of the heathen weaken the feeling of their enormity!'

What a savour of a true minister of Christ has this holy man left behind him; and what a bright example to successors. Wherever Corrie lived, there his very name is as ointment poured forth; and every one who came after him could not but feel in some measure its influence.

In the year 1831, Dr. Parish having been appointed to the chaplaincy, established, together with other influential persons, what was designated, the 'Agra Relief Society.' Each successive year, its operations and its funds increased. In the years 1838, and 9, the time of the great famine—this society was found to be foremost in affording an asylum to the poor half-starved wandering destitutes out of the duab, &c. The effects of the famine were not sensibly felt till the month of September, for while in August, only 105 beggars had been relieved, the number in September amounted to 18,814. From that period the numbers daily increased. In December the total number of persons relieved, was upwards of 20,000; in January, 31,210; from this period, the influx was beyond all calculation; the numbers who crowded to the established alms-houses daily amounted to upwards of 2000.

The Rev. Mr. Chambers was at this time the military chaplain, and the Rev. J. J. Moore, missionary. Subscriptions were solicited from other stations, and sermons preached, &c. to enable the Society if possible to meet the existing distress ; and when this means failed to be sufficient, the application was successfully made to the government. The Bishop and his clergy in Calcutta were also written to, begging their assistance. The manner in which these appeals were met, both by the government and private individuals, reflect honour on the Christian name and British rule in India. Within a few weeks in Calcutta alone, one lack, and one thousand rupees, were subscribed and collected, and forwarded to the scene of misery and death, and every station throughout the province, nobly responded to the pressing and urgent call. Among the various means of relief, an hospital was established, which together with other relief-institutions were under the direction of a Committee. The general superintendence was given by the Rev. Mr. Moore, and especially that of the hospital, in which thousands* died and were buried in masses within and without its precincts.

During the time of this unexampled distress, an orphan refuge was established, into which all who were willing were received. Their parents having died, they were of course houseless and homeless, and in every way destitute. The Church Missionary Society were applied to after a time by the Committee, to undertake the responsibility of the charge, and to supply the necessary superintendence, &c. the Committee promising to use all possible effort to procure subscriptions for its support. To this they readily acceded, and 200 boys and 150 girls were retained at Agra, and the surplus distributed among various other stations. The institution at Agra was placed under the Catechist, David Batavia, who took a lively interest at once in this new sphere of missionary labour, and heartily devoted himself to the various department of occupation.

The Report of the Orphan Asylum in 1840, is too interesting to be omitted here.

* Nearly twenty thousand.

'REPORT OF THE AGRA ORPHAN INSTITUTION, 1840.

'The time having arrived, in which it seems desirable, that the friends and supporters of the Agra Orphan Institution should be made acquainted with its existing condition and resources, as well as with the measures that have been adopted and are in progress, to insure greater efficiency of management, and under the Divine blessing, a fair prospect of success; the Committee have now the pleasure of presenting a statement of their labours from the origin of the Institution to the present period.

'It is necessary to state that during the calamitous famine of 1837-8, the maintenance of upwards of 500 destitute male and female orphan children, devolved upon the benevolence of the public, through its organ the Agra Relief Society. Of these one hundred and fifty were sent to benevolent institutions at other stations, and the remainder continued to be supported by that Society, until the close of its operations; when the orphans, with a portion of the surplus funds, were transferred to a committee of management, composed of gentlemen of the station. All further responsibility rested upon them, and it became a subject of earnest solicitude, to provide for the future support of these destitute children, and, at the same time, to bring them up as useful members of the community.

'Accordingly through the liberality of Government, at the recommendation of the Commissioner, Mr. Hamilton, who has evinced himself a warm friend to the Institution, a spacious building near Akhbar's tomb at Secundra, was obtained for their accommodation, and one hundred bigahs of land were rented from a Zemindar, with the view of instructing them in agriculture, and of eventually locating them on this ground.

'It was also considered advisable that they should be taught in addition some useful trade, so that during those seasons of the year, when little field occupation is pursued, they might be profitably employed in handicrafts;

besides, as agriculture may not be practicable to all, it was judged desirable that they should be possessed of other resources and means for earning a livelihood.

'It is necessary to state these premises, in order to show the ultimate intentions of the Committee, which are, to render these helpless remnants of the famine, useful members of society; which they conceive will be best attained, in the first place, by having them trained on Christian principles; and at the same time by instructing them in agricultural and mechanical labour, and affording them that measure of general education which may be suited to the humble sphere for which they are intended.

'It is perhaps desirable here to state distinctly, that the Institution is strictly a Christian Institution. The education afforded is based on religion, and the children have already been admitted into the Christian Church by baptism. Some were baptized by the Rev. F. Wybrow, when on a visit to Agra—the remainder by the resident missionary, the Rev. Mr. Moore.

'With the views of the Committee for his guidance, Mr. Moore, at their request, undertook the temporary superintendence of the male department, in order to organize a system of instruction, and to provide the necessary machinery for the efficient working out of the Committee's plans, so as to insure a rational hope of success.

'The Committee are happy to state, that considering the difficulties usually attending all such undertakings, and the short period since the establishment of the Institution, experience has proved their measures to be as feasible as the objects are in themselves praiseworthy.

'There are at present in the male branch of the establishment 155 children, and in the female 140.

'The various trades and occupations pursued by the boys are as noted below.* One half of the day is devoted to the acquisition of the rudiments of learning in

* 1 Dyer, 2 Carpet-makers, 3 Sutringie-makers, 4 Shoe-makers, 5 Tailors, 6 Carpenters, 7 Weavers, 8 Blacksmiths, 9 Bhiesties, 10 Shepherds, 11 Gardeners.

the vernacular dialects. Some, however, of the more intelligent, in addition to these studies, are instructed in English; and it is the intention of the Committee to afford those a superior education, in order to qualify them to become eventually teachers and instructors among their countrymen. Considering their age, and the time they have been under instruction, many can read with tolerable fluency, and in general, discover great aptitude for learning.

'To give variety to the young mind, as well as not to burthen the teachers with a large number of scholars at the same time; those children that read in the morning, work in the afternoon, and *vice versâ,* so that both branches of the establishment are constantly employed. This arrangement insures a greater efficiency of supervision; and it has this great and decided advantage, that learning ceases to be considered irksome by the children, nor is the young mind wearied and eventually stunted, by being the whole day employed in study.

'The female department which owes its origin to the benevolence of the ladies of the Station, is at present under the kind superintendence of the lady of the Rev. Mr. Hœrnle; and although it is not to be expected that it should exhibit the same variety of occupation as that of the male branch, yet rescued as these children have been from misery and infamy, they cannot but possess a peculiar interest.

'As the male orphans are brought up in the hope of being useful and Christian members of the native community, so the female orphans are trained with the view of being hereafter suitable wives for native Christians; our primary object therefore, is to rear them in the nurture and admonition of the Lord, and accustom them to habits of industry. They are taught fancy needle work, and spend a portion of the day in acquiring the rudiments of learning; many can already read Hindui and Urdu, and have attained to some skill in needle work. They spin cotton and wool, the latter is transferred to the orphan boys' work-shops, where it is manufactured into carpets. They make their own clothes, grind their own corn, dress their own food, and perform the other domestic offices for themselves.

'The total expenditure during the last seven months for the maintenance of the male department alone, amounted to 2120 rupees 11 as. 8 pie. or a monthly average of about 302 rupees—ranging from 1 rupee 14 annas to 2 rupees each child. This includes food, clothing, medical charges, and instruction, with other incidental expenses.

'The work-shop establishment though at present expensive, will eventually be scarcely an item of expenditure, as the value of the work done will meet the actual cost for instruction; indeed, as the children advance in skill at their respective trades, it is naturally to be expected, that there will always be an increasing surplus for the benefit of the institution.

'The cost of establishment amounts to 853 rupees, 11 as. 8 pie—the value of work done, to 495 rupees, 11as. 10 pie. But this is not a fair criterion of the earnings of the orphans; for owing to the recent formation of the institution and its removal to Secundra, the labour of the boys has been available in sundry repairs requisite, and in the various departments of the workshop, so that a considerable saving has thus been effected. Independent of these, the purchase of tools, instruments, &c. for the different departments of work, constituted at first a heavy item of expenditure.

'The expenses of the female department for the same period, amount to 2298 rupees, 12 as. 8 pie, or a monthly average of expenditure of about 328 rupees,—which will exhibit the cost for the maintenance of each child to be about 2 rupees 6 as. per mensem. This includes—besides food, clothing, and medical charges—the salary of the school-mistress, as well as other incidental items of expense.

'Since the establishment of the asylum, four girls have been married out of the institution. Two to youths educated in the male department, and two to native Christians—who are at present located at Secundra.

'The Committee are happy to be able to state that since the removal of the institution to Secundra, there has been little or no mortality, and the general health of the children has greatly improved. Numbers have been transferred from the Relief Asylum during the famine, in a state of inanition and exhaustion that can scarcely be described. Of these, a large proportion died; and those who survived, did not fully regain their health and strength till months after; added to this, small-pox and ophthalmia raged among the children; and indeed, for nearly the first year and a half, the Orphan Asylum might be considered merely an hospital of diseased and famished children, and little could be done in the way of instruction or organizing any settled system.

'Mr. Moore having, agreeably to the request of the Committee, carried their plans into effect, and organized a system of instruction, intimated his intention of resuming his ministerial duties in the city, and requested to be relieved from the labour of constant and daily superintendence. The Committee accordingly were necessitated to seek for a successor, and were happy in being able to avail themselves of the services of Mr. J. G. Driberg; who had already, under the Rev. Mr. Moore rendered valuable assistance to the institution, and who was perfectly conversant wiḥh the details of management, and with Mr. M.'s various plans, &c.

'It remains to be stated that the institution has hitherto been mainly supported by the surplus famine funds, and that the balance at present in hand amounts only to 2700 rupees; whereas the monthly expenditure for 300 children, with superintendent's salary, &c. exceeds 700 rupees.

'This simple statement, the Committee conceive, will be sufficient to call forth the active benevolence of all friends to the orphan throughout India, and more especially the North Western Provinces.

'The Committee have confined themselves to a brief outline of facts. To any one interested in the progress of the institution and the system at work, a visit to Secundra would, they are persuaded, if practicable, prove highly gratifying. They who are precluded the animating pleasure of seeing with their own eyes these numerous orphans rescued from starvation and misery, and now overflowing with health and happiness, as in the best conducted boarding-schools in England, will however believe our assurances, and have their liveliest feelings of compassion excited. A much deeper interest must be raised for them, when we view them as drawn out of heathen darkness and vice, and likely by the blessing of God, to prove holy Christians themselves; whilst they may be the effectual means of diffusing the blessedness of genuine and healthy Christianity among their countrymen.

'Some security for their continuing to be attended to, may be derived from their being under the control of the Local Missionary Association, which in fact constitutes the Committee of Management, and is immediately connected with the Church Missionary Society.'

The misssion is at present occupied by the Reverends the missionaries Kearnley, Pfander, Kreiss, assisted by catechists and schoolmasters, &c. The mission compound in the heart of the city comprises a church, two mission-houses, and the widows' almshouses. There are also schools in the city and surrounding villages. At the close of last year there were 122 orphan girls, and about 160 boys.*

The Rev. *Amund Massih* also labours in connection with this mission, principally in itinerating excursions in the neighbourhood. An interesting account of his conversion, &c., may hereafter be published in a separate volume, which it is proposed to publish, of eminent converts from Hindoo and Mahomedanism.

GARUKHPORE is another of the Church Missionary

* See Missionary Record for May, 1842.

stations. It is situated about 500 miles N.W. of Calcutta, and about 160 miles N.E. of Benares. It was first occupied by the society in 1823. Its present establishment comprises a church, parsonage, and seminary at Garukhpore, and a native Christian colony, about three miles from the station, on the borders of a forest nearly twenty-four miles deep, and girting the station on the north of the river Raptee, and to a considerable distance south. At this settlement there is also a church, called 'the Church in the Wilderness,' and an orphan asylum. The Reverends J. P. Menge and Charles Wendnagel, from whom recent accounts have been received, are at present the Society's missionaries. An account of its origin and progress may be seen in the publications of the Church Missionary Society.

The last station taken up by the Church Missionary Society is, AGRA-PARAH. This mission arose out of the Orphan Refuge established by Mrs. Wilson. This mission, being of modern origin, is so well known to the public as to render any detailed account unnecessary. A reference to the Society's publications will supply any information that can be desired.

In closing this sketch, the author begs to signify that should it be favourably received he has much more interesting matter to communicate relative to various Christian establishments, and especially relative to the operations of the Society for the Propagation of the Gospel in Foreign Parts, and the Society for the Promotion of Christian Knowledge. With reference to other bodies of Christians, it is thought sufficient to make a short reference to them as taking an active and zealous part in every good word and work, and in many instances as having been foremost in the field. It has been his privilege to have occasionally met them in conference, and to know sufficient of them and their labours to love them for their works' sake, and to bid them God speed.

SOCIETIES FOR THE PROPAGATION OF THE GOSPEL AND THE PROMOTION OF CHRISTIAN KNOWLEDGE, RESUMED.

Bishop Middleton's arrival in Calcutta infused new life into these two oldest societies connected with the Church of England. Previous to leaving England the bishop attended a meeting of the 'Society for Promoting Christian Knowledge,' which had testified their confidence and esteem by placing at his disposal a credit of £1000 for the promotion of their views and designs in India. His lordship therefore as soon as practicable after his arrival, applied himself to the formation of a diocesan committee. A short account of the Society was printed and circulated by him, and other necessary steps were taken for the establishment of the committee, which was consequently formed in May, 1815, and commenced its proceedings under the best possible auspices. In a letter to Archdeacon Barnes of Bombay his lordship thus notices this auspicious event, 'We have had our primary meeting, our members are already thirty-six, and many more may be expected to drop in. The point at which I aim is to proceed quietly ; by the blessing of Providence the society may become a powerful engine of good.' And subsequently in the same month, 'Here we are proceeding admirably well, we make no parade, and we publish nothing, our immediate objects are European and half-castes ; and we shall avoid everything which can reasonably excite apprehension. On the 1st of June of the same year his report is equally encouraging, 'We are remitting to London £650, two-thirds of which will be returned in books, one-third being the property of the parent society. We have a prodigious field before us. Our true policy is to avoid anything which can alarm the most timid ; I do not mean among the natives, *for nothing that we could do would alarm them.'* *

* On another occasion the Bishop writes, 'They,' the natives, 'certainly display no bigotry, and betray no alarm with regard to the

It was by measures of this prudent unostentatious character that the bishop hoped to give life to the profession of Christianity in India, and he certainly had the gratification of seeing his views seconded to a considerable extent, so that in February 1816, he was able to announce to a correspondent in England, that members of the Society for the Promotion of Christian Knowledge, were then to be found all over India, from Delhi to Cape Comorin.

In 1818 his lordship thought himself fully justified in attempting something for the mental and moral improvement of the natives, experience having shown that it was safe and practicable; in reference to which he writes, 'The Church Missionary Society is labouring in this department, and as I have reason to believe, with good success, and experience upon a pretty large scale has afforded us the information required, and the change of sentiment among our European residents has been at least proportionate. At a time when all classes of Christians among us, and some of the natives themselves, are coming forward in the work of education. I could no longer consider it consistent with the honour of the church in this country, or of our Church Society, to remain passive in a scene of such activity.

'At a numerous meeting, holden for the occasion, it was resolved therefore, That schools be established for the purpose of diffusing useful knowledge among the inhabitants of the territory, subject to the presidency of Bengal, &c.'

With reference to this movement the Rev. Mr. Thomason writes—'To the joy of many, our Bishop has come

diffusion of our religion.' An instance in point to which the Bishop refers, was on occasion of the Establishment of the Hindoo College. The Superintendent, a European, to avoid the appearance of seeking to make converts, tore out or pasted over all passages relating to Christianity contained in the books that had been adopted. Upon which the managers, who were all Hindoos of wealth and consequence, desired him not to do so again; two of the managers avowed that they had read the Bible, and had found nothing in it which could do their children harm.

forward on behalf of the heathen. The public was moved—a school committee formed—a noble fund raised for school purposes,—what could the heart desire more? We are not straitened for means, or for patronage; we want only instruments. As a member of the school-committee I have felt it my duty to rise to the great occasion, and have laid my shoulders to the work, and have for some time past been engaged in studying the Bengalee language, organizing schools, examining classes, looking out for teachers, &c.'

The operations of the Committee in pursuance of these plans, were commenced at a place called *Rassipugli,* where, and in the vicinity of *Kali-Ghant,* four schools were immediately established. A second circle of schools was contemplated for Cassipore, thus comprising two of the most populous districts in the vicinity of Calcutta. They were patronized with surprising liberality; between £1400 and £1500 were contributed towards their support in donations, besides £500 in annual subscriptions.

The Bishop some months after the establishment of these schools, writes—'I am convinced that great changes are taking place. Our schools are giving rise to a great deal of discussion. The people seem very much disposed to send their children, notwithstanding they perceive the tendency of the knowledge acquired to make them Christians. They suppose '*it must be.*'

In 1822, in a letter bearing date the 7th of January, the Bishop writes—

'I have this morning been presiding at a Christian Knowledge Committee, to settle the last year's Report. All very harmonious and comfortable. We are printing the parables, miracles and discourses of our Saviour in three different native characters, 2000 copies of each, 18,000 in the whole! The cost will be 3000 rupees, to be taken out of the Society's fund. I am also printing at the Society's cost "Sellon's Abridgment" in two native characters.'

These were prepared and translated by the late Bishop

Corrie. The translation of 'Sellon's Abridgment' is an elegant specimen of the mixed vernacular dialect of Hindoostan, commonly called Urdu.

SOCIETY FOR THE PROPAGATION OF THE GOSPEL IN FOREIGN PARTS.*

In the middle of September 1818, Bishop Middleton received intelligence of a most animating nature, which amply indemnified him for a long period of anxiety. At the commencement of the year his Grace the Archbishop of Canterbury, as president of the Incorporated Society for the Propagation of the Gospel in Foreign Parts, stated to the Board of that Institution, that time having been now allowed for the due settlement of episcopal authority in India, it appeared to him that the moment had at length arrived when the operations of the Society might be safely and usefully extended in that quarter of the world, and that with the security derived from proper diocesan control, it now became the Society to offer their co-operation with the Lord Bishop of Calcutta in such places as with the concurrence of the constituted authorities for the government of India, his Lordship might be inclined to recommend. In pursuance of this intimation, it was resolved that the sum of £5000 should be immediately placed at the disposal of the Bishop of Calcutta, to be used at his Lordship's discretion, for the furtherance of the objects contemplated by the Society, without the loss of time, which must necessarily be incurred by previous communication with Europe.

This intelligence was as the breath of life to Bishop Middleton. It was this liberal grant, receiving it as a pledge of future support, that confirmed the Bishop in a resolution he had previously formed in his mind, of attempting the foundation of a Mission College at Calcutta. From this period the proposed Institution was

* See Report of the Society for 1819, p. 76.

the central object in all his designs for the advancement of Christianity in the East. The Bishop proposed to the Society that the College should embrace the following objects:—

1. That of instructing native and other Christian youth in the doctrine and discipline of the Church, in order to their becoming preachers, catechists, and schoolmasters.

2. For teaching the elements of useful knowledge and the English language, to Mahommedans or Hindoos, having no objects in such attainments beyond secular advantage.

3. For translating the Scriptures, the liturgy, and moral and religious Tracts.

4. For the reception of missionaries to be sent out by the Society, on their first arrival in India.

This communication reached the Board in London early in May 1819, and was received with the most lively interest. It was made known to the public in general as early as possible, and responded to in liberal contributions by the public. The appeal throughout the kingdom made to congregations from the pulpit, was met by contributions amounting to the heretofore unequalled sum of £50,000. Other religious Societies also munificently aided the work.

At a meeting of the Committee of the Christian Knowledge Society, the sum of £5000 was voted to be placed at the disposal of the Bishop for the proposed establishment. The Church Missionary Society also promptly added a similar donation; and soon after the British and Foreign Bible Society munificently contributed another £5000 towards the expences of translating the Sacred Scriptures into the Asiatic languages, reserving to themselves no control or inspection of the work, and leaving it to be accomplished solely under the auspices of the Bishop, and the supervision of the College.

Application was made to the Vice-Chancellors of Oxford and Cambridge, requesting them to make inquiry for persons properly qualified to fill the several Professorships proposed by the Bishop, and on the terms recommended by his Lordship, namely, 400 sicca rupees per month to the senior Professor, or £600 per annum; and that of his colleague or colleagues 300 sicca rupees each per month, or £450 per annum.

While the Society in England were thus furthering the Bishop's views, his Lordship was engaged in looking out for a suitable spot on which to erect this anticipated Eastern University. Its locality, advantages, &c. are thus stated by the Bishop, in a letter addressed to the Propagation Society, in the November following his proposition.

'I have now the pleasure to acquaint you for the information of the Society, that through the favour and distinguished liberality of his Excellency the Marquis of Hastings, I have obtained from the supreme Government, a piece of land as a site, which in reference to the purpose contemplated, is not surpassed by any other whatever. It will contain I believe about twenty acres. Its distance from Calcutta is hardly three miles, and yet by being on the opposite side of the river, which is much wider than the Thames at Westminster, but without any bridge, the College will afford to the students all the privacy and retirement which can be desired. At the same time it will be a conspicuous object, presenting itself to the notice of our countrymen, on their first approach to this capital. I have every reason to hope that the situation will be found healthy; the College grounds being open to the south, whence the wind blows constantly, from the month of March to September or October. Close adjoining to the westward is the Hon. Company's Botanic Garden, and to its beautiful and shady walks near the river, the Professors will no doubt have free access, with the further advantage in case of sudden illness, of medical aid close at hand, in the superintendent of the garden. Nor is it perhaps to be altogether disregarded in an establishment of this sort, that the scenery is such as to gratify and soothe the mind.'

The Bishop's heart was so fully set upon this noble

object, that he never lost sight of it for a day—all his correspondence breathes an air of holy fervour about it. In his eye it was to be the ark of the Christian cause in India. 'If,' he writes, 'it shall please God only to spare me till the work is complete, and the machine effectually set in motion, I shall seem to have attained my *euthanasia. At this moment I would not exchange my duties for those of any individual in my profession.* The college alone is quite sufficient to engage much higher powers than I can boast of, and to reward much greater exertions than I can make. My mind in truth cannot contemplate any thing greater or more worthy of a Bishop of the Church of England, than the foundation and organization of such an Institution.' To another correspondent—'The college is a project which has been in my mind for the last three years, and is all that I can contribute towards an *university* near this capital, and with the blessing of God, (to which I seem to myself to ascribe more and more the longer I live,) it may bid fair to be the foundation of what in future ages may become the University of Calcutta. Can you forgive the feelings of a founder if I tell you that the other day, as I listened to the woodman's axe employed in clearing the ground, I actually began to muse upon what might hereafter be the studies and the glories of the place.'

In December 1820, all the preparatory measures for the building were fully matured. The whole plan and arrangement of the intended edifice were the work of the Bishop himself. The style adopted was the pure, ancient, collegiate Gothic. The building was to occupy three sides of a quadrangle, each 150 feet in length. It was to comprise within itself all the usual requisites of a college; a hall—a chapel—and a library; together with additional advantages of a press. It was to present its open front to the river; the chapel and hall forming the centre, the houses of the principal and professors, the lecture-rooms and the apartments for students, being distributed along the wings.

Of the College, designed to stand on this favoured spot, it was the Bishop's wish that the Society for the Propagation of the Gospel in Foreign Parts should become the proprietors. The Bishop of Calcutta, for the time being, was to become the visitor. Its title was to be 'Bishop's Mission College.' It was founded originally for a Principal and two Professors, and for as many students as its funds should enable the Society to maintain during the period of study, and to provide for afterwards, in the situations of missionaries, schoolmasters, and catechists, at its various stations. These stations were to be under episcopal jurisdiction in all matters ecclesiastical or spiritual ; and in all other respects were to be responsible to the Bishop in his character of Visitor. As the object of the institution was expressly the propagation of the Gospel, no students were to be admitted who should not propose to devote themselves to that object. Its design was widely and charitably comprehensive, since it embraced all such portions of insular or continental Asia, as should, at any time, be under the protection or authority of Great Britain.

At length, all preliminary difficulties being surmounted, on the 15th of December 1820, the Bishop had the inexpressible delight of laying, with all due and impressive solemnity, the foundation-stone of this noble seminary. That day must have been among the brightest, perhaps the very brightest of his whole existence. He had lived to see the prosperous beginnings of a work, which had cost him many a laborious day, and many a sleepless night, but which had often made his pulse beat high with hope, and had given an excitement to his powers that kept them in vigorous and salutary action.

In the year 1821, in a letter addressed to the Rev. Charles Webb, the Bishop adverts with pleasure to the appointment of Mr. Mill to the office of Principal of the College: 'I am glad,' he says, 'that my principal professor (for the Principal must profess, and even teach), is a Fellow of Trinity, Mr. Mill, a man of great talent, I expect. He, and Mr. Alt, his colleague, of Pembroke, arrived soon after my departure. Mr. Alt is said to be eminent in Hebrew,' &c.

It is not necessary to detail minutely in this sketch the commencement and progress of the institution under the superintendence of the Bishops Middleton, Heber, and Turner, as the records are before the public, and, the writer would hope, familiar to all who feel any interest about the spread of the Gospel. A very important query presents itself to the mind, namely,—How far the objects proposed by the venerable bishop have been realized.

It is deeply to be lamented, that after a vast expenditure of money on buildings, principals, and professors, &c., scarcely anything of good has been accomplished. I say not this acrimoniously, but with the deepest and most heartfelt regret. I loved the institution—I watched its progress with more than common interest, and when it was proposed to have a Church Missionary seminary in Calcutta, I gave my opinion against it, fearing it might look like a rival institution; I loved Bishop's College, and I looked forward to the sending of my own sons *to graduate* there with intense pleasure.

1. But what has it done in instructing native youth, &c. in order to their becoming preachers, catechists, and schoolmasters, during a period of more than twenty years?

2. For the teaching of the elements of useful knowledge and the English language to Mussulmans and Hindoos, &c.

3. For translating the Scriptures, the Liturgy, and moral and religious tracts.

4. For the reception of English missionaries, &c.

Scarcely *anything* has been done in either of these departments. Not a portion of the Scriptures, or of the Liturgy, has been translated by any of the College Establishment, and now, nothing is being done but what had better be left undone. Sure I am, that if sainted spirits can weep, Bishop Middleton is now weeping in heaven over the idol of his heart.

Something, however, has been done in the way of translation, or rather original effort, in the year 1830. Dr. Mill published a work in parts, which he called *Christa Sangita*, or the Sacred History of our Lord Jesus Christ in Sanscrit verse.

The preface to the first edition of the first book, entitled, "Yeshú Utpatti; or, the Origin of Jesus,' commences thus:—

'To give to the historical truths of Christianity a dress borrowed from the metrical legends of the Hindoos, is no novel idea; but the attempt to do this without violating, either in the facts or the spirit of the narrative, the chaste simplicity of scripture, may have greater pretentions to originality. Such is the present undertaking; for which the plain style and easy versification of the standard Sanscrit mythological epics of Vyasa and Valmiki, afford far greater facilities than are presented by the vernacular muses of Southern India, in whose most meretricious forms the same sacred history has been before conveyed, but with singular adulteration, by the genius of the Jesuit Father Beschi.* The style of these mythological poems has been indeed before attempted by Christian imitators for a different purpose,—but one to which from Indian usage, it is equally well adapted, as the celebrated episode of the Mahábhárata, the Bhagavad Gita, may suffice to shew, that of conveying moral or metaphysical instruction in the form of dialogue. The attempt in this manner to restore the great truths of natural religion, which the Brahmanical system has obscured or depraved; to refute by arguments drawn from themselves, the polytheistic and pantheistic systems, to which the vulgar and the sage are severally addicted, is a work strictly

* Of the great Tamil work of this extraordinary author, entitled Tembarani, or The Unfading Garland, recounting the early history of our Lord, some description may be seen in the Preface to Mr. Babington's translation of the adventures of the Gooroo Paramarthan (a work ascribed to the same author,) in Hough's Answer to the Abbe Dubois, and in Hoole's Journey to Southern India.

within the province of a Christian instructor; and, if executed with as much of good faith as of spirit and ability, would have reflected undoubted honour on that celebrated Society from which the project originated. But when, as if to defeat the success of the design with all heathens of knowledge and integrity, we see the names of Narada, Jaimini, and other venerated teachers of Brahmanic theology, introduced as refuting and denouncing it, and the name of the most ancient and sacred of all Hindoo writings, prefixed as the real title of the composition (though the Vedic style is widely different from that of the Puranas in which these pretended Vedas are written) no skill in the execution can screen from censure the authors and abettors of a forgery equally disingenuous and imprudent. The work, of which the part containing the false Yajur-Veda in a loose French translation was printed at Yverdon in 1778, imposed on some even of real sagacity in Europe, where an eagerness to see genuine Vedas had before been strongly expressed by Mosheim and others. But strong suspicions of its genuineness had been excited, even before the discovery of the manuscripts of the original forgery, formerly belonging to the Jesuit's College at Pondicherry, which is the subject of Mr. Ellis's satisfactory dissertation in the fourteenth volume of the Asiatic Researches.

'The poem, of which the first book is here published, is as far from claiming kindred with the Brahmanical assumption of the last-mentioned composition, which it resembles in language, as with the Hindoo embellishments of the former, which it resembles in its subject; but it has in one sense a more decided Indian original than either; its first projector being neither Jesuit nor missionary, but an unconverted Gentile Pundit, Ramachandra Vidyabhushana of Burdwan. The curiosity of this Brahman had been sometime before excited by the perusal of the gospels of St. Matthew and St. John in his own vernacular Bengalee idiom. From this he was led, while at Bishop's College, to conceive the design of making in his own words, a Purana of this history, by a metrical translation of it into the sacred language of his tribe : and conceiving from a version of the Commandments and Creeds which I had sometime before executed in the same style of Sanscrit versification, that I would approve and support his undertaking, he brought the Introductory Canto, which he had composed from St. John's first chapter, with a request that I would assist him to continue it. The perusal of these verses (of which an account will be subjoined hereafter,) the ingenious production of one who yet frankly avowed himself a Hindoo in religion, was calculated to excite more surprise than pleasure, and yet more of hope than of any other feeling. I encouraged him in the strongest manner to persevere in the work he had commenced, though my voyage to England very soon after this time, in August 1828, precluded any active assistance on my part.'

On Dr. Mill's return to India, he fouud that the Pundit had not succeeded in the attempt :

'He evidently needed more to guide him to the spirit of the original narrative, than the versions in his possession supplied ; and I soon found, with his assistance, that some passages of the evangelists were capable, with no more departure from the literal construction, and with far less from their real style and manner, of such adaptation to the genuine Puranic stanza as was satisfactory to himself and other native scholars. From this time, agreeably to his first request, I took the direction of the work, not only in the selection and supply of the materials, but in their Sanscrit rendering also, using in this occasionally the aid of other Pundits beside Ramachandra. The approbation of Bishop Turner and other members of our College Syndicate being obtained to the undertaking, the work was pursued in the second and subsequent cantos on the plan which I will now more fully explain, which in respect of the citation of prophecies, &c. enlarged upon me as the work proceeded.

'The first mentioned canto, which differs from the

rest in being, with two very slight exceptions, the unaided production of Ramachandra; opens with a question of a disciple to a Guru, or religious teacher, respecting the means of deliverance from the universal prevalence of sin. The question delivered in quasi-alcaic undecasyllabic measure entitled Indra-vajra, is answered by the instructor in the ordinary iambic tetrameter of the Puranas. He directs his inquirer to Christ the Son of God, as the only deliverer from the power of sin. The disciple inquiring who is Christ, and how he is thus identified with the eternal deity, is commanded by the Guru to hear the divinely-revealed account of this mystery. Then opening with the declaration, "In the beginning was the word," the sage describes with St. John, but more paraphrastically, the co-eternity and consubstantiality of the Divine Word with the Father, the eternal communication of all divine attributes to this only-begotten Son of God and Light of Light, in full and undivided perfection; his participation in the creation of the universe, as the expressed intelligence, the power, and the wisdom of God. He concludes with stating that he, the true image of the invisible God, "without whom nothing was made, that was made," yet descended to reveal him afresh to his creatures lost by sin; that this Divine Word became Man, that he might re-unite man to God. The actual history of this incarnation and how the true light shone uncomprehended in the darkness of his own world, he now proposes to inform the yet uninstructed disciple. And this announcement of the coming history concludes the singular composition of the Burdwan Pundit, entitled Sabda-Avatra adhyaya, or Canto of the Word's Incarnation, which consists of 22 distichs.

'The history opens in the second canto with the statement that in the reign of Augustus, Emperor of Rome, in a general peace of the world, fifty years from the commencement of the great Indian era of Vicramaditya, the angel Gabriel was commissioned to deliver the message of the incarnation to the blessed Virgin of

Nazareth in Galilee. The events are then told as in the first chapter of St. Luke from ver. 26—45, with no greater deviation from the words of the original than would be required for a prose translation in any Asiatic language.'

The hymn ver. 46—55 is given in another measure, but closely rendered. The third Canto recounts the circumstances of John's nativity. The fourth is entitled 'The Promise to the Fathers,' and is meant to explain the allusions made to the ancient patriarchs, prophets, &c., without some idea of whose history the gospel narrative must often be unintelligible. A sketch is accordingly given of the history of the chosen people of God, from the call of Abraham to the accession of David. The Canto concludes with the promise of God to David, 2 Samuel vii. 8—16, &c. In Canto fifth the disciple asks, 'how the conditional part of the remarkable promise just quoted was answered in the subsequent fortunes of David's offspring,' and is told that the unconditional part of the promise points to Christ, while according to the conditional part, David's royal descendants were punished with loss of empire, &c., for their transgressions. The history of Israel and Judah is then sketched, down to the birth of Christ, and 'a rapid but comprehensive description of the evils of Israel at this time, the alien rule, the extinction of prophecy, the corruption of traditional religion, and consequent depravation of manners, all leading the faithful people to desire earnestly the accomplishment of the long-deferred promises to their fathers, concludes this canto of ninety-two distichs, entitled *David Vansas*, or the stem of David.'

The sixth Canto, entitled *The Birth from a Virgin*, details the particulars connected with the birth of Jesus, and cites the prophecies in Isaiah vii. 14, Micah v. 2, and Isaiah ix. 1—7. The seventh relates the circumcision and presentation of Jesus in the temple, (giving also an explanation of these ordinances) and the homage paid by Simeon and Anna to the infant Lord.

This beginning of the glory which was to mark the second temple, and the interest which ALL NATIONS have in the promised Messiah, are then adverted to. The eighth Canto is entitled '*The rising of the Star to guide the nations*,' and ascends to the origin and fall of man, relating the promise that the seed of the woman would crush the serpent's head. The teacher then tells that this promise formed a ground of faith and obedience to a series of good men,—Noah (the true *Manu*) Melchisedek, Jethro, and Job, and was not utterly lost 'even when the tumultuous waves of error (the Mahá Máyá of Indian Mythology) causing the reflection of innumerable false forms of the one true God, had covered the earth with idolatry and sin.' The ninth Canto records the flight of Jesus with his parents to Egypt, the tenth his return to Judea, and the changes in the rulers of that country. In the eleventh the teacher answers the queries of his pupil about the religious institutions of the Israelites and the Scriptures of the Old Testament, which are detailed with some grounds for crediting 'the integrity of these inspired writings.' The apocryphal books are also mentioned and distinguished from the canonical.

In Canto twelfth, the origin of the Sabbath is deduced from the Mosaic account of the creation, the Jewish festivals are described, and the history which concludes the second chapter of St. Luke respecting the visit of the Saviour to the temple when twelve years old, is related. In the thirteenth, the disciple enquiring whether, as the Jewish Scriptures are held sacred, the Jewish festivals are observed by Christians, is instructed as to the Christian Sabbath, and some of the other festivals of the Christian Church as the annunciation, nativity, Epiphany. The fourteenth and last Canto of the first book consists of a hymn to Christ, consisting of a eulogy of Thin, an ascription of praises to Thin, and a series of prayers of which the description cannot be here extracted.

This first part of the Christa Sangita, entitled Yeshu-

Utpatti,' or the origin of Jesus, was first published in 1831. A second edition has just appeared, somewhat altered, and without the English preface and interesting genealogical and chronological table which accompany the first edition.

Book second of the Christa Sangita, entitled 'Putra-Abhishekas,' or 'The Unction of the Son,' was published in 1834, and 'comprises our Lord's inauguration to his public office, all the acts of his forerunner to the close of his life, and the events of his own early ministry down to a period a little more recent, that of the feeding of the five thousand.' It consists of twenty-three cantos, and differs from the first book (which is chiefly preliminary in its character) in being almost entirely a harmonized narrative taken from the evangelists, whose language, though in verse, it preserves with remarkable closeness.

The third book, entitled 'Sat-pálaka-charitram,' or the 'History of the Good Shepherd,' extends to the last passover, and appears to have been but recently finished. It also consists of twenty-three cantos. The fourth, entitled 'Moktri Máhátmyam,' or the Saviour's magnanimity,' embracing the history of his death and resurrection with their attendant and following circumstances, has not yet reached the writer of this notice.

The above abstract, however meagre, may serve to give an idea of the plan of Dr. Mill's noble and magnificent,—I might perhaps say wonderful,—performance, which every friend to the diffusion of Christianity should use his best endeavours to disseminate widely among the Pundits of Bengal, Hindoostanee, and indeed of all India. I will end with the author's own sentiments as to the probable usefulness of his work, with which he concludes his preface to the first edition of the first book.

'Of the probable utility of the work, those whose interest in its contents may have led them to accompany me thus far in the description, may perhaps expect to hear. A poem of this nature has, if tolerably executed, an access to many of the higher orders of Hindoos, which no tracts or scriptural versions in any of the ordinary spoken languages can, in the present state of feelings and prejudices, possibly attain; while in the greater extent of country over which it is read, (the Sanscrit being studied by the learned in every part of this vast Peninsula,) it has a compensatory advantage for the more limited number of its readers. It may therefore be auxiliary to the vernacular translations, by bespeaking attention to them with some of that influential class, who would otherwise despise and reject them without examination; more particularly by showing, in the compass of one history, and in the genuine Hindoo manner, the coherence of the several parts of our scriptures, in their common reference to the one great subject whom that history describes; and in fixing, by occasional specimens introduced naturally in the course of the narration, a sense of the sacredness and sublimity of their contents, in minds far from insensible (as all who know them truly will bear witness) to the impressions of moral grandeur and beauty. And while exertions of no common zeal and ability are directed to the intellectual improvement of the wealthier of our native fellow-subjects at the capital of this presidency, it may not be unimportant to supply in this manner to a class which includes most of these, and many more than these, in its number,—what is there not only not imparted, but I fear in some instances sedulously excluded,—the knowledge of the one object to which the religious feelings, the deepest seated and most important of all, can be safely and beneficially directed. While some might even seem desirous to eradicate from their minds the few good impressions of the Supreme Power that their wretched system has allowed them to retain, it may not be useless to let him hear through this Hindoo medium, but without compromise or concealment, of that higher truth, which is not merely the rectification of their depraved theism, but the mystery of human recovery 'hidden from ages and generations,' concealed rather than signified in the

Avataras of their distorted tradition,—the knowledge of which among ourselves, with the happy freedom and other blessings resulting from it, constitutes, in the opinion of the best minded among us, the true principle of our mental and moral superiority,—on adherence to which we can alone rest any confident hopes of its permanence.'

'It is difficult to judge of the probable success of this undertaking, by any present appearances. Many Brahmans have expressed a strong desire to read this work: and one heathen Pundit now teaches it to his heathen pupils. In the temple of Calighat, the principal object of religious attraction in the neighbourhood of this city, I have witnessed what I may term its eager reception by a number of priestly devotees from various parts of India, who in those precincts would have rejected even with contumely the gift of any Bengali or Hindoo tract, but who read and chanted this, with a full knowledge of its anti-idolatrous tendency, even close to the shrine of their impure goddess, and on the floor stained with the blood of her hundreds of daily slain victims. No one acquainted with India will rate these facts at more than their real worth, and to those who, in the ignorance of the genius of paganism, might found erroneous conceptions on them, it may be sufficient to recal to mind what is the most melancholy moral trait in the account of this work, the readiness* with which these devotees of superstition can assume the ideas and expressions of a faith most opposed to it. But to such as believe that the only power which can raise India from moral apathy and degeneracy, is that

* 'In no instance have I seen this more strikingly exhibited than in the positive pleasure with which every Brahmin that I have consulted has seen and criticised the Sanscrit imitation which I have placed as the motto of this work: where well known instances of Indian superstition, closely corresponding to those Greeks and Egyptian ones which the excellent father renounces in such unsparing terms of condemnation to his pagan friend Nemesius, are commented upon in precisely the same terms to the Hindoos. So little has moral approval, or a sense of *what is true*, in the objects of religion, to do

of which this work, however imperfectly executed, is the subject,—even these appearances may not be destitute of hope; and such will not refuse their good wishes to an attempt to displace, with any number of readers, or in any degree however inconsiderable, by a pure and holy substitute, the monstrous and demoralizing legends of pagan worship.'

The following passage from a Sermon, preached by Dr. Mill, at the consecration of Bishop's College Chapel, on the 15th of May 1828, pp. 23—25, touches partly on the philosophical Pantheism of the Hindoos :—

'And if such is our feeling generally towards the condition of unconverted Gentilism, that of the country in which Divine Providence has so remarkably placed us, has surely not inferior claims on our interest. No system of paganism indeed ever stood more complete in all the character of St. Paul's description than that of India. Were we required to produce from the history of mankind a system, in which the most sublime truths of natural religion were most successfully perverted, so as to be ineffectual to the mind and conscience of the votary; in which the grand distinction of creature and Creator was most systematically set aside, and that ascription of pure goodness to the latter, that is the only source of all piety, most utterly destroyed, by making evil essential to his very creation: in which all natural

with the Brahminical system, that this passing sympathy with the known disapprobation and scorn with which the unholy foreigner regards the same objects, is no impeachment of the devotee's own allegiance to them. It would be extremely erroneous to infer from that apparent indifference to the object of *faith*, in which the Brahmatic votary so differs from the proselytizing Mahommedan, that he is not equally sensitive with the Mussulman or any other religionist, to every thing in which the religion of his system is involved, the ever-recurring ordinance and perspective rite which is so inseparably interwoven with every habit of his life. This is the case even with the Pundit Ramachandra Vidyabhushan, to whom I owe the first idea of this work: of whom also I may remark, that though sufficiently enlightened to confess freely the moral superiority of the Gospel to the exoteric superstition to which he conforms, he declares with equal frankness, his decided preference of the mystic Theology of the Bhagavad Gita to any thing which he has seen in Christianity.

inducements to real penitence were most subtily removed, while the most entire priestly subjection was maintained; in which the attention of the votary was most studiously diverted from the morality of life to unprofitable ceremonies, or yet more useless and wretched abstractions: and in which (setting aside those particular precepts of conduct which the preservation of order makes necessary) the sense of the true rule of life, and end of being was most thoroughly corrupted, even by religion and law,—and the strongest barriers opposed in every part of its elaborate institute for that purpose to the social spirit of our common nature,—much more to the benevolent equalizing spirit of Christianity;—we could in no place or time find this more entirely or elaborately effected than in the system established here—a system which, whether considered by the side of the superstitious idolatry that occupies the vulgar worshippers, or of the esoteric philosophy engaging the speculative few that aspire to rise above the illusions of worldly existence to essential union with the Divinity, appears in both, to the attentive and impartial observer, most dark and demoralizing; so that it may well excite a doubt whether the gross corruptions of the one, or the deeper spiritual vices (admired as they are and commended to the highest praise of sanctity) in the other, are most fatal to the principle of goodness. The system that embraces both these, and frequently presents both in singular and unlovely combination, retains, to a degree that it is difficult for an European mind even to conceive, firm possession of every habit of thought and action in the interesting people amongst whom we live; its principles rendering them to a degree, rare probably even amongst heathens, insensible to the very existence of objective truth considered as independent of what is taught and prescribed to the several classes of mankind: and thus no less closing their understandings to the evidence of truth, than their hearts to the willing admission of a better virtue. It should seem as if the heathenism of apostolical description, after being banished from every other region known to us by ancient recollection,—banished either by the true faith, or that partial semblance of the true which the Arabian impostor planted, had taken undisturbed position here, and invested its last stronghold with a character of deadly evil proportionate to the greater length of possession.'

The sketch about to be given of Book IV. of the Christa Sangita, may be suitably prefaced by the following extracts, first, from 'A Valedictory Address from the Bishop, Archdeacon, and Clergy* of Calcutta and its neighbourhood' to Dr. Mill on his final departure from India, and secondly from the Address of the Asiatic Society of Bengal to the same learned person on the same occasion :—

'We must be forgiven, however, if we dwell for a moment on that which is attracting the notice of oriental scholars both in Europe and India—your History of the Life of our blessed Saviour in the sacred Sanscrit language of religion and poetry. This most rare and difficult, and indeed unexampled, undertaking, we have many of us had the opportunity of knowing, is sought for with eagerness by the learned Pundits of India—nor do we think any means more likely to pave the way for a calm inquiry into the nature and evidences of the Gospel amongst the learned classes of Hindoos, than a publication which unites, for the first time their own admired poetical style in their own ancient language and consecrated in their Shastras, with the elementary facts and doctrines of the Christian revelation. Had you accomplished nothing else, dearest Sir, in India, besides this remarkable work, you would have placed your name in conjunction with that of the college over which you preside, in the highest rank of oriental benefactors and scholars.' (Address of the Bishop and Clergy, pp. 5, 6.)

'But the most valuable of your literary undertakings

* The names of twenty-one Clergymen are subscribed to it.

is your Sanscrit Poem the Christa Sangita. In that beautiful work the praises of Our Redeemer have been for the first time sung in the sacred language of the Vedas. It is your peculiar boast that you have caused the purest doctrines to flow in the stream of this noble language. To the whole body of the learned Hindoos you have thus rendered accessible the sublimest truths, by conveying them in a channel to which, as their own venerated river, they ascribe the power of purifying all it touches. To a mind like yours this must be an inexhaustible source of gratifying reflection.' (Address of the Asiatic Society of Bengal to the Rev. Dr. Mill. See the Society's Journal, No. 60, for Sept. 1837, p. 800).

The Fourth Book of the Christa Sangita is entitled, 'Moktrimáhátmyaparvva, or the Book of the Redeemer's Glorification, and extends to the length of 1578 slokas. The First Canto is entitled 'Mumùrshudehábhyanjanam, or the Anointing of the body of Him who was about to die.'

The teacher then proceeds with the sacred narrative of our Lord's acts after his arrival at Bethany, and describes the Supper there, and the unction of the Saviour by Mary. The preparatory circumstances to the entry of Christ into Jerusalem are then noticed; and in Canto Second, called 'Sadrájapravesas, or the Entry of the Holy King,' the triumphal and jubilant entrance, and other events, of the Sunday with which the Holy Week began, are narrated. In Canto Third, named 'Sárvvánoayaprárthanálayasodhanam, or the Purification of the House of Prayer for all Nations,' are described the events of the Monday. Canto Fourth is entitled, 'Saddhantrimandaguruparájayas,' or the defeat of the wicked teachers, the murderers of the righteous, and details the events and discourses of the first part of Tuesday preceding the crucifixion, as given in the twenty-first, twenty-second, and twenty-third chapters of St. Matthew, &c. Canto Fifth, bearing the appellation of 'Naraputradvitiyá gamanádesas,' or 'The Announcement of the Second Coming of the Son of Man,' details the sacred history of the latter portion of the holy Tuesday. Matt. xxiv. xxv. The Sixth Canto is called, 'Abhishikta gháta kálaprastutis,' or 'The Preparation of the Time for the Murder of the Anointed,' and contains the events of the Holy Wednesday. The Seventh is entitled, 'Sadbhojanásírvvádas,' or, 'The Benediction of the Holy Food,' and, as its name imports, relates to the institution of the Eucharist, and gives the discourses in the thirteenth and fourteenth chapters of St. John, &c. being the events of the earlier portion of the Holy Thursday. The name of the Eighth Canto is 'Mahámadhyasthacharamopadesas,' or, 'The last Instruction of the Great Mediator,' and is taken from the twenty-sixth chapter of St. Matthew, the fourteenth of St. Mark, the fifteenth, sixteenth, and seventeenth of St. John, comprising the latter events of the Holy Thursday. The Ninth Canto bears the title of 'Udyáníyavyathanam,' or, 'The Agony in the Garden,' and details the events which occurred between the night of Thursday and morning of Friday. The Tenth Canto is called 'Varopalanirákritis,' or 'The Rejection of the Costly Stone.' It contains a narrative of the earliest events of Good Friday. The Eleventh Canto is denominated 'Pàpihasteprabhusamarpanam,' or, 'The Delivering up of the Lord into the hands of sinners,' and comprises the second portion of the history of the Friday. Canto Twelfth is named 'Mahàyajnyasampúranam,' or 'The Consummation of the Great Sacrifice,' and describes ths concluding events of the holy Friday.

'The events immediately following the crucifixion are then described. Canto fourteen is called 'Paramavisrámas,' or 'The excellent Rest,' and comprises the events of the holy Saturday; and Canto fifteenth 'Tamabalapará jayas,' 'The defeat of the power of darkness,' the earlier events of the Sunday of the resurrection. The sixteenth Canto bears the appellation of 'Mrityunjaya pradarsanam,' or 'The manifestation of the victory over death,' and describing the latter transactions of the Sunday. The seventeenth is called 'Sátpratyayaprasansá,' 'The commendation of Holy Faith,' and comprises the events of the eight days following the resurrection, being taken from Mark xvi. and John xx. Canto eighteen is named 'Nityapálakávabhásanam,' or 'The appearance of the Eternal Guardian or Shepherd,' and narrates the events of many days following the week of the resurrection. The nineteenth Canto is called 'Swargárohanam,' or 'The ascension into Heaven,' and details the events of the Holy Thursday and the nine preceding days. Canto twentieth is called 'Sadátmasásitamandaliprabandhas,' or 'The history of the Churches ruled by the Holy Ghost,' and Canto twenty-first, 'Sarvvsaktimanmoktristotram,' or 'A Hymn in honour of the All-powerful Saviour.' The latter is a translation of the Te Deum; the former is a brief sketch of the history of the Christian Church. First the miraculous descent of the Holy Ghost on the day of Pentecost is described,—with its consequences, the power of speaking in foreign tongues unknown before, the discourse of St. Peter, the conversion and baptism of three thousand persons,—the gradual increase of the Church by the power of Him who led captivity captive and dispensed gifts to men, and in spite of human opposition, the martyrdom of Stephen,—the dispersion of the disciples who went every where preaching the word,—the admission of the Gentiles into the Christian fold, the conversion of St. Paul, his enrolment in the apostolical order, his special mission to the Gentiles and journeyings to proclaim the faith, the Nerorian persecution,—the crucifixion of Peter, the death of St. Paul and others,—the preaching of the Gospel by St. Bartholomew in India, (dese Bháratíye) in Malabar, and on the Coromandel coast, &c. (Keraladrávidádyeshu) by St. Thomas, who was killed by the Brahmins,—the death of all the Apostles except St. John, &c. the destruction of Jerusalem and of the Temple and the subversion of the Jewish economy,—the establishment and regulation of the Christian Church by the three orders (ásrama) of her ministers, bishops, priests, and deacons,—(Adhyaksha, Jyeshtha, Paricharin) the death of St. John,—the persecutions of the Church by the Persians and Romans,—the conversion of Constantine,—the apostacy of Julian,—the irruption of the barbarians, and their conversions,—the rise and conquests of Mohammed, with the diffusion of his creed,—the capture of Constantinople by the Mussulmans,—the corruption, declension and punishment of the Church by the loss of her members,—her indestructible character notwithstanding,—the doctrine of Christ and his Apostles handed down by a succession of Bishops,—the Syro-Malabaric and Anglican churches referred to as branches of the Christian Church. The pupil here expresses his desire to be admitted by baptism into this church, which his teacher agrees to do after consulting his bishop. He then details to him in order the sacred books of the New Testament, which he is to study.

'Felix faustumque sit! May many follow the example of this imaginary student, after the same course of instruction!

'No specimens have been given of those portions of the work which are not explanatory but narrative. It may be sufficient to observe that the sacred histories are followed with remarkable closeness; and yet a wonderful fluency, ease and elegance of versification maintained.

'Thus has a noble attempt been made to employ that powerful aud beautiful instrument, the Sanscrit language, for the instruction of the learned Hindoos. But,—though this specimen is not likely to be ever excelled or even equalled,—it ought to be regarded only as a prelude to other works on kindred subjects and in a similar form.'

SOCIETY FOR THE PROPAGATION OF THE GOSPEL.

'The labours of this Society are confined to five stations: viz. the city of Moorshedabad, where a mission has just been commenced, Cawnpore in Upper India, Howrah, Tallygunge, and Barripore, the latter three being situated round about Calcutta, and to the south of it, looking to Bishop's College as a centre. At these stations five missionaries are labouring, assisted by four catechists, twenty native Christian teachers, and twenty heathen schoolmasters, educating twelve hundred heathen children in twenty-one vernacular schools, besides three English schools and three Christian seminaries. Referring to these heathen schools it is said—

'With regard to the general working of Mission schools upon the minds of the heathen youth (a question attended with serious difficulties to many zealous and judicious friends of missionary effort) the Society's missionaries in the immediate neighbourhood of Calcutta afford on the whole a favourable testimony, though they do not appear able to point to any instance of actual benefit having been effected through their instrumentality. To judge from the testimony of some natives themselves, adduced in one of the subjoined Reports, the schools are considered as having a powerful tendency to detach the young from the superstitions and errors of their fathers; though in most cases the desire of obtaining instruction for their children leads the parents to overcome their apprehensions on this score.'

'Boishkotty is the most central of a circle of villages. in which scarcely any but the people employed by the Zumindar, can either read or write. Indeed, in one village named Jeypoor, the only person who could read a little, was a man who had been taught for a few years in our school at Bally; so that when I wished to distribute the Scriptures and tracts, to leave a more permanent impression than I could by verbal explanation, I found none but this man who could at all understand them. The usefulness of schools for the progress of the Gospel in such places as these is evident.

'I have myself more than once been told by the people of that village that they would all send their children if these books were discontinued, and writing and arithmetic taught. And on inquiring what objection they had to the books, they have replied, that there was no immediate danger to apprehend, but that the reading of Christian books seduces the minds of their children, and leads them to forsake the religion of their fathers. The conversion of a native youth named Joygopal Duft (several of whose relations used to attend the school,) his admittance into Bishop's College, and my connexion with that institution, seem also to have alarmed the people. A native newspaper has added to all this, by publishing Bengalee doggrel verses, warning children to abstain from attending missionary schools, or even from loitering in the streets when a missionary passed. Time will, I hope, remove this prejudice.'

The Committee, in consequence of the Parent Society being obliged to contract their annual supply of means, (they having entered into new and necessary engagements in other parts of the world,) and in consequence of the Government having taken up extensively the education of the natives, have given up their large circle of schools at Chinsurah, near to which place (Hooghly) a very popular and extensive college has been opened.

The stations of Howrah, Tallygunge and Barripore, which furnish very useful detailed accounts of chapels, congregations, &c. appear to have twelve places of worship, one of which as well as a school-house had since the issue of the last report been erected at the expense of the Christians, thereby giving a practical proof of the value they set on the change which has come over them. This is gratifying, and it is to be hoped the time will soon come when we shall see many churches erected by the joint endeavours of the native Christians. It will be when they voluntarily come forward and make sacrifices for such purposes that we may expect to find a firm and lasting foundation for Christianity in India.

With regard to the labours of the Rev. the missionaries, we find them saying that in addition to the Sunday ministrations, they have been able to continue their usual pastoral visits during the week, on which occasion prayers are read at the house of some Christian, or the glad tidings of salvation made known to the heathen as opportunity offers, they (the Christians) are further attended by native Christian teachers, whose duties are to instruct the catechumen in catechisms and to read portions of Scripture to them. Two fresh extensions of the mission are recorded, at the extremes of the circle to the north and south of Calcutta, and many families are stated to have abandoned the superstitions of heathenism and to have enrolled themselves in the body of catechumens, where a long trial of sincerity and moral conduct awaits them previous to admission by baptism within the pale of the Church. It appears that since the publication of the last report twelve months ago, one hundred and forty-three individuals have been added to the Church, principally to the south of Calcutta. It will be advantageous and interesting to learn what the missionaries say regarding the conduct of their flocks generally, with which intention we copy extracts. The Rev. D. Jones of Tallygunge says—

'With regard to the general conduct of the baptized, I would say that with a few exceptions they are walking in the faith and fear of God; but with regard to the catechumens, I fear there are numbers who have come forward with motives not strictly pure, and with mistaken notions of Christianity. This we must expect, and not be surprised if we find tares mixed with the wheat. To have a Church unspotted, free from all vices, is next to an impossibility. If in the days of the Apostles, wicked men crept into the Church, (witness the state of the Corinthian Church, and individuals whom we find made mention of in the Acts of the Apostles, and in the Epistles of St. Paul,) how much more now, when we possess not the like gifts they did. So that the ill walk of some of the members of our Christian community, should not dishearten or discourage us in our work, but we should go on "making the crooked ways straight, and the rough paths smooth," with entire dependence on the Almighty, praying that he would bring them under the sanctifying influence of the Holy Ghost, and cause them to act in conformity with the religion they have embraced; and "that they might walk worthy of the Lord unto all well-pleasing, being fruitful in every good work, and increasing in the knowledge of God."'

Report of the Rev. C. E. Driberg of Barripore:

'With reference now to the state of the congregations under my care, I have experienced alternations of sorrow and gladness. How often is ardour damped and hope depressed by witnessing indifference and coldness in those for whose eternal welfare the missionary is so deeply interested. But thanks be to God, these seasons of trial are occasionally cheered by some brighter prospects, affording some token that, although unworthy and insufficient, our labours have not been altogether unacceptable, thereby filling our hearts with joy and gratitude to Him in whose vineyard we are called to labour.'

The following extract will exhibit the means employed with any of the flock who fall away:—

'It is our earnest endeavour to maintain Church Government and Discipline among the members of the Church, but this we find a matter of no small difficulty. It is our custom (as was that of the Primitive Church) in cases of notorious and flagrant crimes to excommunicate, and in slighter offences to make the delinquents stand in a conspicuous place during the whole of the service, partly to put them to open shame, and partly to deter others from the contagion. In some cases this has proved effectual towards exciting that contrition and abhorrence of sin, and dread of its consequences, which it was intended to produce; but, alas, in how many instances has the end been defeated. When the offender finds that his crime has been detected, rather than be openly reproved, he generally goes over to some of the different communities of Christians, in hopes of a reception; while others, though they do not betake themselves to another communion, yet sullenly refuse to attend the means of grace, turning a deaf ear to all our entreaties.'

A VISIT TO THE MISSIONS OF JANGERA AND BARRIPORE.

The Bishop of Calcutta went down to the centre of the mission at Jangera on the 30th of December last. As he was threading the narrow rivulets in the mission canoe, he enquired of the Reverend missionary concerning the state of his flocks. Eighty-six have been baptized, including children, this last year, making the whole number since 1829, three hundred and twenty-seven. The Catechumens under instruction are about seven hundred in twenty different villages. One great discouragement has occurred at Rajahunpore, where forty catechumens have fallen back from attending church and from receiving the missionary's instructions in their village, and had attempted to regain their lost caste among the Hindoos. The Bishop was grieved, but not surprised: such failures and perhaps more lamentable cases must be expected, if a great work is indeed going on. What was the state of the Corinthian and Galatian churches, in the earliest times; and what of the seven Asiatic ones at the close of the first century, the last of the Apostles still living? The offence in this case was taken by a leading person or two in the village, because some little secular advantage in their petty law suits was not granted; this touchstone detected the shallowness of the impression made by the Christian doctrine, and led to the relapse of the forty people who composed the little enquiring flock, of whom not one had been baptized.

The way in which accessions to the mission circle are commonly made, both at Jangera and Barripore, appears to be this. The report of the new religion spreads from one village to others around—the increased diligence and happiness of the Christians are observed—the weekly visits of the missionary are known—the instruction given to children is talked of—the new domestic peace and quiet are noticed—the connection of the religion with the governors of the country is perhaps taken into account—the equal justice dealt out by the Christian magistrate is extolled—the little Christian churches erected in the principal spots are seen—the rest and worship of the Lord's day after every six days labour, together with the prayers, and singing, and preaching, which accompany it, are spoken of.

A few leading persons come over to the nearest church to judge for themselves—no one observes them—they crowd in with the rest—they come a second and third time—they confer with their friends, (the villages are small, twenty families perhaps, and from that to a hundred) if their minds are at all touched and awakened to serious inquiry, they send a message in form to the missionary, to beg him to come and instruct them in the new faith; the misery of their own they know well enough, though not the cause. The Reverend missionary dispatches first a catechist to them—the plan of the Gospel is generally opened—the fallen state of man unfolded—the origin of idolatry traced—the One Living and true God proclaimed—the incarnation of this eternal, self-existent God in the person of his co-equal Son is stated—the true sacrifice of his death explained—the Holy Ghost, the author of grace and spiritual life in the human heart described—the holy morals of Christianity declared—the duty of every human being to turn to this true religion "from idols, to serve the living and true God, and wait for his Son from heaven, whom he raised from the dead, even Jesus, which delivereth from the wrath to come" is plainly urged—and the grace of the Holy Spirit to strengthen their feeble resolutions, and renew and create afresh their hearts, and sustain them against temptation, is exhibited.

The necessary sacrifices are then honestly detailed to them: 'You must renounce caste; you must forsake all idolatry and its attendant festivals and usages; you must live chastely with one wife, and one wife only; you must attend church on the Lord's day; you must welcome the missionary to your villages; you must not expect earthly profit or advantage of any kind, except the blessings, temporal and spiritual, flowing from Christianity itself; you must wait a long, long time under instruction (generally about two years) before you can think of being admitted to holy baptism.' "Choose you," adds the missionary or catechist, "whom you will serve." If they confirm their wish to be received as catechumens, they are welcomed into the verandah of the Christian temple. The missionary observes their regular attendance or otherwise at church; he visits them almost weekly at their houses; he sends them native and if possible European catechists (the missionaries have youths from the college, agreeably to Bishop Middleton's directions, with them) he notices whether they really break off from idolatry, whether they forsake all uncleanness, whether they dread telling lies and cheating, whether they pray in secret, whether they show something of a genuine sorrow for sin, and shame for their past idolatry, whether they behave well to their wives and children, whether they are more diligent and cleanly in their habits, whether they seem really to believe that except they forsake all evil practices and believe in the name of Jesus Christ they cannot be saved—lastly, whether any just complaints are brought against them, either by their brother catechumens or the heathens, of moment.

By these kinds of evidence the missionary judges. After two years or more, he communicates to the Bishop or the Archdeacon the number whom he thinks prepared for baptism. If possible they come down and examine the candidates and assist at their baptism. If not, they request the missionary to act on his own judgment.

The village of Rajahunpore is the first that has failed in a body.* The missionary at Barripore had however a sore trial of another kind. At Andermanie one Christian turned back and drew away five or six with him. He had been baptized by the late missionary, the Rev. Mr. Tweddell, many years since, and had never been a satisfactory character. He was refused some petty secular request very properly. He joined himself to the heathen zemindar of the village, and disputed the purchase of the land on which the church had been built. He collected a mob, and prevented the Christians from attending church. He forcibly assaulted the missionary, who was at first very much distressed; as he did not know how far the defection might have spread. The Bishop wrote to him from Dacca to "comfort him concerning his faith, and that he should not be moved by these afflictions," to which, indeed, we ourselves "know that we are appointed." 1 Thess. iii. 24. He hastened over, on his return to Calcutta. The magistrate had previously composed the tumult, by sending down three or four police officers to protect the missionary and his flock. The thing had died away. The partners in the apostacy had openly confessed their folly, and solicited, with the ringleader, to be re-admitted to the congregation. A long probation in the verandah is appointed them.

In the meantime, this obstruction has "turned out rather to the furtherance of the gospel." The heathen are astonished at the firmness of the missionary and the flocks, they notice the interference of the magistrate, they begin to enquire themselves after the new religion. The missionary has just received a message from an adjoining village of about 106 souls, to come over and

* These, however, are now showing a desire to return to the Christian fold.—Feb. 16.

teach them. The catechist went and was cordially welcomed. Andermanie, the seat of the disturbance, is resuming her sabbaths and sacred assemblies, and is in more than her former peace.

A specimen of the examinations may now be given. The answers were translated by the missionary, and taken down as nearly as possible word for word.

Examination of Catechumens.

Q. 1. Who made the heavens and the earth?—A. God.

2. What else did he make?—Man, and all the living animals, and everything.

3. Can God be seen?—He is like wind, and cannot be seen.

4. Where is he?—Everywhere; no place where he is not.

5. Is idolatry sin?—Yes, because it breaks the second Commandment; it is very wrong, very wicked to make images of God: Hindoos very wrong.

6. Who is Jesus Christ?—You have showed Him to us, He came to save sinners.

7. Whose Son is He?—The Son of God.

8. Are you all sinners?—Yes, from our infancy we were sinners.

9. What is a sinner?—A breaker of God's Commandments.

10. In what state did God make man?—Pure, and holy, and happy.

11. How did he become a sinner?—By eating the forbidden fruit.

12. How is that state now to be altered?—By believing in Jesus Christ.

13. What did Christ do to wash away sin?—He gave His life.

14. Can the Ganges wash from sins?—No.

15. What do they do, who put mud from the Ganges in their aged parents' mouths, and leave them on the bank?—They break the fifth Commandment.

16. Who is the Holy Ghost?—He is God.

17. What is the work of the Holy Ghost?—He sanctifies the heart.
18. What do you mean by sanctifying the heart?—He makes it clean.
19. Is the heart sanctified by nature?—By nature our hearts are corrupt.
20. How are you to obtain the help of the Holy Spirit? —By praying to God for it.
21. What are the fruits of the Spirit?—Love, truth, peace.
22. Are anger and envy fruits?—No.
23. What is Christian marriage?—One man and one woman.
24. What is the man's duty?—He ought to love his wife, and have only one.
25. How does he treat his wife?—He looks upon her as his own flesh, and eats and drinks with her.
26. Why do you desire Baptism?—To receive Eternal Salvation.
27. Who ordained Baptism?—Jesus Christ.
28. In whose name are you to be baptized?—Father, Son, and Holy Ghost.
29. What benefit do you expect from it?—If not baptized, we cannot be of God's elect people.
30. What do you mean by being born of water and of the spirit?—The water is a sign; there is no benefit, but as it is a sign of God.
31. Who gives the grace?—Jesus Christ.
32. How do you expect the grace?—We expect the blessing of the sign as to the water? and the spirit as to the grace—we forsake our sins and obtain a new heart.
33. What blessing do you especially hope for?—We are to hope for God's Holy Spirit in Baptism.
34. What is to become of man after death?—Those who do good will go to heaven; those who do bad, to Hell.
35. What will become of the body after death?—It will be raised again.
36. By what power?—By Jesus Christ.

37. What meanwhile becomes of the spirit?—It goes to God.
38. Is there any hope for the wicked after the judgment is passed?—No hope.
39. By whose power are idolaters to be converted to God?—God's, they must pray for the Spirit.
40. How do men grieve the Spirit?—By doing sin; we must beware of sin.
41. Who are God's people?—Those who believe in Him, love Him, and pray to Him.

Such is a specimen of the answers made by the Catechumens, some of them six, others twelve, others eighteen months under instruction—the questions were classed under certain heads.

I proceed to the class of baptized persons; for them miscellaneous questions were prepared, as follows:—

Q. 1. What will be the effect of believing in Christ?—A. We get salvation. By receiving the Holy Ghost we become good.
2. What do you mean by a sacrifice for sin?—Christ became a sacrifice for sin, He died for sin, He is the true sacrifice.
3. What is the origin of the Hindoo sacrifices?—Nothing to be obtained from them.—They make offerings of goats, which can never take away sins.
4. Why cannot the Hindoo offerings take away sin?—Unless the Saviour gave His life, nothing can take away sin.
5. Is idolatry a sin?—Yes? it is full of obscenity and sin.
6. Who delivered you from idolatry? —The Lord Jesus Christ.
7. Was it done by your own power and wisdom?—No; by the power of the Holy Ghost: we could not of ourselves.
8. Did God show you great mercy thereby?—Yes, great mercy.
9. How are you to shew your thankfulness to God?—By worshipping God with our heart, by cleansing our

hearts, forsaking all sin, amending our lives, and keeping his commandments.

10. Have you a body and a soul?—Yes?
11. What does the soul do?—It keeps the body in motion; by it we praise God and worship Him.
12. Where will the soul go after death?—It goes to the owner, that is God.
13. What is heaven?—A place of pleasure.
14. What is Hell?—A place of punishment.
15. Who is the light of the world?—Jesus Christ.
16. Are men all in darkness?—Yes; in great darkness—all are in darkness who are not enlightened by Jesus Christ, they do not worship God, but idols of their own making.
17. How are the children of light to walk?—According to the Commandments of God.
18. Can you merit anything by keeping God's Commandments?—No, man cannot merit anything by obedience to them.
19. Did Jesus Christ rise from the dead?—Yes.
20. How?—He raised himself by His own power.
21. Where will the body of man be at the day of judgment?—United again to the spirit, and judged by God.
22. Who is the Holy Ghost?—He is the third person in the Holy Trinity; He is the Sanctifier.
23. What is the heart of man?—Full of sin, vanity, and idolatry.
24. What can change the Hindoo's heart?—The Holy Ghost.
25. What is the difference between a Christian's behaviour to his wife, and a Hindoo's?—The Hindoos have no love to their wives, and look upon them as their servants—the Christian loves his wife, and lets her eat with him.
26. What is prayer?—Whatever you have in your mind to make known to God.
27. Why should you pray?—Because we are sinners, and need to be delivered from our sins.

28. How should you behave in your duties in life?—A man must be diligent in his business, and tell the truth; if not, he is not a Christian.

The general state of these missions, so far as can be judged, is this, that there are about eleven hundred altogether under catechetical instruction, including children, from 60 or 70 villages around Jangera and Barripore—that about 400 have been baptized, of whom between one and two hundred were adult converts—that one village, as above stated, with 40 catechumens, has fallen away—that the threatening disturbance at another has enlarged, instead of diminishing, the Christian flock—that in many of these 60 or 70 villages a considerable portion of the inhabitants has received the joyful sound.—At Raggapore, indeed, a full half of the inhabitants with the head-man—and at Devipore 20 families out of 25—whilst at others only a few individuals out of the 100 or 120 have welcomed the gospel—that there are eight Christian churches, erected principally of bamboo, in the chief villages, by the Society for Propagating the Gospel, for the most part, and by that for Promoting Christian Knowledge—that in these churches divine service according to the Liturgy and Rubric of our Apostolical Church, so far as they are translated, is regularly celebrated (the responses to the Litany at Barripore by the 150 simple people, charmed the Bishop and Archdeacon: there was a heartiness and devotion quite peculiar) that Christian domestic habits are in slow, but regular progress,—that diligence in their calling is increasing—that the markets are now open for their usual commerce, which they frequent with new sobriety and truth—that many are becoming, from the moral influence of Christianity, a little independent in their circumstances—that the residence of an excellent gentleman engaged in the Salt Department, is a singular aid (he has actually built a Christian village of twelve neat huts, entirely separated from the heathen bazars, and full of promise) and also the impartiality of the Honourable Company's local magistrate :—and that the whole of this gradual dawn of the Gospel, with its holy effects, is to be attributed under the great Author of mercy and grace (to whom only be all glory in the Church) to the pious, mild, sensible, meek, enlightened, persevering labours of the Rev. Missionaries constantly resident on the spot, aided by their European and Native catechists.

One main object of the visit was to examine yet more minutely, after five years since the Bishop's first going down to them, the real present state of things, the amount of spiritual good, the depth or otherwise of their religious convictions—and the steadiness of their faith and love. He was assisted in this fatherly enquiry by his friends the Archdeacon, and the Reverend Professor of the College. He was especially jealous lest secular motives should have swayed the converts ; and turned his closest attention to the state of their hearts before God, so far as he could come to a judgment, and to the "fruits meet for repentance" in their spirit, temper, family habits and general conduct.

The Bishop's impression is that "a great and effectual door" is here opened—that as much of real knowledge of the gospel and stability of faith is apparent as amongst such a people under such circumstances could perhaps be reasonably expected—that the grace of God is at work amongst them, and is showing itself, as it did in the Philippian or Thessalonian primitive churches, according to their measure—that there has been nothing sudden in their conversion ; nothing perhaps very deep ; nothing as yet in the way of spiritual attainment striking or elevated ; but a solid and holy, however slow and feeble progress in the illumination of the Spirit of God, contrition for sin, reliance on the sacrifice of Christ, renewal of the heart, separation from the pollutions of an idolatrous world, and a godly, sober, and righteous conversation.

Few have adequately attained what the apostle calls "peace with God" through the blood of Christ ; some appear to have done so, but comparatively there are few: the most are desiring, learning, waiting, praying for the forgiveness of their sin—are babes and infants in grace—and are exceedingly in danger of relapsing into what would be unbecoming the gospel, if constant care and vigilance be not exercised by their pastors.

And here the adaptation of our Protestant Anglican Church to such a country as India becomes every year more apparent. Her liturgy and services—the solid education which Bishop's College gives her ministers—her scriptural platform of Church government—the stability and spirituality of the religion she aims at diffusing—the bond of union which all her administrations constitute—the steady, unostentatious progress in heartfelt religious discipline and habits, which she urges—the subjection to the different ranks of spiritual teachers, masters and pastors, which she recommends and exhibits—all seem exactly suited for a timid prostrate population, incapable of guiding themselves in any thing, but disposed to lean on the energy and example of her European instructors.

The Christian reader may now judge whether these "first fruits of the Gentiles" in our Calcutta, agricultural, isolated villages, warranted the hopes which those who were on the spot conceived. The Bishop could not avoid saying, "Can any forbid water, that these should not be baptized who have received" (in his ordinary and incipient influences for sanctification) "the Holy Ghost, as well as we?" Those whom the Reverend missionaries presented were then baptized; about twenty-five adults; the entire congregation audibly undertaking to be their sponsors and guardians in the fulfilment of their vows—the sponsion was affecting beyond description.

SKETCH OF THE TALLYGUNGE MISSION IN CONNECTION WITH BISHOP'S COLLEGE.

A few schools for the imparting of knowledge, were its first beginnings—these were established by the venerable Society for Promoting Christian Knowledge, about the year 1820, and were afterwards transferred to the incorporated sister Society in the year 1828. Before the arrival of any of the Society's missionaries, these schools were under the superintendence of a Mr. Van Eriecken, a layman.

In 1824, the Rev. Mr. Morton, upon his arrival in India, was directed to take the superintendence of this circle of schools; it was then thought necessary, in order that the schools might be under the immediate eye of the missionary, that he should take up his residence somewhere in the neighbourhood, and a suitable residence being at that time vacant and for sale, it was purchased, and Mr. Morton took possession, and continued in the active superintendence of seven native schools, containing an average of 700 boys, until the year 1826, when that gentleman was removed to Chinsurah. The care of the schools thence devolved on the Rev. W. Tweddle, then residing at Howrah, on the other side of the Ganges. The appointment of the Rev. Mr. De Mello soon after to Howrah, enabled Mr. Tweddle to remove to Tallygunge.

In August 1829, after having finished the prescribed course of studies in Bishop's College, Mr. Jones was directed to join Mr. Tweddle in the capacity of catechist. The idea of establishing an English school, suggested itself to Mr. Tweddle, and a small building was erected, which soon filled with scholars.

In April, 1830, two young men from a village called Sulkeah, twenty miles south of the Mission house, called to make inquiries about Christianity. The result was, they were baptized, and became the first fruits of the mission. Immediately after this, the Rev. Mr. Tweddle, accompanied by his catechist, visited their village, and exhorted the heathen whom he met, to follow the example of those two, and become disciples of the holy Jesus, &c. Shortly after, four more came forward, and earnestly requested baptism, and in proof of their sincerity, brought and delivered up their images.

The number soon increased to twelve. Such was the commencement of this mission.

On the appointment of the Rev. J. Bowyer to Barripore, this little flock was given over to his care, being at too great a distance to be visited efficiently by the missionary at Tallygunge.

It was not long after this arrangement that a man came from an adjacent village, called Jangira, and attended regularly at the Mission-House for instruction. After a few days, he returned to his village, and declared to his family his intention of embracing Christianity. They, at first, of course, used all possible thought or argument, to dissuade him from such a step, and on finding him firm and resolute in his purpose, excluded him from the family circle. Upon this he returned, and told his tale, and begged earnestly that his village might be visited by the missionary, which wish was complied with, and shortly, as the result of several visits, a temporary school was opened at his house, upon which the whole family was excluded from all communion with their own caste. After much teaching, the whole family were baptized, and received into full communion. The work of God progressed, others were added, and a small cottage in the village was at length appropriated for divine worship. A school-house was also erected, which was attended by the Christian and heathen children promiscuously.

In Dec. 1832, Mr. Tweddle fell a sacrifice to a malignant jungle fever, while superintending the erection of a more commodious place of worship, the number of hearers having considerably increased. The building was, however, completed, and now stands conspicuous in the village of Jangira, about eight miles south of the Mission House, and being situated on a little rising ground, can be seen from several miles around, a monument of Christian love and of Christian charity.

After the death of Mr. Tweddle, the Rev. Mr. D. Mello superintended this mission till June, when, by the direction of the Bishop, Mr. Jones, having been ordained, took charge of it. Mr. Driberg, a student of Bishop's College, was appointed to assist as catechist. In the various schools, about four hundred at this time attended, besides the English school, which numbered about fifty. Many converts have since been added, and the writer of this sketch had the pleasure of witnessing the baptism of several, he thinks from fifteen to twenty, in company with Bishop Wilson, his then chaplain, and the professors of the College. The congregation filled the place of worship at Tallygunge. The candidates were arranged around the font, and the Bishop proceeded to examine and exhort them. It was what one might be led to think of a primitive scene. There was no excitement—no show—no crowd—a quiet introduction of a few idolators into the fold of Jesus Christ. The Bishop and his chaplain—the missionary and his catechist—and the native converts ;—the one proposing his questions, the other translating them, the third party earnestly and simply answering them. The examination was taken down with scrupulous accuracy, and was as follows :—

After a few words of encouragement, they were examined in Dr. Watts's first Catechism, which, being translated into Bengallee, they had learnt. Afterwards, the Bishop proceeded to question them as follows :

'Is man a sinner, and do you feel yourselves to be so?—We all do.

'What does sin deserve?—The wrath of God. God is angry with sinners. Hell (from different individuals).

'Does God know the hearts of men?—Yes.

'What sin has God seen in your hearts?—All sin ; all manner of sins.

'How long ago did you begin to feel, and know that you were sinners?—Some few, some three, some two, some one year, and one about eight months.

'Who is the Saviour of us sinners?—Jesus Christ.

'Who is Jesus Christ?—The Son of God.

'What has Jesus Christ done for us sinners?—After suffering many indignities, He died upon the cross.

'By what means are our hearts to be changed?—By praying to the Holy Spirit.

'Who is the Holy Spirit?—The third person, who sanctifies our hearts.

'How many persons are there in the Godhead?—Three; Father, Son, and Holy Ghost.

'Are there three Gods then?—No: three in one, and one in three.

'Then how many Gods are there?—Only one God.

'Who made heaven and earth?—God.

'What is God?—A Spirit; cannot be seen—all-powerful—pure—everywhere present. He knows the hearts of all.

'Why do you come to baptism?—It is the command of God, and the sign of the pardon of sin.

'Who appointed baptism?—First, John; then Jesus Christ.

'Can you give the text appointing baptism?—"Be baptized in the name of the Father," &c.

'Besides the sign, what does the water represent in baptism?—By the water of baptism we are washed from our sins.

'But does the water do this?—No: the Holy Spirit, not the water.

'What do they promise who are baptized?—That after baptism they will forsake the ways of sin, and keep God's Holy will and commandments.

'Will you give up all heathen caste?—We have left them altogether, and will not return.

'If the heathen try to persuade you, what will you do?—Not listen.

'What kind of life will you now try to lead?—What God commands, and what Jesus Christ has shown us.

'With regard to deceit, concealment of the truth, fraud, &c., what do you say about it?—We will not do these things.

The examination proceeded to a greater length.

As the bishop left the place, he observed, 'So interesting, and yet so simple!'

'FIFTEENTH REPORT OF THE CALCUTTA DIOCESAN COMMITTEE OF THE SOCIETY FOR PROMOTING CHRISTIAN KNOWLEDGE.

'It is with much pleasure we find room for a notice of this Report for the information of those friends who feel interested in the operations of this Society, and in publishing the efforts it has successfully made to extend the circulation of the Sacred Scriptures, and the Society's valuable publications. Our readers are doubtless aware that this Society directs its labours exclusively to the Scriptures; Common Prayer Book; books and tracts; schools and churches; and within this sphere makes itself extremely useful. In proof of this we extract from the Report of the Parent Society for 1835; that during the year reported on, including the issues of the Committee of General Literature and Education, which is a branch of this Society, the amazing number of 7,025,235 works were circulated: we also note from the same source the following most gratifying fact, that while the parliamentary report exhibited an increase between the years 1817 and 1835 of a little more than 100 per cent. in the number of children under instruction in the kingdom, the accounts of the National Society during the same period show an increase of above 300 per cent. It is this Society's glory to have been the first body in the kingdom which came forward in the year 1698 to promote the education of the poor upon Christian principles; this work was afterwards taken up on a more extensive scale by "the National Society for promoting the education of the poor in the principles of the Established Church," but it continues to supply all the religious books used in these schools, and probably in the greater part of all the charity schools in the kingdom connected with the National Church.

'Our business however lies at present with the Report of the Diocesan Committee, and we are glad to see that depôts of the Society's books have been formed at Penang and Singapore, at the former of which places a most encouraging commencement had been made: a Branch Society had been formed at the suggestion of the Lord Bishop at Nusserabad, and a supply of books had been forwarded there, considerable supplies of bibles, prayer-books, and tracts have been despatched to Moulmein, Agra, Cawnpore, Chunar, Allahabad, Mhow, and Dinapore. Lending libraries have also been supplied to Benares and the Calcutta Free School Church. We take this opportunity of introducing to the notice of the numerous libraries now forming throughout India the highly moral and useful publications of this Society, which we observe have been uniformly, as regards size and binding, published in England in forty-one volumes.

'The Committee report that they have under their care three schools in Calcutta, two of which, a boys' and a girls', being for the offspring of the poorer Portuguese, are likely to become very useful. The St. James's school continues in a healthy state; and the examinations very satisfactory.

'With respect to the funds of this Society, the Committee make a strong appeal to the liberality of the Indian community, and certainly not without cause, for although the exertions of the Society are small, comparatively, still it appears to be contemplated to reduce them if the means for their support are not increased in this country. The subscription list is unusually small, and has dwindled from 1236 rupees in the year 1834, to 284 rupees in the year ending with April 1836.

'We will, in recommending the affairs of this Society to the notice of our Christian friends, conclude in the Committee's own words, they say—

"'Before closing their Report, the Committee would earnestly solicit the liberal subscriptions of the public towards the support of the schools; it having been intimated by the Parent Society, that, in consequence of the many calls upon their funds, they cannot supply the sum necessary for carrying on the schools in Calcutta. The Committee trust that the Christian public will not suffer these schools to fall to the ground, and thus deprive so many children of the advantages of a Christian and useful education, which hitherto has been afforded them under the immediate superintendence of the Lord Bishop and the Calcutta Diocesan Committee. They trust their appeal may not be in vain; but that funds will be forthcoming, which will enable them to carry on these schools, in which they are deeply interested."'

SOME MORE PARTICULARS ABOUT CAWNPOOR AND FUTTEHPOOR.

At Cawnpoor I made a very short stay, and therefore could not notice *much*, considering ALL that is being done there;—and it would be unjust and presumptuous if I insinuated that this communication contains a full account of the proceedings at the station. I request you, therefore, to understand me as intending to impart only *some particulars* respecting them. Indeed, what I am going to mention in this letter does not include almost any thing connected with the labours of the ordained missionary gentlemen at this place, into whose proceedings I had not time to inquire.

The Female Orphan Asylum at Cawnpoor deserves notice in the first place. Forty-six girls, collected from out of the heathen world, are here under Christian education. This of itself is a very cheering fact, and is calculated to make a pious person thankful to Almighty God for his gracious providence in ordering so happy an event; and the change which has palpably taken place in the feelings and sentiments of the wards appears to be a great evidence of his blessing upon the institution. Although they had but lately been grovelling under heathenism in its most wretched form, and only for a short time emancipated from its bonds, yet their sense of propriety has already become very remarkable; and did I not previously hear any thing about them, I could not infer, from any features in their general conduct, that they had ever been heathens, much less could I suppose that they had only recently been brought out of that community. With the exception of a very few, they all appeared to me to be quite different creatures from their cotemporaries still under their native yoke. Their attention to their studies, their quickness in answering questions, and above all their respectful behaviour towards their superiors, struck me very much when I visited them. They are all simultaneously taught in the English and Hindui languages, and although I only heard them in the former, yet I dare say that they were equally able to bear an examination in the latter. I was much pleased by what they had actually learnt of the English language, considering the short time they had been at it, and I was more delighted by what they seemed to promise. If they continue, as I trust they will, to make progress in the same ratio in which they have hitherto done, I hope, under God's blessing, there will be a still more wonderful change in them.

There are several native schools at Cawnpoor, but I only visited two. The Magazine School, as it is termed, contains sixty boys, twenty-one of whom learn English. For a long time there was no regular master to teach this language, and what lessons were given in it were owing to private and individual benevolence. Lately, however, a native has been sent up from Benares, who gives instructions in English, and is much liked by his employers. The first-class boys read the following books:—The New Testament, Murray's Abridged Grammar, and the English Spelling Book, No. 2. This implanting of sound principles into the minds of children still within the pale of heathenism is equally remarkable and desirable. The waters, it is said, wear away the stones, and such exertions must tend to loosen the cords which keep young minds bound to a system of degrading superstitions. This school had long owed its maintenance to the liberality of a single gentleman, and although he has since been seconded by others, yet he still continues to take the same interest in it, and contributes largely to its funds.

The Free School, supported partly by Government and partly by the contributions of private individuals, has ninety-eight boys in its list, about seventy of whom are in daily attendance. It is conducted by a European master, with two assistants under him. There is a female department attached to it, besides a class of Persian students. Formerly there had also been a Sanscrit class connected with it, but this has been given up. The books read in the first class of the English department are the following:—Goldsmith's History of England, Archdeacon Corrie's Ancient History, Goldsmith's Geography, and Murray's Grammar.

Futtehpoor is a very small station, and as a city has nothing remarkable. More, however, is being done there than could be expected from the patronage of only four Europeans. A male orphan asylum, an English seminary, and three Hindui village schools are the instruments with which the work is here done. Considering how few of the Europeans are resident in it, one must be surprised that so much is going on in it. The orphan asylum contains forty children, and is a very useful sphere of labour. The care with which the boys are brought up is as astonishing, as the results, under God's blessing, have already been cheering. They were collected from out of the same community, and in the same manner as the girls in the Cawnpoor Asylum, and the former have undergone as great a change in their habits and sentiments as the latter. All these boys learn English and Hindui at the same time, and the progress they have made is very surprising. Within a short time they have learnt to read and explain the New Testament in both these languages, without much difficulty, and to work simple sums in arithmetic. But what is the most remarkable in them is, the change that has taken place in their habits and feelings. Although but lately brought out of the most wretched state of heathenism, yet the propriety with which they behave towards themselves and others, and the general spirit of morality which they breathe, would do credit to any European children. The gentleman in whose house they live, nay, within whose rooms they pass the greatest part of their time, has seldom had occasion to be in any way disturbed by them. They are quiet and steady, intent upon their own work, seldom prone to play except for the sake of bodily exercise, and always ready in an instant to do any thing which they are desired by their superiors. Their living costs their benevolent guardians and instructors but very little. They cook their own dinner, very young though they are, and feel satisfied with plain and simple things. Are not all these striking proofs of the blessing of God upon the exertions of the Christian gentlemen here? Oh, what pious mind can reflect without gratitude, that so many poor creatures, snatched from the jaws of misery and starvation, have not only been provided for in their bodily wants, but also placed under the influence of such happy circumstances?

The English school contains sixty-three boys, and is conducted by a young Bengali gentleman, a convert to Christianity, who was taken up to Futtehpoor nearly two years ago by the Venerable Archdeacon Corrie. The progress made by the boys will appear best by mentioning the books read in the first class:—The New Testament, Goldsmith's History of England, Goldsmith's Geography, and Murray's Grammar. The Baboo who is at the head of the school has also to superintend the Hindui bazar schools. The chaplains of Cawnpoor, within whose district this station is included, take much interest in all these institutions, and visit them whenever they pass this way.

APPENDIX.

A.

The population of Calcutta by the last census is near 250,000 within the ditch, and five or six hundred thousand are supposed to reside in the immediate suburbs. Within a circuit of twenty miles the population is generally estimated at *two millions.* Of the number within the city about 130,000 are Hindoos, 60,000 Mahommedans, 3000 English, and 3000 Portuguese, or Indo-Britains; the rest are French, Chinese, Armenians, Jews, Moghols, Parsees, Arabs, Mugo, Madrasees, &c. The whole number of houses is about 70,000, of which nearly 15,000 are of brick or stone, the rest are of mud and unburned brick.

Officers stationed at the avenues of the city ascertained that an average of 100,000 persons enter daily from the surrounding villages, chiefly sircars, servants, fruiterers, &c.

Literary, charitable, and religious institutions are now numerous. Of literary institutions is the 'Hindoo College,' established in 1816 by wealthy natives. There are generally from four to five hundred scholars. English and Sanscrit are taught in two separate departments.

The *Mahomedan College.* This also has two departments; English and oriental. There are about two hundred scholars in daily attendance. In the one they are taught their own literature and faith, through the medium of the Persian and Arabic languages. In the other the ordinary routine of a good English school, including natural philosophy, and the different branches of mathematics.

The *Hoogly or Mahomed Mushen's College* is richly endowed, and now possesses an annual revenue of no less than a lac of rupees, (100,000.) It has of late been reorganized and taken under the superintendance of the English Government. It numbers nearly two thousand students, the greater number of whom are instructed in English literature. Arabic and Persian are also taught, but not more than three hundred of the students ever attend the oriental department.

The *Medical College* which was instituted by a general order of the Supreme Government, is another noble and promising Institution: medical science is taught on the most enlightened principles, and in the English language. It is deservedly a favourite Institution with both natives and Europeans. In these and other Literary Institutions, not less than five or six thousand Hindoos and Mahommedans are receiving a liberal English education : from those above-mentioned, religion is excluded.

Those in which Christianity forms the basis of education, are principally conducted by missionaries of various Societies. Among these the General Assembly's School is pre-eminent. It was founded by Dr. Duff, who has since been joined by several other gentlemen by whom the Institution is conducted conjointly. It has existed now above twelve years, and at present numbers nearly seven hundred pupils. The education is of the highest order. Several have already made a profession of Christianity, others have gone forth as teachers to their countrymen in the suburbs of Calcutta and further up the country.

The *Benevolent Institution at Serampore,* a few miles distant from Calcutta, has existed now nearly forty-years, without interruption, and several hundreds of natives and others have passed through the routine of education, and numbers are at present employed as teachers, writers, and clerks, &c.

The Boarding and Day-schools at Chitpore, and which have been eminently blessed, were established in 1822. This is decidedly a Christian Institution, and in every respect a most valuable one. The boarding-school consists wholly of the children of native Christians. The day-school is for heathen, and numbers generally above three hundred scholars, and is not inferior even to the General Assembly's.

The *Martiniere* is a school founded by a munificent legacy of the late General Martin. It was opened in 1835. It is intended wholly for the children of Europeans, and has a Principal and two Professors.

The *High School* established by the late Bishop Corrie, is of the highest order of such schools as are numerous in Calcutta, and its discipline excellent.

Benevolent Institutions are numerous, and are generally supported with great liberality, putting to shame the cold-hearted and close-handed charity of the western world. It is true in more senses than one, that an eastern sun warms. Among these are the Leper Hospital established by Dr. Cary,—various Orphan Societies,—District Charitable Society,—Widows' Fund,—Marine Pension Fund,—the Presidency General Hospital,—the Native Hospital,—Lunatic Asylums, &c.

FREE SCHOOL CHURCH.

Perhaps more attention has not been paid to any one existing institution than that of the Free School, or been more liberally supported. Its funds have always been more than ample for its expenditure, and on the arrival of the good Bishop Turner, at his instance a surplus fund was applied to the erection of a very handsome and substantial church, with a beautiful and commanding spire, which stands now among several others a monument of Christian liberality, and serving to point the passing idolater to God in the heavens, and whom the heaven of heavens cannot contain. It was consecrated by Bishop Wilson in the year 1833, on Saturday February 2nd, and called St. Thomas's Church, but is better known by the name of Free School Church. Besides the children and establishment of the school, European families residing in the neighbourhood, who were before destitute of Church accommodation, are allowed to hold sittings, &c.

The ceremony of consecration was, in a heathen land, deeply interesting, and hundreds of natives were assembled on the occasion to witness it. It was to them a sermon which they could *feel*. The bishop was received at the principal entrance, where the petition of consecration was delivered to him, and afterwards read by the registrar. The bishop then entered the body of the church, and walked to the communion-table, followed by the ministers, who were to officiate, and a number of the rest of the clergy, repeating the twenty-fourth Psalm, the bishop one verse, and the clergy another, alternately. The regular service appointed for the consecration of a church was then gone through by his Lordship ; the Rev. Dr. Mill, acting as chancellor, read the sentence of consecration, which, after receiving the signature of the bishop, was laid upon the communion-table.

The state of the School is stated to be—a plain course of education, comprehending geography, English grammar, writing and arithmetic, the History of England, together with reading books of a simple kind ; and moreover the nature and principles of the Christian religion from the Holy Scriptures, catechisms, and other books, constitute together, with morning and evening prayers, the daily instruction ; the female department is also instructed in plain-work as well as in lace and straw-work, the disposal of which appears to have realized 140 rupees.

We rejoice exceedingly to see these useful arts taught in the female department, for we are sure that in whatever ratio the female character can be elevated by education and honest industry, in a much greater ratio will the men be raised through their indirect instrumentality. No country in the world shews more distress among the widowed part of mankind than Calcutta does, but by thus in early life putting those whom it may please the Almighty to reduce to that forlorn condition in the way of honestly relieving their necessities, is charity indeed! and we look with great faith and hope on this experiment both in the female departments of the Free School and the District Charitable Society. We remember having seen some very tasty and well-executed straw-bonnets, manufactured by the wards of this institution.

The number of children maintained and educated in the school on issuing the report was 394, of whom 248 are boys, and 146 girls. We conclude this notice in the words of the Committee : 'The Governors cannot conclude this report without once more adverting to the state of the funds, and in doing so they beg to reiterate their entreaties for increased support. They rest the grounds of their appeal on the important benefits which result from the establishment; and they trust that the single fact, that 400 children are rescued from destitution, ignorance, and vice, brought up in the fear and love of God, instructed in the Christian religion, and enabled by what they are taught in the school to earn a livelihood when they have left it, is more than enough to recommend the institution to a benevolent and discerning public.'

THE DISTRICT CHARITABLE SOCIETY.

The proceedings of this Society during the past year present few particular occurrences deserving to be brought under the notice of the public. The system of the Society has been long organized in a way well adapted to the efficiency of its operations, so that the whole now moves on in one continued uninterrupted stream of labour.

The Report states 'that the expenditure of the Society in all its districts has been economical without curtailing unnecessarily the relief given to the deserving poor. The rate of regular disbursements from the Central to the District Committees has been lessened in some degree, and in consequence the Society have had the means of supplying the increased demands of the Native Committee, the Leper Asylum, and the Workhouse under the superintendence of the Ladies' Committee.'

The Ladies' Committee in connection with the Society have given in their first Report, by which it appears, that they have occupied a house wherein 'the females, whether adult or children, supported by the funds of the District Charitable Society, are assembled in a room provided for the purpose, to perform needle-work, if competent to do so, under the superintendence of a person engaged for that object, and if unable to work, to receive instruction in the same, from the same person.' The superintendant of the work-room is required to give instruction in reading for two hours in the day to such children as are unable to read, and also to such of the adults as being able to read, are willing to be instructed.' It appears that those who have attended have done so cheerfully, and it is hoped their number will increase. The workers receive a fixed price for all work done, two-thirds of which is deducted from their monthly pension, so that the willing and industrious receive, besides their pension, one-third of the value of whatever work they can perform. The sum earned within the two months that the plan had been in operation was small, but it is expected that when once understood the number of hands will increase, either to employ themselves at the work-room, or else to take work home as they may be permitted. It is devoutly to be hoped that the experiment of employing these women, hitherto supported in idleness, has so far succeeded, that they may look forward to the continuance and eventual perfecting of a system which shall improve the moral condition, while it relieves the bodily wants, of the poor who come within its influence.

'During the past year the receipts have consisted of

	Co. Rupees.
Congregational Collections and Donations, .	16770
Donations from the Supreme Government .	14450
General Subscriptions	16183
	47403
Balance of last year (Jan. 1, 1836.)	14000
Total	61403

THE CALCUTTA CHRISTIAN SCHOOL-BOOK SOCIETY.

To report continued healthful existence, on the very fie. of change and decay, is to declare the special kindness of God to us above many others; to report existence, active and influential, for good, is to proclaim the peculiar mercy of God rising above us, and that on the very scene of our sin and demerit. Yet such is the report, which, on behalf of the Calcutta Christian School-Book Society, we have now to make. It exists healthfully, actively, influentially—it exists for good, for supreme good, for that good for which the Lord Jesus Christ lived, died, and lives again for evermore—for the glory of God in the salvation of man! This is the noblest end for which a man can live—the sweetest work in which man can engage—the dearest cause for which a man can suffer or die—the grandest, widest, happiest service in which a man can ever be absorbed or sunk. We give thanks to God, that during one other year we have been enabled to pursue this our chosen work upon our chosen field; and that, in quiet and silence, we have been enabled to forward the educational commissariat of our Indian Christian band!

I. The income of the society for the year, from June, 1841, to June, 1842, has been about 3,000 rupees. This includes the money arising from the sale of books, together with the various direct contributions received throughout the year for the objects of the society.

II. The expenditure during the same period has been about 2,900 rupees. There are, however, claims which turn the balance slightly against the society, so as to leave it under temporary obligation to its treasurer. This state of accounts, in a mercantile point of view, may be satisfactory, because it keeps the society in a state of pecuniary safety; but, in a higher point of view, it is not so. By resources so limited, however well balanced (as they ought to be), we are disabled from extended spiritual enterprise; so that, instead of being able to promote a great demand, by presenting a large supply, we are only able to meet a small demand with a scanty supply. Our sale of books during the past year has been about 1,600 rupees, which, considering the fewness of Christian schools, is no small encouragement in our third year.

III. The society's book-list remains, as to numbers, much as last year. Considerable alterations have been made, however, in the substance of some of the society's lesser works, as in the Second and Third Instructors. Translations are still in progress, such as of the Second, Third, and Fourth Instructors; but we have learned by experience to promise but little as to times and seasons of completion, in a country where agents are few, opportunities precarious, and work always so uncertain.

LIST OF BOOKS.

1. The Bengalee Spelling-Book, a small work, for Vernacular Classes—1½ annas.
2. The First Instructor—English, new edition—1 anna.
3. The same in Anglo-Bengalee—3 annas.
4. The same in Anglo-Urdu—3 annas.
5. The second Instructor—English, 4 annas.
6. This Instructor is now being translated into Bengalee and Urdu.

7. The Third Instructor. A new and improved edition,—price 12 annas.

8. The Fourth Instructor. A large selection of useful extracts,—price 1 rupee (in course of translation into Bengalee.)

9. The Poetic Instructor. A selection from our best poets,—1 rupee.

10. Macculloch's Course of Reading—highest prose reading-book—chiefly scientific and religious, with poetry,—1 rupee 12 annas.

11. Maculloch's English Grammar—12 annas.

12. Arithmetical Instructor—with English and Indian tables—12 annas.

13. Elements of Euclid—six books—1 rupee 8 annas.

14. Solid Geometry, Spheric and Conic Sections—1 rupee 8 annas.

15. Marshman's Brief Survey of History—two parts, each 1 rupee 2 annas.

16. Marshman's History of India—1 rupee 2 annas.

17. Marshman's History of Bengal—1 rupee 2 annas.

18. Barth's General History on Christian Principles—with maps—for upper classes—2 rupees.

19. Manual of the Evidences of Christianity—12 annas.

20. Letters on the Evidences of Christianity—12 annas.

21. The Shorter Catechism—by the Westminster Assembly of Divines—with Scripture Proofs.

22. Also in preparation, on Geography, A Manual for beginners—in the press, to be ready in a few weeks.

23. Maps of the World, in sets of six, viz., Europe, Asia, Africa, America, Eastern Hemisphere, Western Hemisphere;—in sheets, 30 rupees a set. They may also be had varnished and mounted, at an increased expence.

24. Globes, terrestrial and celestial—of 9, 12, and 18 inches, have been ordered from Britain, and may be expected in a few months.

IV. We subjoin a list of our contributors or supporters, from the date of the Society's formation in June 1839, until the present time;—and though some of those, whose names are here given, be now dead, or departed from India, yet their names are still ours, and we put them into our basket of fragments, that "nothing may be lost."—We give this list in order to show *who* have supported our cause—a cause, of which they cannot be ashamed,—and in order also to remind a few of our former friends, that they once helped us, and so suggest the question, why do they not help us *now?* Is India less needy? Is our cause less worthy? Is our bond less catholic? Is our Society less trusty? Is our object less Christian? If not, why not help us *still?*

V. We publish again the principles of our Society, in the form of its original Laws.

'I. The name of the Society shall be, the "Calcutta Christian School Book Society."

'II. The bond of the Society shall be, those grand Christian doctrines in which the Protestant Evangelical churches are agreed.

'III. The special object of the Society shall be, to obtain and furnish a supply of books in the English and native languages, for promoting education on Christian principles.

'IV. Such general school-books only shall be kept by the Society, as are not inconsistent with the word of God:—and such religious school-books only, as are decidedly scriptural.

'V. The necessary supply of books shall be obtained by original composition, republication, or by purchase, as may seem best.

'VI. The Society's works shall be sold at the lowest price consistent with pecuniary obligations, and the necessary expense of agency: and the Society shall retain a power, in special cases, to dispose of books at reduced rates.

'VII. The Society shall also be at liberty, if expedient, to use its influence, in any more general form, for the advancement of the grand object of Christian education.

'VIII. There shall be a "General Committee" for managing the business of the Society, with a special "Sub-Committee" to superintend the preparation and publishing of books.

'IX. Subscribers, to whatever amount, shall be considered members of the Society.

'X. The formation of Local Committees throughout the country shall be solicited and promoted, in order to co-operate with the General Committee in Calcutta.'

VI. The General Committee of Management consists of the following gentlemen :—

Alexander, J. W., Esq.—Boaz, Rev. T.,—Boswell, Rev. R. R.,—Byrne, Wale, Esq.,—Campbell, Rev. J.—Charles, Rev. J., D.D.,—De Rodt, Rev. R.,—Duff, Rev. A., D.D.—Hæberlin, Rev. Dr.,—Hawkins, J. Esq.—Ewart, Rev. D.,—Mackay, Rev. W. T.,—Meiklejohn, Rev. W. H.,—Roxburg, Capt.,—Sandys, Rev. T.,—Small, Rev. G.,—Smith, Rev. T.

Sub-Committee of Publication.—Messrs. Alexander, Campbell, Ewart, Long, Macdonald, Mackay, and Drs. Duff and Hæberlin.

VII. We now beseech our Christian friends to grant us more help. At present, we stand alone here, as a Society to furnish a complete store for Christian Education in India. We have embodied this purpose in our corporate existence; we have taken up our own division of labour in accordance with our vital principle; and our desire and our aim is, if God permit, in due time, to aid in furnishing a store of Christian literature for the Christian schools of India: yea of all India, if our brethren in other presidencies will not bestir themselves, and take the enviable work out of our hands. Our aim is quite practicable; and we fear not, little by little, to accomplish it.

Is not our object Christian? Do we not lay all literature at the feet of Christ? Is not our end Christian? Do we not seek to convert all to Christ? Is not our Christianity simple, to obey Christ's command? Is not our Christianity catholic? Does it not include every one who follows Christ, under whatever human banner? And is not catholicity of spirit and work more sweet than diversity? India sees the catholicity of death, in its universal agreement to sin; shall she not also see the catholicity of life, in the universal agreement of grace by one Jesus Christ? Shall not the Christianity, which demands the whole world to be one Church, stand forth in its own self as one? And if all Christians cannot co-operate in everything, shall they not the more gladly, on that very account, work together wherever they can possibly unite? The habit of uniting on earth in the service of Christ, prepares us for our everlasting union in the presence of God in heaven. May the Christian School Book Society be helpful in promoting the everlasting happiness of the world, and the eternal union of the Church!

(Signed) J. MACDONALD, *Corresponding Secretary.*
J. CAMPBELL, *Minute Secretary.*
J. W. ALEXANDER, *Cash Secretary.*

Calcutta, August, 1842.

B.

DEFINITIONS OF BRAHMA.

The system of the Vedanta state him to be void of shape and natural distinction.

Eternal and without distinguishing marks.

Unalterable and void of attributes: void of form and immortal, pure and void of joy, viz. producing pleasure from intellectual joy.

The system of Logical Philosophy describes him thus:

He is the fountain and ocean of all thought, not to be comprehended by thought: inexpressible, immeasurable, his existence can only be proved by reason.

Brahma is in knowledge the form of knowledge; known only to the wise by knowledge; his nature is spirit.

The system of the Meemangsha describes him to be the form of activity.

The system called Shankya states him to be out of the reach of creatures.

The system of the Patanjul is, that the Eternal has a body of an enormous size, so as to fill the earth and sky.

The Grammarian system states him to be in the form of words or *sounds*.

The system of the Puranas and the Agomon say, that the Eternal is matter, and the form of idols.

Thus according to the various Shasters, Brahma is variously represented, and hence the different opinions, I suppose, of the various sects among the Hindoos.

Nothing can be more unquestionable, than this statement of the *Vedantic* doctrine, i. e. the theory and practice of those contemplative spiritual teachers among the older Hindoos who have been so unblushingly held out to the world, as if they had been asserters of pure *Deism*, or *Mono-Theism*.

It is the principle of this system, that whoever can by diligent abstract meditations, rid himself of the *illusive* notion of *diversity*,—a process avowedly and systematically distinguished from *active virtue*, and from the exercise of *charity of every kind*, (since all affections as implying diversity of person must be extirpated,) this person by the very act that raises him above idol-worship, sets himself equally above *all* worship: he is himself God, absorbed into that all-pervading essence of Deity which they call *Brahma* in the neuter gender. And why then, (say these sages themselves,) should he then worship that of all whose attributes, omniscience, omnipresence, &c. he is then essentially partaker? though that infinite essence, in its various and multifarious manifestations to *inferior* mortals that are still subject to the *illusion of diversity*, may be and is still, in proportion to that variety, a proper object of worship to *them*.

It were a wide field of speculation to trace the effect of this persuasion both on the minds of these professed sages themselves, and on the minds of the vulgar, who are all taught to believe and reverence, the system upon which this absorption and self-deification proceeds: particularly to point out its strict compatibility with the practice of the grossest and most complicated idolatry by the *latter*, and with its most complete encouragement, nay confirmation and establishment by the *former*. To do this thoroughly, would be to explain in a very great degree the whole mystery of iniquity connected with Hindoo worship. Certain it is, that the ΠΡΩΤΟΝ ΨΕΝΔΟΣ of *all* heathenism, but of this *gnostic heathenism most eminently and systematically*, is the confounding the creature with the Creator.

The following is in substance a conversation with a learned Brahmin in the course of my missionary excursions while in India, illustrative of the popular view of Hindooism as now held.

At the close of this most interesting day's labour, a young sharp-faced, keen-eyed looking Brahmin in the fore-front of an immense crowd, caught my eye while preaching. His appearance interested me greatly, and as his eye caught mine, I exclaimed, 'No God—no God—the Hindoos have no God! They acknowledge no God—they live without God—they deny His existence.' Upon which I observed his interesting countenance change from long to short, and from the grave to the ridiculous. I added—'Alas, how sad! What a pitiable condition.' I here observed him anxious to speak; and he did speak as follows,—'How without God—what do you mean by without God?' I replied—'You acknowledge no God superior to and diverse from yourself. No knowledge of the only living and true God,—and therefore no fear—no love—no worship of God.' Hastily interrupting me, he said—'How wildly you talk.' I asked him if he could prove the Hindoo belief of a God supreme above, and distinct from, his creatures,—an object of worship, from the Veda.' After further observations made upon the doctrine of the Veda, he submitted, but observed that the *unilluminated* could not understand it, and spoke of the idolatrous system as *compatible* with its profession, when properly understood.

It may *prima facie*, seem difficult to reconcile the inculcation and actual practice of idolatry with the Pantheistic belief; but on a closer view of the subject, it will be seen to arise necessarily out of it, and is wholly and altogether compatible with it—that both in fact are ONE AND THE SAME *system of religious belief*.

We have only to conceive clearly that the doctrine of the Veda is simply this: 'That there is nothing existent in the universe *but* God,'—that this universe *is* God, (their *neuter* Brahma,) and that every other *supposed* agent, visible or invisible, is *illusive* in respect to its *apparent* diversity from God.'

'From Brahma,' says the Veda, 'springs a power capable of *division*—even as a wave from the ocean,' so that this refined intellectual system, so far from being incompatible with the popular idolatry of India, as frequently maintained, is the very *life and soul* of it,—for whilst they hold that all is *illusion*, they maintain, what is very true, that this illusion is nevertheless inseparable from man's intercourse with his fellow-creatures in active and civil duties. To which they always add, his intercourse with higher beings in sacrifice and other religious duties. Hence it is clear as day, (on this admission) that to persons so circumstanced as the mass of mankind are, the same Vedantic system that maintains all things to be God, should both countenance and presuppose the obligation of a Polytheism as various as the (illusive) diversities of existence; and that as the only practical mode in which *such* persons *can* worship the all-pervading deity. The Pantheism is here the very soul and principle of the Polytheism, as far as mankind at large are concerned. And according to the Vedantists' declared opinion, 'A man commits no other error in his polytheism and the works connected with it, than what he equally commits in the works of his ordinary civil life:' i.e. he errs in all, simply by conceiving either gods, family friends or country, to be distinct from himself, and from the one all-comprehending deity. The contemplative sage gets rid of all these diversities at once: nor is there on this system any other escape from Polytheism, than in that which is equally the escape from all other relations and duties whatever; even from the duty of worshipping the one sole-existing Spirit, with whom the sage then knows himself to be identified. And we may add, that the same process, which by thus raising a man, as they speak, above all notion of *I* and *thou, mine* and *thine*, and discharging him of all notions, but that of his absorption into the one infinite Essence, makes him superior to *all duties*, idolatry always included,—does at the same time make him the object of idolatry to others who yet walk in the regions of diversity.

THE SOUL.

'The soul is not a thing of which a man may say, it hath been, it is about to be, or is to be hereafter; for it is a thing without birth; it is ancient, constant, and *eternal*, and is not to be destroyed in this, its mortal frame. How can the man that believeth that this thing is incorruptible, eternal, inexhaustible, and without birth, think that he can either kill, or cause it to be killed! As a man throweth away old garments, and putteth on new, even so the soul, having quitted its old mortal frames, entereth into others, which are new. The weapon divideth it not—the fire burneth it not—the water dissolveth it not—the wind driveth it not away;—for it is invincible, indivisible, inconsumable, incorruptible, eternal, universal, permanent, immoveable;—it is invisible, inconceivable, and unalterable.'—*Bhagavat Geta.*

The above is a conversation between Krishna (an incarnation of Brahma) and his chief disciple Arjùn, in reply to a very reasonable request that he might be excused inflicting death on the nearest relations of life. A god instructing a creature that it was no sin to murder a Gúrú (spiritual instructor), or any created being, because indestructible!!! It follows:—

> *'Pap o pun jag mo nahin manio,*
> *Jo kuch lakho—so mohe janiyo,*
> *Hai jago moihin mahin banan,*
> *Nat putli sam sab nachau.'*

which at once stopped the mouth of the disciple. The meaning is,—

There is no such thing as vice or virtue.

Whatever is visible is a manifestation of myself.

I made the world, and I, (not govern it) but I am the hand that causes all to move, like the hand that turns the crank that moves the puppets in a puppet-show. In other words, the world, with all its peopled inhabitants, is a machine, and God is the mainspring, or, in plainer language, the world is a fiddle, and God is the fiddler. How awful!

ANOTHER ABSTRACT.

Even I was not at first not any other thing; that which exists unperceived, supreme; afterwards I am that which is; and who must remain am I.

Except the first cause, whatever may appear, and may not appear in the mind, know that to be the minds *maya* or *delusion*, as light, as darkness.

As the great elements are in various beings, entering, yet not entering (that is, pervading, not destroying) thus am I in them, yet not in them.

Even thus far may inquiry be made by him who seeks to know the principle of mind in union and separation, which must be *everywhere always*. A sublime definition of the Deity, says a Christian writer; and so it is in a Christian sense.

The world is *illusion;*
Ideal, not real.

This doctrine naturally arises out of the question. 'If all be Spirit, what is substance?' The early teachers of the *Vedanta School* asserted, that it was *Sakti*, the perceptible power, the active energy, or the manifested instrumentality of the ONE SPIRIT! and *ergo*, though not substantially, yet essentially one and the same. This solution was possibly found too subtle to satisfy the understanding of later teachers of the Vedanta, therefore they went a step further, and boldly cut the knot by maintaining, that '*there was no such thing as substance.*' Matter exists not independent of perception, and that all substances are indebted for their seeming reality to the ideas of the mind.'

They went still further, and maintained, that until our intellects are purified by abstraction—until we have attained a just appreciation of our *own nature*, and of that of *universal spirit*, our ideas are *all wrong*. 'Until the day of true knowledge dawn upon us, we are asleep —in a dream—we *misconceive* of all we *perceive*—v. g.

we take a rope for a snake—an oyster-shell for mother of pearl—mirage for real water.' All that we see in our unilluminated condition, is *maya*, deception — illusion, *nothing!* There are not two things in existence. There is but *One* in ALL—no second—no matter—there is spirit alone. The world is not God, but there is nothing but God in the *world*.

The following scene in one of my missionary excursions at a Mela, will convey perhaps a better idea of living modes of thought upon this subject.

To-day, at the fair, I met with a very extraordinary character. He was covered with a dark coarse blanket, made of sheep's wool, and his whole appearance was that of a rustic day-labourer. A crowd of people were assembled before a Pundit, who was engaged in reading a portion of one of the Poorans, among whom this man was standing, very near to where we took our position. A conversation was soon begun by asking the Pundit what he was reading, and afterwards to what school he belonged. He first defended the idolatrous system, and when driven to a dilemma, merely said, it was all *illusion*, and took refuge in the Vedant system, with which he showed himself pretty well acquainted as a system of *Pantheism*. 'God is one, and there is no second,' was his thesis. He was asked what was the nature of this one sole self-existing being; to which he replied, 'His nature is inexplicable.' Is He matter or spirit? 'Both.' In His original existence he was pure spirit, this material system is a body with which he has clothed himself as with a garment—as a spirit He is without attributes—now that he is in the power or under the dominion of matter, he is subject to passions: i.e. you mean the original pure spirit is? 'Yes.' Is it so voluntarily, or by constraint? 'Voluntarily.' Then He was originally a being *capable of volition*. He willed to be under the dominion of matter. How can you call a pure simple spirit, capable of volition, (nir-gún) i.e. without attributes or qualities, properties, &c., volition is the property of a thinking being; it results from reflection, and *action* is the result of both. Nothing can act but spontaneously. It is impossible therefore for any but a thinking being to act. There can be no liberty where there is no idea of the action to be performed. 'It is not so written in the Vedas. The Vedas describe Brahm, the self-existent in his original state, wholly without *thought*, and the Vedas are eternal truths. But who awoke him from this apathetic state? You say no external power existed save himself: admitting this, how came he to awake from this state of slumber? mind! no external power existed. The poor man's features were quite contorted from anger, and with such a satanic look, he said violently. 'Did you come here to falsify our holy books?' He was simply told that truth could never suffer from candid investigation. The sentence was scarcely finished, when the rustic-looking man, who was standing just by, roused himself, and poured forth such a flow of real eloquence as I never before heard from any Pundit I had ever before conversed with. The idolatrous system he condemned as childish and foolish. This was pretty well received? but on denouncing the Vedas in the most unqualified and in very unmeasured terms, he was interrupted by a sneering sarcastic rebuke from the disputant. This was too much, and with eyes striking lightning, he quoted for several minutes most beautifully and fluently, passages from the Vedas, contradictory of each other. It is impossible to conceive of a more intense silent interest than the whole crowd manifested. Every countenance seemed all astonishment, while the orator concluded by telling them they were all fools, following cunning-devised fables, the dupes of the priesthood. He then walked off, and we followed him, when the following conversation took place:—

'Do you live near here?—I have now no settled residence.

'How long have you thought as you now do on the subject of the Hindoo religion?—Several years. I have read the Vedas over often, and found them inconsistent with themselves, and contrary to reason. Hence so many sects have arisen. No one understands them, and no one interprets them alike.

'What is your own opinion with respect to God and religion?—' I believe all religions to be the invention of interested men, and reject all.'

'Do you find peace of mind in your infidelity—does your soul find rest in anything?—No, I am in the world like a child in the womb.

'What idea have you of your origin and end? Whence you are, and whither going?—My mind is like a mirror that reflects a thousand images. Sometimes I have fancied that I had got the thing (truth), but it always makes a fool of me: I find it like the will-with-a-wisp.'

'Did you ever hear of the Christian religion?—Never till this morning, and what I heard was very reasonable; give me a copy of your Scriptures, and I will investigate them.'

He was immediately presented with a copy, accompanied with an earnest prayer, that he might read, mark, learn, and inwardly digest its sacred truths. I saw him no more.

A crowd remained, and I preached to them Jesus Christ and Him crucified. All were serious, and many seemed deeply impressed. O that a lamp were lighted up in every inhabited place throughout India. "Awake, O Lord, awake, as in the ancient days, let thy light and thy truth go forth!"

To-day met the old Shastree again. After saluting him, and being seated, yesterday's conversation was resumed. He observed, that it had been unsatisfactory, and that he wished to argue the matter over again; but without giving me an opportunity of speaking, he quoted a number of lines from one of the shasters, the purport of all which was, to show the self and sole-existing spirit was enveloped in matter merely for his own amusement, and that after a time the elements would all return to their original state, and the pure spirit would return to its primary unembodied state of existence.

It was replied, that this doctrine destroys the divine unity for the present at least, and so far contradicts the Vedas: there is such a contrariety of thought and feeling, and consequently of action, that the impossibility of such confusion and disorder proceeding from one sole and single existing being, must be visible to every one. You see how much we differ in our opinions. You see between us no *accordance*, no *oneness of thought, sentiment, feeling, any thing*. Is this sole self-existing being at war with himself? Interrupting me, he replied in an angry hasty mood, 'That is all the effect of his connection with matter.' I said, 'Is it not matter, inert, passive,' &c. 'No; it is the cause of all the sin and all the disorder, and all the misery we see in the world.' 'And not subject to the Divine control, of course the pure spirit being itself subject to *maya* (matter). He has lost his sovereignty, and is the *slave* of what you call *maya*, and which to all our senses is inert?'—'*You* say it is inert, and *you* know of no instance to the contrary?' I replied, 'Does it depend on the pleasure of this ideal being (for so you consider this material world) when the pure spirit shall be emancipated?' 'No, emancipation is procured by *penance and works of merit*.'—'Performed by whom?' 'By the all-pervading spirit.'—'To whom? i. e. who exacts these, for what sins is the penance performed?' The poor man now assumed a sulky fit and made no reply. I left in the hope of a better opportunity, which in a few hours occurred.

On my return from perambulating the fair, observing a crowd about the Pundit, one of the readers was directed to read the poem in Hindoo, published at the Church Missionary press, and called 'The Essence of the Scriptures.' (This little tract in Kythee always attracts attention.) It commences with a description of the divine attributes as set forth in the scriptures. As the reader proceeded, observing the Pundit's attention fixed, I took the tract myself, and repeating the few lines which relate to the peculiar incommunicable attributes of the Deity, such as omnipotence, omnipresence, &c. I observed (passingly) See what a contrast! how different to the spirit which inhabits these bodies, viz. omnipotent! This, pointing to the breast, is indeed capable of great things, but not *omnipotent*. God made the world, can you create an ant? Omniscient—seeing all things. The eye of the Lord runneth to and fro through the whole earth, in every place beholding the evil and the good. Surely you have no such powers? 'Yes, I have!' 'Where was I last week?' Of course the poor creature could not tell, and the multitude shouted. Again, Omnipresent—you recollect a couplet in the Ramayan of Toolsee Das, wherein he says, on being asked, Where is God? Tell me where He is not. The man instantly repeated it. Well now surely you cannot claim for yourself such a power? During the pause the crowd seemed in breathless anxiety to be waiting a similar answer as before, when to the utter astonishment of all, the poor fellow got up and walked away. Several requested me to go on.

"True and righteous altogether"—Now how can this apply to us poor fallen sinful people. A wise-looking sort of fellow pushing himself forward, called out, 'Why not, what sin did I ever commit?' As I had never seen the man before, I could not charge him with any particular sin, and so replied by asking him why he came here? He replied, 'For the same reason that others come.' 'That is, said I, 'to bathe in the Ganges?' 'Yes,' and turning round to a Pundit standing by me, 'And you bathe in Gunga to wash away sin?' 'Yes, *Gangá jí ká dhára, páp káte ká árà*,' i. e. The stream of the Ganges is a saw that cuts away sin. Then your own conduct is witness against you that you are all sinners. The errand you are upon is to wash away sin. Herein you acknowledge a being superior to yourselves, one who takes cognizance of human actions. To that holy, sin-hating God you stand responsible, and to Him you and I must render an account, and O what an account. Every thought of the heart, every word good or evil spoken, every deed done in the body. "We must all appear before the judgment-seat of Christ," the judgment seat, a judgment so strict, so impartial, exact, the judgment-seat of *Christ*, God's fellow, compeer, Him hath God ordained to be the judge of quick and dead, Jesus Christ, the Saviour, the anointed of God. "Jesus Christ came into the world to save sinners." He taught in our world, and did many wonderful works, and then was crucified, cut off, made an offering for sin, an atoning sacrifice, and at the end of the world he shall appear again without a sacrifice, a bloody offering to take vengeance on them that know not God, and to be glorified in all who believe on his name. All were silent, and I departed.

BUDHISM.

The following was communicated to me by a Budhist Priest who had been converted to Christianity :—

'According to the tradition and belief of the sect of the Budhists on the island of Ceylon, in the history of Budha the founder of their religion, are some striking analogies to that of Christ, and the points of resemblance are far too numerous to be the result of mere accident.

'Budha was miraculously conceived: born of a princess while on a journey of state ; at his birth the angelic host rejoiced. He fasted for a long period, during which he was incessantly tempted by an evil spirit,—which temptations he overcame, and the evil spirit was cast into a place of punishment. Budha likewise abolished sacrifice, and had eighty-two followers, answering to the twelve apostles and seventy disciples of our Lord.

'There are other resemblances which seem conclusive that Budhism, either at its origin, or at some subsequent period, has had many facts of the Christian history engrafted into it. If at its origin, then the date assumed by its professors must be false, as they assign the birth of Budha to have taken place 250 years before the Christian era.

About three years since, I visited the coast of Arracan, where Budhism is generally professed, and where I conversed with some of the chief among them, on their principles and profession, their creed, and rules of life, &c. I was fully convinced from all the information I could obtain from them, that their principles were thoroughly atheistic. And that *Nastic*, (the name given them by the orthodox Hindoos) is strictly applicable, i. e. *Destructionists,* or *Annihilists.* They have no object of *worship.* Their places of assembly are filled with images of Budh, &c. but they do not worship them—together with these images are placed almost every article of European, as well as Asiatic manufacture they can procure, particularly pictures, glass, and earthenware. In one, on the right hand of the principal image of Budh, was placed a chamber-utensil, innocently enough I am persuaded. It was merely considered like china on the chimney-place—more for ornament than use.

During my stay at Kuac Frew, a singular ceremony took place, illustrative of their principle of destruction, &c. which principle is, that the spirit's alliance with this body is a hell of punishment; and by performing a certain number of virtuous acts (as they are pleased to call them) *liberation* is to be obtained, i. e. *annihilation.*—Any person who does so, becomes an object of veneration. When he dies a contest takes place for the possession of his body. The victorious party immediately grasping whatever is nearest, or available, sets about macerating the poor lifeless body—flesh and bones, into a mummy, which done, they shapen it into a human form, place it in a box or coffin, which they fill with '*Castor oil,*'* &c. and hermetically seal. This precious treasure is then kept for a whole year; at the end of which, the lid is taken off, the poor body is taken out, a

* The oil is afterwards sold in the Bazaar as a sovereign remedy for body and mind.

pile is erected, and barrels of gun-powder are placed in the midst. The body is then put on the top of the pile, and the pile ignited, the body of course is *destroyed* and scattered to the four winds of heaven. This is emblematic of *destruction!* Each particle goes into its own, *element!* And *bus!* there is an end of it!

C.

The following description of a Sabbath at Sea, may be interesting to such as never witnessed such a scene.

Our ship was bound for Madras and Calcutta. Two sabbaths passed in the Channel, without the semblance of rest, or of holy-day. All was labour, hurry, confusion, and deafening sounds. The third Sunday was otherwise. It stands in my recollection full in beautiful contrast. On going upon deck early in the morning, we were rejoiced to find that it was possible to make a difference between the Sabbath and other days, even far out at sea. The awning was stretched over the poop, the deck beautifully clean, the long end of the halliards, sheets, tacks, and all the nautical assemblage of robes, lay coiled in circles upon the deck with almost geometrical exactness; the ship's officers were in their Sunday dresses, and the hardy crew in their new and clean clothes. These trifles, combined with the sweet and balmy air for which these latitudes are famed, gave to the scene and to the day, an appearance of tranquillity and sanctity of peculiar kind.

They who are accustomed to watch the movement of their own hearts, full well know the influence of outward things in disposing or indisposing them for devotional exercises. David loved the stillness of the night, for communion with his God, and for diligent searching of his own heart. The blessed Son of David also when on earth *retired* into a mountain *apart* to pray, and He loved Gethsemane as a fit spot for holy meditation, and converse with God his Father, whose will He was come down to do, proving that he was *very man*, and as man alive to all the susceptibility of man's nature and manifesting by His own bright example, that

> The calm retreat, the silent shade,
> With prayer and praise agree.

Impressed with these feelings, we trod the poop of our little floating world. The water was remarkably smooth, having only that peculiar swelling and undulation usually attendant upon a calm, and though we beheld not the might of the Lord when he bloweth with his wind, and the waves thereof rise and swell, we confessed it in that power which could say to so fickle an element, "Peace be still!"

At five bells, (half-past ten) '*prayers and muster*' was the order issued by the officer of the watch, and with ready obedience the crew assembled on the quarter-deck; their names were called over, and their respective posts assigned them. When this was done the men unbonnetted, and took their seats on some capstan bars which had been arranged in parallel lines for their accommodation, supported on water-buckets. The Rev. —— took his place in front of the cuddy, the capstan covered with a flag, served for a pulpit. The officers and passengers then took their seats above and below, on poop and deck, &c.

Precious at all times are the devotional services of our Church, but especially were they so to us in these novel yet interesting circumstances; with our then peculiar anticipations, and after the turmoil of the two preceding Sabbaths, "even as cold water to a thirsty land." The sun shone brightly, though the intenseness of his rays was shaded from the little audience by the awning and the mainsail, which scarcely was filled by the light breeze which waved about our heads.'

The service was quietly and solemnly performed, all in keeping with the scene. Mr. —— touched upon our past feelings, our present interesting situation, and our hope of a successful voyage, in a manner deeply interesting.

A poor pigeon which had escaped from his confinement, continued for some time to hover round the ship, like the dove of Noah finding no rest for the sole of her foot, save the sea-girt citadel. Like her, O my soul, when thou dost madly forsake the shelter of thy Redeemer's bosom, may'st thou find no repose, till thou fleest thither again!

Bounding along the obedient surges,
Cheerily on her onward way,
Her course the gallant vessel urges,
Across the stormy gulf—Biscay!
In the sun the bright waves glisten—
Rising slow with measured swell;
Hark—what sounds unwonted!—Listen,
Listen, 'tis the Sabbath-bell.

Hushed the tempest's wild commotion,
Winds and waves have ceased their war.
O'er the wide and sullen ocean
That shrill sound is heard afar.
And comes it as a sound of gladness
To thy tried spirit, wanderer, tell?
Or rather does thy heart's deep sadness
Wake at that simple Sabbath-bell?

It speaks of ties which duties sever,
Of heart so fondly knit to thee;
Kind hands, kind looks, which wanderer, never
Thine hand shall grasp, thine eyes shall see.
It speaks of home and all its pleasures,
Of scenes where memory loves to dwell—
And bids thee count thy heart's best treasures,
Far, far away, that Sabbath-bell.

Listen again! thy wounded spirit,
Shall soar from earth, and seek above,
That kingdom which the blest inherit,
The mansions of eternal love.
Earth and its lowly cares forsaking,
(Pursued too keenly, loved too well,)
To faith and hope thy soul awaking,
Thou hear'st with joy the Sabbath-bell.

D.

PROVIDENTIAL ESCAPE.

Extract of a Letter, giving an account of the providential escape of the Rev. H. F. from murderers, on the night of July 28th. 1816.

You will already have learnt from imperfect reports in the newspapers, my wonderful and providential deliverance out of the hands of a set of brutal murderous ruffians, who had undertaken, in the capacity of Dawk-bearers, to convey me from the first stage on my way to Saharunpore: I readily comply with your wish to know the particulars, which are indeed so decidedly a proof of an over-ruling and merciful interference of the mighty arm of God in my behalf, that I must at all times thankfully rejoice to call this providence to remembrance. Never can it be forgotten by me! Many of the circumstances which I now have it in my power to communicate have been brought to light by subsequent legal investigations; but as they will enable me to relate the whole affair in more regular detail, I shall not interrupt my story by any needless references to those authorities, any further than to premise that they were ample and satisfactory enough to connect the whole series of their cruel and blood-thirsty designs against me; but "the Lord was my helper:" I can only attribute it to Him that I live to relate the mercy.

I was solicited to go to Saharunpore for the purpose of uniting in marriage Mr. Grindall, the Judge and Magistrate there, and Miss Munn. The distance is about seventy miles, and not far from the Himalaya mountains, about thirty-six miles, which range in a north-westerly direction towards the regions of Tartary. It was particularly desirable to the parties that I should reach Saharunpore on the morning of the 29th July, which obliged me therefore to set off on Sunday night the 28th, after the sabbath services were finished. You know they are rather laborious, particularly at this time of the year. In India the most scrupulous attention is paid to the necessity of selecting the cool hour of the early dawn for the morning Church, so as to get into the shelter of a house by eight o'clock, before the sun is too high. I have a second service in my own house at ten, when about sixty soldiers usually attend, with whom I am personally acquainted, and several of the humbler classes of society. My son Henry superintends the Hindoostanee service with Anund Mussee in the afternoon, and at night I am lecturing on the Gospel of St. John in the Church. I am, you may therefore conclude, somewhat weary when the day's work is done. After a cup of coffee I turned into my Palanquin, and soon composed myself to sleep. It was about ten o'clock. As I passed the hospital, about eight or ten of my soldiers (as I call them) were waiting to say once more farewell, and to commend me to God's gracious care. They drew my attention to the ill-looking set of bearers who were carrying me, and truly they were a most truculent villainous party, one man in particular, I could not help almost shuddering to look at. He was very tall, very black, with an enormous quantity of rough shaggy hair on his head and beard and breast, his grumbling voice when he spoke was scarcely human, resembling more the savage growl of a wild beast than any thing else. He also limped on his right leg, as he trotted on with his flaming Mussaul, and seemed particularly curious to pry into my Palanquin. I had no arms and was merely dressed in my night gown and trowsers. After a few parting words with the dear pious soldiers I closed the doors and was soon buried in sleep. I however heard the bearers talking and laughing with each other about some expected '*Tamasha*,' fun; and '*buhot uchha nuseeb*.' The fates favour us, i. e. we are in luck's way. There were ten bearers and two Mussaulchees. I was of course utterly unconscious how far I had travelled, when I was suddenly awakened by what appeared to me to be a smart blow with a stick upon the roof of my Palkee, and which was instantly but very gently lowered to the ground. I threw open the slide and enquired what was the matter. The answer was a dreadful blow on the breast, with a heavy laden Lattee, (a solid bamboo, with iron rings round the butt end) which laid me upon my back forthwith, and the pannels of the slides were in a moment beaten in. As I endeavoured hastily to jump out to make the best defence I could, not liking to die in my nest, I distinguished the tall Mussaulchee standing with an uplifted sword, ready to make a cut at my head, and which happily for me I saw in time. As I sprang up from my left hand, I struck him with my right with all the strength I could muster, and he fell like a log, not however without inflicting with his falling sword a severe wound across the jaw-bone, which instantly gushed out a torrent of blood. Of course I concluded it was mortal, but in the anxiety and confusion of the moment, felt only that my desperate situation called for as desperate a defence. Yet the cowardly villains did not close upon me as I expected, but stood in a semicircle in front of me, gazing on their prostrate companion. He speedily got up however, and flourished his sword, and encouraged the men by his gestures to resume the attack. Several of them had lattees in their hands, with which they kept threatening me in the way in which the natives usually practice fencing, leaping forward and retreating and ejaculating a sort of grunt, 'huh ! huh !' at every feint. They observed (with that exception,) a death-like silence. I retreated before them, asking them what they wanted, and assuring them I had nothing about my person. There was for some time no reply. At last the Mussaulchee growled out the word Rooh-pee, (pronouncing it deliberately as I spell it) I said, 'All are in the Palkee !' They interchanged looks with each other, but followed me up as I retreated. From the exceeding loss of blood I suddenly became faint and sick, my knees trembled under me, and I was sinking to the ground. I had turned at the moment to ward off a threatening blow from another of the party, when the Mussaulchee made another successful cut at the back of my neck, but happily the wound was slight. I still kept retreating with my face towards them, and remonstrating with them, but my weakness and faintness increased so visibly, that the ruffian seemed encouraged to make a rush at me, and with his uplifted sword to cut me down, when one of the bearers seized his arm, exclaiming in a sort of suppressed whisper, 'marro mut, marro mut!' The man hesitated. There was a large sheet of water close behind me, and having no alternative, as they followed me up to the very edge, I waded into it. They followed me a little way into the water, and then stood and *watched* me across. It was not more than one hundred yards over, and not deeper than my waist. On my reaching the opposite bank, they all hurried back and began to break and plunder the palanquin. The dawk jungle was very high, I therefore went down upon my hands and knees and crawled a considerable distance into the thicket, and lay down, as I hoped, secure from further molestation. The cold water had refreshed me much, and I was able to twist the wet bed-gown into a kind of rope and bind it fast round my throat to staunch the bleeding. I had not the slightest conception where I was. It was star-light, but there was no moon. I looked for the north star to afford me some guiding direction, whither to turn my steps, when just at that moment I heard the Ghurree of H.M. 67th Regt. strike eleven o'clock. It was as the cheering voice of a friend inviting me to a safe place of refuge, and I was much delighted to find that I could scarcely be three miles from my own home, a distance which I thought I could easily accomplish. I need not say how fervently and gratefully I lifted up my heart to God, and how much my whole soul was engaged in ejaculatory prayer and thanksgiving to my Almighty Deliverer. Never have I before or since so realised the apparent actual approach of death, and never before or since have felt, deeply felt, how in the midst of life we are in death. I had closed my eyes to sleep in robust health and strength, dreaming of no danger, and fearless in consequence, and now I was tottering along like a helpless infant, scarcely able to make an effort to seek assistance. I sat awhile on the ground to gather a little revival of spirit, and to bind up my wound more securely. There had been a heavy fall of rain a few days before, which was most fortunate for me, as by washing my parched mouth now and then, I felt wonderfully refreshed. I had lost my shoes in the struggle, which rendered walking rather painful, nevertheless I made tolerable progress by resting now and then, and washing my face with cold water. When I got out of the jungle into the open plain, and saw the glimmering of the distant light in the guard-room, I was able to keep a straight course. But fainting continually returned, and I was obliged in consequence to lie down, thinking I must die. I had, you may be sure, many very anxious and serious thoughts, the benefit and savour of which I think I feel to this day, though alas not with suitable and sufficient strength. I thought of my large and interesting flock, of my *peradventure* widowed wife and eight fatherless children, and I prayed to God to protect and preserve me for their sakes. Another somewhat alarming reflection crossed my mind: I had on this very spot only a few mornings back met two fierce-looking wolves, and the bare possibility of meeting them under my present helpless circumstances in the dead of the night, was by no means agreeable. I roused up my spirits and renewed by efforts to proceed. At last I reached the burial-ground, and a little in advance of it I heard the voices of two soldiers in conversation. I hailed them with some difficulty. 'Who's there?' was the reply. 'Mr. Fisher!'—'*What!*' and they talked to each other. 'Depend upon it,' said one, 'it is that drunken artilleryman. Let him lie, he will be sober enough in the morning.' 'No, no!' said

I, 'Mr. Fisher, the chaplain.' They were with me in a moment. 'Who has used you thus? how came you in this sad plight? where are the rascals?' accompanied with a few indignant execrations, uttered with a true-hearted Irish energy. I replied, 'Never mind, take me to the guard-room, and send for the surgeon. They caught me up, as if I had been a child, and soon conveyed me into the centre of the crowding soldiers, who came gathering round. The surgeon soon came and skilfully dressed my wounds, and expressed a hope that they might heal with the first intention, (as the phrase is,) and that I should soon be well. The soldiers were all apparently filled with the most indignant rage, particularly the Light Company, who were most of them personally known to me, from having seen a good deal of them in the hospital, &c. and were exceedingly anxious to turn out, and hasten in the direction over the plain from whence I had come, hoping to seize the villains. I assured them this would be utterly hopeless, from the length of time which they had unavoidably had to accomplish their escape. The Light Infantry Company however obtained permission to go under the serjeant-major's command, and off they set double quick. A most extraordinary circumstance had in the meantime occurred, which I shall proceed to relate as illustrating the apparent overruling providences which attended the whole adventure. The soldiers speedily reached the small village of Sofeepore, behind which the attack on me had been perpetrated, the villagers were all retired to rest and all was silent as death, but in *one* house, a light was observed to be burning. Corporal Macginnis hurried towards it. It was extinguished as he approached the door. He however demanded admittance, threatening 'to ram the butt end of his musket through the door' if they did not open it. Happily for Macgennis, a sudden shout from his comrades, proclaiming, 'Here they are! they are all here!' called him to the outside of the village wall, I say *happily*, for behind that threatened door, stood ready the armed Mussaulchee, fully prepared to cut him down, as the man afterwards declared. I must here inform you that at that time, it was customary for a patrol of the 8th Dragoons to ride two or three times during the night in that same direction, and also a mounted patrol of the Begum Sambroo's were directed to meet there and interchange the usual military 'All's well!' The murderous bearers were aware of this, and had carried me, while I was asleep, out of the high road into the adjoining jungle, where the scene I have related took place. Some time had elapsed before they could return into the road again, and in making the attempt to do so, they were seen by the Begum's patrol, who instantly rode up to them and compelled them to halt till the Dragoon patrole should come up. They complied of course, and sat conversing on the ground. In the meantime I had accomplished my melancholy march, and the active Light Company had reached the spot, in time to secure the fellows. 'And so please your honor,' said Corporal Macgennis, 'as soon as I found we had hit on the right track and nabbed the rascals, I brought my bayonet to the charge, ordered them to fall in, and here they all stand!' They were placed in secure guard till the morning, and then lodged in the jail to take their trial before the Judge, Mr. Gorton.

A very diligent investigation took place, and the result was a clear exposition of the whole affair from beginning to end. I have already stated that the ruffian armed with the sword had concealed himself in the hut which Corporal Macgennis was about to enter, when the shout of his comrades called him off. The discovery of this fellow was singular enough. There happened to be in Meerut at the time a man of suspicious character, who went to Mr. Gorton the Judge (probably under the idea of obtaining some reward) and voluntarily offered to betray the Mussaulchee's hiding-place, as he knew where he was. He deposed to the following effect:—

'About a week ago this same Mussaulchee came to my house, and after condoling with me on my apparent poverty, said he could put me in a way to get a good booty, if I would join him and some others in a scheme which they had resolved to execute. Would I swear secrecy! I promised of course. Then said he, I can tell you, that the Padre Sahib is going off to Saharunpore by Dawk on Sunday night to a Shaddee,* and he carries with him two thousand rupees,† and a casket of jewels for the bride. We have engaged ourselves to take him the first stage, and if opportunity serves, we will take him into the jungle, kill him, and throw his body into a well, and carry off the prize. It will be many days before he is found, and we shall have time to make our escape certain. But said the witness, he may have pistols and shoot some of you. No, he replied, that is not likely. He is not a soldier, and we can surely overpower him, if we are true to each other. The witness declined joining with the party, however, because Mr. G——'s police *knew* him, and the moment the Padre is missing, I shall be the *first* sought after, as my character is bad. I wish you success, but there is great danger.'

The witness said also, that the Mussaulchee had fled into the village, and concealed himself in a hut in Sofeepore when first the patrole came in sight, (while the bearers were endeavouring to regain the road with the broken palanquin, purposing to say, that the Padre had been attacked by Dacoits, and had fled into the jungle, wounded). There the Mussaulchee remained all that night, and the following day. He then returned to his own home, where he now is! 'How do you know that he is there?' I have just left him, said he.

* Marriage.

† The origin of this absurd report can only be conjectured. Captain Gwatkin had requested me to take charge of a packet of books which he was anxious to send to Mr. Grindall, and which I readily undertook to do. He being *the Paymaster*, I suppose the people conjectured that *it might* probably contain rupees; and so fond are the natives of rupees, and so reckless of human life with such a temptation before them, that I do well believe for such a sum, they would have had no objection to cut as many throats, if convenient opportunity should serve.

I went to his house to hear all particulars, as everybody was talking about it, and I said, 'Now you have got 2000 rupees, you must give me *half*, or I will inform against you!' He asserted, that it was all a lie, *jhoot bat*, that there was not more than sixteen rupees in the drawer, and some silver clasps and edging of a little book, (it was my favourite little pocket Bible, *a Pasham*, given me by a dear brother. They tore off the clasps, &c. and threw away the book,) and some clothes. Here's my share of the plunder, take it, and don't betray me. The false friend (what is the friendship of the wicked worth,) received the proffered gift, and carried them immediately to the Judge, who, having furnished him with a strong guard, the culprit was soon seized, and lodged safely in the jail.

One of the prisoners was admitted king's evidence and substantiated all that the first witness had said. Another remarkable circumstance tended to prove that the bearers had carried me *out* of the direct road, which they at first denied stoutly. The soldiers from whom I had parted near the Hospital, had sauntered back to their barracks, but stood a considerable time near the guard-room in the sun-dial chabootra, watching the progress of the blazing Mussauls, and conversing with each other. They distinctly saw the light turn rapidly to the right into the jungle, (the Saharunpore road turns almost at right angles *to the left*). They became stationary a few seconds, and then were extinguished. 'About three quarters of an hour afterwards, Mr. Fisher returned to the barracks severely wounded, and all his clothes steeped in blood.'

While the surgeon was engaged in his charitable office, a messenger was despatched to communicate to my son Henry the unfortunate, or rather let me say the providential circumstances attending my proposed journey. He came, poor fellow, in haste. The shock was almost overwhelming, and indeed to my whole family, a source of exceeding sorrow, but also of exceeding thankfulness for my miraculous escape. After a few days, when I was able to bear moving in a tonjaun, I accompanied Mr. Gorton to point out the spot where I had been attacked. It was in the thickest part of the jungle, and the place easily ascertained from the trampled state of the grass; a pair of bearer's slippers, a lattee, and the broken fragments of the palanquin, lay scattered round, and the footsteps marked in the mud at the side of the talao, evidently imprinted by some one who had been staggering about from some cause or other unable to walk steadily. The marks exactly fitted my feet, and were a sufficient proof that I had been attacked *there*, and not, as the men asserted, in the highroad. Notwithstanding the guilt of these atrocious villains was so fully substantiated, they were, by *Mahommedan law* (as I was informed) and in opposition to Mr. Gorton's opinion, acquitted, inasmuch as I was not actually killed, but the case was referred for closer reconsideration, and to the final decision of the Circuit Judge, and I believe to Calcutta, and the whole gang received some corporal punishment, and were transported to Prince of Wales's Island. One man contrived to make his escape, and was not heard of for some years. He was, however, subsequently taken up for housebreaking and murder, and was hanged at Meerut. The poor wretched creature was sent to me before his execution to ascertain if I could identify him. But the only man I could and did swear to (for I never could forget him) was the black and limping Mussaulchee.

Truly the Almighty God was with me and compassed me as with a shield. How can it ever be blotted from my memory and heart, that his marked interference in my behalf was beyond dispute or doubts. I stand amazed when I call to mind his undeserved mercies. Was it not a strange sort of infatuation that these fellows should be so blinded by their eager impatience for the prize, that they would not wait a far more convenient and distant place, three or four miles more in advance, where in all probability I must have perished for want of assistance. The wildness of the place, the increased distance, the continued bleeding, exhausting my remaining strength, would have rendered it hopeless for me to escape. How could I have explored my way or travelled so far on foot in my exhausted state, or how understand in what direction to move! Again, how wonderful that they should have had any apprehensions of an unarmed defenceless victim, yet evidently they were kept from letting loose their rage, from some cause or other ; they appeared to imagine, I had perhaps some secreted dagger in my hand, when the swordsman fell so head over heels, and never came near enough to be hit, only reaching out their lattees at a distance and springing back again, with some token of alarm when I attempted a blow. And that timely and unexpected voice too! 'Marro mut, marro mut!' Was it not the restraining mercy of God! "Slay not my servant, though he be a frail sinful man, I will spare him, I will remember his wife, his children, his flock, I have prepared for him mercy and truth and will preserve him?" Yes, my dear brother, so I consider it, let others call it lucky, good fortune, &c., I call it mercy, free, mighty, undeserved. To God be all the praise. He has delivered my soul from death, and He will deliver my feet from falling, that I may walk before God in the light of the living. How extraordinary it was that the moment of attack should be just at that particular point of time. Five minutes later, and I had heard no Ghurrhee, and what was to guide me in a dark night through a pathless waste to a place of refuge. To my heart the bell spoke intelligibly, Turn this way, come hitherwards, there are your friends, this way lies your home, and who led me by the hands, supported my unyielding spirits, staunched the bleeding, and finally healed the wounds! The Lord he is the God, the Lord he is the God. Oh! may I never forget His tender care of me and mine, but render Him faithfully, love for his love. My dear soldiers seem to have been wonderfully wrought upon by all these circumstances, and to draw round me with a degree of affection that can only be appreciated by those who feel as they feel, and love as they love, even in the fellowship of Jesus Christ our Lord. I bless God I am nearly well, but am suffering still from weakness through the loss of blood, and severe pain in the breast from the blow of the lattee. I have also lost the free use of the muscles of the neck on the right side, and have a strange and constant nervous sensation in the jaw, which is uncomfortable, but not painful. The surgeon tells me my escape is *a miracle.* The sword passed close to the glands which secrete the saliva, and yet they were untouched. And my speech is not affected, although, from the depth of the wound in so dangerous a place, it was most likely I should have been for ever disabled as a preacher, even if I escaped as I did with life. May I ever rejoice to bless and praise His holy name, who has approved himself my guardian and my God. HALLELUJAH!

E.

SKETCH OF THE LIFE OF THE REV. CHARLES KNORPP, LATE MISSIONARY OF THE CHURCH MISSIONARY SOCIETY AT BENARES.

How soothing and consolatory to the mind of the believer are the assurances contained in the word of God, that all his dispensations in providence, and all his dealings in grace towards his church, are ordered and arranged by infinite love and wisdom! The influence and impression of these truths are felt peculiarly powerful, when his honoured and faithful servants are removed in the bloom of life, and in the zenith of activity and usefulness. That "precious in his sight is the death of his saints," is a delightful thought, and we know their lives are equally precious to him also, and are never cut short, but for some wise, though perhaps hidden reason, which if we know not now, we shall know hereafter.

It is a solemn and heart-stirring event that both husband and wife were carried off so nearly together, and so unexpectedly, Mr. Knorpp dying on the 29th of March, and Mrs. K. on the 2nd of April last, at the early ages of 32, and 28. Loudly does it speak to those who remain, to "work while it is called to-day," for O how soon may the night come on *us*, "when no man can work." Humanly speaking, none could have calculated on a longer life of usefulness in India, than both of *them*, especially Mrs. Knorpp. But the Lord's ways are not as ours, and he saw fit thus early to withdraw them.

Mr. Knorpp was a native of Stuttgart, the capital of the little kingdom of Wurtemberg in Germany, which though it contains considerably fewer inhabitants than London, has produced and sent forth during the last twenty years, one third, or nearly one half, of all the missionaries who have entered the field. He had the privilege of being born of truly pious parents, in whose abode it could be seen and felt, that religion reigned pre-eminent. Their incessant prayers for their offspring were, that they might become the children of God; and it is believed that the gentle and unceasing efforts of his kind and affectionate mother on his behalf were not unblessed. O how much is in the power of mothers, when their hearts are bent upon "the one thing needful,"—when the early conversion of their little ones is their prominent care! As in nature, so in grace, early sowing will produce early reaping, and usually the most abundant harvest.

Mr. Knorpp was the first among many children, who appeared to be religiously impressed. His younger years were spent in school, and when that period of his life was over, his parents placed him with a friend, for the purpose of learning a trade; but his heavenly Father had chosen him for a nobler calling, as was soon made apparent.

During his apprenticeship a family affliction,—the severe illness of his beloved mother,—and the faithful preaching of a devoted young minister, led him to deep reflection, and finally to strong conviction, and it was at this interesting period, in his sixteenth year, that he truly and entirely gave himself up to the Lord.

The minister alluded to was the celebrated Hoffacker, whose labours at Stuttgart effected immense good, particularly among the young. Several pious youths in the warmth of their first love united together for prayer, under the direction of a holy and highly advanced Christian, and Knorpp was one of their number.

It was there that the germ of missionary zeal was planted, and in some degree developed, and after the lapse of a few years, he, with several of the other youths, publicly offered himself to become an evangelist to the heathen, and by applying to the Committee of the Mission seminary at Basle in Switzerland, he was received as a student into that institution.

It will be interesting to mention here, that this seminary, from which so many missionaries are sent out, is conducted upon the most purely scriptural principles, and appears particularly well calculated for the education of those, who in the self-denying spirit of the apostles, desire to go forth among the heathen. The plan of education is well contrived to advance the spiritual growth and intellectual improvement of the students. The domestic arrangement is also peculiarly fitted to produce those habits of simplicity and diligence, which every missionary ought to possess.

The Principal, Mr. Blumhardt, is a man of considerable talents, great erudition, and practical piety, in whom are united what we so seldom witness—the characters of an affectionate father and counsellor, as well as most able tutor to his pupils. The whole establishment, consisting of about sixty individuals, presents the beautiful picture of a *family*, living in the most undivided harmony; humility, peace, and love, reign there in a higher degree than the writer ever remembers to have witnessed elsewhere. A sweet spirit of prayer pervades the place, which is fostered by voluntary meetings between the members of the various classes and the teachers. It may truly be said that prayer and praise resound through the dwelling continually, and this doubtless is the keystone to the happy spirit of its inmates. It were indeed devoutly to be wished, that every missionary who leaves that place might ever retain the spirit of simplicity and piety which he brings from thence, and keep alive in its full warmth, the feeling which so animates both teachers and students there,—that a missionary needs more than the mere frame-work of human learning, and that his own soul must stand in the right position before God, if he wish to become a useful and efficient labourer among the heathen.

At this favoured place our sainted brother studied upwards of five years, during which he diligently redeemed his time, aud made a truly satisfactory progress, evincing good abilities, and improving every opportunity for enriching his mind. His intercourse with the tutors and brethren was very beneficial to him ; he grew in knowledge and in grace, and gave pleasing promise of becoming a missionary indeed ; nor was such promise disappointed.

After leaving the seminary he once more visited his beloved parents, and bade them a final farewell. The hour of separation was bitter to their natural feelings, yet both rejoiced in seeing their son depart on such an holy errand.

Having arived in England with several other brethren, he entered into connection with the Church Missionary Society, and prepared for ordination, to which he was admitted as a Deacon by the Bishop of London, and after this, following the call of the Committee, he proceeded to labour in North India. Himself with three missionary brethren, had the privilege of making the voyage with our present reverend diocesan, from whose society and instructive example be derived great benefit. He often mentioned afterwards with gratitude the high esteem and cordial affection he conceived and retained for his Lordship, as his last journal abundantly testifies.

Soon after landing in Calcutta he was ordained Priest, and he then proceeded to Benares, with Mr. Leupold, his fellow-labourer. There, after diligently studying, and attaining a sufficient knowledge of Hindee and Ordoo, he preached his first sermon to the heathen, at the expiration of nine months from his arrival, and from that period to his death he proclaimed the gospel regularly twice a day in the city of Benares.

From his own journals we learn that he pursued his noble course in the true spirit of a holy and devoted messenger of God, deeply mourning over the darkness and ignorance of the Hindoos, and grieving like Paul, when at Athens, to see that great city so wholly given to idolatry.

We cannot forbear to remark here, that perhaps none but those who are actually engaged in preaching to the heathen, can fully understand the peculiar difficulties and trials connected with this arduous work. Day after day the servant of God goes out, declaring salvation through Jesus to the perishing sinners around him; but when he beseeches them in Christ's stead to be reconciled to God, himself and his message but too generally meet with opposition, derision, and scorn. Far different is the situation of the missionary, to that of the minister over a professedly Christian congregation. The former has, as it were, to intrude his message in many cases upon unwilling and prejudiced hearers; and as an intruder he is frequently disregarded and opposed.

Our departed brother deeply felt this, especially in a place like Benares, which may well be termed the head-quarters of Hindoo bigotry and superstition, and he feelingly alludes to it towards the close of his last journal, at the very termination of his labours; after which he remarks, that 'had not a missionary a gracious Saviour, before whose throne he may come with all his cares and anxieties, there would be no possibility of bearing up under the trials of his faith, and of keeping his hand to the plough.' But "they that wait upon the Lord, shall renew their strength;' and this promise was fulfilled in the experience of our beloved brother. Grace was given him to persevere to the end; he fought the good fight, he kept the faith, and has finished his course.

In November 1834, Mr. Knorpp was united to a pious partner, Miss West of Islington, with whom he had formed an engagement in London. She proved a sweet-tempered, affectionate, and useful helpmate to him, and became the mother of two dear infants, who are now left orphans. From April 1836, Mrs. Knorpp took an active part in the management of the Benares Church Mission Orphan Institution, which has lost much by her removal.

The following interesting extract of a letter received from Mr. Leupold, contains the affecting account of the last illness and death of these valuable missionaries:

'On my return from my excursion I found dear brother Knorpp in a weak state of health, but my presence seemed to revive him. He was very anxious to go into tents for a week or a fortnight, hoping to be able to ward off a sickness, of the approach of which he had some presentiment. Circumstances over which he had no controul compelled him to postpone going for a week, and we therefore spent a few happy days together. I was stopping with them, and never before observed them so earnest in prayer;—they were both preparing for heaven. A holy earnestness rested on dear Knorpp's brow, whilst his wife was more affectionate than ever. She had prepared several little things against my arrival, to welcome me, and her husband and myself could not but smile at her ingenious inventions.

'During their absence from home I had several letters from them, expressive of their desire for the coming of Christ's kingdom, and their affection towards me. In one of them brother Knorpp after complaining of his unprofitableness, says, 'O that I had the love of a John, the zeal of a Paul, and the strength of a Goliah.' And Mrs. Knorpp's desires were most ardently expressed, for living more to the glory of God, and more in communion with him.

'After being a fortnight in tents, they returned home, but it appeared to me that neither of them had derived much benefit from the trip. Knorpp had evidently become weaker, but his partner stated that she never felt better in her life than she did then.

'As poor Knorpp suffered more daily, I pressed him to consult the doctor, and on Friday the 9th of March prevailed on him to do so; but he did not think Knorpp's case a dangerous one. What made me uncomfortable, was a bad cough which he had, and at the same time I observed that the health of Mrs. Knorpp became impaired. Her rosy cheeks grew pale, and a languor was perceptible in her eyes, with a depression of mind, which alarmed me. Soon after this they both lost their appetite, and on the tenth, Knorpp was obliged to remain in bed, and his poor wife was much excited, for her impression was, 'my husband will not live.' During two days and nights she was incessantly engaged in nursing him; though I entreated her not to exert herself so much, yet I could not prevail. I shall never forget the impression I received on entering their house the day after Knorpp took to his bed; both were asleep beside each other, one as pale as death, and the other flushing red, as though a burning fever were raging in her veins. That evening I begged much to stay during the night with brother Knorpp, but she would not permit it.

'On the following Tuesday when returning from the city, I found her really ill with fever, still she wished to go on attending her husband, but here I interfered, and prepared a couch for her in his study, on which she reclined. From that hour they saw each other no more in this world. During the day, the fever continued to increase on her, yet the doctor thought nothing of her illness, supposing it, as we all did, to be merely the effect of excitement and anxiety of mind. He ordered both to be kept quiet, and I went from one room to another, endeavouring to administer spiritual and temporal comfort to each of them.

'On Wednesday in the afternoon Mrs. Knorpp came out of her room towards the place where I was sitting, and looked with intense anxiety upon me. I smiled at her, and she went away; but a few minutes after she called me, and said, 'As I lay here on my couch, my husband stood before me as if prepared to go out. He was in a great hurry and wished to kiss me, but as I hesitated, he disappeared.' She wept much, and added, 'He is dead.' I cannot express with what anguish of mind she related this, and I was exceedingly affected too, but endeavoured to show her, that the whole was in consequence of excited imagination, which she allowed.

'But on Thursday the sickness took a serious turn with both, and I found my strength not equal to my task. I therefore thankfully accepted the kind offer of our dear missionary brethren to share with me in my labour of love. About eight o'clock at night I prepared to retire, having been four nights without rest, but when giving dear Knorpp some barley-water, I perceived to my sorrow his countenance changed, his teeth closed, his eyes become fixed, and death seemed to spread over his whole frame. The doctor immediately applied a blister to his head, and being greatly fatigued, I lay down, though the impression of my dying brother was too vivid in my mind to allow me to sleep. At one o'clock I was sent for, as he was supposed to be dying; we prayed with him, and he prayed also. It seemed that at the beginning of the night his prospects of eternity had been gloomy, but when I saw him, they were bright. He exhorted the servants, spoke to me in German, and then said, "Come, Lord Jesus, come quickly!" Being asked how he felt, he replied, 'Peace, peace, peace is in my soul, a bright light shines before me. I could tell you more, but I must not.' His countenance beamed with heavenly joy, and every one could see that the Lord was gracious to him. Some time afterwards he said to me in German, 'Ah it is a hard thing before the thread of life is cut through. I am dying, there is no more hope of life; a little while, and I shall be with the Lord.' I could not reply for tears; he was so resigned, and looked with such longing joy towards his approaching dissolution.

'The doctor requested me to inform Mrs. Knorpp of the danger in which he was, to prepare her for the final stroke. I therefore mentioned to her the whole of what had transpired during the night, to which she listened with joy and great interest, exclaiming, 'O how happy to be in such a frame of mind, and so prepared; but he will die, and not survive, though he may be somewhat better this morning;' at the same time adding, 'I hope the Lord will spare me, for I am not yet prepared, I have not prayed enough, or been so faithful as I ought.' I then pointed her to Jesus, as the all-sufficient Saviour of such unfaithful sinners as we are, and I also begged her to prepare for the sad tidings of her husband's going home, because though he was then better, he was still in such danger, that a relapse of fever might open his way into heaven. She calmly looked at me and said, 'I am prepared, and have been so from the beginning.'

'Brother Knorpp lingered on notwithstanding these very unfavourable symptoms, but on Sunday the 25th, he became very weak, and believing his dissolution to be at hand, he called for me: he was perfectly sensible, but unable to speak, and therefore called for pencil and paper, and wrote a few sentences containing his dying request to me. He then wished to write to his dear wife, but perceiving that it cost him too much exertion, I took the paper from him.

'After that day he became frequently delirious, sometimes fancying he lay in quicksand, at other times in fire, or between red-hot stones. Poor Mrs. K. too became very ill; for six days she slept scarcely an hour, and took medicine but to little purpose. I despaired of her life, yet I hoped against hope; but she was evidently aware of the approaching crisis, and requested me to destroy all her papers after her death; and then she exclaimed, "I die, I die; I trust the Lord will pardon me, and receive me to himself."

'My own sufferings, as you may imagine, were most intense, not bodily, but mentally, yet as my day, so was my strength. I could now and then speak to my God as it were face to face, and this was my consolation. But though the spirit was willing, the flesh was weak, and I felt truly thankful to the dear missionary brethren, who all regularly relieved me in turn. Their good ladies too watched Mrs. Knorpp day and night, and when she was so far reduced as to be obliged to give up nursing her babe, Mrs. Mather kindly offered to take him along with her own little girl. Mr. Nicholls likewise took dear Sophia, and how deeply I felt their kindness, you can better imagine than I can describe. I am sure their reward, and indeed that of all the dear missionary brethren and sisters, will be great in heaven, for their deep sympathy and unceasing kindness.

'About this time I was myself seized with the same malignant fever, and retired to bed with the deep impression that I should never rise again. I therefore took leave of my dear brother, who was then perfectly sensible. We parted with the assurance on both sides of *never seeing each other again* in this world, nor did we see each other again, as I became dangerously ill, and during the height of my attack, our dear brother departed. His end was peace; his prospects of eternity remained bright to the last, he breathed hard, I was told, for two hours, and then fell asleep. I was deprived of the privilege of closing his eyes and attending his funeral, and my feelings were acute, but the Lord was my consolation. Never in all my life was He so gracious to me as on that day; tears of sorrow and of joy mingled, and I could not help calling out. "O for a thousand tongues to sing, my dear Redeemer's praise."

'As soon as I was somewhat recovered, I went to see poor Mrs. Knorpp; she had heard of my illness, but nothing was told her of her husband's death, nor did she ever hear it. She asked but once after him, and the question was not answered. How she will have been rejoiced at finding him in heaven, ready to welcome her there! I was with her for about two hours; she was perfectly sensible, and said she felt better, but to me she appeared dying. We parted in tears; I was wavering between hope and fear, but the latter predominated, and in the morning when I awoke, I heard that her spirit too had left its earthly tabernacle, and taken its flight to its eternal mansions. It seems that after I left her, her illness took a decided turn, she complained of being obliged to lie in iron and hot water, just as her husband had done, and like him she breathed hard for two hours, and fell asleep on the 2nd of April. Her countenance in death bespoke the peace which must have filled her soul at her departure; and she seemed to smile at my tears.

'She was interred the following day, and lies to the left hand of her beloved husband, and there they both repose together, till the archangel shall awake them with his trump.

'This sickness was not quite apparent, perhaps it was the putrid fever, for it seemed to seize from the beginning on the very vitals, and I still feel the effect of my four days' illness. All the care and attention possible, were rendered to our beloved friends; two most clever and intelligent medical men were constantly with them, one of whom always passed the night in the house.

'As I remarked before, *all* our missionary brethren and sisters watched over them in turn, night and day, with unceasing solicitude, and fervent prayers were offered for them both in public and in private, but the Lord was pleased not to grant them, and who shall ask, Why? We shall ere long perceive what now appears mysterious, and this is enough.

'And now what more shall I say? They are gone home, and are safe. I shall perhaps soon follow, and I declare with sincerity that, though I pray to live a little longer for my work's sake, I long to be with Christ.

'These cutting bereavements have, I hope, created in me a stronger desire than I ever before felt, to live more to God's glory, and to cleave closer to Him from whom death cannot separate me; and although my intense feelings of joy and sorrow will pass away, these desires I trust *never will.*'

It is unnecessary to add anything to these extracts, as they speak for themselves all that might otherwise have been said. We can abundantly perceive from them the truth of the remarks with which this sketch commences, and likewise that the last days of God's faithful servants are a true comment upon their lives; and we cannot do better than exclaim, "May we die the death of the righteous, and may our last end be like his."

BENARES.

City of idol-temples and of shrines,
Where folly kneels to falsehood, how the pride
Of our humanity is here rebuked!
Man that aspires to rule the very wind,
And make the sea confess his majesty.
Whose intellect can fill a little scroll,
With words that are immortal: who can build
Cities, the mighty and the beautiful,
Yet man, this glorious creature can debase
His spirit down to worship wood and stone
And hold the very beasts which bear his yoke,
And tremble at his eye, for sacred things!
With what unutterable humility,
We should bow down, O holy Lord, to Thee,
Seeing our vanity and foolishness,
When to our own devices left, we frame
A shameful creed of craft and cruelty!

LOSS OF LIVES AT A BATHING FESTIVAL.

DEAR SIR,

I have just received a letter from a missionary friend, who was on the spot, stating that a day or two before he wrote, a bathing festival had taken place at Benares, at the junction of the Barna and the Ganges, not a quarter of a mile from his own house, at about three in the morning, when, awful to state, *three hundred persons* were literally trodden to death. After day-light the Thanader went to the spot, and on taking the depositions, was told that that number had perished. He however deemed it too appalling to make such a report to the magistrate, and therefore after some consultation, determined upon reporting the death of one hundred and seventy. And whilst this was going on, the friends of the deceased were busily employed in extricating their friends and relations, and consigning them to the flames. In the evening of the same day the missionary went to the spot, and saw more than thirty corpses still lying in the spot, and the domes were dragging them into the Gangá.

This is not the first time that such deadly scenes have taken place at Benares, for not more than two or three years ago, a similar catastrophe took place at one of the Ghåts *in* the city itself; when, about two o'clock in the morning a sacred bathing took place during an eclipse of the moon, and the Sepahees from Secrole rushed up the narrow lane leading to the river, and upwards of forty persons were trodden to death.

If idolatry and superstition have made such havock in one single city of Hindoostan in one year, what must they have done in all parts of India—surely tens of thousands must have been its victims annually! And this is the system that is considered *innocent* and *harmless*. And this is the religion that is countenanced and defended by the Court of Directors and the Supreme Government of India for the sake of filthy lucre! This goddess is worshipped by a body of men calling themselves Christians! Alas! why not throw off the mask! renounce Christianity, and openly profess Hindooism at once? They would then be acting consistently. But no, they will not do this, on account of the odium attaching to it—their pride must also be fed. But they must expect their reward as a Government. The Most High will not suffer such a line of conduct to pass unpunished. They will doubtless suffer in time; and if they do not repent and retrace their steps, rue it to all eternity! May the Lord in rich mercy prevent their destruction, and open a way for the liberation of these poor deluded beings from the power of sin and Satan, and make them freemen of the Lord.

Yours,

A. MOFUSSILITE.

JOURNAL OF A MISSIONARY AT BENARES.*

Feb. 24, 1837.—We had the pleasure to meet the bishop this evening at the chaplain's house. His Lordship and Mr. Bateman received us with expressions of affection. It was a great joy to see each other again after an interval of more than four years. We dined at the chaplain's in company with some other gentlemen. His Lordship as well as Mr. Bateman looked exceedingly well.

Feb. 26.—The Bishop preached this morning a very interesting sermon on Heb. xiii. 8, and agreeably to our request had a collection for our Mission; after which we had the Lord's Supper. The collection amounted to about 460 rupees. The Rev. Mr. Bateman preached a good sermon in the evening.

Feb. 27.—The Bishop held a confirmation and then proceeded to Bengalee tola for an examination of all our schools. His Lordship principally carried on the examination, and expressed himself much pleased with the progress of the different boys. After the examination, his Lordship and Mr. Bateman returned to the Mission-compound much exhausted from the fatigue of the day. The day was unusually hot. With many kind and paternal wishes the Bishop left us, expressing a hope to see us soon again.

March.—This has been a month of much trouble and anxiety to me. At the middle of this month I was

* This interesting Journal of Missionary labours, is that of the excellent and lamented Rev. C. Knorpp, who died at Benares on the 29th of March 1838, aged 31 years, and was survived by his wife only four days. They have left two infants.

taken ill with a severe fever (which I fear was produced by too much exposure to the sun,) which lasted four days, and to our great surprise and alarm the small-pox made its appearance. As it may be supposed, this was a time of much anxiety and fear. But the Lord was gracious to me and to my family, and preserved me in the midst of danger. The small-pox was of the distinct kind, and of a very mild nature. On all sides nothing but death was to be seen and heard. The small-pox carried many off, and then the cholera commenced raging in an awful manner. Europeans as well as natives died of these diseases. Thirty, forty to fifty according to police calculation, died daily of cholera in Benares. Many persons came daily to me for medicine. Still no impression is made on the natives. Death has lost its horror among them, and none asketh, "What must I do to be saved?" The disease went to such a pitch that persons being quite well this moment, fell down dead the next. A lad in my employ, whilst drinking water, vomited once, fell down, and was instantly dead. Oh that men would consider the awfulness of appearing before a righteous Judge, and repent of their evil works and idolatry and turn to the Lord Jesus Christ!

The missionary work was partly iuterrupted by my illness, but by the mercy of God I shall again be enabled to commence preaching in the city. The small-pox has left great weakness of body behind, and the doctor will not allow me any exertion as yet. A Bairagee visits me frequently. He met us in the city. I had many interesting conversations with him, and he appears to have received a conviction of the truth of Christianity. The last time when he was with me he expressed himself strongly convinced that Christ is the only true God and Saviour. 'I have chosen him, he said, as the only object of my meditations and worship, and wherever I may go to, I shall keep my heart and soul fixed upon him.' The Bairagee expressed a strong desire to go to Adjudia (Faizabad), but had postponed his journey, in order to have some more conversations with me on our religion. I suppose from his long absence that he is gone upon his journey.

April.—I had several very interesting discussions with pundits in the city. But it is really awful to see these men struggling against the convictions divine truth is producing upon them. Their blasphemous expressions, imputations against the God of heaven, cannot be uttered. Oh I fear many harden their hearts and give themselves up to all kinds of iniquities! On the 20th instant was an eclipse of the moon. People from all parts of the country were flocking to the holy city, and gave us opportunity to preach to them the word of God. I met with some very interesting men, who listened with great desire to our conversations, and confessed the folly of seeking pardon of sins in the water of the Ganges. I think that above all, the people in Benares are the worst and the most profane and shameless sinners. As soon as they see any one attentive and making interesting questions, they laugh him to scorn and frighten him away. I fear they are growing worse and worse, like the people of Sodom and Gomorrah. At different times respectable Brahmins seeing the attention of the people, and being enraged, and some also with cold blood, asserted this horrible doctrine, that God is the doer of good and evil actions —He is a liar, a thief, a murderer, &c. The heart bleeds to hear men of sound understanding and much knowledge declare and assert the most holy God to be such an abominable creature, and that all merely in opposition to holy doctrines explained to every one who likes to listen. May God have mercy upon them!

May 3.—I had a most interesting morning in the city at Dassa Somed. This place being near the river and leading to it, is one of the most populous, and much frequented by Brahmins. We were listened to by many of the Brahmins, and several of them entered into conversation. One appeared to be very attentive. He spoke very calmly and candidly, and entered into a regular argument about Hindooism and Christianity. He dropped the arguments in favour of Hindooism, and my conversation assumed more the form of an address. An elderly man, most bitter against Christianity, and a decided enemy, who had on former occasions annoyed us in every possible manner, coming up to us, was very angry when seeing the attention of the people, and commenced his railing. Already had he succeeded in getting a few men over to him who joined in his sins. But I continued to speak, taking no notice, and becoming more serious in my address, I saw the old man gradually moving nearer and nearer, until he reached the wooden pillar of the verandah under which I sat. He listened with great seriousness and never spoke a word. The Brahmin, with whom I had conversed, testified that our doctrines were the truth, and desired a Gospel, which I gave him with a tract. A Bairagee observing the Brahmin's seriousness, commenced to abuse him. 'Will you forsake your religion and accept that of strangers?' said the man. 'And what is that to you?' replied the Brahmin, 'if I find the truth in it, I shall.' They quarrelled for some time. The Bairagee demanded that he should return the books to me, which he would not, nor did. The old man then took the Brahmin's part, saying, that in those books are only words of righteousness—'Read them,' said he, 'it will do you no harm.' I was surprised at these expressions of this our bitter enemy, who at other times would rather have knocked the Brahmin down than taken his part. The old man went away. Who knows, perhaps this morning's conversations have made a lasting impression. Another bitter enemy came up to us. He wanted to dispute with me, and charged me with robbing his people of their righteousness and religion. I gave him a practical question to solve, saying: You know that Vishnoo in his nine incarnations exhibited his character. It behoves God to give men moral lessons by words and deeds, and thereby to direct them in the way of holiness. Now observe the nine incarnations committed all kinds of crimes: fornication, adultery, thefts, lies, and having shown you their immoral actions, teach you thereby and encourage you to do the same. Now Jesus Christ, the incarnation of our shasters, never committed any thing which was sinful—no sin was found in him. He was full of righteousness and holiness, and his words corresponded with his character; for he said—Thou shalt not commit adultery, and whosoever looketh on a woman to lust after her, hath committed adultery already in his heart; he said, Thou shalt not make a lie; thou shalt not covet, &c. Now, I continued,—please tell me which do you consider righteousness? that which Vishnoo taught in his incarnations, or that which Christ taught in word and deed? He would not answer, only replied, When we are alone together, then will we speak about it: he went off making a salaam. Another Brahmin asked what opinion I taught respecting God? Sargoon or Nirgoon? Neither the one nor the other, was my answer. According to the doctrine of Sargoon, you believe that God is a stone, a river, a plant, &c. and according to Nirgoon, you make him a nullity in the universe, and besides this believe that the principle of life in man and beast is God. I went over the old ground of arguments with him, showing Hindooism in its pure light, and explained the fundamental doctrines of the Christian religion to him. He had nothing to say, and before he left, received some tracts at his request.

We had a great storm last night with some rain, which cleared and cooled the atmosphere. This morning was very pleasant, and I could spend my time till nearly ten o'clock in the city.

May 30.—Since the very hot weather, I can only spend the mornings amongst the people; the evenings are so excessively oppressive that it would be highly imprudent to act otherwise. However, once or twice, when it is my turn to preach in the chapels, and which custom we wish to keep up, it cannot be avoided. Nothing of much interest has occurred to me of late. The Bairagee who has paid me visits some time since, and appeared in earnest, has fully disclosed his design. He wants money from me to go with ease and comfort to Adjudia (Fyzabad). But I told him plainly that if he sought money from me, he was deceived. My reader being present, told him afterwards that he considered him a great hypocrite, and that he had need of repentance. He told him that he had been likewise such a deceiver, as he had travelled from city to city and sought rest for his soul, but could not obtain it until he came to the knowledge of Christ, where alone peace could be found.

We had to fight against wild beasts in human shape this morning. Several Brahmins united to defend the greatest blasphemies against God, whom they declared to be the worker of all vices and crimes. One might fight in the conflict and despond of every hope of success in a city where 25,000 Brahmins, full of all subtlety, cunning and viciousness, are daily labouring against the efforts of seven missionaries. Oh it is heart-rending to see the state of this city! The only consolation for us remains in the daily practice *to strengthen ourselves in the Lord,* as David did. I feel more and more the necessity of earnest and intense prayer for them, that the Lord may give them repentance unto life before they fall into a reprobate mind. Oh may he give me a spirit of prayer and a heart of faith!

A Brahmin followed me this morning to my house. He had listened to us in the city. He came from Adjudia and appears to be in some temporal distress. From his statement it appears that the few articles he brought with him, had been stolen at the ghat of Benares, in sight of the daily-worshipped Deota the Gunga. I asked him to stay here and hear more of our shasters, which he seemed to like.

A Bengalee met me this week in the city. He complained most seriously against the people of Benares as being such a set of thieves, rogues and fit for all kinds of vice, and intimated his doubts whether I could ever do any good here. However, he said, Go on preaching your religion—who knows but some may accept it and give up their bad habits. A Brahmin hearing him, immediately began to abuse us and to say, Oh who will ever accept your religion, do you not see that all the people are in our power? They worship us even as gods; for you must believe that God is in me. He made a dreadful noise with scolding and railing against me and our religion, wishing to draw the people off. He repeated frequently such words as, God is in me and I am the master of the universe. I spoke little, seeing him to be full of rage, and merely required him to prove here before all, that he was God, by a fact, such as to heal a leper or to give sight to the blind. The people approved of this proposition, but he being unable to do it, scampered off, and gave me a good opportunity to address the by-standers.

June 3.—The above-mentioned Brahmin left us today. He desired me to advance him money that he might be enabled to marry his daughter to a Brahmin. His thoughts are merely bent upon this subject, as he fears, his daughter being of age, he might by further delay, bring a family reproach upon him. This was according to his own statement, the reason why he left home in search of such a person who might open his bountiful hand towards him. When he saw that this would not do with me, he proposed to Treeloke * to intercede for him with me, that I should give him at least fifty rupees, and then he would bring his family to live with us. However when he saw that this expedient would not succeed, he thought best to set off, but not before he had made sure of a rope for drawing water out of a well. How true the assertion of the Apostle: "there is none that seeketh after God." All seek for money. *Money* is the *greatest idol* at Benares. The God of this world has blinded their eyes. I had a long argument with a Mussulman or rather with two. Salvation, the sonship of Christ, the prophetship of Ma-

* The native reader.

hommed, the divine origin of the Koran, were the topics of discussion. Much anger and hatred were manifested by them, but they could not advance any reasonable argument in favour of Mohammed or his Koran. One of the Mussulmans, at the close of the discussion, asked me for the Pentateuch and a New Testament, which I promised him.

June 5.—We had a pleasant morning, and two Hindoos appeared to be fully convinced of the truth of the Christian religion, and especially of the truth that Christ alone is and can be the Saviour of mankind. But there is no courage with these people to break through their caste, &c. May God give them grace! Some books and gospels were taken.

June 13.—More than three hours were spent this morning in the city. We had great crowds of hearers. Much discussion took place. A Brahmin maintained that God must be worshipped in every shape and form, using this simile, viz. a blind man cannot see the sun, but when his eyes are opened he sees him and admires him. As long as man does not see and worship God in every form, he is blind; but when his eyes are opened, he admires the deity in every thing which his eyes behold. I just turned it and showed him that the contrary is the case. When he saw that he might be hard pressed for arguments, he ran off. The people called him a katchha admi (a man of little understanding.) Another Hindoo asked: If only the Christian religion is true, what became of our forefathers, they have not heard it: have they received salvation or not? I answered his question, and told him that it was for him and us who hear and know the gospel to believe it and accept that salvation which is offered in it, or else our damnation would be certain. Another Hindoo asserted that *the heart* (man) which he called true, and not the image or idol or any thing else, was God—the heart in man that is the deity itself. Answer: "But out of the heart proceed evil thoughts, murders, adulteries, fornications," &c. Is this true or not? Yes, yes, the by-standers called out, how then can it be God, who is full of holiness and righteousness, the hater of sin and the judge of all evil doers? You greatly err. The nature of God and the sinfulness of man were now described, and the Saviour declared who is able and willing to deliver all from error and sin. Another respectable Hindoo, who had been quietly listening for two hours, entered now fully into a most interesting conversation. He appears to be a man in earnest search after the truth. From his statements he seems to have given up idolatry and the doctrine of pantheism as unworthy of God. How to receive forgiveness of sins and to live a holy life were the main topics of conversation. He requested me not merely to go and preach in the streets, but to visit respectable men in their houses.—There are many who believe your doctrines and your book to be true, and wish to do accordingly. I requested him to introduce me to them,as I was exceedingly glad to have such an opportunity. He promised to do so, and first to pay me a visit in company with them, then he would take me to his house. He said further: I cannot call your religion bad, as others do, for I think, who knows but this may be the one which comes from God. Some Brahmins immediately began to abuse him, seeing his earnestness. One even went so far as to ask him, whether he was one of their religion or a Christian? I am one of your's, but not like you—I cannot call that bad which is good. He walked along with me when returning home, and promised to come to me to-morrow: he would not allow me to pay him a visit first. He is a Benares-man, and appears to be very rich. O may the Lord open his heart like Lydia's! All the tracts and Gospels we had, were taken. The heat was already excessively oppressive, and made me hasten homeward.

July 9.—The Lord's day. Had divine worship on the premises with our Christian orphan boys and native Christians. My school-boys, who are attending every Sunday, brought with them a respectable young man. He also was present during divine service. He was very attentive. When I inquired who he was, he told me that some years ago he had been in the very school which is now under my superintendence, and learned to read our books. It was evident from his countenance that the recollection of those days was pleasant to him, and that some love to the truth had taken hold of his heart. He came for the very purpose of receiving a Gospel, expressing his high approval of the good words contained in our books. I was happy to see in him an instance that bazaar-schools may after all be quite in vain. When he received the desired book, he was pleased, and expressed a wish now and then to call on me for some instruction in our books. Soon after, another Hindoo came and desired the Ten Commandments. He had heard them in the bazaar, but could not at that time obtain a copy of them. He would have no other tract but that with the commandments. When I gave him a copy, he desired me of his own accord to explain them to him, which I did, and took occasion to enter into some important conversation, shewing the evil tendency of the Hindoo religion and the excellency of the Christian. I felt rather poorly and weary after the service, and having spent more than an hour with him in conversation, I called for Treeloke, who spoke with him and instructed him about two hours longer, in the principal doctrines of our religion. The man complained of want of time before he left, or else he would come more frequently and hear about our doctrines; however he promised to come when at leisure.

The above-mentioned Hindoo met me again, and we had a very long discussion (I mean with the Benares-man.) He has picked up something of our religion, and thinks these few fragments sufficient for his salvation. He says that he believes in the invisible God, who is neither in an idol nor in the breast of man, and that this God will be served and honoured by the abhorrence of every bad action, and by the performance of every good deed. The acting upon this rule procures to man the lost favour of the great and glorious Being. I succeeded several times in upsetting his castle, into which he has thrown himself, and showed clearly and strongly the utter impossibility of man's justification by his own so-called good works and consequent acceptance with God. A large crowd was present all the time, and I was able to bring into our discussion a great deal of Gospel truth, and to explain the only way of free salvation through the blood of Christ.

July 13.—The weather is exceedingly trying: fever is prevalent. Mrs. Knorpp is suffering from an attack of it.

August 8.—We have dreadful weather—the heat is great and no rain falling for some weeks. Mr. Leupolt and myself have suffered from fever last month. To-day was a large Mela in honour of Doorga. Treeloke and myself posted ourselves at the Daureeabeer Chapel, where all the people passed by, and we were constantly engaged in giving away tracts, for which there was a great demand. Most respectable men came up to us and asked for them. One native gentleman, a rich Brahmin, was very desirous to receive some, and told me that he had himself read part of the Gospels, though he did not possess the book himself, but a boy near his house who has received a New Testament came frequently to him, at which occasion he usually reads in the book. As I had no gospels with me I promised the Brahmin a copy of the New Testament, which my reader would deliver to him at his residence. Treeloke immediately inquired after his name and the place of his dwelling, which the Brahmin told.

August 11.—I had a long dispute with a Mussulman this morning. The poor man has quite Hindoo ideas about religion, and defended their system very much. I took him upon his own ground. He wanted to prove his prophet's Mission from the passage in Isaiah xxi. 7, —his prophet riding upon a camel and Christ upon an ass. He was told that if he knew a little of profane history, he would be ashamed to interpret this passage as referring to his prophet. I explained the meaning of it, and the fulfilment of the prophecy, to which he had nothing to say. He wished now to know the difference between Christ and the Hindoo Ram, (the Mussulman confessed that he had been a Hindoo not long ago.) As there were a great many Hindoos present, I did not deny him the gratification of comparing the two characters with each other. The comparison put the two persons in their real light. The Hindoos listened with much attention—Ram appeared a mere man in all his origin and actions; Christ the true God, from his being conceived by the Holy Ghost, to his ascension. Except one Hindoo, all my hearers admired the holy character of Christ. The Mussulman had only to cavil about the birth of Christ by a virgin. I appealed to my hearers and told them that all Mussulmans know that the Gospel (Injil) was six hundred years before the appearance of Mahommed and the Koran; that in the Gospel it was written that Christ was conceived by the power of the Holy Ghost and born of a virgin—the same was said in the Koran six hundred years afterwards—now my friends, the Mussulmans believe in the Koran, have they a right to deny and to scandalize a fact contained in their own book, merely because it is written in the Gospel? This appeal had a good effect. The Hindoos turned against the Mussulman, as he could produce no proof against the doctrine of the wonderful conçeption and birth of Christ, which he admitted was contained in his Koran. A great step was gained. The Hindoos heard a testimony of Christ's divinity from their own countrymen whom they call brothers (bhai,) and saw his divine character in his life and resurrection in opposition to the mere pretensions of Ram. Two Hindoos were quite affected—they had come from the up-country, they took tracts and promised to come to my house. But I fear the good impressions will soon be destroyed by the Brahmins, who are day and night busy in terrifying every one who appears seriously inclined towards Christianity.

The unusual heat and dryness of the season is carrying off many a one to the grave, and frequently am I interrupted in my preaching in the city by the passing by of a corpse and a host of people after it, constantly repeating with a loud noise the blasphemous words, Ram nam satya hai (the name of Ram is true or Ram is true.) But alas! death seems to have lost all its terrors, with this people.

August 15.—I was at the Daureabeer chapel this morning and had a long discussion on the nature of God, with a pundit. He was rather a man of candour, though bigoted. He asserted the doctrine generally held by the Hindoos, that God is the author of good and evil. When he saw that his arguments failed, and that his doctrine was incompatible with a holy God, he candidly asked, whence sin, the moral evil, originated? I took occasion to show him first the origin of this doctrine of Hindooism—which consists in the ignorance of the real history of the fall of man—and turned then to the first three chapters of Genesis which I had in my hand, and explained the fall of man. He had nothing to object, and took afterwards the book, commencing to read, but soon returned it to me, saying, that they themselves had books enough, what should he do with this too. When I looked about me I saw a Hindoo whom I recognised to be the same man who had been with me in my house on a Sunday to receive the commandments. He appeared pleased to see me and asked for a tract. When all the people had left us, I asked him whether he remembered the conversation we had together on that day, to which he answered in the affirmative. He then began to say the ten commandments by heart, which he did with a very simple and serious expression of countenance. He promised to come to me in a few days.

The great Doorga-mela took place to-day. I sent Treeloke early in the afternoon and followed after, when the heat of the day, which was almost intolerable, had subsided a little. Immense multitudes were flocking towards the temple of Doorga. Hundreds of tracts were given away by us to persons who had first proved to us that they could read. It was dreadful work. The people pressed upon us and almost suffocated us; as it is my principle not to give a tract, until I have heard people read before me. This makes the distribution of tracts difficult and wearisome. I was surprised several times this evening to hear persons repeat portions of our tracts and Scripture, when I expressed my doubts about their reading the books they received. To some respectable brahmins I gave some copies of Genesis and Gospels; of the latter I have very few.

Sept. 17.—The conduct of Barshat produced in my own heart great humiliation before my God, and made me more earnest in prayer for the conversion of this benighted city; and behold the Lord heard my supplications. A remarkable instance of conversion took place in Kesar Gir, whom I baptized to-day before the Hindoostanee congregation in Secrole. Kesar Gir is the son of a brahmin, and was adopted as son and heir in his infancy by a Gosain of Benares, a man of great property; besides several great stone houses at Benares, he possesses several villages. This Gosain having no relations and no family of his own, (this sort of Hindoos observing celibacy) rightly instituted his adopted son Kesar Gir as his lawful heir in case of his decease.

In his early years, Kesar Gir was sent to the bazaar school now under my superintendence, for instruction in reading and writing; where he imbibed some knowledge of Christianity by reading the Gospels. After having stayed some years at this school, the Gosain, who was at the same time his Gooroo, took a Brahmin to complete the boy's education, after which he was initiated into the Gosainship by mantras and ceremonies. It is curious to observe that the very mantra which was whispered into his ear contained the name of Christ, tato Miash—the essence (Masih or) Christ; in fact the whole mantra is nothing but a repetition of 'I am the supreme Being.' As he was now a youth of some independence, he followed the bad example of his Gooroo in some of the vices practised by him, especially that of fornication and adultery. For three years he lived in this state of sin; but as his conscience reproved him for his conduct, he endeavoured to quiet it by a more rigid observance of the idolatrous rites of his sect. This however was to no effect. At last a Gospel came again into his hands; he read it diligently and soon received such strong convictions thereby of his former conduct, that he earnestly set about to reform himself, and at once gave up his beloved mistress. The change which his mind underwent did not escape his Gooroo's observation. Kesar Gir had already fixed his mind to become a Christian, and had only waited till he could find opportunity to open his heart to me. Several times he came to Treeloke, but appears to have been treated as a suspected person by him. However soon an opportunity offered for a complete decision in his choice. One day his Gooroo observed him as usual reading the Gospel with great attention, at which he became so enraged that he took the book out of his hand and tore it in pieces. Kesar Gir was so hurt by his Gooroo's conduct, that he felt the greatest pain in his heart, and could not eat from sorrow of mind for two days. He now would no longer stay with his debauched Gooroo, and set out with a full determination to come to me. It was that very day when he met me in the city, examining the school where he had first received an impression of the truth of Christianity. He followed me to my house and commenced to live on our premises. His love of the divine truth and his sincerity were obvious to every one. I took him now under a regular course of instruction, and his progress in divine knowledge was very rapid. His former sinful life came with power back to his recollection, and he confessed all his former sins to me, and desired, as soon as practicable, to be joined to the people of God and to become the servant of the Lord Jesus by the administration of baptism. Whilst he was with me he had every inducement to go back again, but he refused every offer and cheerfully gave up all the property of his Gooroo which would have been his by inheritance, counting the knowledge of Christ greater riches than his Gooroo could give him. He was accordingly baptized on Sunday the 17th of September, 1837. He had drawn up a short statement, why he had embraced the Christian religion, and read it before the congregation, as follows: 'I was brought up in the Hindoo religion, which has established thirty-three millions of false gods, and was kept in this darkness of ignorance of the true God, until I read the Gospel, by the reading of which I was convinced of the divine origin of Christianity, and the falsehood of my religion. I examined the Christian religion and found that this is the only true one pointing out a sure way of salvation. I did not find Christ a deceiver, as all the Hindoo incarnations, for the true God does not practice deceit and sin as they did, and therefore no salvation can be expected from them, nor from the Hindoo religion, where God is made the author of sin. When I read of the life and actions of Christ, I found nothing but goodness and holiness, and was convinced of his divinity, and faith in him was produced in my heart. I was convinced that I could only find salvation through him, and as I have seen the Hindoo religion to be nothing but a construction of lies, I forsake it and all the gods I formerly served, and believe now in Jesus Christ and his true religion, and for the forgiveness of my sins I look to him alone; for he has suffered for my sins also, and made an atonement, being convinced that without shedding of blood there is no forgiveness.' He received the name of Timotheus at his baptism. His countenance cleared up, and he looked very happy. He told me that whilst he was receiving baptism, a new light sprung up in his soul, and he felt happy as he never did before.

Timotheus is now about twenty-four years of age, naturally strong, of an open and clear countenance, considerable talents, bold and energetic in character, and of an humble demeanour. He is well acquainted with his own religion, and reads and writes his own language well. He will be a useful man as a reader, and is very anxious to speak and preach the Gospel to his countrymen. May God the Holy Spirit enlighten his mind and fit him for every good work!

Having been prevented from keeping a regular journal, I beg to introduce here a few particulars that occurred during several months. Mr. Smith having left in the beginning of August for his trip up the country on account of his health, the current duties of the mission were left to Mr. Leupolt and myself. The publication of a religious periodical by our Tract Association was finally agreed on. The particulars have since appeared in the 'Christian Intelligencer,' and need not be repeated here again. The paper is to be printed in the Hindostanee language, and published every month, and having been appointed to be editor with the Rev. Mr. Mather of the London Society, my missionary duties have consequently increased. I am happy to say that this periodical has already an extensive circulation, and is considered by every friend of the spread of Christianity as the instrument of doing much good to our native Christians and others.

On the 19th of September we were blessed with an increase to our family by a healthy male child, and a few days after we had the pleasure of seeing Mr. —— with us, a member of our Calcutta Committee. We rejoiced to make his acquaintance, and were thankful to the Lord to find that we have truly pious men in the Committee, who desire to further the good cause not only with their contributions and counsels, but also with their earnest prayers. Mr. —— was made acquainted with all the particulars of the mission, both as to its temporal and spiritual concerns, and he will be best able, as an eye-witness, to give a faithful statement of its progress and prosperity.

At the beginning of October our highly-esteemed Bishop resumed his visitation, which was broken off in March at Allahabad, and we had the pleasure to meet his Lordship at the Brigadier-General's. We were, however, sorry to observe, that the Bishop had taken a severe cold in the steamer coming up from Calcutta, which brought on a troublesome cough, and his Lordship, during his stay at Benares, was prevented from more extensive usefulness in consequence of it. The Bishop, nevertheless, preached several times in the English church, held two ordinations, one for Mr. Moore, of Agra, for priest's orders, and the other for Mr. Richards, of Meerut, for deacon's orders; an English confirmation in the church, and a Hindustanee one in the Line Chapel, when sixteen of our elder orphan boys were confirmed, and several others baptized. On the same day of the Hindustanee confirmation, our beloved Bishop united to the visible church by baptism, our own little boy.

I must not omit to say, that we enjoyed his Lordship's visit to Benares more than any one in the station. His Lordship's health becoming more unfavourable every day, we proposed a little change of air, by removing from the Chaplain's house, where the Bishop lodged, to our premises at Segra, which was kindly accepted. The house of Mr. Smith, who was absent, was consequently occupied by his Lordship, and thus we had his advice and prayers for our own and the mission's prosperity. This was indeed a blessed season to us, which will never be forgotten. His Lordship went several times with me to the city, visited our three chapels, and addressed himself several times to the assembled crowds in Hindustanee. Our Free School and the Orphan Seminary were examined likewise by the Bishop, as well as the Orphan Female School of Mrs. Smith, and of all he saw, he expressed his great pleasure and satisfaction. I accompanied his Lordship to the Government School and Sanscrit College, at the latter of which an interesting discussion took place with the greatest Pundits of Benares, who were so discomfited that they angrily ordered their disciples who were attentively listening to the discussion, to go to their respective apartments.

The Bishop, in consequence of Mr. Bateman's illness,

and subsequent embarkation for England, was deprived of his private chaplain. After a stay of about three weeks, the Bishop left Benares for Ghazeepore. The latter place being without a chaplain at the time, the Bishop expressed a desire that one of us should accompany him thither, to assist him in the duties to be performed there. Upon an understanding between myself and Mr. Leupolt, it was agreed that I should accompany his Lordship. The journey was by water. His Lordship's stay at Ghazeepore was about ten days, during which time the Church was consecrated. I assisted the Bishop as far as I was able, by reading prayers and preaching on the two Sunday evenings we spent at this station. Three very interesting sermons were delivered by the Bishop. I spent some very happy days with his Lordship and his doctor, and the little change of air which I enjoyed was beneficial to my health. The Bishop was exceedingly kind to us at Benares, and likewise to me at Ghazeepore, and we felt that we had a father with us, and not merely superior. Our beloved Diocesan has greatly endeared himself to us, and has a full share in our affections. Our prayer to the Lord is, that he may be long preserved to India, and be a blessing whithersoever he goes. Oh may He sustain him by His Almighty grace in so difficult an office!

At the close of November, Mr. Leupolt, for various reasons, proceeded on a trip to Calcutta, from which he returned again at the beginning of February 1838. The Mission, with the schools and Orphan seminary, was now to be attended to by me, which, though labouring night and day, could not be done by me satisfactorily. To all these duties was added another, though entirely a voluntary one.

Previous to the Bishop's departure from Benares, he had asked us, whether at any time when there was no chaplain in the station, we would voluntarily undertake to perform once on a Lord's-day divine service, until the arrival of a chaplain? This reasonable request we gladly agreed to, as it appeared to us wrong to have the Church shut up when there are three clergymen in the station. The Bishop made mention of this to the General, requesting him to ask us when our services required. The chaplain was leaving the station, the General of Benares requested me in writing, if practicable and agreeable, to perform Divine service in the English Church. From that time hitherto regular service has been performed in English. It was certainly too much at the time when I was alone, and I had to labour more than my strength was sufficient, to do at least some justice to all my duties, but my brethren have all returned now. English preaching does not interfere with our primary duties, and we shall continue to do so, until a chaplain be appointed to this large station.

On the 21st of December 1837, a Hindoo widow was united by baptism to our congregation in the lines. She is a young woman of about twenty-four years of age, and of an intelligent mind. She had become acquainted through the native Christians in the lines with the Christian religion, and manifested a desire to forsake idolatry. Two respectable men, the one a fife-major, and the other a drum-major of the regiments here, introduced her to me for Christian instruction. She came consequently daily to my house, and received instructions in the truths of the Bible, and when I could judge her prepared for the holy rite, baptism was administered on the above-mentioned day. I was much pleased with her progress in Divine knowledge, and she evidently felt, on the day of her baptism, something of the Divine grace vouchsafed to humble believers on such holy occasions. Towards the latter end of January I made an excursion towards Mirzapore, partly for missionary purposes, and partly for a little change, as my spirits began to sink under the pressure of business. I found the people at Mirzapore very ready to hear us, and I preached several times on the river-side, and in the city to great assemblies, who listened attentively without much objection to our doctrines. My time was too much limited to make a long stay there, as I could only travel by marches, which took me three days to go there, and the same back, and long I could not be absent from Benares. One Sunday I spent there only, on which I preached to the resident Europeans and East Indians, and administered at their request the Sacrament of the Lord's Supper. It is really a pity that our Society has not yet appointed a missionary to this place, which, I believe, from all appearances, is a most promising station, and the missionary might be likewise acceptably useful among the Europeans who are destitute of the regular ordinances of religion. Mr. Woodcock, the Magistrate there, was exceedingly kind to us, and knowing that our encamping-place was infested with robbers, sent us two watchmen for the night from the Thania (police). There is now a neat little Gothic chapel building by the contributions of the few residents of the place, which would be open to a missionary of the Church of England. Oh could I for once prevail on the Committee to send one of their missionaries from England to this place. A good man would receive certain assistance in his work by the residents.

After Mr. Leupolt's return to Benares, I started off a second time to spend a few days more in the country, and pitched my tent at Sydepore, twenty-four miles from Benares. Here our preaching among the natives was on the whole acceptable, few objected or mocked, but on the whole a great reserve, mixed with some fear, was discernible. The people were so afraid we might prevail against them in arguments, that the very mentioning to give up idolatry and to serve the living God, or in other words, to become a Christian, struck a panic in their minds. Some, however, took tracts gladly. The principal men of the village, Mussulmans and Hindoos, came one day to my tent for some religious conversation, when the respective merits of Mahomedanism and Christianity were discussed, and, as usual, the religion of the Koran was found unable to adduce its proofs for its Divine origin and authority. Several people amongst the Hindoos and Mussulmen gave me some encouragement, and perhaps the day is not far distant when they will renounce that which is false, and accept that which is true. May the Holy Spirit guide their inquiries!

At the close of this I must observe, that Paschat, the Bairagee, who left me as mentioned in the preceding journal, came back again in December last. He begged very hard that I would receive him again, confessing his folly in having left our premises. Since that time I am happy to observe, that his conduct is different to what it was before, and his mind more attentive to the concerns of his soul, though I say it with trembling that his case is hopeful. Whoever knows a little of this country, is sufficiently acquainted with the temptations that assail our native inquirers and Christians. There is outward and inward temptation which they have no grace to withstand, and Satan is busy enough in all in his power to bring those that stand to fall. The peculiar circumstances, in which a missionary is placed, make the work consequently so much more difficult and trying. His hopes are frequently frustrated when most promising. Has he received a few as a seal of his ministry from among the heathen? then he must ever be upon his guard like a watchman not to lose them again by being drawn by their own lusts and the temptations of their former companions and associates into their old sins again. No one knows the trials of a faithful missionary, and no one can sufficiently sympathize with him. Had he not a gracious Saviour, before whose throne he may come with all his cares and anxieties, there would be no possibility of bearing up under the trials of his faith, and of keeping his hand to the plough. May the Lord not forsake us by reason of our unworthiness, and many mistakes and omissions we are guilty of in his righteous and holy cause. May the sympathy of our Christian brethren and sisters be more excited towards this country so full of idolatry, vice, and all abominations, and may they pray more for the latter rain—the gracious outpouring of the Holy Spirit on all flesh!

OBITUARY OF STEPHEN LAPRIMAUDAYE, ESQ.

This "aged disciple" departed this life at the Old Church Parsonage on Sunday morning Aug. 9th. He had attained to more than the appointed years of man's life, having reached the advanced age of nearly seventy-five, most of which had been passed in this debilitating climate.

His death was attended with all those mitigating circumstances which follow a life of faith on the Son of God. It was like the composed setting of the evening sun, or the gathering of the full ripe grain into the garner—all was peaceful, and calm, and serene, and joyful.

The friends who surrounded his dying bed, had seen him under circumstances, which left but little expectation of his revival, about three years before, and the faith which he then expressed, and the hope which then supported him, shewed how firm was the foundation on which his eternal views and expectations were based. The same faith and hope, strengthened by the exemplary patience of the three subsequent years, sustained him amidst the last conflict. He died on the day of sacred rest—at the time that God's people were worshipping within the walls of the earthly sanctuary, and within hearing of the organ's peals, which just at the moment were guiding and accompanying the voices of those who "make melody in their hearts to the Lord:" happy emblem, we trust, of that eternal sabbath on which he at the time entered,—of that glorious society of angels and the spirits of just men made perfect which he then joined; and of that happy choir of the "heavenly sphere" who praise God day and night in his temple, and who sing the song of Moses and the Lamb without weariness and without cessation, whose voices he was then permitted to emulate.

The faith of this aged saint had been evidenced by holy fruits through a long series of years. He was simple-hearted, docile, benevolent, desirous to know and do his Master's will. No one could be near him without being impressed with the conviction, "Behold an Israelite indeed in whom is no guile."

But he rests from his labours and his works follow him, and if ever surviving friends felt the force of the admonition, "not to sorrow as others who have no hope," it will be felt and is so in the present case. "Blessed are the dead which die in the Lord; yea, even so saith the Spirit."

MEMORIAL OF CAPT. W—. OF THE BENGAL ARMY.

1 Thess. ii. 13.

There is nothing in this transitory life more calculated to impress us with a firm belief in the truth of the Word of God, than attending the death-bed of a Christian:—to mark the consolation he derives from a knowledge and heartfelt persuasion of its efficacy, in the hour of need, when this world is but as a shadow passing away, and eternity appears in view, cannot but seal upon the minds of those who witness it, the necessity of seeking the Lord whilst He may be found; that, in the same trying hour they may be enabled with equal confidence and certain hope to look to the throne of grace.

I know little or nothing of ——'s early life, except what he may casually have mentioned to me. A friend who was intimately acquainted with the deceased, before he went to England on furlough in 1830, said to me, 'W. was then much as other men; and I was astonished at the change which had taken place in him, when I again met him, after his return from furlough.'

I had first the pleasure of becoming acquainted with the deceased in January 1843, when he was living with a religious friend at Chinsurah: he had then the truth of the gospel at heart.

I know not whether this blessed truth first took root in England, or after his return to India; but as he often talked to me of the excellent preachers he had heard at home, I am led to think that it was planted there; and that on his return to this country, the death of a dear relation, and the accounts of his glorious death-bed, were, through God's blessing, the means of making it grow and flourish. That the latter event made a deep impression on his mind, the following interesting document, found amongst his papers after his demise, will abundantly shew:—

'*Chinsurah, Feb.* 6, 1834.

'The frame of mind I find myself in is so pleasant, that, as an incentive to the future, I write it down. For some two months,—since indeed, the time I received the tidings of my dear and ever to be lamented brother W——'s death, I have felt an inward satisfaction and delight in prayer, I never experienced before: his being so suddenly called from this world, and at a time of perfect health, after a residence in this country of upwards of thirty years, when on the very eve of leaving it, to join his dear wife and family in England, so shocked me, so brought to my mind and in so vivid a manner, the power of the Almighty, that I looked up to him from my heart as my Father, my only hope through his blessed Son Jesus Christ.

'The cares and anxieties of this fleeting life will soon pass away; but his kingdom shall endure for ever.

'Oh! that I may have faith without wavering,—that I may resist the manifold temptations so constantly set in my path, and strive to be good from a nobler motive than fear.'

Circumstances prevented my seeing much of my deceased friend, till near the close of 1834, when, our corps being at the same station, he asked me to live with him; an offer which I most readily and thankfully accepted.

Pascal observes in his 'Thoughts,' on the vanity of man: 'We wish to live an ideal life in the minds of others; and for this purpose we constrain ourselves to put on appearances.' Man's heart will tell him the justness of this remark, yet I will venture to say, to few was it less applicable than the deceased. He led a very retired life, indeed so much so; that his brother officers (who loved and respected him) often complained to me, of so seldom seeing him. When I have told him of this, his answer has been, 'I cannot help it, I shall always be happy to see any of them here. But I feel happy living as I do, and I seldom go out without finding some trifle or another annoy me. Time perhaps may give me more confidence.' He had nothing of moroseness in his disposition, indeed, I never recollect meeting any one who was invariably so cheerful. He remarked to me, 'I think there is no inconsistency in a Christian being cheerful, indeed I am convinced that a firm belief in and acquaintance with the work of God, must make a man so. I cannot tell you how happy I feel, what an altered man since I began to seek for the truth,' and then he mentioned several pious men of our acquaintance, as examples of the truth of what he had said.

About the beginning of the month in which he died, he said to me, 'During your absence' (I had been some time away on duty) 'I have been reading several of your books—Pascal's Thoughts amongst others: it is a most delightful book; Pascal was indeed a wonderful man; I have also had the loan of Abbott's Young Christian, which I strongly recommend to you.'

On another occasion, he said, '—— has just been calling, and we have had a long conversation about religion; his heart seems inclined that way; but he has raised doubts in his mind by reading Paine's Works, and wishes now he had not done so.'

A trait in my deceased friend's character, I cannot leave unnoticed, it bears its own peculiar stamp: "Blessed is he that considereth the poor." (Ps. xli.) He was very fond of drawing, and for a fortnight previous to being laid on the bed of sickness, he was indefatigable in preparing a number of sketches with the intention of sending them to a friend in Calcutta, to be sold at the next fancy sale which might take place.

I shall now mention some passages which occurred during the deceased's last fatal illness, which will shew the delightful frame of his mind, and how with regard to him the words of the Psalmist were verified—"The Lord will strengthen him upon the bed of languishing; Thou wilt make all his bed in his sickness." For the first five days after feeling unwell, he tried to bear up, thinking it only a slight bilious attack. But as the disease (a remittent fever) grew upon him, he was confined to his couch and was very restless. On the fifth day, I think, before his demise, he said to me, 'I never felt so unwell as I do now, it cannot last long. O! what a comfort it is in such an hour to have a Saviour to flee to; all my trust is in Him, and I feel happy: He will never forsake me.'

The fever increased much on the evening of that day. He said, 'I feel that I am getting worse; O God do thou in mercy grant that I may retain my reason.' To the Doctor, who came in shortly after, he said, 'Do not think the worse of me for what I may say, for I have no command over myself.' It pleased God to keep him calm and tranquil during the night. About three o'clock in the morning, he commenced talking to me in a delightful manner, of his trust in Christ, and how happy he was, in having for many months past been thrown so much into the society of good men, men whom he believed to be sincere Christians. 'Give my affectionate regards,' he said, 'to ——,' naming the chaplain who was at Chinsurah when he was living there as before mentioned—'I wish I could see him, and also to G——, he will take it kind of me remembering him now.' A few minutes after, an officer of his regiment (who had kindly come to attend upon him,) standing by his couch, addressed him by his Christian name, he said, 'Ah! if you but knew what a comforter Christ is: I feel quite happy in Him.' In the course of the day, Mr. C—— the chaplain kindly called, and as my friend had expressed a desire to see him, he was admitted. I am happy to see you,' my friend said, 'I pray that the Lord may remove me.' Mr. C—— told him he ought not to wish so. My friend rejoined, 'but I have always added, "Thy will be done,"' and turning to me, 'Have not I always said, "Thy will be done."'

He seemed and expressed himself much pleased with the short and beautiful prayer, Mr. C—— offered up at his bedside. And although he was too unwell to receive another visit from him, he twice or thrice expressed the pleasure his visit had given him.

On another occasion, (referring to an offer I had made to read a Psalm to him, to which he was too unwell to accede,) he said to me, 'we must commence reading the Scriptures to-morrow.' A dear friend who was standing by, remarked, 'It will not be a commencement with you, for you have constantly read them for long past.' 'Ah yes! yes!' my friend said, and appeared lost in pleasing recollections.

Two evenings before his death, a dear friend came from Calcutta to see him. My friend was lying quite still at the time, and had been speaking to me calmly a minute before. I whispered to him that his dear friend G—— had come from Calcutta to assist in nursing him. 'Who? he asked: 'Who? Christ come to nurse me?' From this time he sunk rapidly. The medical gentlemen (who had been most attentive) did all in their power to alleviate his sufferings, and they were successful, for after lingering thirty hours longer, he fell calmly into the sleep of death. The last words he distinctly uttered were 'Wonderful! how wonderful!'

DEATH OF MRS. SCHNEIDER.

'*Benares, July* 31, 1839.

'In writing to you this time, I do not know whether I shall speak of the goodness of God, or of the afflictive dispensation with which the Lord has again been pleased to visit us. Mercies and chastisement are so mixed, that I do not know whether I shall sing psalms, or sit down in the dust and weep : my heart is sad, yet I have cause to magnify the good will of my God towards me. I rejoice in the Lord, and yet sorrow and tears mingle with my joy.

'You will understand better and rejoice with me, when I tell you that it pleased our heavenly Father to present us with a sweet little daughter, on Friday night about 10 o'clock, but you will also mingle a tear of sorrow with ours, when I inform you that the same gracious Father, according to his heavenly wisdom, was pleased to remove our dearly-beloved sister Schneider to a better land.

'On Thursday Mrs. Schneider had a slight attack, which seemed to increase on Friday. In the morning, however, she was pretty well. We finished the book of Daniel, and spake together on the blessed hope of the resurrection. Our hearts were full, and we rejoiced at the prospect before us. The invisible world seemed to be more united to the visible one than ever. We enjoyed the presence of the Lord. Life and immortality were before us, and we rejoiced in the anticipation of that blessed morn, when the believer's expectations shall all be realized, when mortality shall be swallowed up of life, our souls reunited to our glorified bodies, and we all enter with the Lord the realms of eternal bliss. But little did we think, that she, in whose society we promised ourselves yet many enjoyments, would so soon be permitted to realize all these blessings, and that within two days after, we should have to commit earth to earth, ashes to ashes, dust to dust, in *sure* and *certain* hope of the resurrection to eternal life through our Lord Jesus Christ. But thus it pleased the Lord, and our duty is to be still and know that the Lord is God!

Dear Brother Schneider sorrows deeply, but not as such who have no hope. He is resigned, assured that all is well, though he is unable to fathom this mysterious dispensation. He has lost a jewel such as there are few in this world. Dear sister Schneider was a pattern of humility, modesty, devotedness, and affection ; and, during the short time she was among us, she endeared herself much to our hearts, and her removal cast a general sadness upon all around her. Her end was peace. When beginning to traverse the valley of the shadow of death, she looked upon me with deep anxiety, and lifting up her eyes, she exclaimed in German : "Lord, help me through this hour." I said to her, "Be of good cheer, He will not forsake you." The only subject which appeared to weigh upon her mind, was her dear husband. "I am very sorry," she said, "that I must leave him alone." Yet this sacrifice was also made, and with it the last earthly tie seemed to be severed. As the hour of her dissolution approached, her countenance became serene, and seeing me shed tears at her side, she smiled and pointed towards heaven ; and then stretching out her hands, exclaimed, "Come! Come!" and her Saviour came!—she fell asleep, her spirit having taken its flight to that land, where there are no more tears!

'A loud call on us all! to live nearer to our God, and to work whilst it is called to-day. Oh, dearest brethren, what is our life! How soon will our twelve hours be accomplished. How powerfully the Lord reminds us that we should not imagine we have an abiding city here, but feel that we are pilgrims and strangers, destined not for an earthly but heavenly abode, not for time, but eternity. But shall we then sorrow? No! no! but rather let us rejoice at the hope set before us in Christ. Let us be more faithful in our work, in praying for ourselves and each other. United with each other in the bond of love, let us work together, and live, labour, suffer, and die for the Lord and his work, and the day will come when we shall be united to the Lord, and to each other, and all those near and dear to us, and then we shall join with sanctified lips the choir of saints and angels, in ascribing praise and glory to our Lord God and Saviour! 'With our united Christian love,

'Ever your affectionate Brother,

'C. B. LEUPOLT.

E.

SIR HENRY BLOSSET, CHIEF JUSTICE.

Sir Henry was privileged to have had the prayers and instructions of an eminently pious mother. During his last illness, the remembrance of her piety and maternal love caused him to weep abundantly. The Rev. Mr. Thomason, who attended him in his last illness, particularly mentions this incident as corroborating the many testimonies of a blessing attending maternal solicitude for their children's eternal welfare. His visits are thus alluded to:—

He said, 'I cannot affirm I am not somewhat depressed;' adding, 'It is fit I should be so. Perhaps there is no state of mind more salutary; it would be well for us if we were oftener in such a state. I can, from my heart, declare, that though I am deeply humbled, and have much to make my heart sad; yet I feel the mercy of God so greatly to exceed my own demerits, that I cannot but feel myself overwhelmed with a sense of it.'

He was then led to mention, as the greatest blessing, *his voyage to India.* He looked back upon it with peculiar thankfulness. It was what he needed. A voyage by sea was well calculated to impress the mind with seriousness. He had found this to be a season of solemn recollection, and of *religious enjoyment.* In the retirement of his cabin, he had enjoyed more of God than ever before, and though it was unusually prolonged, he felt sorry when it came to an end. He could bless God for all his afflictions, and could testify that they had been his richest mercies, adding, that he had experienced the fulfilment of that promise in Isaiah xxx. 20, 21, which he repeated with great solemnity and distinctness from beginning to end.

The conversation then turned on the mysteriousness of God's dealings in bringing him to India, and then laying him on a bed of sickness, which, in all probability, would be the bed of death. He had hoped, if it had pleased God to allow him time, to use the influence of his situation in advancing religion, and especially in encouraging the various institutions which had been formed for the benefit of India; but the very serious aspect of his sickness had put a stop to all his plans, and had led him to examine his motives strictly, and to feel that he was *nothing*. His anxious desire was now to acknowledge the hand of God, in the exercise of entire patience and resignation to his holy will. After some further conversation on this topic, at his request I prayed with him, having previously read a portion of Scripture referred to in the Visitation for the Sick. He was visibly affected with a solemn and thankful sense of that passage, that the Father of spirits chastens us for our profit, that we may be partakers of *His holiness*, and added his fervent *Amen*—that it might be so with him. It is impossible to convey adequately the solemn pathos, the tone of *tenderness*, the dignity and humility with which he spoke.

On the following day he complained of great pain, and observed that his disorder was still a mystery. He did not know how it would terminate; but he added, 'One thing we know, *He* doeth all things well, and, in whatever it may end, it *must end well.*' His countenance was illumined with an expression of cheerfulness when he said this, which plainly showed the inward composure of his mind. At nine in the evening, I found him in bed, and much exhausted. He could not converse. I read the ciiird Psalm, making such little remarks as seemed suited to his circumstances, and prayed with him. After prayer, he spoke of receiving the Sacrament. It was his particular wish not to defer it too long. It was an ordinance he much enjoyed. He was in a very happy frame of mind, and repeated the lines—

'Singing, as I wade to heaven,
Sweet affliction, sweet affliction!'

About two o'clock on Friday, I received a message

from the doctor, that he was sinking fast. I went and administered the Sacrament to him, which he had looked forward to with much earnestness. It was a memorable occasion. It was necessary to curtail the service as much as possible. I began with the prayer, 'We do not presume to come to this thy table,' &c. It was delightfully affecting to witness his fervour, his humility, his holy enjoyment of the ordinance. In order to shorten the service, I proceeded to the benediction after the prayer, leaving out the hymn of praise, 'Glory be to God on high.' He immediately noticed the omission, and interrupted me, pronouncing himself with great animation, the whole of that beautiful part of the service. We were all greatly affected. I cordially thanked him for noticing the omission, and *with tears of joy we concluded the service together.*

The service being concluded, he requested me to draw the chair close to his couch, and sit down, at the same time intimating his wish that all others might withdraw. He then most affectionately put out his hand and entreated me to pray for him that he might be delivered *from all false confidence,* adding, that he felt much peace; but that when he reflected on his past life, he could not but feel a trembling sense of his demerit; that he trusted in the mercy of God through Christ, but that at such a season, and in a matter of such importance, he felt it necessary to pray against false confidences. He repeated this expression with great earnestness. I replied that God would not disappoint the hope founded on the merit of his Son. To which he replied, 'That is true; I am perfectly satisfied on that point. My views are strong and clear. I have no cloud or doubt, and long to be with my God and Saviour. O when will the time come? To this time I have looked forward—O God thou knowest. It does not take me by surprise—I have been preparing for it. For some years past I have been endeavouring to withdraw from the world, avoiding as much as possible all new connections, and labouring to be ready for my summons. I greatly long for my rest. Here he dwelt with delight on the blessedness of being with God, varying and reiterating his expressions, sometimes in broken accents, at others more distinctly. I observed that he was now in a state to appreciate those lines of C. Wesley, written when he supposed himself dying. 'What are the lines?' he said, 'repeat them.' I began,

> In age and feebleness extreme,
> Who shall a sinful worm redeem ?

And was then proceeding to the line,

> Oh, let me catch one glimpse of Thee !

but here he took me up, and with great fervour, repeated two important lines which I had missed.

> Jesus, my joy and strength thou art,
> The comfort of my drooping heart,
> Oh ! let me catch one smile of Thee,
> Then drop into eternity.

He was refreshed with these lines, and entered with great delight on another hymn,

> Jesu, lover of my soul, &c.

We repeated three verses together, and every now and then he helped my memory till we came to the end, in which he joined with great emphasis and tone of manner,

> Spring Thou up within my heart,
> Rise to all eternity.

Here I expressed my thankfulness to God for the support vouchsafed to him at so trying a time ; and observed that it was a new instance of the Lord's tender mercy, in that when he most needed comfort, his consolation should be so strong, adverting at the same time to my first interview, when he was comparatively depressed. He said, 'It is indeed a merciful dispensation, but that violent disorders naturally deaden the expression of one's feelings. I have abundant reason to bless God for all his dealings.' 'Yes,' I said, he has not dealt with us according to our deserts.' 'Not according to MY deserts,' he emphatically said, 'I am sure you know not how I have sinned against him; but I can see mercy,' he continued after a pause, 'in all the way by which I have been led, and a gracious reason for every trial, with which he has visited me. All is wonderful, surely "*goodness and mercy hath followed me all the days of my life, and I shall dwell in his house for ever.*"' These last words he added with uplifted hands and great fervour of tone. The scene was animating!

F.

A VISIT TO THE INDIAN FEMALE ORPHAN REFUGE, AGRIPARRAH.

There is a spot near Calcutta, less known perhaps than it deserves, a precious portion of the Lord's garden, where the eye of faith can see many trees of righteousness of His right hand planting, budding, blossoming, and bearing fruit:—it is "out of the city, a place by the river-side, where prayer is wont to be made."

It was on one of the fine days of the past cold weather, that our little family party visited this Bethel. We left Calcutta early in the forenoon, and after an agreeable hour's drive arrived at Cox's Bungalow, where a simple direction-post pointed the way to the Indian Female Orphan Refuge. It is a plain substantial building, situate on the left bank of a sweep of the river, midway between Calcutta and Barrackpore. We were met by its kind owner with her accustomed Christian cordiality, and soon initiated into the routine of her daily operations, and the varied arrangements of her important and interesting institution. Morning school had just terminated as we arrived, and as we were no strangers to Mrs. Wilson's little flock, many cordial greetings passed between us and them.

We soon had the gratification of seeing the dear children at their morning meal, seated on the floor in their usual native mode, around three sides of a long room: one of the eldest of these brands from the burning besought the blessing of the Christian's God upon the food He had given, and praised Him for its bestowment when the meal was done. Their food was simple and good, nor did appetite seem to be wanting. It was a lovely sight to behold so many Indian females so cared for and so blessed—more especially when the mind glanced at what their condition might have been, had not this refuge been opened for them—*slaves*—outcasts—lost for time and for eternity. No approach to European manners, save the important one alluded to, and that too of cleanliness, was observable in their meal, and it is Mrs. Wilson's wise resolve to bring up her interesting flock in a manner which will render them individually fitted for the stations they will most probably be called upon to fill—those of laborious industry. Indeed all here bore the stamp of *consistent* practical piety; and if almost spotless cleanliness, neatness and order, are attractions, friends in the Lord will do well to visit this monument of Christian faith and perseverance.

After this many of the children assembled, and read the Scriptures in English, translating them into Bengalee as they proceeded, in a manner which clearly proved their understanding of the sacred truths they read: and sang several beautiful English hymns to English tunes very sweetly, and with a correctness which surprised us. One large, light, and airy schoolroom contained many classes busily employed in reading the Scriptures in Bengalee and English, &c., while in another apartment twelve or fourteen were engaged in worsted work, which they have learned to do in a manner that would be no discredit to more educated and more privileged young people.

Distant from the contamination of the city, and far

from its noise and tumult, this invaluable institution is working its important way; its inmates being, as much as possible, independent of all without its walls; for the children are taught to labour for themselves and those about them, and their efforts, willingly afforded, are found sufficient, yea, more than sufficient, for the proper discharge of the domestic duties of the Refuge; thus dispensing with that most fertile source of vice in India—heathen servants.

The situation of the Refuge is interesting: standing as it does on the bank of an extensive reach, it affords a lovely prospect of the majestic flood, as it rolls on its way, spotted with barks of all descriptions, not the less beautiful to a British eye because they are rudely constructed. To us the air was balm, and seemed to bring health and strength on its wings as it swept over the mighty river,—nor were our souls untouched, for all things seemed to say, 'Christian, thy God is here.' Pray, ye that love the Lord Jesus, that the blessing of Jehovah may abundantly rest on this oasis in this vast desert of idolatry, that many may be the palm-trees that shall flourish there.

Long has the founder of the India Female Orphan Refuge laboured in this land, and the existence of this institution is one of many proofs that she has not laboured in vain; how should every feeling of grace, yea and many of nature too, lead Christians in India to strengthen her hands and comfort her heart. Look around! we find tributes rising to the honour of the good and great, and sums are lavished on things without profit; but the Parian marble, however fair, the monumental tomb however lofty, the sculptured bust however exquisitely wrought, shall ill stand the convulsion of that day, when earth and heaven shall pass away, and the elements melt with fervent heat. Here is an opportunity for those to whom God has richly lent earthly goods, to prove themselves faithful stewards by erecting a temple of immortal souls, a spiritual building which the terrors of that day shall only beautify, removing it from earth to heaven: then no refuge shall we need, once entering into the eternal kingdom we shall go no more out, then shall there never more be an orphan, for all shall have a *heavenly* Father: "then our notes of praise shall for ever swell the song, and labours, sorrows, pains and griefs, be lost in one eternal joy!" Till that happy day arrive, let us plead for the fatherless, and remember those who labour in the Lord, and esteem them very highly for their work's sake.

CONVERSION OF A NATIVE.

Written by a Native Convert.

On the 23rd of February 1839, with feelings of gratitude and thankfulness to the Lord we were permitted to witness the sacrament of baptism administered at Bishop's College chapel to a native named Bissonauth. The circumstances regarding his conversion are both interesting and encouraging. About two years ago he received some tracts which were distributed by a native Catechist attached to the Baptist mission: he read and examined them carefully, and saw the difference between Christianity and his own religion; subsequently he heard the word preached by a native in a small chapel on the road, and read some more tracts. These led him to a more energetic inquiry—he felt his lost state and the necessity of a Redeemer—he compared the word of God with the Shasters, and soon he was enabled by divine grace to detect the falsity of the latter, and heartily desire to embrace the other. The first step he took, was to renounce Hindooism; he was engaged in the service of a person, where Hindoos, Mahomedans and Portuguese united in persecuting him continually for about twelve months; after which time he lost his employment, and continued to reside amongst them: his persecutions were unabated, his constant desire for the salvation of his soul also remained in vigour and activity by Him who is the Giver of all good—in this situation he was introduced to the writer of these lines. Upon being questioned as to his reasons for embracing Christianity, he replied, 'I know I must die one day, and when this body is dead, the immortal soul within, which can never die, will be sent either to a place of happiness or misery; and I am aware that if I continue a Hindoo my soul must go to a place of torment, because the Shasters do not provide a Saviour, and my sins have been such that I need a Saviour.' Upon another occasion he said, 'What the Hindoos worship cannot be Gods, for every thing regarding their deities is impure; and if there is a God, surely it is the Christian's God, holy and pure, as described in the Testament.' He touched upon several passages of the Testament, proving the holy life and walk of our God and Saviour. He was directed to the Rev. Krishna Mohana Banerjea: he removed from the society of his persecutors, was instructed about two or three months, and afterwards baptized. Are any dear Christian brethren engaged in distributing tracts, or preaching in these small chapels, let them read this and take courage, and may we pray for a blessing upon every tract and every sermon or exhortation. The Lord has been pleased to bless this year, with extraordinary instances of His infinite love and mercy—may He continue them for his own name and merit's sake, "till the whole earth is filled with His glory." Amen.

NOTES OF A JOURNEY FROM THE BANKS OF THE JUMNA TO BOMBAY.

I started from the banks of the Jumna on the 27th of November, and arrived here this morning, (Bombay, Jan. 12, 1837,) just in time for the Hugh Lindsay, which will start on the 13th instant, and in which I have been lucky enough to secure a cabin. I had imagined that I could travel comfortably all the way to this place dawk, so that you can conceive the disappointment I experienced, when on arriving at Saugor I found bearers no longer on the road. By dint of great exertions, I, after three or four days, secured thirty bearers, and these took me to Hoshingabad in five days, distance 150 miles; beyond that, they would not and could not move, and as that country cannot produce a single bearer, I was under the necessity of abandoning the palanquin, and take to riding a tattoo, after sacrificing a considerable part of what I deemed comforts. From Hoshingabad to Poonah I rode my tat, which was a good strong brute, a distance I count of about 500 miles. Saugor I found a most miserable-looking place, the soil as black as soot, the grass parched up, and the surface of the earth covered with large black stones. The lake is the only redeeming quality about the station, and that is certainly very pretty and picturesque; the houses bad and low, and the station, though a large one, as I passed through it, seemed deserted. The country between Saugor and Hoshingabad is wild in the extreme, nothing but a succession of low hills one after the other, all clothed with trees, chiefly teak, but none that I saw large, and the valleys below occasionally slightly cultivated. The villages were very far apart, and the country appeared deserted. You may go for miles without meeting a human being, or in fact any thing endued with life, not even a bird to vary the dreadful stillness that prevails; the same remark holds good throughout the whole of the country subsequently passed through, so that there will be no necessity to recur to the remark. At Hoshingabad I was most kindly received and did not get away till the 11th. The next station reached was Asserghur, distant 150 miles. I arrived there on the 16th, and was most kindly entertained by the officers of the 3rd Bombay Native Infantry. I found them in temporary bungalows down below. In the hot weather they reside in the fort, which is so high as to keep them out of the range of the hot winds. Our system of marching was this, after taking a cup of coffee, started at day-light and rode till 10 A.M., spent two hours at breakfast under a tree, and starting again, rode till 4 P. M. a snail's pace all the way. I thus advanced at the rate of about 25 miles a day. A table servant whom I had secured was mounted on a good strong tat, and the baggage came on by others. As I had no tents, I dined and slept under trees, preferring such shelter to the filthiness of native houses. The country round Asserghur is bleak and blasted to a degree; the only thing worth seeing is the fort: from below it does not appear very imposing, but when after a most steep and laborious ascent, you arrive at the top, you feel how strong it is. A march from Asserghur is Borhanpore, a very large city, inhabited chiefly by Borahs, a singular sect of Mussulmans. In the cemetery are the tombs of three of their priests, well executed and worth looking at: they are square buildings with a dome at top made of the finest chunam, so as to look like marble; the ornamented work in the interior is very rich and in good taste, fountains play all round, and the terrace is paved with painted tiles. In an old palace are some marble baths whose beauties are not quite concealed by the heaps of rubbish which surround them; they are fast going to decay. Here the Taptee is now scarcely knee deep. I left Borhanpore on the 19th; the bleak, deserted, parched-up face of the country continued day after day, with nothing to vary or to relieve the scene, and being all alone, you may fancy how solitary I found it, and what a painful depression of spirits it created. On the 22nd I reached the celebrated excavations of Ajunta, so they are called, but they are situated some six miles from that town; they are certainly wonderful, not as abounding in any thing in the shape of either sculpture or painting that can be compared with the productions of Europe, either of former or of the present time, but they are wonderful because they are evidently the result of considerable skill and immense labour, and were executed at a period so remote as to be beyond the reach even of tradition. The hills in which the excavations have been made are evidently of volcanic origin. Viewed from the centre of the large arched cave, the whole scene before you puts you in mind of a horse-shoe, the tongue of land jutting out is like the frog of a horse's foot; one end of the shoe is formed by a water-fall of 120 feet perpendicular height, (here the stream has its rise) the other by an abrupt turn of the hill. Some of the caves are inaccessible. I saw nineteen only; they are situated about half-way up the hill, and are cut out of the solid rock. They vary as much in size as in superiority of execution. Some are coarsely finished, others scarcely commenced, others again are most elaborately finished; I have no room to give a minute description. The whole interior was at one time painted, and in some of the caves the paintings are still quite fresh. The ceilings were painted in divisions and a circle in the centre, the whole representing fruits and flowers of every description, among them I observed clusters of grapes with little bacchuses entwined among the leaves; this is not an Indian idea! Many of the figures on the walls are very well done, and put you in mind of the copies of the cartoons of Raphael, the countenances are Grecian, and not a bit like the people of this country. Negroes are also strikingly depicted. I also observed among the ornamental parts of one room a female figure very well sculptured, standing on a Dolphin. Where did the natives get this idea? The caves are generally square, at the end opposite the entrance is a recess in which is the large god Jum, always coarsely carved, and within on the sides are excavated cells in which the priests resided, like the monks of Europe I suppose, for these excavations were undoubtedly meant as places for retirement and devotion. All the large colossal figures are in bad taste, coarsely executed and out of all proportion, but the ornamental carving of some of the columns, and the small figures of men and animals on the base and capital, are exceedingly well done. From Ajunto I went to Assaye and spent my Christmas day on the field of battle. Not a vestige of the fight remains, but some broken pieces of cannon. My dinner was but a poor one, consisting of doll rotee and brandy paunie. On the 27th I reached Aurungabad and remained till the 2nd. The city though built by Aurungzebe is now in ruins; the only building it contains worthy of notice is the Begum's tomb, which is nothing to those who have seen Delhi and Agra. The city is well supplied with water, which is brought from the hills, a distance of eight miles, by means of an aqueduct. The climate is said to be good, and the oranges and grapes delicious. I went to see the celebrated fort of Dowlatabad and the caves of Ellora; both of them you know well from description, I will therefore only say that the excavations of Ellora are in my opinion far inferior to those of Ajunta; the latter have in fact never been properly examined or described.

The character is, I think, the same as that on the Allahabad and Delhi columns? These letters are particularly distinct on the face of the large arched cave at Ajunta, but appears to have escaped observation. Two other inscriptions have been copied several times, but I do not know the result. From Aurungabad I rode to Ahmednuggur, and soon got into a good road, which continued all the way to Bombay. I made no stay at Ahmednuggur, but pushed on to Poonah, where I arrived on the 8th, and started again on the 11th, arriving here (Bombay) on the 12th of January. From Talla to Paunell the road is excellent, and bungaloes all the way for travellers. At Poonah I got into a phaeton, which brought me to Paunell in the evening, a distance of seventy miles; there I got into a boat and found myself here in the morning. At Cuclea, half way between Poonah and Paunell, is another arched cave much larger than those either at Ajunta or Ellora; the proportions are good, but the columns, with the exception of the capitals, coarsely executed; the ribs of the arched ceiling are of wood, which is strange. The Bole Ghaut road is splendid, and the scenery very picturesque.